Income Inequality and Financial Inclusion Initiatives in a Global Context

Oytun Meçik
Eskişehir Osmangazi University, Turkey

IGI Global
Scientific Publishing
Publishing Tomorrow's Research Today

Vice President of Editorial Melissa Wagner
Director of Acquisitions Mikaela Felty
Director of Book Development Jocelynn Hessler
Production Manager Mike Brehm
Cover Design Jose Rosado

Published in the United States of America by
IGI Global Scientific Publishing
701 East Chocolate Avenue
Hershey, PA, 17033, USA
Tel: 717-533-8845 | Fax: 717-533-7115
Website: https://www.igi-global.com E-mail: cust@igi-global.com

Library of Congress Cataloging-in-Publication Data

Names: Meçik, Oytun editor
Title: Income inequality and financial inclusion initiatives in a global context / edited by: Oytun Meçik.
Description: Hershey, PA : IGI Global Scientific Publishing, [2026] | Includes bibliographical references and index. | Summary: "The book will focus on how these crises exacerbate inequalities and how different regions, institutions, and policies respond to mitigate their effects"-- Provided by publisher.
Identifiers: LCCN 2025044734 (print) | LCCN 2025044735 (ebook) | ISBN 9798337373607 hardcover | ISBN 9798337373614 paperback | ISBN 9798337373621 ebook
Subjects: LCSH: Income distribution | Financial crises
Classification: LCC HC79.I5 I537 2026 (print) | LCC HC79.I5 (ebook) | DDC 339.2--dc23/eng/20260129
LC record available at https://lccn.loc.gov/2025044734
LC ebook record available at https://lccn.loc.gov/2025044735

British Cataloguing in Publication Data
A Cataloguing in Publication record for this book is available from the British Library.

Table of Contents

Detailed Table of Contents

Environmental crises are among the most pressing global challenges at the present time. Especially, the escalating adverse effects of climate change have exacerbated economic and environmental problems in various regions of the world. In recent years, governments, civil society organizations and researchers have increasingly turned their attention to addressing these critical issues. In this context, the simultaneous rise in income inequality and environmental crises provide a significant clue to the relationship between the two phenomena. This situation indicates that the relationship between the two concepts should be subjected to a more in-depth analysis. A comprehensive academic database such as Web of Science is preferred for conducting literature searches. Following Méjean et al. (2024), a study conducted in was performed queries on environmental crises and economic inequalities. These inquiries focus on the titles and abstracts of the articles, and the analysis resulted in the identification of 312 articles indexed in SCI-Expanded, SSCI, and ESCI, and written in English.

From the dawn of civilization, poverty has been a predominant concern. Among them, the post-Second World War welfare state policies and economic development had a significant effect. Scientific and technological advancements and economic growth increased the GDP of almost all countries. However, it also widened the gap between the rich and the poor. This became evident with neoliberalism, privatization, and deregulation of the economy. The private assets increased enormously, losing the public sector's control over the economic interactions. As a result, income and wealth inequality increased rapidly. The World Inequality Report (2022) affirms the massive concentration of income and wealth in the hands of a few individuals. It adversely affects poverty alleviation strategies as poverty increases along with the rising income inequality. The World Bank (2024) affirms this precarious situation. From this perspective, this chapter examines the significance of the human security approach in addressing these human insecurities.

The distribution of income among people influences both investment choices and risk tolerance and capital distribution patterns and overall financial system stability. The literature shows that inequality produces different market effects based on which income groups are increasing or decreasing in size. This research investigates the connection between income inequality and financial market performance through an analysis of income distribution metrics on stock price changes and variance of coefficients (VC) which represent stock market risk or volatility. A 15-year data set of nine countries are conducted final estimations with Feasible Generalized Least Squares (FGLS) because traditional models failed diagnostic tests. The results show that higher Gini coefficient values lead to decreased stock price growth together with elevated financial market volatility, yet High20 top-income concentration creates market stability. The empirical evidence supports the theoretical framework which demonstrates that inequality affects both investment potential and market operations.

This article examines the effects of income inequality, GDP per capita, inflation, unemployment, and the age-dependency ratio on central government debt in 18 OECD countries over the period 1999–2022 using a Panel ARDL approach. Income inequality, unemployment, and the age-dependency ratio have a positive impact on public debt. Conversely, inflation and GDP per capita are found to have a debt-reducing effect. The Dumitrescu-Hurlin causality test reveals a unidirectional causality running from inequality to public debt. The results highlight the critical role of socioeconomic factors such as income inequality and unemployment in determining public debt dynamics. It also highlights the need for social policy interventions to ensure fiscal sustainability.

This chapter explores the potential of fiscal policy to serve as a multidimensional tool in addressing climate change, reducing income inequality, and promoting economic growth in Türkiye. Employing a Structural Vector Autoregression (SVAR) model, the analysis incorporates macroeconomic and sectoral emissions data to investigate the dynamic relationships between environmental taxes, sectoral CO_2 emissions, inequality, and output. The findings suggest that while environmental taxation significantly reduces emissions, particularly in the industrial and transportation sectors, its redistributive effects on income inequality remain limited. The study highlights the need for complementary social spending and progressive reforms to ensure a just and sustainable green transition. Policy implications are derived to inform a fiscal framework that aligns environmental and socio-economic goals.

This study analyses the role of the housing affordability crisis in the reproduction of economic inequalities within a multi-dimensional framework. Based on a descriptive analysis, inequalities in the housing market are assessed along three main dimensions: inequalities in access to housing, the burden of housing on household budgets and the role of housing as a means of wealth accumulation. First, evidence indicates that rising house and rental prices impact housing affordability especially for low-income and young households. Second, the cost burden of housing varies both across countries and different income groups, disproportionately affecting low-income households. Finally, transformation of housing into a financial investment instrument and wealth transfer pathways deepen wealth-based inequalities. In conclusion, the housing market crisis is a multidimensional crisis requiring economic, social integration, and welfare solutions.

This chapter offers a theoretical and visual analysis of the distribution of crime rates across Europe, focusing on various crime types over time, and examines their correlation with income inequality—one of the most highlighted determinants in the empirical literature—to shed light on the structural drivers of crime. Moreover, this chapter provides spatial representation of crime rates as a descriptive overview of crime across Europe, focusing on three decades, i.e., 2000s, 2010s, and 2020s, to further observe how crime rates evolve over time. By combining visual tools and descriptive statistics, we provide a concise yet insightful perspective on the evolving nature of crime within the European region and its relationship with the income inequality. Our findings reveal a significant heterogeneity in the distribution of crime rates across European countries. Moreover, this variation is observed despite the geographical proximity, common historical background, similar institutional structures and the existence of shared social and economic policies under the umbrella of the Europe.

The study investigates the impact of FinTech adoption on the financial empowerment of women in Delhi's NCT region. Using a quantitative design, data were collected via structured questionnaires from 200 women in urban and semi-urban areas. Grounded in the UTAUT and Diffusion of Innovation frameworks, the study analyzed factors like performance expectancy, social influence, and perceived complexity. Results reveal a positive correlation between FinTech use and financial empowerment—reflected in increased savings, financial confidence, and income generation. However, barriers such as low digital literacy and socio-cultural norms hinder broader adoption. The findings highlight FinTech's potential in reducing gender disparities in financial access. Targeted awareness, inclusive tech design, and digital literacy campaigns are crucial for enabling greater adoption and impact.

Preface

As the editor of *Income Inequality and Financial Inclusion Initiatives in a Global Context*, I am privileged to present this volume, a collaborative endeavor that seeks to illuminate the complex interplay between economic inequality and the multifaceted crises that define our global landscape. In an era marked by financial volatility, social upheavals, political instability, and escalating environmental challenges, the persistence of economic disparities remains a central obstacle to achieving equitable and resilient societies. This book is born out of a pressing need to understand these dynamics, not in isolation, but as interconnected forces that shape and are shaped by inequality across diverse contexts.

The convergence of crises, from the reverberations of the 2008 financial meltdown to the social fractures exposed by the COVID-19 pandemic, the unrest fueled by political polarization, and the disproportionate burdens of climate change, has laid bare the fragility of our global systems. These crises do not merely coexist with inequality; they amplify it, disproportionately affecting the most vulnerable while often sparing those with greater resources. Yet, within this complexity lies an opportunity: to rethink how we address inequality, to design innovative policies, and to foster resilience through inclusive frameworks. This volume rises to that challenge, offering a comprehensive exploration of how economic inequalities interact with crises and how we might chart a path toward a more equitable future.

The chapters within this book reflect the collective expertise of a diverse group of scholars, policymakers, and practitioners who bring interdisciplinary perspectives to bear on these pressing issues. From the historical and contemporary drivers of global inequality to the intersectional impacts of crises on marginalized populations, the contributions span a wide range of topics. They examine the role of public policy, the influence of globalization, the potential of technology, and the efficacy of international cooperation, while grounding these analyses in rich case studies from around the world. The book also proposes forward-looking frameworks for resilience and equity, bridging theory and practice to offer actionable insights for addressing these challenges.

CHAPTER OVERVIEW

Chapter 1 employs a bibliometric analysis to map research trends on environmental crises and economic inequalities, drawing on 312 articles from the Web of Science to highlight the growing academic focus on this nexus. By analyzing titles and abstracts, the study reveals the escalating adverse effects of climate change on economic disparities across various regions, underscoring the need for deeper investigations into how environmental challenges disproportionately burden marginalized communities. This chapter sets a critical foundation for the book's exploration of the interconnected dynamics of crises and inequality.

Chapter 2 adopts a human security approach to examine global poverty amidst rising income inequality, analyzing how neoliberal policies, privatization, and deregulation have widened the gap between rich and poor. Drawing on the World Inequality Report (2022) and World Bank (2024), it highlights the massive concentration of wealth and its adverse impact on poverty alleviation efforts. By emphasizing human security, this chapter offers a compelling framework for addressing economic disparities in the context of global crises.

Chapter 3 investigates the divergent effects of income inequality on stock market performance, using a 15-year dataset across nine countries and Feasible Generalized Least Squares estimations. The findings show that higher Gini coefficients correlate with reduced stock price growth and increased market volatility, while top-income concentration fosters stability. This analysis provides critical insights for investors and policymakers, illuminating the complex relationship between inequality and financial market dynamics.

Chapter 4 explores the impact of income inequality, unemployment, and age-dependency ratios on public debt in 18 OECD countries from 1999 to 2022, using a Panel ARDL approach. The results demonstrate that inequality and unemployment drive debt accumulation, while inflation and GDP per capita have a debt-reducing effect. By revealing unidirectional causality from inequality to debt, this chapter underscores the need for social policy interventions to ensure fiscal sustainability.

Chapter 5 examines fiscal policy's potential to address climate change, inequality, and economic growth in Türkiye, employing a Structural Vector Autoregression model with macroeconomic and sectoral emissions data. The findings indicate that environmental taxation reduces emissions, particularly in industrial and transportation sectors, but has limited redistributive effects on inequality. This chapter advocates for complementary social spending and progressive reforms to support a just and sustainable green transition.

Chapter 6 analyzes the housing affordability crisis as a driver of economic inequality, assessing disparities in access, cost burdens, and wealth accumulation through housing markets. Based on a descriptive analysis, it highlights how rising house and rental prices disproportionately affect low-income and young households, while housing's transformation into a financial investment deepens wealth-based inequalities. This chapter calls for multidimensional economic, social, and welfare solutions to address the crisis.

Chapter 7 provides a theoretical and visual analysis of crime distribution across Europe over three decades, examining its correlation with income inequality. Using descriptive statistics and spatial representations, it reveals significant heterogeneity in crime rates despite shared social and economic policies in the region. By highlighting structural drivers of crime, this chapter underscores the need for targeted interventions to address inequality's role in social instability.

Chapter 8 investigates technology-driven financial inclusion in Delhi's National Capital Territory, focusing on FinTech's impact on women's financial empowerment. Based on a quantitative study of 200 women, it reveals a positive correlation between FinTech use and increased savings, financial confidence, and income generation, while identifying barriers like low digital literacy. This chapter highlights FinTech's potential to reduce gender disparities and the need for inclusive tech design and literacy campaigns.

Chapter 9 assesses India's public policy framework for gender equality, analyzing initiatives like Beti Bachao, Beti Padhao and identifying barriers such as social norms and economic exclusion. Through case studies, it illustrates successes and limitations, advocating for integrated approaches involving institutional reform, data-driven policies, and community-led interventions. This chapter enriches the book's focus on intersectionality and actionable strategies for equity.

Our ambition is to provide a resource that speaks to a broad audience: scholars and students in economics, sociology, political science, and environmental studies; policymakers crafting responses to crises; practitioners in NGOs and the private sector; and engaged citizens seeking to understand the forces shaping our world. By integrating rigorous academic research with practical recommendations, this volume aims to advance the discourse on economic inequality and inspire transformative solutions.

I extend my deepest gratitude to the contributors whose scholarship and dedication have made this book possible. Their willingness to engage with these complex issues and to offer fresh perspectives has enriched this project immeasurably.

It is my hope that *Income Inequality and Financial Inclusion Initiatives in a Global Context* will serve as both a catalyst for dialogue and a foundation for action. As we navigate an increasingly uncertain world, this book invites readers to explore the intersections of inequality and crises, to question existing paradigms, and to contribute to the creation of more inclusive, resilient, and sustainable societies.

Chapter 1

Bibliometric Analysis of Research Trends on Environmental Crises and Economic Inequalities

Şeyma Sertçelik
https://orcid.org/0000-0003-0403-4972
Istanbul Esenyurt University, Turkey

ABSTRACT

Environmental crises are among the most pressing global challenges at the present time. Especially, the escalating adverse effects of climate change have exacerbated economic and environmental problems in various regions of the world. In recent years, governments, civil society organizations and researchers have increasingly turned their attention to addressing these critical issues. In this context, the simultaneous rise in income inequality and environmental crises provide a significant clue to the relationship between the two phenomena. This situation indicates that the relationship between the two concepts should be subjected to a more in-depth analysis. A comprehensive academic database such as Web of Science is preferred for conducting literature searches. Following Méjean et al. (2024), a study conducted in was performed queries on environmental crises and economic inequalities. These inquiries focus on the titles and abstracts of the articles, and the analysis resulted in the identification of 312 articles indexed in SCI-Expanded, SSCI, and ESCI, and written in English.

DOI: 10.4018/979-8-3373-7360-7.ch001

1. INTRODUCTION

Environmental crises have been escalating rapidly since the 1950s (Steffen et al., 2011). These crises have led to various negative changes (Millennium Ecosystem Assessment, 2005) and climatic deteriorations (IPCC, 2013) in the ecosystem. Therefore, biodiversity and ecosystems are increasingly under threat. In particular, the acceleration of global warming has intensified environmental stress and ecological degradation, pushing ecosystems towards critical thresholds. In this regard, the escalating severity of environmental crises presents a highly complex and challenging issue. This situation, which affects the world and global warming and destroys the global carbon cycle, is a vital issue that is attracting more and more attention from governments (Adebayo & Kirikkaleli, 2021).

One of the most pressing challenges facing contemporary global society is the growing concern about income inequality (Kopp & Nabernegg, 2022). Disparities in income or wealth among individuals are referred to as economic inequality (Yoganandham, 2022; Butler, 2022: 22). Among the main determinants of inequality are differences in countries' levels of development and economic structures. Economic growth and rising prosperity have proved insufficient to close the income gaps both at the national level and between countries. In many countries, the distribution of income and wealth has become increasingly concentrated in the highest income groups. This unequal distribution not only affects the economic, political, and social domains but also causes a negative impact on environmental indicators. As a result, degradation of the natural environment and economic inequality are emerging as critical issues. The rising trends of both economic inequality and environmental degradation necessitate an in-depth analysis of the relationship between these two phenomena (Ali, 2022).

Reducing inequalities and ensuring environmental protection are among the main priorities for policy makers in the process of sustainable development process. It is an ideal scenario to realise both objectives simultaneously, i.e. to reduce inequality and enhance environmental quality (Hubacek et al., 2017). In particular, the process of urbanization driven by intensifying population and expeditious industrialisation poses assorted environmental challenges like air and water pollution, changes in land use and waste management (Bai et al., 2017; Wang, 2024). In this respect, it's very pivotal to consider the relationship between the environment and inequality in economic research and policy design processes. Otherwise, if these issues are analyzed independently, the interaction between them is not fully understood and there will be deficiencies in highlighting future research needs. The United Nations head also emphasises the importance of this issue, stating that the world faces "the harsh realities of a deeply unequal global landscape" (World Social Report, 2020: 2; Ching et al., 2023).

More than 70% of the global population feels the effects of rising income inequality, which slows down the socioeconomic development process (United Nations, 2020a). From a global perspective, the share of the richest 1% in total wealth is increasing over the years (World Inequality Database, 2019). Therefore, mitigating environmental degradation and enhancing income distribution are among the main issues that will be given the most importance. For that purpose, the United Nations has adopted the 2030 Sustainable Development Goals (United Nations, 2025; Li et al., 2023). These goals aim to achieve sustainable economic development, eradicate poverty, struggle injustice and inequality, environmental protection and combat the impacts of global climate change (Ali et al., 2024). In this context, policymakers have increasingly prioritizing both issues in their national and global agendas. With this growing interest, there has been a significant revival in academic research on understanding the causes and consequences of economic inequalities. Studies suggest that through the destruction of ecosystem, reduced agricultural productivity, deaths from extreme weather events, and social disruption, climate change is expected to have long-term economic impacts (Cai & Lontzek, 2019; Donadelli et al., 2017; Balakrishnan & Tsaneva, 2021; Kim, 2021, Chisadza et al., 2023). To this respect, it addresses the following research questions:

- Which key research themes related to environmental crises and economic inequalities have been developed between 2000 and 2025,
- Which countries, authors and journals have made significant contributions, and which countries have entered into bilateral or multilateral cooperation agreements,
- How did the overall transformation in this field has taken shape?

2. LITERATURE REVIEW

The raising environmental crises have boosted critical problems regarding the role of inequality in environmental degradation (Berthe & Elie, 2015: 191). For years, research on these troubles has been analyzed independently, resulting in the disregard of pivotal interactions between them. Thus, the relationship between environmental degradation and income inequality continues controversial, featured by discrepancies in the theoretical and empirical literature, and lacking a obvious consensus (Golley & Meng, 2012; Baek & Gweisah, 2013; Berthe & Elie, 2015; Hao et al., 2016; Wolde-Rufael & Idowu, 2017; Grunewald et al., 2017; Masud et al., 2018; Kousar et al., 2023; Wang, 2024).

Researchers from diverse disciplines have improved various theoretical approaches to illuminate the impact of income inequality on environmental quality. These varied theoretical frameworks constantly put forward divergent perspectives (Pata et al., 2022); while some studies allege that income inequality exacerbates environmental degradation, others claim that it has a negative impact (Wang, 2024). For example, some researchers argue that income inequality results in overconsumption of natural resources (Baloch et al., 2020; Ekeocha, 2021). Other perspective allege that considerable levels of income inequality encourage pollution diminution as income inequality rises, the marginal inclination to emit diminishes. (Liu et al., 2019a; Huang & Duan, 2020; Wu & Xie, 2020). As can be seen; scientific research on the relationship between the environment and inequality has revealed divergent results (Wang, 2024).

Many studies in the literature claim that fair income distribution encourage environmental protection and a healthy environment plays a vital role in eradicating profound poverty (Cho, 2018; Khan et al., 2022). Several research have also stated the relationship between environmental impacts and economic inequality, but almost all have examined this relationship from a regional/production-based aspect (Ravallion et al., 2000; Grunewald et al., 2017; Jorgenson et al., 2017; Hailemariam et al., 2019; Knight et al., 2017). In summary, heightening income inequality is one of the vital cause of rising environmental contamination with regard to ecological footprint. In addition, the lack of education, sufficient purchasing power, and awareness resulted in increased dependency on non-renewable energy and thereby widening the ecological footprint, and exacerbating environmental impacts.

The rest of the chapter is organized as follows; Section 3 presents the research methodology, database selection, data and method. Section 4 describes the result, performance analysis and mapping research themes. Section 5 reports discussion and future research directions.

3. RISKS RELATED TO ENVIRONMENTAL CRISES

3.1. Sustainability

Climate change poses not only a future threat but also immediate hazard to both ecological balance and human well-being. The main cause is that the accelerated release of greenhouse gases into the atmosphere due to human activities. In particular, fossil fuel use, expansion of industrial processes and elevated energy consumption cause disrupting nature systems, as evidenced by growing global temperature, altered precipitation patterns and extreme weather events (IPCC, 2021). Such environmental degradation has directly impacted sustainable development, constrains economic growth, exacerbates challenges to environmental justice.

Carbon emission and intensive energy use are among the most critical indicators that trigger environmental crises. These factors threaten the sustainable natural environment and resource utilization, emerging both in household energy consumption and national energy policies. In this context, fossil fuel-based production is unsustainable over the long term in view of limited resources and the profound ecological damage they inflict. Therefore, the transition to renewable energy systems is essential in both mitigate global warming by reducing the carbon footprint and supporting economic growth by reducing reliance on external dependency sources (REN21, 2023).

3.2. Economic Vulnerabilities

From an economic growth perspective, the relationship between environmental crises and growth has extensively been investigated. This relationship is explained with the conceptual model known as the Environmental Kuznets Curve (EKC) in the literature. The EKC hypothesis argue that environmental degradation initially worsens as income levels rise, however beyond a certain welfare threshold, increases in environmental awareness and technological innovation in society lead to improvements in environmental quality (Grossman & Krueger, 1991). Especially in the 1960s, environmental concerns were not taken into consideration to ensure growth. From the 1970s onward, this relationship was tried to be integrated into environmental policies. In this direction, developed countries had widely adopted ecologically sensitive production techniques since the 2000s. On the other hand, many developing countries continued to expand production, despite the negative impacts on the environment and its costs (Cetintas et al., 2016: 58).

Environmental crises simultaneously amplify risks both economic and social domains. Beyond their impact on income levels, they exacerbate vulnerabilities in agricultural production, water scarcity, health equity, food security and migration flows. These complex dynamics hinder policymakers' ability to anticipate and manage emerging threats, thereby necessitating interdisciplinary approaches in both policy formulation and implementation. Moreover, such crises create cascading vulnerabilities that deepen socioeconomic challenges-particularly poverty, inequality, income losses, infrastructural deficits, and limited institutional capacity (Carter & Janzen, 2018; Costella et al., 2021). As a result, effective risk management in the face of environmental crises must require an integrated framework in terms of environmental justice, global cooperation and vulnerable populations.

3.3. Environmental Justice: The North-South Contradiction

Environmental justice encompasses the equitable distribution of environmental benefits across all societal groups, equal participation in decision-making processes, and compensation for damaged communities (Schlosberg, 2007). Climate risks produce cascading effects—ranging from ecosystem disruption to social dislocation—that constrain livelihoods and generate new socioeconomic vulnerabilities, notably through rising poverty and social fragility (Bene et al., 2013; Schaffrin, 2014; IPCC, 2022; Besnili, 2023; Sengül & Murat, 2024). In this context, these interlinked threats give rise to a dynamic structure in which environmental hazards intersect with existing social inequalities and institutional capacities (Awojobi & Vloveret, 2017; Costella et al., 2021; Kundu et al., 2021).

While the East-West reflects cultural differences in the world, whereas the North-South highlights wealth disparities. Poverty tends to be less pervasive in the Global North, while it's more intense in the Global South. Historical patterns of environmental injustice, including the export of polluting industries and hazardous waste from developed to developing countries—have exacerbated these divides, contributing to economic crises and environmental degradation in less affluent regions. This practice has created serious challenges at every stage of the waste lifecycle, from production and transport to storage and disposal, and underscores the need for stronger international regulations and reparative justice mechanisms.

Historically, Western countries have instrumentalized injustice as a defining feature of their material and political expansion from the slave trade and human trafficking to colonial domination entrenching unequal power dynamics that persist today. Despite proposing solutions to contemporary environmental crises, developed countries frequently prioritize their own strategic interests over genuine remediation, resulting in policy prescriptions that are both insufficient and self-serving (Kilic & Tok, 2014). As a result of this approach, it seems to be a crucial for industrialized societies to observe global justice and the fair use of their ecological resources, and for prosperous countries to reduce their use of resources and abandon their colonial policies (Shiva, 2019).

4. RESEARCH METHODOLOGY

4.1. Database Selection

A wide range of databases are available for scientific research in the field of social sciences. For example; WoS (Web of Science), Scopus, Google Scholar, PubMed, etc. Web of Science holds a notable advantage over Scopus and Google Scholar by providing such as optimising search results, cited references and advanced search filters (Norris & Oppenheim, 2007). Furthermore, WoS is widely recognised and frequently used at internationally due to its has high quality standards (Merigó et al., 2015: 2647; Gaviria-Marin et al., 2019: 196) and widespread acceptance in academic publication analysis (Chen, 2017; Dzikowski, 2018; Nunen et al., 2018; Gaviria-Marin et al., 2019; Yan & Zhiping, 2023). The WoS Core Collection database also provides a distinctive citation tracking capability using an objective measure (Dzikowski, 2018: 83). For these reasons, the WoS Core Collection database was preferred for this research. This ensures linguistic and terminological consistency among the analyzed articles and facilitates the data review and analysis process.

4.2. Data and Method

The bibliometric method can be used to investigate, systematize and analyse historical data, track citations, assess the development of knowledge in a specific field and possibly even predict the future (Daim et al., 2006: 983; Liu et al., 2011). This research uses the bibliometric analysis approach to integrate the findings of studies in the literature and evaluate them from a broader perspective. By providing a holistic analysis of the interaction between economic inequality and environmental crises interact, it offers insights that can support the development of effective adaptation policies. The research aims to define emerging trends, key themes and research gaps from previous studies. In this regard, bibliometric analysis serves as an effective method for understanding the relationship between environmental crises and economic inequalities.

Academic publications can be evaluated on the basis of specific units of analysis. Journals, authors, cited references, institutions and countries are the most prevalent units (Dzikowski, 2018). As stated by Chen (2017), "a science mapping approach involves multiple components; a scientific literature, visual analytical tools, indicators that can emphasize critical patterns and tendencies, and scientific change theories that guide the discovery and interpretation of dynamic patterns".

As part of the bibliometric analysis, it was selected studies indexed in the SCI-Expanded, SSCI, and ESCI collections of the Web of Science database. Thereby ensuring the inclusion of peer-reviewed articles of demonstrated quality. Additionally, enhancing both the international consistency of our bibliometric indicators and the reliability and comparability of citation data across high-impact journals. And the articles published between 2000 and 2025 were taken into consideration. This period was selected to capture both the historical development and current trends in research on environmental crises and economic inequality, providing sufficient temporal depth to examine the contemporary evolution of methodological and thematic frameworks.

In various databases, the most common retrieval methods include full-text, subject, title, and abstract searches (Li & Chen, 2016: 15). In this study, following Méjean et al. (2024), various queries were conducted on environmental crises and economic inequalities in March 2025. These search queries focus on the titles and abstracts of the scientific articles. Additionally, with the Citation Topics Meso filter, topics that are not related to the research field, such as Smell & Taste Science, Zoology & Animal Ecology, Legionellosis, Dentistry & Oral Medicine, Marine Biology, and Membrance Science, were excluded from the analysis. This analysis, resulted in the identification of 255 articles within the WoS database between 2000 and 2025.

Figure 1. Query Structure

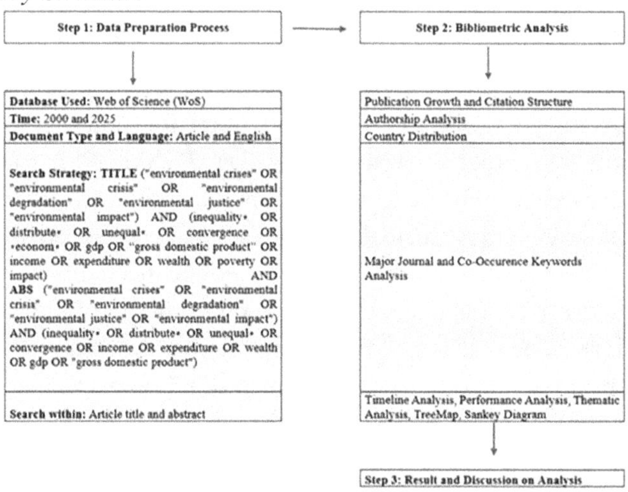

5. RESULT

This section presents both a performance analysis based on bibliometric indicators and a thematic mapping of research trends. First of all, an outline of the research field is provided by clarifying the main information and key statistics. This refers to "performance analysis," which is one of the two main components of a bibliometric analysis (Lim & Kumar, 2023). Subsequently, the conceptual foundations and research trajectory in the field are examined to offer a comprehensive understanding of its intellectual landscape.

Figure 2. Main Information

5.1. Performance Analysis

In this section covers the studying topics such as published documents, the total citations, the publications of different authors contributing to the relevant topic, the leading journals and countries analyzed through a descriptive approach.

5.1.1. The Trajectory of Publication Trends

Figure 2 illustrates the evolution of all publications in the WoS database over time, categorized by year of publication. The observed trend indicates that the relationship between environmental crises and economic inequalities is gaining increasing attention from the academic community. Thus, it can be said that the studies in literature have notably expanded, especially since 2015. After 2020, there is a significant acceleration in both the number of publications and citations. Despite annual fluctuations in the number of publications, the global research trend has been constantly upward, reflecting the growing interest in this interdisciplinary relationship. There may be several reasons for this increase:

Figure 3. Annual Scientific Production related to Environmental Crises and Economic Inequalities

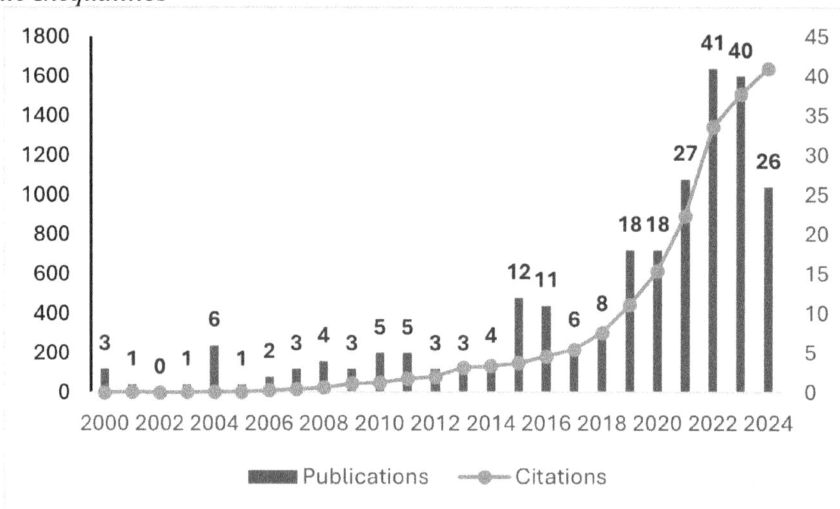

- The adverse affects of the global impact of environmental crises: Climate change, drought, natural disasters and their socio-economic impacts are receiving more attention in the academic literature.
- Sustainable Development Goals: The SDGs accepted by the United Nations in 2015, may led to the prominence of issues of environmental justice and economic inequality in academic studies.
- The expansion of research support: Incentives from funding bodies and governments may have fostered a growth in studies in this area.
- Advancements in Technological developments: Increased access to databases has facilitated a more comprehensive analysis of publications in this area.

5.1.2. The Most Salient Authors

There are a total of 778 research articles written by researcher on the research topic examined. Figure 3 highlights the most relevant authors in the worldwide. Accordingly, Wang, Adebayo and Kirikkaleli can be described as productive authors.

Figure 4. Author Productivity overtime and Publication Frequencies on Environmental Crises and Economic Inequalities. The size of the circles shows the volume of publications, and the gradient of the color indicates the volume of citations per year.

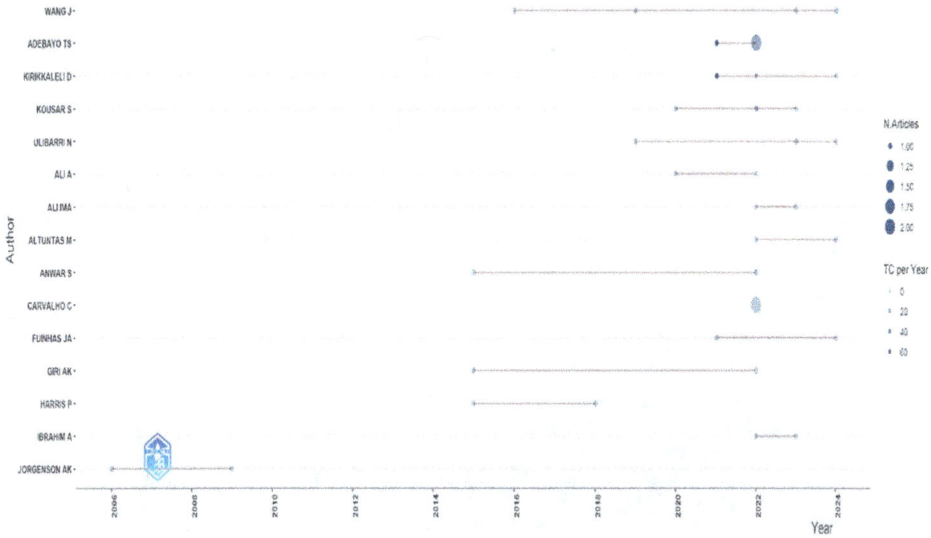

The fact that some authors have published 3 articles indicates that their research is an important reference source in the literature. These results show that some authors have become pivotal references in the field by receiving many citations, but their work is less frequently repeated in terms of prevalence. On the other hand, authors with fewer citations but more frequent mentioned authors in the literature may be researchers who contribute to the field from different perspectives. In terms of bibliometric analysis, it can be said that highly cited authors generally carry out effective studies in the methodological or theoretical framework, while authors who are more frequently referenced play a supporting or complementary role in different studies. This evaluation can be useful in understanding the basic academic trends in the field of research and in determining which sources are important for future research.

The fact that most authors have only conducted one study may indicate that no comprehensive literature reviews were carried out and that only articles known to the authors were cited. Some researchers may have executed a paper on environmental crises and economic inequalities except their field of expertise after that focused on to different subjects. This situation may also express the interdisciplinary approach, and evolving nature of the field, and the contributions of researchers from diverse disciplines. It is possible to say that academic studies in the literature are based on specific pioneering studies and that many researchers have made restricted contributions because of the interdisciplinary nature of the field. Thus, it may be beneficial to investigate the authors prevailing areas of research and other studies with a more extensive analysis.

5.1.3. The Most Productive Countries

Figure 5. The Most Productive Countries and Average Number of Citation

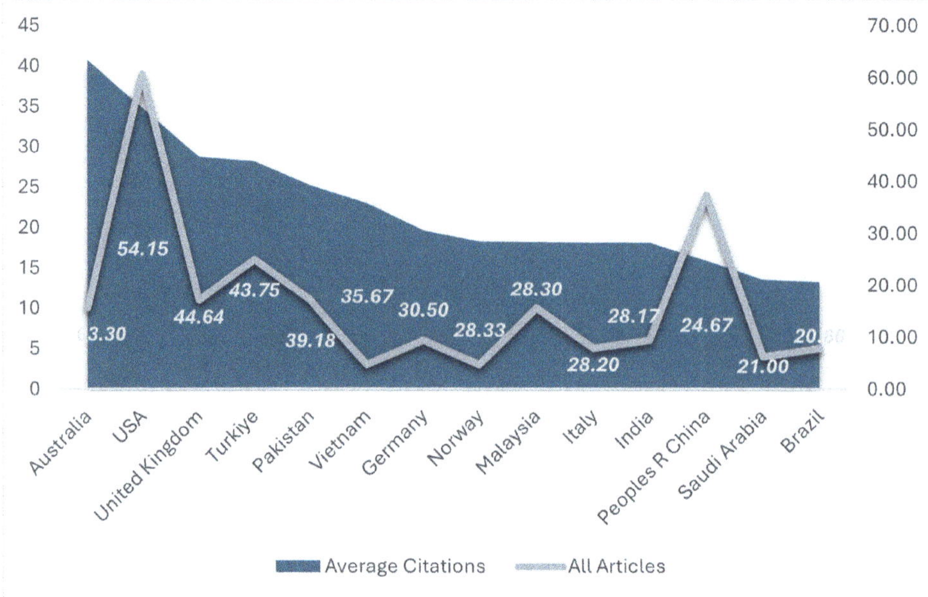

The graph shows the number of academic works on environmental crises and economic inequalities in different countries and the average number of citations to per countries. This is crucial in highlighting the significance and impact of a research area. Therefore, instead of the total citations, the average number of citations per study was used. The variation in citation averages from one country to another may be related to a number of factors, such as the quality of the studies, the extent of international collaboration and the degree of visibility in academic circles.

The various publications include research articles from a total of 51 countries and 778 authors. Australia and the USA are the most productive countries in terms of average citation. It suggests that studies from these countries have a greater impact on the literature and are cited more frequently. It is also worth noting that Australia and the United Kingdom, despite their low number of articles, are the top countries in terms of average citations. Turkey, the United Kingdom, and Pakistan have also contributed to the scientific literature. The fact that countries such as China and

Saudi Arabia have a high number of publications but lower citations may indicate that these studies are less influential in the literature. In Vietnam, Germany, Norway, Italy, India, Saudi Arabia and Brazil, studies in this area are still limited, it highlights the need for further research to gain a better understanding of the impacts of climate change and to advance a range of adaptation strategies.

5.1.4. The Most Productive Sources & Wos Categories

Figure 6. The Most Productive Sources

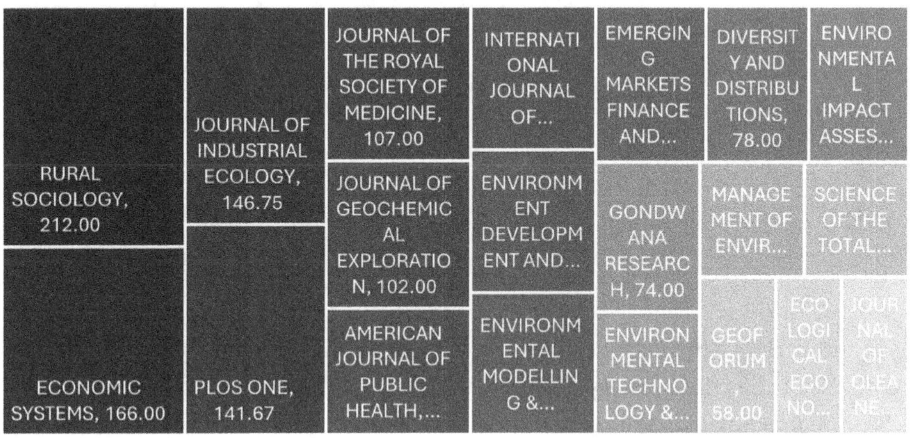

Figure 6 shows the 20 most productive journals in the field according to average citation values. Rural Sociology ranks first with 212 citations for a single article published by it. Economic Systems ranks second with an average of 166 citations and Journal of Industrial Ecology ranks third with 146.75 citations. The prominence of Rural Sociology as the most prolific journal in our bibliometric analysis underlines the alignment of our research theme with rural environmental and socio-economic issues. This suggests that scientific attention is being focused on the intersection of environmental and economic challenges within rural contexts.

Figure 7. Number of Documents and Average Citations related to WoS Categories

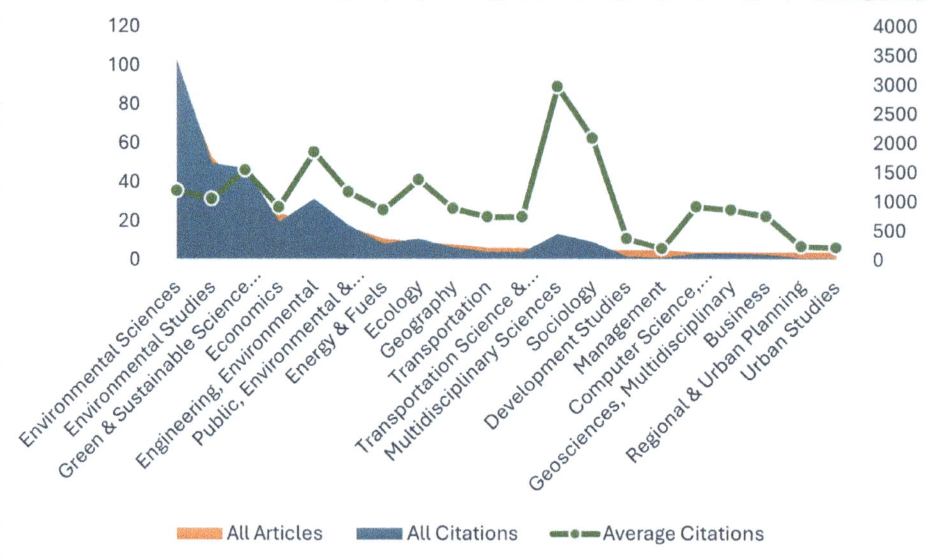

Figure 7 shows the distribution of documents by WoS category. While Environmental Science is the primary category with 97 documents, it is followed by Green & Sustainable Science & Technology with 34 documents. In addition, Economics, Environmental Engineering, Public, Environmental & Occupational Health and Energy & Fuels contributed a significant number of documents with 24, 19, 17 and 11 respectively. It is particularly striking that the average number of citations is highest score in the Multidisciplinary Sciences category. The high number of citations for these studies suggests that researchers from different disciplines are interested in environmental degradation and economic inequality. Although studies in the field of environment and energy lead with regard to number of publications, the average number of citations is more evenly distributed. This distribution shows that studies on economic inequality and environmental crises are interdisciplinary and cover several interrelated fields of study. The dominance of environmental and social sciences underlines the importance of interdisciplinary approaches in understanding and addressing the challenges posed to society by climate change. In addition, many interdisciplinary studies have emerged, including transport, sociology, computer science and interdisciplinary applications.

5.2. Mapping Research Themes

Science mapping is often used to complement the analysis carried out in the previous section and to reveal in greater depth the dynamic characteristics of the research field (Cancino et al., 2017; Merigó et al., 2017). The visuals obtained in the study were generated using VOSviewer 1.6.20 and the Biblioshiny package via RStudio. These visuals allow us to identify prominent authors, countries and journals, and to analyse the links between researchers working in the field and keywords (Blanco-Mesa et al., 2017; Martínez-López et al., 2018). It is also possible to observe the evolution of conceptual development and research hotspots (Laengle et al., 2017; Demir et al., 2024). This makes it possible to examine the diversity of research interests, the scientific network, and the potential to develop different research areas over different over time (Merigó et al., 2018; Tur-Porcar et al., 2018; Iskandar et al., 2024). Therefore, more comprehensive analyses such as Thematic Progression and Citation Burst Analysis are needed to deepen our knowledge of the economic impacts of environmental crises.

5.2.1. Co-occurrence Keywords Analysis

Keyword analysis aims to examine the conceptual structure of a research area. It is pivotal to carry out this analysis, incorporate a wide range of literature and observe the core concepts examined (Callon et al., 1983). A node in a graph depicts the occurrence of a keyword and its size represents its level of significance. Different colors are interpreted in the context of a category. The proximity between keywords reflects the strength of their relationship, and different colors are used to indicate different clusters (Demir et al., 2024; Yan & Zhiping, 2023). As shown in Figure 8, 24 keywords were included in the analysis by setting a threshold of five in the VOSviewer software.

While the most commonly used keywords in the field are concepts such as environmental degradation, CO2 emissions, economic growth, renewable energy, EKC hypothesis and environmental justice, panel quantile regression stands out among the methods. When the visualization is examined, four clusters are identified.

Figure 8a. Mapping of Co-Occurrence of Keywords

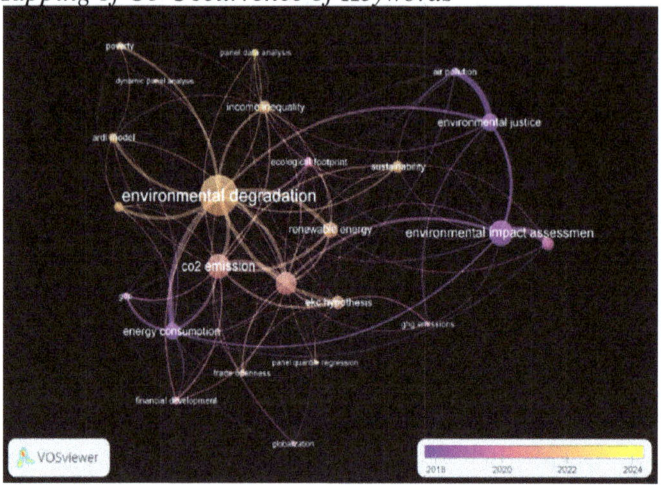

Figure 8b. Co-Occurrence Keyword Word Cloud

According to the color scale foregoing, keywords close to yellow represent more recent research (2023-2024). Words close to purple are topics studied in previous years (2018-2020), indicating that research in these areas has been present in academic literature. It can be seen that topics such as environmental degradation, CO_2 emissions and energy consumption have been studied for a long time, but areas such as environmental justice and impact assessment have been addressed by more recent studies.

Cluster1: It is shaped around topics such as CO_2 emissions, economic growth, EKC hypothesis, energy consumption, panel quantile regression. This cluster comprises studies that focus on the relationships between environmental and economic variables. CO_2 emissions, energy consumption and economic indicators are closely linked, particularly in relation to economic growth and environmental sustainability.

Cluster2: It includes topics such as environmental degradation, income inequality, poverty, ARDL model, dynamic panel analysis, and addresses the links between environmental impacts and income inequality.

Cluster3: It includes topics such as environmental justice, environmental impact assessment, air pollution, life cycle assessment, and studies examining the social dimensions of environmental policies.

Cluster4: This cluster focuses on the use of panel data on environmental issues such as renewable energy and ecological footprint.

5.2.2. Co-Authorship Network and Sankey Diagram

Co-authorship networks represent authors by nodes in their structure and co-authorship relationships by links. These networks are used to explore collaboration between authors, research communities and the structure of scientific topics (Newman, 2001). The co-authorship network visualizes the global distribution of the literature by showing the countries that have produced the most academic output and impact on the themes of environmental degradation and economic inequality. The colors represent the intensity of countries contributions to the topic: red areas represent the highest density (greatest number of publications, citations or collaborative networks), yellow and green areas represent moderate density and blue areas indicate low density.

Figure 9. Mapping of Co-Authorship of Countries

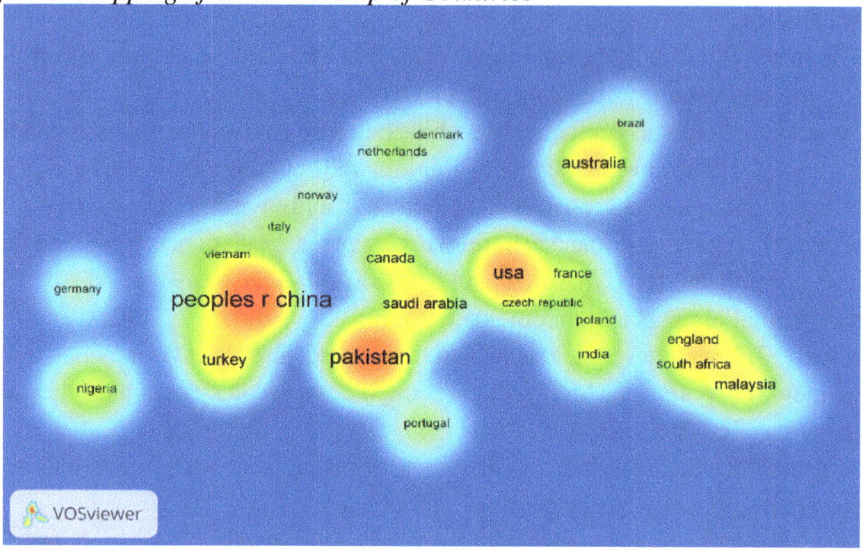

China, Pakistan and the USA stand out as countries that significantly contribute to the literature. In addition to producing high-impact publications, these countries are also central to collaborative research networks. This may indicate a growing academic interest in environmental and economic issues in these regions. Turkey, Saudi Arabia, Canada, Malaysia, Australia, England, South Africa and India make moderate contributions. Countries such as Germany, Italy, Portugal, Denmark, Poland and Nigeria are less prominently represented on the map.

The table and Sankey diagram below are valuable in showing which countries are collaborating and where there may be gaps in the literature. They can also guide the development of regionally focused analyses or strategies for international collaborations for future research.

Table 1. Countries with the Highest Total Link Strength

Country	Article	Total Link Strength
China	40	28
Pakistan	25	22
USA	47	16
Australia	14	10
Turkey	23	9

Figure 10. Sankey Diagram for the Keyword, Country and Author

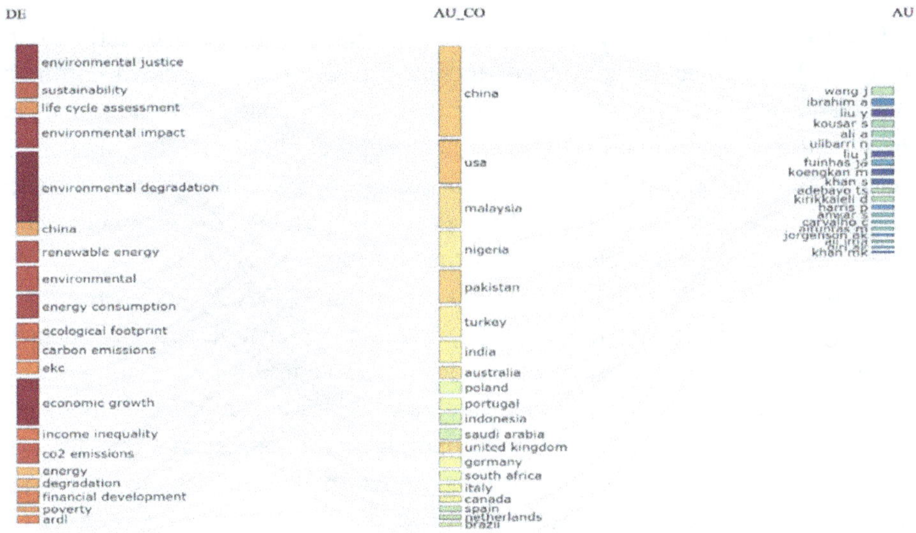

The network structure between keywords (DE), countries (AU_CO) and authors (AU) is illustrated in Figure 10. The visualisation highlights the geographical concentration of thematic areas and identifies the researchers contributing to these studies. Keywords include environmental justice, sustainability, life cycle, environmental degradation, renewable energy, energy consumption, carbon emissions and economic growth.

- Environmental justice and sustainability are the most pivotal themes, focusing on environmental inequalities and sustainable development policies.
- CO_2 emissions and energy consumption show that environmental degradation is analyzed in conjunction with its economic dimensions.

China and USA stand out as the countries with highest academic contributions. Pakistan, Nigeria and Malaysia also reflect the growing importance of environmental sustainability and economic inequality in developing economies. Turkey, India and Poland are among the countries that play an active role in the global academic network. This indicates that research on environmental and economic crises is not only concentrated in developed countries but also in emerging economies. The significance of interdisciplinary research and international academic cooperation is rising.

5.2.3. Thematic Progression

Thematic analysis involves classifying key research themes based on their relevance and density. Themes are categorized into four distinct categories accordingly their relationships with keywords. Centrality on the horizontal axis and density on the vertical axis, along their ranking values (Cobo et al., 2011). The size of the circles is commensurate to the number of documents/publications related with each keyword in the respective quadrant. This analysis helps to identify the major trends in the research field and to outline a roadmap for future researches.

Motor Themes: The topics in the top upper-right quadrant are referred to as motor themes (in other words; hot topics) because they exhibit both high density and high centrality. These are the most active and central topics in the research area, widely discussed in the scientific literature and leading to new developments. In particular, the relationship between economic growth and energy consumption and the impacts on public health stand out among the most notable themes in the scientific literature. **Themes:** Economic growth, energy consumption, health, CO2 emissions, exposure, equity.

Basic Themes: Themes located in the lower-right quadrant are the core themes. They represent the keywords that are central to the research field but haven't yet been developed. Themes with high centrality but low density serve as the fundamental building blocks of the research area and usually correspond to the theoretical or methodological foundations of the discipline. **Themes:** Pollution, life cycle assessment, quality, air pollution, carbon footprint, greenhouse gas emissions.

Emerging or Declining Themes: Themes in the lower-left quadrant are referred to declining or emerging themes. They represent underdeveloped areas with low centrality and density. This indicates either emerging areas of research or topics of declining academic interest. **Themes:** Design, Dynamics, Life, Fuel. Design and fuel dynamics, in particular, may have been more prominent in earlier studies on sustainable energy and carbon footprint. However, fuel dynamics and design processes may regain significance with the development of new sustainable energy solutions.

Niche Themes: In the upper-left quadrant have internal ties but insignificant external ties and thus they are of only marginal interest to the field (Adisa et al., 2020). Themes with high density but lower centrality scores are studied in depth within specific research community but are less prevalent in the broader academic literature. **Themes:** Justice, power, childhood asthma, emissions. Environmental justice and policy debates are primarily examined by a specific academic community. In particular, research on environmental justice and the health effects of air pollution in the United States appears to focus on these themes. These issues are highly relevant in specific contexts but aren't yet central enough in the literature with a broader context.

Figure 11. Thematic Progression in Research Area

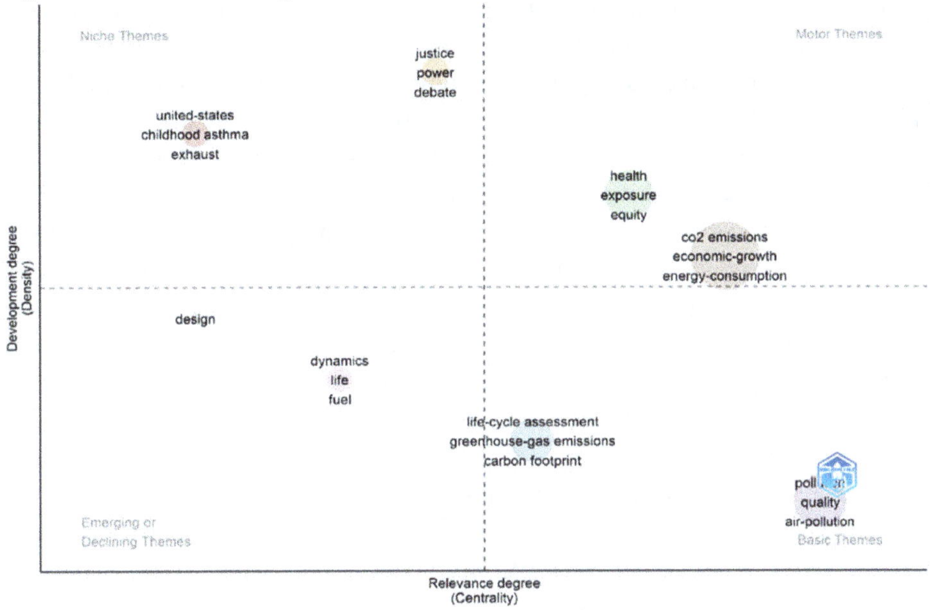

6. DISCUSSION

The purpose of this research is to procure an overview of scientific researches on environmental crises and economic inequalities through bibliometric analysis. Bibliometric analysis reveals research trends in the field by determining interdisciplinary interactions and provides guiding information. In this context, a bibliometric analysis was conducted using Bibexcel, VOSviewer and the Biblioshiny package in order to examine the interaction between environmental crises and economic inequalities. This research primarily focuses on performance analysis to evaluate the quantitative and qualitative impact of publications in a specific field. After that the analysis is completed by visualizing the formation of keywords, academic collaborations between countries and thematic progresses with science mapping. Thus, the research both reveals current research trends and tries to identify potential research gaps for future research. The findings of the research highligt the current status of the interaction between the two fields and shed light on which academic studies focus more.

From general perspective, it's possible say that research on this topic has increased significantly, particularly in the last decade. The most efficient countries in terms of number of publications and total number of connections indicating academic collaborations are the USA, China, Pakistan and Turkey. The growing effectiveness of these countries shows an expansion of both funding and interdisciplinary collaboration in the field. Moreover, this finding partially mitigates the "collaboration gap in developing countries" highlighted by Wang et al. (2022). The most productive countries in terms of average citation values are Australia, USA, United Kingdom, and Turkey. This result underscores the robustness of these countries' research infrastructures and their strategic investments in fostering international collaboration networks.

The most productive academic journals also are seen as Rural Sociology, Economic Systems, and Journal of Industrial Ecology. This finding indicates that researches emphasizes the intersection of rural areas socio-ecological dynamics and industrial ecology frameworks. In addition, Multidisciplinary Sciences stands out as the WoS category with the highest average citation value, followed by Sociology and Engineering categories. This distribution demonstrates that the field's social and technical dimensions are examined through an interdisciplinary perspective.

The most used keywords by the authors are Environmental Degradation, Co2 Emission, Economic Growth, Energy Consumption, Environmental Justice and these words are in a central position in research on the relationship between environmental crises and economic inequalities. These keywords reflect a literature that conceptually and empirically examines the interaction between ecological degradation and inequality. In addition, the clusters "emissions", "energy consumption" and "public health outcomes" have the highest citation density, indicating that the interaction between the environment and public health has become central to scientific discourse.

Thematic progression is crucial for tracing the evolution and depth of scientific discourse within a field. In the environmental and public health literature, prominent themes include the links between emissions, economic growth, energy consumption and public health outcomes. Key focus areas such as air quality, air pollution, life cycle assessment and carbon footprint analysis are extensively explored, reflecting ongoing research and policy interest, while emerging niche topics such as environmental justice, power dynamics and childhood asthma are gaining scholarly attention. These areas, while currently less central, are increasingly recognised for their importance in understanding the broader impacts of environmental issues on vulnerable populations. Accordingly, it is imperative to develop preventive interventions for specific health indicators, including air quality and childhood asthma.

7. CONCLUSION

Although the database used in this research is the Web of Science, it should be noted that other databases, such as Scopus and PubMed can also provide significant contributions to similar analyses. It should also be noted that there are scientific studies in the literature that are not indexed in WoS but may contain significant publications in various journals that can make significant contributions to their fields. Another limitation of the research is that only English publications were included in the analysis. Therefore, excluding studies conducted in different languages may limit a comprehensive assessment of global research trends.

There are many components affecting environmental crises. In this chapter themes with high bibliometric density were examined primarily; weak clusters can be discussed in detail in other scientific researches under the title of Future Research Directions. For that reason; Sustainability, Economic Vulnerailities, and Environmental Justice: The North-South Contradiction are the main topics focused on in the theoretical framework.

Based on the principal findings, some policy recommendations can be developed to overcome the main challenges related to environmental crises and economic inequalities. Breaking the cycle of poverty and inequitable distribution combined with environmental crises requires considering the mutually reinforcing nature of these problems. In this context, implementing policies that focus on equal access and inclusion of resources and services is of critical importance. Governments should prioritize programs that strengthen the economic resilience of poor and vulnerable communities, especially in the fight against and adaptation to climate change. In addition, diversifying livelihoods not only reduces communities' dependence on agriculture-based economies, but also allows for the creation of a more sustainable economic structure against shocks caused by climate change. Such strategies allow for the establishment of stronger social structures, especially those that are less affected by environmental crises and economic inequalities.

As a result, issues such as environmental justice, renewable energy and sustainability have become increasingly popular and a notable research trend at the global level. This development shows that environmental policies are not only focused on environmental impacts, but also on their social dimensions such as inequality and justice. In this context, international collaborations and multidisciplinary research are becoming an increasingly necessary and important research network.

In addition, the impact of environmental crises on economic inequalities has increased, especially in the context of energy consumption and economic growth. This situation provides an important research area for understanding the relationship between energy policies and economic inequalities. In this way, researchers and policy makers can assess the current situation from a more holistic perspective. This can help to shape future policy and research agendas. An integrated approach that takes into account political-economic dynamics, societal needs and environmental challenges will provide a crucial basis for reducing social inequalities and building a resilient future.

REFERENCES

Adebayo, T. S., & Kirikkaleli, D. (2021). Impact of renewable energy consumption, globalization, and technological innovation on environmental degradation in Japan: Application of wavelet tools. *Environment, Development and Sustainability*, *23*(11), 16057–16082. DOI: 10.1007/s10668-021-01322-2

Adisa, O. M., Masinde, M., Botai, J. O., & Botai, C. M. (2020). Bibliometric Analysis of Methods and Tools for Drought Monitoring and Prediction in Africa. *Sustainability (Basel)*, *12*(16), 6516. DOI: 10.3390/su12166516

Ali, I. M. A. (2022). Income inequality and environmental degradation Egypt: Evidence from dynamic ARDL approach. *Environmental Science and Pollution Research International*, *29*(6), 8408–8422. DOI: 10.1007/s11356-021-16275-2 PMID: 34490558

Ali, M., Kirikkaleli, D., & Altuntaş, M. (2024). The nexus between CO_2 intensity of GDP and environmental degradation in South European countries. *Environment, Development and Sustainability*, *26*(5), 11089–11100. DOI: 10.1007/s10668-023-03217-w

Awojobi, O. N., & Vloveret, M. (2017). Social protection and climate resilience: A review of Sub-Saharan African case studies. [IJOEAR]. *International Journal of Environmental & Agriculture Research*, *3*(12), 100–103.

Baek, J., & Gweisah, G. (2013). Does income inequality harm the environment? Empirical evidence from the United States. *Energy Policy*, *62*(Nov), 1434–1437. DOI: 10.1016/j.enpol.2013.07.097

Bai, X., McPhearson, T., Cleugh, H., Nagendra, H., Tong, X., Zhu, T., & Zhu, Y. G. (2017). Linking urbanization and the environment: Conceptual and empirical advances. *Annual Review of Environment and Resources*, *42*(1), 215–240. DOI: 10.1146/annurev-environ-102016-061128

Balakrishnan, U., & Tsaneva, M. (2021). Air pollution and academic performance: Evidence from India. *World Development*, *146*, 105553. DOI: 10.1016/j.worlddev.2021.105553

Baloch, M. A., Khan, S. U. D., Ulucak, Z. S., & Ahmad, A. (2020). Analyzing the relationship between poverty, income inequality, and CO2 emission in Sub-Saharan African countries. *Sci. Total Environ 740*, 139867. https://doi.org/. scitotenv.2020.139867.DOI: 10.1016/j

Bene, C., Cannon, T., Davies, M., Newsham, A., & Tanner, T. (2013). *Social protection and climate change*. OECD Development Co-Operation Workinp Paper., DOI: 10.1787/5jz2qc8wc1s5-

Berthe, A., & Elie, L. (2015). Mechanisms explaining the impact of economic inequality on environmental deterioration. *Ecological Economics, 116*, 191–200. DOI: 10.1016/j.ecolecon.2015.04.026

Besnili, M. O. (2023). İklim Değişikliği ve Sosyal Adalet: Sosyal Politika ve Dayanıklılık Çerçevesinden Bir İnceleme. *Uşak Üniversitesi Uygulamalı Bilimler Fakültesi Dergisi, 3*(2), 20–37.

Blanco-Mesa, F., Merigó, J. M., & Gil-Lafuente, A. M. (2017). Fuzzy decision making: A bibliometric-based review. *Journal of Intelligent & Fuzzy Systems, 32*(3), 2033–2050. DOI: 10.3233/JIFS-161640

Butler, E. (2022). *Introduction to Economic Inequality*. Institute of Economic Affairs.

Cai, Y., & Lontzek, T. S. (2019). The social cost of carbon with economic and climate risks. *Journal of Political Economy, 127*(6), 2684–2734. DOI: 10.1086/701890

Callon, M., Courtial, J. P., Turner, W. A., & Bauin, S. (1983). From translations to problematic networks: An introduction to co-word analysis. *Social Sciences Information. Information Sur les Sciences Sociales, 22*(2), 191–235. DOI: 10.1177/053901883022002003

Carter, M. R., & Janzen, S. A. (2018). Social protection in the face of climate change: Targeting principles and financing mechanisms. *Environment and Development Economics, 23*(3), 369–389. DOI: 10.1017/S1355770X17000407

Cetintas, H., Bicil, İ. M., & Türköz, K. (2016). Türkiye'de CO2 Salınımları Enerji Tüketimi ve Ekonomik Büyüme İlişkisi. *Finans Politik ve Ekonomik Yorumlar*, (619), 57–67.

Chen, C. (2017). Science mapping: A systematic review of the literature. *Journal of Data and Information Science, 2*(2), 1–40. DOI: 10.1515/jdis-2017-0006

Ching, S. L., Lau, L. S., & Choong, C. K. (2023). Income inequality, educational attainment and environmental degradation: Evidence from global panel. *Environmental Science and Pollution Research International, 30*(15), 43056–43067. DOI: 10.1007/s11356-022-19256-1 PMID: 35508851

Chisadza, C., Clance, M., Sheng, X., & Gupta, R. (2023). Climate Change and Inequality: Evidence from the United States. *Sustainability (Basel), 15*(6), 5322. DOI: 10.3390/su15065322

Cho, E. Y. N. (2018). Links between poverty and children's subjective wellbeing: Examining the mediating and moderating role of relationships. *Child Indicators Research, 11*(2), 585–607. DOI: 10.1007/s12187-017-9453-z

Cobo, M. J., López-Herrera, A. G., Herrera-Viedma, E., & Herrera, F. (2011). An Approach for Detecting, Quantifying, and Visualizing the Evolution of a Research Field: A Practical Application to the Fuzzy Sets Theory Field. *Journal of Informetrics, 5*(1), 146–166. DOI: 10.1016/j.joi.2010.10.002

Costella, C., McCord, A., Van Aalst, M., Holmes, R., Ammoun, J., & Barca, V. (2021). *Social protection and climate change: Scaling up ambition. Social Protection Approaches to COVID-19 Expert Advice Service (SPACE).* DAI Global UK Ltd.

Daim, T. U., Rueda, G., Martin, H., & Gerdsri, P. (2006). Forecasting emerging technologies: Use of bibliometrics and patent analysis. *Technological Forecasting and Social Change, 73*(8), 981–1012. DOI: 10.1016/j.techfore.2006.04.004

Demir, G., Chatterjee, P., & Pamucar, D. (2024). Sensitivity analysis in multi-criteria decision making: A state-of-the-art research perspective using bibliometric analysis. *Expert Systems with Applications, 237*, 1–18. DOI: 10.1016/j.eswa.2023.121660

Donadelli, M., Jüppner, M., Riedel, M., & Schlag, C. (2017). Temperature shocks and welfare costs. *Journal of Economic Dynamics & Control, 82*, 331–355. DOI: 10.1016/j.jedc.2017.07.003

Dzikowski, P. (2018). A bibliometric analysis of born global firms. *Journal of Business Research, 85*, 281–294. DOI: 10.1016/j.jbusres.2017.12.054

Ekeocha, D. O. (2021). Urbanization, inequality, economic development and ecological footprint: Searching for turning points and regional homogeneity in Africa. *J. Clean. Prod. 291*, 125244. https://doi.org/. jclepro.2020.125244.DOI: 10.1016/j

Gaviria-Marin, M., Merigó, J. M., & Baier-Fuentes, H. (2019). Knowledge management: A global examination based on bibliometric analysis. *Technological Forecasting and Social Change, 140*, 194–220. DOI: 10.1016/j.techfore.2018.07.006

Golley, J., & Meng, X. (2012). Income inequality and carbon dioxide emissions: The case of Chinese urban households. *Energy Economics, 34*(6), 1864–1872. DOI: 10.1016/j.eneco.2012.07.025

Grossman, G. M., & Krueger, A. B. (1991). Environmental Impacts of the North American Free Trade Agreement. *John M. Ohlin Program Discussion Paper*, No. 158, Princeton. https://www.nber.org/papers/w3914.pdf

Grunewald, N., Klasen, S., Martínez-Zarzoso, I., & Muris, C. (2017). The trade-off between income inequality and carbon dioxide emissions. *Ecological Economics, 142*, 249–256. DOI: 10.1016/j.ecolecon.2017.06.034

Hailemariam, A., Dzhumashev, R., & Shahbaz, M. (2019). Carbon emissions, income inequality and economic development. *Empirical Economics, 59*(3), 1139–1159. DOI: 10.1007/s00181-019-01664-x

Hao, Y., Chen, H., & Zhang, Q. (2016). Will income inequality affect environmental quality? Analysis based on China's provincial panel data. *Ecological Indicators, 67*(8), 533–542. DOI: 10.1016/j.ecolind.2016.03.025

Huang, Z., & Duan, H. (2020). Estimating the threshold interactions between income inequality and carbon emissions. *Journal of Environmental Management, 263*, 110393. DOI: 10.1016/j.jenvman.2020.110393 PMID: 32174532

Hubacek, K., Baiocchi, G., Feng, K., & Patwardhan, A. (2017). Poverty eradication in a carbon constrained world. *Nature Communications, 8*(1), 912. DOI: 10.1038/s41467-017-00919-4 PMID: 29066777

IPCC. (2013). Summary for policymakers. In Stocker, T. F., Qin, D., Plattner, G. K., Tignor, M., Allen, S. K., Boschung, J., Nauels, A., Xia, Y., Bex, V., & Midgley, P. M. (Eds.), *Climate Change 2013: The Physical Science Basis. Contribution of Working Group I to the Fifth Assessment Report of the Intergovernmental Panel on Climate Change*. Cambridge University Press.

IPCC. (2021). Climate Change 2021: The Physical Science Basis. Contribution of Working Group I to the Sixth Assessment Report of the Intergovernmental Panel on Climate Change [Masson-Delmotte, V., P. Zhai, A. Pirani, S.L. Connors, C. Péan, S. Berger, N. Caud, Y. Chen, L. Goldfarb, M.I. Gomis, M. Huang, K. Leitzell, E. Lonnoy, J. B. R. Matthews, T. K. Maycock, T. Waterfield, O. Yelekçi, R. Yu, and B. Zhou (eds.)]. *Cambridge University Press*, Cambridge, United Kingdom and New York, NY, USA, 2391, https://doi:DOI: 10.1017/9781009157896

IPCC. (2022). *Climate Change 2022: Impacts, Adaptation and Vulnerability. Contribution of working group II to the Sixth Assessment Report of the Intergovernmental Panel on Climate Change. H.-O. Pörtner* (Roberts, D. C., Tignor, M., Poloczanska, E. S., Mintenbeck, K., Alegría, A., Craig, M., Langsdorf, S., Löschke, S., Möller, V., Okem, A., & Rama, B., Eds.). Cambridge University Press.

Iskandar, I., Anas, A., Bahri, S., Menne, F., & Baharuddin, T. (2024). Social vulnerability and climate change: A bibliometric analysis. *Cogent Social Sciences, 10*(1), 1–15. DOI: 10.1080/23311886.2024.2402849

Jorgenson, A. K., Schor, J. B., & Giedraitis, V. (2017). Income inequality and carbon emissions in post-soviet nations, 1992-2009. *Ekonomika (Nis)*, *96*(3), 33–43. DOI: 10.15388/Ekon.2017.3.11557

Khan, S., Yahong, W., & Zeeshan, A. (2022). Impact of poverty and income inequality on the ecological footprint in Asian developing economies: Assessment of Sustainable Development Goals. *Energy Reports*, *8*, 670–679. DOI: 10.1016/j.egyr.2021.12.001

Kim, S. J. (2021). Environmental shocks, civil conflict and aid effectiveness. *Conflict Management and Peace Science*, *38*(6), 674–695. DOI: 10.1177/07388942211015240

Knight, K. W., Schor, J. B., & Jorgenson, A. K. (2017). Wealth inequality and carbon emissions in high-income countries. *Social Currents*, *4*(5), 403–412. DOI: 10.1177/2329496517704872

Kopp, T., & Nabernegg, M. (2022). Inequality and Environmental Impact-Can the Two Be Reduced Jointly? *Ecological Economics*, *201*, 1–12. DOI: 10.1016/j.ecolecon.2022.107589

Kousar, S., Bhutta, A. I., Ullah, M. R., & Shabbir, A. (2023). Impact of economic and green growth on poverty, income inequalities, and environmental degradation: A case of South Asian economies. *Environmental Science and Pollution Research International*, *30*(12), 35200–35213. DOI: 10.1007/s11356-022-24191-2 PMID: 36527550

Laengle, S., Merigó, J. M., Miranda, J., Słowiński, R., Bomze, I., Borgonovo, E., Dyson, R. G., Oliveira, J. F., & Teunter, R. (2017). Forty years of the European Journal of Operational Research: A bibliometric overview, *European Journal of Operational Research,* 262(3), 803-816, ISSN 0377-2217, DOI: 10.1016/j.ejor.2017.04.027

Li, J., & Chen, C. M. (2016). CiteSpace: Text Mining and Visualization in Scientific Literature. *Capital University of Economics and Business Press.* 193-206.

Li, X., Wu, K., & Liang, Y. (2023). A Review of Agricultural Land Functions: Analysis and Visualization Based on Bibliometrics. *Land (Basel)*, *12*(3), 561. DOI: 10.3390/land12030561

Lim, W. M., & Kumar, S. (2023). Guidelines for interpreting the results of bibliometric analysis: A sensemaking approach. *Global Business and Organizational Excellence*, *43*(2), 17–26. DOI: 10.1002/joe.22229

Liu, C., Jiang, Y., & Xie, R. (2019a). Does income inequality facilitate carbon emission reduction in the US? *J. Clean. Prod. 217*, 380-387. https://doi.org/. jclepro.2019.01.242.DOI: 10.1016/j

Liu, X., Zhang, L., & Hong, S. (2011). Global biodiversity research during 1900-2009: A bibliometric analysis. *Biodiversity and Conservation*, *20*(4), 807–826. DOI: 10.1007/s10531-010-9981-z

Martínez-López, F. J., Merigó, J. M., Valenzuela-Fernández, L., & Nicolás, C. (2018). Fifty years of the European Journal of Marketing: A bibliometric analysis. *European Journal of Marketing*, *52*(1/2), 439–468. DOI: 10.1108/EJM-11-2017-0853

Masud, M. M., Kari, F. B., Banna, H., & Saifullah, M. K. (2018). Does income inequality affect environmental sustainability? Evidence from the ASEAN-5. *Journal of the Asia Pacific Economy*, *23*(2), 213–228. DOI: 10.1080/13547860.2018.1442146

Méjean, A., Sowah, P. C., Guivarch, C., Piontek, F., Soergel, B., & Taconet, N. (2024). Climate change impacts increase economic inequality: Evidence from a systematic literature review. *Environmental Research Letters*, *19*(4), 1–22. DOI: 10.1088/1748-9326/ad376e

Merigó, J. M., Blanco-Mesa, F., Gil-Lafuente, A. M., & Yager, R. R. (2017). Thirty Years of the International Journal of Intelligent Systems: A Bibliometric Review. *International Journal of Intelligent Systems*, *32*(5), 526–554. DOI: 10.1002/int.21859

Merigó, J. M., Gil-Lafuente, A. M., & Yager, R. R. (2015). An overview of fuzzy research with bibliometric indicators. *Applied Soft Computing*, *27*, 420–433. DOI: 10.1016/j.asoc.2014.10.035

Merigó, J. M., Pedrycz, W., Weber, R., & de la Sotta, C. (2018). Fifty years of Information Sciences: A bibliometric overview, *Information Sciences*, 432, 245-268, ISSN 0020-0255, DOI: 10.1016/j.ins.2017.11.054

Millennium Ecosystem Assessment. (2005). *Ecosystems and Human Well-being: General Synthesis*. Island Press.

Newman, M. E. J. (2001). Scientific collaboration networks. I. Network construction and fundamental results. *Physical Review. E*, *64*(1), 016131. DOI: 10.1103/PhysRevE.64.016131 PMID: 11461355

Norris, M., & Oppenheim, C. (2007). Comparing alternatives to the Web of Science for coverage of the social sciences' literature. *Journal of Informetrics*, *1*(2), 161–169. DOI: 10.1016/j.joi.2006.12.001

Nunen, K. V., Li, J., Reniers, G., & Ponnet, K. (2018). Bibliometric analysis of safety culture research. *Safety Science*, *108*, 248–258. DOI: 10.1016/j.ssci.2017.08.011

Pata, U. K., Yilanci, V., Hussain, B., & Ali Naqvi, S. A. (2022). Analyzing the role of income inequality and political stability in environmental degradation: Evidence from South Asia. *Gondwana Research, 107*, 13–29. DOI: 10.1016/j.gr.2022.02.009

Ravallion, M., Heil, M., & Jalan, J. (2000). Carbon emissions and income inequality. *Oxford Economic Papers, 52*(4), 651–669. DOI: 10.1093/oep/52.4.651

REN21. (2023). *Renewables 2023 Global Status Report Collection*. Renewables in Energy Supply.

Schaffrin, A. (2014). The new social risks and opportunities of climate change. In *International Handbook on Social Policy and the Environment*. Edward Elgar Publishing. DOI: 10.4337/9780857936134.00007

Schlosberg, D. (2007). *Defining Environmental Justice: Theories, Movements, and Nature*. Oxford University Press., DOI: 10.1093/acprof:oso/9780199286294.001.0001

Sengül, B., & Murat, G. (2024). Küresel İklim Krizinin Sosyal Boyutu ve Sosyal Politika Önlemleri. *Süleyman Demirel Üniversitesi Vizyoner Dergisi, 15*(41), 342–358. DOI: 10.21076/vizyoner.1310015

Steffen, W., Grinevald, J., Crutzen, P., & McNeill, J. (2011). The Anthropocene: Conceptual and historical perspectives. *Philosophical Transactions. Series A, Mathematical, Physical, and Engineering Sciences, 369*(1938), 842–867. DOI: 10.1098/rsta.2010.0327 PMID: 21282150

Tur-Porcar, A., Mas-Tur, A., Merigó, J. M., Roig-Tierno, N., & Watt, J. (2018). A Bibliometric History of the Journal of Psychology Between 1936 and 2015. *The Journal of Psychology, 152*(4), 199–225. DOI: 10.1080/00223980.2018.1440516 PMID: 29611782

United Nations. (2020a). UNDESA World Social Report 2020a. Retrieved from https://www.un.org/development/desa/dspd/world-social-report/2020a-2.html

United Nations. (2025). The 17 goals. Retrieved from https://sdgs.un.org/goals

Wang, J. (2024). Renewable energy, inequality and environmental degradation. *Journal of Environmental Management, 356*, 1–14. DOI: 10.1016/j.jenvman.2024.120563 PMID: 38479288

Wolde-Rufael, Y., & Idowu, S. (2017). Income distribution and CO2 emission: A comparative analysis for China and India. *Renewable & Sustainable Energy Reviews, 74*, 1336–1345. DOI: 10.1016/j.rser.2016.11.149

World Inequality Database. (2019). Data. Retrieved from https://wid.world/data/. Accessed: 12 Apr 2025.

Wu, R., & Xie, Z. (2020). Identifying the impacts of income inequality on CO2 emissions: Empirical evidences from OECD countries and non-OECD countries. *Journal of Cleaner Production, 277*, 123858. DOI: 10.1016/j.jclepro.2020.123858

Yan, L., & Zhiping, W. (2023). Mapping the Literature on Academic Publishing: A Bibliometric Analysis on WOS. *SAGE Open, 13*(1), 21582440231158562. Advance online publication. DOI: 10.1177/21582440231158562

Yoganandham, G. (2022). Global Economic Inequalities and Environmental Problems in relation to the Job Market, The Economy, and the Ecosystem as a whole-Atheoretical Assessment. *Mukt Shabd Journal, 11*(8), 640–658.

KEY TERMS AND DEFINITIONS

Bibliometric Analysis: It is a method that examines the quantitative data of scientific publications—such as article counts, citation numbers, and author or country collaboration networks—and reveals the contribution and impact trends in various disciplines. Additionally, it evaluates the development of knowledge and provides inference about trajectories of future publications.

Economic Inequality: It means that the unequal distribution of income, wealth, and economic possibilities between individuals or households in a society.

Economic Vulnerability: It is denotes an economy's susceptibility to external shocks—such as financial crises, price volatility, or natural disasters—that may undermine its capacity to sustain stable economic activity.

Environmental Crises: Environmental crisis is a severe disruption of natural ecosystem functions driven by both anthropogenic activities and natural phenomena that results in widespread ecological imbalance and threatens biodiversity and human well-being.

Environmental Justice: It encompasses the equitable distribution of environmental benefits across all societal groups, equal participation in decision-making processes, and compensation for damaged communities.

Performance Analysis: It refers to the quantitative evaluation of the productivity and impact of research actors (authors, journals, countries, institutions) within a given field. It generally covers total number of publications, number of citations, the most productive sources, countries, and authors.

Research Methodology: It refers to the set of methods selected to address a research problem in accordance with the study's objectives. It also provides a systematic framework that specifies what is investigated, why, and how.

Research Trend: It refers to a discernible shift or pattern in the methods, themes or result of scholarly inquiry within a given field over time.

Sankey Diagram: It is used to visualize the flows of scientific information such as citations, co-authorships, or keyword transitions (e.g., authors, institutions, countries, or research topics).

Sustainability: It is an approach that seeks to use resources efficiently and preserve ecological balance to compensate the needs of present and future generations, supported by a shared commitment to these principles.

Thematic Progression: It is an analytical approach that examines the temporal evolution of key concepts and topics within a research field, analysing their appearance, strengthen, and decline.

Chapter 2
Navigating Global Poverty in the midst of Rising Income Inequality:
A Human Security Approach

Jipson Joseph
https://orcid.org/0009-0005-1795-5051
Christ University, India

Achyutananda Mishra
https://orcid.org/0000-0002-4113-0974
Christ University, India

ABSTRACT

From the dawn of civilization, poverty has been a predominant concern. Among them, the post-Second World War welfare state policies and economic development had a significant effect. Scientific and technological advancements and economic growth increased the GDP of almost all countries. However, it also widened the gap between the rich and the poor. This became evident with neoliberalism, privatization, and deregulation of the economy. The private assets increased enormously, losing the public sector's control over the economic interactions. As a result, income and wealth inequality increased rapidly. The World Inequality Report (2022) affirms the massive concentration of income and wealth in the hands of a few individuals. It adversely affects poverty alleviation strategies as poverty increases along with the rising income inequality. The World Bank (2024) affirms this precarious situation. From this perspective, this chapter examines the significance of the human security approach in addressing these human insecurities.

DOI: 10.4018/979-8-3373-7360-7.ch002

1 INTRODUCTION

Poverty has been one of the constant challenges to humanity, affecting the survival and standard of living of millions of people. Although the percentage of the poor population is decreasing, it still exists significantly in many parts of the world (Fan & Cho, 2021). The understanding of poverty also changes with time. Poverty was primarily understood as a lack of nutritious food. It was then perceived as an absence of a minimum standard of living. From the second half of the 20th century, it was understood to be connected with consumption and income. The World Bank is the leading proponent of the monetary understanding of poverty. It led to an easy measurement of absolute and relative poverty. However, many criticized it, arguing that the unidimensional (income) understanding of poverty cannot present an exact picture. Accordingly, towards the end of the 20th century, with the United Nations Development Program (UNDP) initiative, poverty is understood as multidimensional. It affirms that poverty lacks vital dimensions, such as income, nutritious food, healthcare, and other essentials. Besides, the latest data from the World Bank (2024) and the UNDP (2024) affirms that poverty exists in almost all parts of the globe. Although poverty is more explicit in the developing world, the data states that it is also notably present in the developed world, pointing to the global nature of poverty.

Poverty was seen as quite a normal thing, which some people are supposed to suffer throughout their lives. Thomas Malthus (1798) claimed that human beings' suffering from a lack of want is an inevitable law of nature. Roser (2022) argues that it was unimaginable in the 18th century that poverty could be alleviated. According to Moatsos (2021), almost three-quarters of the global population during the 1820s lived in extreme poverty. However, economic growth over the last two centuries has significantly alleviated poverty. With economic development, society increased its production of goods and services, helping to resolve a situation where the majority could not access basic goods and services (Roser, 2023). For instance, in 1820, almost 90% of the population in Sweden was poor, but by 2024, it was reduced to just 15% with the support of massive economic growth (Roser, 2022; Hasell et al., 2022). However, along with economic development, income inequality also increased, causing an increase in the number of people living in relative poverty (de Vita, 2007).

History attests to various poverty eradication and income inequality reduction strategies by national governments and international bodies. The welfare government's origin has significantly contributed to accelerating this objective. However, the 2022 World Inequality Report discloses the massive income and wealth disparity. While the bottom 50% of the global population owns just 8.5% of total income and 2% of total wealth, the top 10% owns 52% of total income and 76% of total wealth. The latest report of the World Bank (2024) affirms that almost 700 million people live below the $2.15/day mark. It shows that poverty and income inequality are present on a large scale. Poverty has been a growing concern around the globe since the dawn of civilization. Although many believed that the economic growth of the 20th century would help eradicate poverty, it increased income inequality and suffocated people experiencing poverty. That is, poverty and rising income inequality make people's lives more insecure than ever. The United Nations (UN) initiated many programs in the last decades of the 20th century to eradicate poverty and income inequality (Moatsos, 2025). Among them, the UNDP's human security approach has more significance as it stands for a global policy approach that incorporates the fundamentals of human rights, human development, freedoms, capabilities, and sustainable development in its policy framework.

In line with the above, this chapter critically evaluates the present scenario of human insecurity caused by global poverty and income inequality and their intersection. Since they harm people's meaningful and peaceful lives, it is worth addressing them from the perspective of the human security paradigm, as many argue that poverty and income inequality occur due to policy failures. The chapter will suggest some policy guidelines to confront the complexities of poverty and income inequality and ensure security for all people across the globe.

2 LITERATURE REVIEW

Critically examining the Indian income inequality during 1922-2015, Chancel and Piketty (2019) affirm that income inequality is very high in India, pointing to a transition from British Raj to Billionaire Raj. Such an increased economic inequality will adversely impact the poverty eradication strategies. Fan and Cho (2021) delve into the various possible ways for poverty eradication across the globe, like increasing agricultural productivity, limiting rural-urban migration if agrarian productivity has not reached a desired level, and social security nets. They argue that, along with rural poverty, urban poverty also should become a prime concern of policymakers. Lawrence (2021) argues that inequality between and within countries is increasing swiftly. The COVID-19 pandemic reinforced the already existing income inequality. He notes a strong relationship between threats to security and inequality, which requires urgent policy interventions. Focusing on the West African scenario, Kouadio and Gakpa (2022) examine whether economic growth and institutional quality reduce poverty and inequality. They affirm that economic growth and overall improvements in institutional quality enhance the attempts for poverty eradication and inequality reduction.

Ferreira et al. (2022) state that inequality has become a significant concern in international development challenges. Inequality harms growth, development, and governance. When these vital concerns are damaged, it increases the percentage of poverty in society. Bhoi (2022) examines the financial plight of the scheduled castes and affirms that education can promote their economic growth and development, which will help them to overcome poverty and societal inequality. Although it does not explicitly focus on the human security approach, it underlines the importance of a people-centered approach. Miyandazi et al. (2023) and Liebenberg et al. (2023) focus on the issues of poverty and inequality through the lens of human rights. While the first focuses on the Kenyan situation, the second studies the South African scenario. Both agree that poverty and income inequality affirm society's existing human rights violations. Giang (2024) affirms that poverty is a crucial concern for both developing and developed countries. Some consider it a fundamental threat to humanity and the root cause of all global issues. Various governments, like that of Vietnam, have taken up the idea of multidimensional poverty and attempted to perceive it through the lens of human security due to its all-encompassing nature. Parolin et al (2025) examine the intergenerational persistence of poverty in five high-income countries, such as the USA, the UK, Australia, Denmark, and Germany. However, it does not address the role of the human security approach.

The literature affirms that global poverty and income inequality are serious concerns of the academic world. However, except for Giang (2024), none of them addressed it through the lens of the human security approach. His study was limited to the Vietnamese approach of human security. This chapter, therefore, intends to advance the human security framework on a broader horizon by examining poverty and income inequality across the globe.

3 METHODOLOGY

The chapter employs the critical analysis method of doctrinal methodology for examining global poverty amid rising income inequality. The chapter uses the data from the World Bank, UNDP, World Inequality Lab, and various researchers to explore the interconnection between global poverty and income inequality. The chapter also makes a comparative study of the developed and developing worlds to explore their differences regarding the percentage of poverty and income inequality. Although the chapter does not precisely use any tools of the qualitative and quantitative methodologies, it heavily depends on the primary data from the international and national institutions and research agencies.

4 GLOBAL POVERTY AND INCOME INEQUALITY

Although the globe has been concerned about poverty and income inequality for centuries, the global efforts for poverty eradication became more visible only in the second half of the 20th century, especially with the UN initiatives. Although poverty was seen as an issue in the developing world, the latest trends affirm that it is equally visible in the developed world. Besides, globalization's interconnectedness affirms that insecurities like poverty and income inequality in any part of the globe will have repercussions in other parts (Kant, 1795). It leads to an understanding of global poverty and inequality, especially with the latest trends in privatization and multinational and transnational corporations. Both poverty and income inequality cause insecurities in human life. This section, therefore, analyzes the meaning and implications of these two concepts.

4.1 Global Poverty

Poverty has been an ongoing concern for humanity. It is defined in material, financial, relational, and spiritual perspectives. Pogge (2005, p.1) calls poverty "an ongoing harm." How does it become harmful or insecure? Many people consider that since poverty refers to a lack of material things, it causes alarming insecurities in human lives. Some others perceive it from the viewpoint of income and wealth and hold that it affects people's aspirations for a standard of living. It leads to relational poverty, which is considered in relation to the living standards of other people in a society. Underlining the spiritual perspective, Hunter (1904) argues that poverty is not a mere lack of things but "the fear and dread of want." Sen (1992, p.109) defined poverty as the "failure of basic capabilities to reach certain minimally acceptable levels." With the theoretical support of Sen's capabilities approach, poverty is examined in the context of well-being (Costa, 2008). Hunter (1904) explains the essence of poverty as the pressure "to live miserable we know not why, to have the dread of hunger, to work sore and yet gain nothing." The real situation of the poor is extremely pathetic as they experience hunger, fear, social exclusion, and marginalization. The country's huge income generation and GDP growth adversely affect the market balance as it prioritizes only the interests of the affluent people. People experiencing poverty are again forced to experience insecurity and economic burdens in their lives due to imbalanced economic growth and distributional failures despite their hard work.

Global poverty is often measured using two different parameters: subjective and objective, and absolute and relative. Subjective poverty measurement is calculated based on the interaction with people, asking whether they experience poverty. On the other hand, objective poverty is the impartial fixing of specific parameters for measuring poverty. An individual's subjective perception is not counted in the objective poverty measurement (Moatsos, 2025). However, compared to the objective poverty line, where the researchers or policymakers fix a standard of reference without really understanding the life situations of people, the subjective understanding of poverty has more value as it can epitomize the genuine concerns and insecurities of those who experience poverty (Narayan et al., 2000). Whether the quantification or measurement of poverty, using any measuring tool, will provide the whole picture is a complex question. Poverty measurement does not consider or analyze the real experiences of poor people. It just provides some numbers. Their day-to-day experiences are essential for understanding poverty's true nature. Besides poverty statistics, the globe requires knowing poor people's living circumstances, their daily obstacles, and expectations about possible solutions (de Schutter, 2021).

From 1990 onwards, the World Bank initiated the income-based calculation of poverty. Accordingly, the understanding of absolute/extreme and relative poverty has evolved. Both absolute and relative poverty lines are objective measurements. The World Bank fixes an international poverty line to measure absolute poverty across the globe and updates it in specific periods. It helps efficiently estimate the number of people experiencing extreme poverty worldwide. Such a method will help devise particular policies and strategies for their empowerment. The UNDP's Multidimensional Poverty Index (MPI) also follows an absolute poverty line calculation but uses a different method. Although these two international institutions follow specific parameters to fix a relative poverty line, relative poverty understanding revolves around inequalities in living situations and people's access to the bare essentials in society (Moatsos, 2025).

It would be impossible to fix a common reference standard for measuring subjective poverty, as individual perspectives differ depending on the person. The World Bank has made a significant effort to give voice to the people experiencing poverty through its considerable contribution of 2000 (Narayan et al., 2000). However, as Moatsos (2025) claimed, no subjective measurement or approach to poverty has been published. The following points examine various objective measurements to provide an exact scenario of global poverty.

4.1.1 Lack of Nutritious Food

Nutritious food is an essential requirement for survival. Poverty is identified as the lack of healthy food necessary for human existence. It revolves around the quality and quantity of food. The WHO has identified the required food calories for an average individual, and the inability to obtain the needed quality food is considered poverty (Allen, 2017). The UN and several national constitutions affirm the right to food in the context of poverty and famine. Both poverty and famine endangered the right to life of millions of people, even when there were sufficient resources in the world to feed them. It shows that while some people had surplus food, many were denied basic food requirements, exposing societal inequalities. Researchers argue that more people die of hunger and famine than war and armed conflicts around the globe (Gráda, 2007). The right to food imposes certain corresponding obligations on the State. Like any other human right, the State must respect, protect, and fulfill people's food rights. The first obligation (to respect) implies that the State should not prevent people's access to food. The second obligation (to protect) points to the duty of the State to take preventive measures against institutions or individuals that challenge people's access to food. The third obligation (to fulfill) implies that the State should actively provide sufficient food security to people. It also stands for the state's direct responsibility to provide adequate food if individuals fail to achieve it for any reason (CESCR, 1999).

4.1.2 Lack of Minimum Standard of Life

The minimum standard of living refers to satisfying the bare essential needs. It implies the satisfaction of goods and services without which people will be forced to live in some form of deprivation, affecting their security and meaningful life (Moatsos, 2025). Most low- and middle-income countries consider poverty in the light of a lack of basic needs. Understanding the minimum standard of living depends on the economic scenario of each country. It would be impossible to devise a globally accepted minimum standard of life as it depends on each country's social, cultural, economic, and political circumstances (Jolliffe & Prydz, 2021). The minimum standard of living of the USA or the UK would be larger than that of Uganda or Bangladesh. The history of identifying poverty with the lack of basic needs for a minimum standard of living started with the contributions of Adam Smith. Thereafter, Rowntree (1901) and Booth (1904) advanced this approach (Moatsos, 2025). Reddy and Pogge (2010) claim that understanding poverty in the light of basic needs has the potential for better internationally comparable poverty estimates. Even when enlisting the drawbacks of this method, Authors like Moatsos (2025) argue that if systematically designed, this method has more scope to outshine the dollar-a-day (DAD) method. While the DAD method uses a specific poverty line for years, applicable to all countries, the CBN (cost of basic needs) method changes with country and year. Townsend (1979, p.915) rightly argued that "the necessities of life are not fixed. They are continuously being adapted and augmented as changes take place in society and its products." However, the DAD method is relatively easy, whereas the CBN method requires detailed specifications and more data.

4.1.3 Lack of Income and Wealth

Poverty is predominantly understood in economic terms as a lack of income. From this perspective, poverty is used with three suffixes: extreme, moderate, and relative. Extreme poverty is a severe situation in which individuals and households cannot meet basic survival requirements. Moderate poverty points to a situation where the basic needs are barely met. Relative poverty states that the income of some individuals or households is comparatively lower than that of most people in the region (Sachs, 2005). Relative poverty helps to measure inequalities and disparities as it compares the income and wealth of individuals in a given society. While absolute poverty speaks of deprivation in absolute terms, relative poverty explains it compared to other people's lives in a society. Both absolute and relative poverty point to a situation where people live in a deprived state. Their basic requirements for a significant life are challenged due to their poor financial condition. Accordingly, they fail to adapt to the growing demands of society.

Measuring poverty using the income parameter started in India (1962), where a working group calculated the minimum required income to meet basic needs for a healthy life. It fixed 20 in rural areas and 25 in urban areas as the poverty line. An attempt to measure worldwide poverty started with Ahluwalia et al. in 1979, in which they took the details of 36 developing countries. Thereafter, the World Bank led the initiative to understand poverty in connection with consumption and income. From 1990 onwards, it started to provide a fixed poverty line. It began with fixing $1/day as the official mark for measuring extreme poverty. Ravallion et al. (1991) fixed this line based on consumption-based household surveys. They used income as the second-best choice if the consumption details were unavailable. This method is widely recognized as an income-based calculation. In September 2022, the World Bank fixed $2.15/day as the contemporary poverty line for calculating absolute poverty. The basic premise of the World Bank scholars for measuring poverty in terms of income is that the lack of income and wealth affects people's consumption patterns, leading them to poverty (Moatsos, 2025).

4.1.4 Multidimensional Poverty

Multidimensional poverty affirms that understanding poverty from the monetary perspective alone will not be just. A fundamental understanding of poverty requires comprehending it from different angles. Economic deprivation and income inequality are the most visible expressions of poverty. However, it does not mean that poverty is only a financial issue. As mentioned above, poverty includes a lack of food, a minimum standard of living, and a shortage of other vital elements, leading to the multidimensionality of poverty. The UN agencies try to define poverty within a larger horizon, covering almost all essential aspects of human life. They state that poverty is not a matter of single deprivation but interconnected deprivations. Measuring poverty in terms of multidimensionality began in the 21st century. Its definitions cover deprivations in resources, capabilities, choices, security, and power, essential for realizing various rights (CESCR, 2001). Based on Article 25 of the UDHR, Pogge (2011) defined poor persons as individuals who lack access to a standard of living adequate for their or their family's health and well-being, including food, clothing, housing, and healthcare. All these underline that poverty has many vital dimensions.

The UNDP and the Oxford Poverty and Human Development Initiative (OPHI) developed the MPI in 2010 based on the Alkire-Foster methodology to understand the multidimensional nature of poverty. Based on the MPI, a household is poor if it experiences deprivation "in at least a third of the weighted indicators" (Atkinson, 2019, p. 157). The fundamental premise of MPI is that no two persons experience poverty similarly. The 2024 MPI provides data from one hundred and twelve countries, including twenty-one low-income countries, eighty-seven middle-income countries, and four high-income countries. The MPI covers 92% of the global population. Among the covered 6.3 billion, 1.1 billion people experience poverty, and 83.2% are in Sub-Saharan Africa (553 million) and South Asia (402 million). One hundred four million poor people are in East Asia and the Pacific, 53 million are in the Arab States, 34 million are in Latin America and the Caribbean, and 2 million are in Europe and Central Asia (OPHI & UNDP, 2024).

4.1.5 Current Scenario of Global Poverty

Although there has been significant growth in poverty eradication efforts over the last two centuries, the international poverty line and the current number of people experiencing extreme poverty affirm that poverty is still a reality affecting every tenth person in the world (Roser, 2023). Poverty was mainly considered a problem in the developing world. Since the developed world has higher income and social security nets, the issue of absolute poverty was not considered part of its life. However, the data confirms that developed countries also experience large numbers of poverty. Compared to absolute poverty, relative poverty is higher in the developed world. Gough and Eisenschitz (2021) argue that a general parameter to understand and measure poverty in the developed world may not be suitable. Each high-income country's particular context and period are to be considered when measuring poverty. In 2019, almost 17.5% of the US population was poor (Brady, 2023). Analyzing the scenario of five high-income countries, like the USA, the UK, Australia, Germany, and Denmark, Parolin et al. (2025) affirm the intergenerational persistence of poverty even in the developed world.

4.2 Economic Inequality

The evidence of the last two centuries affirms that economic growth has substantially contributed to poverty alleviation. The globe has various models of economic growth and poverty alleviation, such as a free and open market system with minimum taxes and state regulation for attracting investment and stimulating growth (Hong Kong & China), extensive government investment in education, infrastructure development, and healthcare (Kerala, India), and some protectionist measures for incubating industries to enable them internationally competitive (South Korea) (Pogge, 2005). These models have provided positive results. They also affirm that economic growth is essential for society's overall growth. The last decades of the 20th century witnessed a resurgence of economic growth with the theoretical support of neoliberalism (Bhoi, 2022). Privatization and an open economy were the immediate results of this paradigm shift. The changes from public ownership to private engagement in economic exchanges strengthened the economy and increased the GDP per capita (Joshy, 2021). The Bretton Woods Institutions, the Marrakesh Agreement, and the Washington Consensus also increased economic interactions (Drabek, 2024). Globalization and its interconnectedness further broadened the scope of global economic life. All these contributed to an unparalleled increase in financial matters. However, with the rise in GDP, poor people's living situations did not change. It only benefited a few people in society. This resulted in a massive concentration of income and wealth in a few hands, leading to two opposite groups: haves and have-nots. There has been an enormous increase in the average global income, but the data shows that millions still experience extreme poverty (Pogge, 2005). It shows that the benefits of economic growth are not equitably distributed. The lack of equitable distribution points to income inequality.

Economic inequality, whether income or wealth, is not an issue in the developing world alone. It exists in the developed world as well. Analyzing 34 years (1980-2014) of American economic history, Stiglitz (2016) argues that the real income of the wealthiest 0.1% increased by 281%, and they hold more than 22% of America's total wealth. This phenomenon is widely visible in countries like Britain, Germany, and Russia. Piketty and Zucman (2015) also note the growing inequality in the developed world, especially concerning inherited wealth. By comparing the GDP per capita of the top 25 countries with the bottom 25 countries of 1960 and 2019, Lawrence (2021) states that inequality is rising globally. Chancel et al. (2022) affirm that income and wealth inequality have become a global phenomenon affecting developing and developed countries equally. While the European Union and China experience a relatively minor increase, countries like the US, Russia, and India have spectacular increases in inequality. In some countries like India, inequality has become extreme, inviting attention from policymakers and other actors (Chancel &

Piketty, 2019). Higher inequality is always a serious concern for the nation. However, many European countries claim comparatively less inequality. The Gini Coefficient notes that Slovakia has the lowest global inequality (0.23) (Statista, 2025). It shows that inequality exists across the globe in varied degrees.

4.2.1 The World Inequality Report of 2022

The World Inequality Lab affirms that inequality evolves from the distributional failures of economic benefits. Many countries publish reports of economic growth, but do not report how the benefits of economic growth are distributed. Accordingly, the World Inequality Report has added value as it provides data on world inequality, which is provided nowhere else. Through this report, the World Inequality Lab wants to conscientize people, policymakers, and global leaders about the distributional failures, unbalanced concentration of income and wealth, and rising inequality. The assessment is based on the purchasing power parity (PPP). The report states that the wealthiest 10% of the world population earn more than 50% of global income, and the poorest 50% own just 8.5%. It shows that an enormous gap exists in society. Concerning wealth, the top 10% own about 76% of the global wealth compared to just 2% of the bottom 50%. This uncontrollable concentration of income and wealth into the hands of a few individuals results from growing privatization and higher engagement of multinational and transnational corporations. The report also notes that inequality is drastically increasing in some countries compared to others. It shows that economic inequality can result from political choice and economic interactions (Chancel et al., 2022).

4.2.2 Concentration of Income and Wealth

The data above affirms that the globe experiences a massive concentration of income and wealth in the hands of relatively few individuals, corporations, and countries. It also points to the distributional failures of the economic system (Lawrence, 2021). Some researchers claim that global inequality is being reduced with economic growth (Kouadio & Gakpa, 2022). A thorough research into the present scenario of economic interactions affirms that inequality is rising between and within nations. Comparing the GDP per head of the top 25 countries with that of the bottom 25 countries affirms an enormous gap between them. The top countries on the ladder are 52 times richer than the bottom countries (Lawrence, 2021). Pogge (2005) argues that the colonial era was the prime responsible agent for the growing inequality between nations that exists even in the present time. Most contemporary affluent countries ruled the present poor countries by trading people like mere cattle, abolishing their culture, traditions, and political institutions, plundering their land

and natural resources, and enforcing foreign products and customs against their will and interest. He thus argues that the global poor have a moral claim to some of the affluence of high-income countries.

The Gini Coefficient is the widely used method to estimate inequality within countries. It is based on the measurement of income distribution. According to it, the higher the Gini Coefficient, the higher the income inequality in that country. It shows the depth of the gap between a country's rich and poor sections. The latest Gini Coefficient notes that countries like Slovakia, Slovenia, Belarus, Moldova, the Czech Republic, Azerbaijan, the United Arab Emirates, Algeria, Iceland, and Ukraine have a low level of inequality. On the contrary, countries like South Africa, Namibia, Zambia, Mozambique, Jamaica, Angola, Colombia, Brazil, Zimbabwe, and Botswana have a high rate of inequality. While Eastern European countries dominate the list of countries with less inequality, African countries dominate the list of high inequality (Statista, 2025). When income and wealth inequality rise, it causes societal disparities. There is a misconception among some people and researchers that the concentration of income and wealth among a few people will lead to the country's economic development, as they are the primary job creators (Stiglitz, 2016). However, an OECD report claims that the economic growth of countries like the US, the UK, and Italy would have been 6-9% higher if income inequality had not risen in the last two decades (Cingano, 2014). Lawrence (2021) argues that if the concentration of wealth is not correctly used for productive activity, it will cause a crisis of overproduction, a slump, and mass unemployment. It shows that the concentration of income and wealth in a few hands does not benefit the country in the long run.

4.2.3 Multidimensionality of Inequality

Inequality is often identified with income and wealth. Measuring inequality in economic terms is easy. However, inequality is not a unidimensional reality; it has many faces. It has social, political, and environmental dimensions. It is also closely associated with inequalities in education, healthcare, the realization of human rights, and security (Wilkinson & Pickett, 2010). Income and wealth inequalities affect the nutrition and health demands, educational possibilities, and the satisfaction of essential needs. For instance, in developing countries like India, there is a general belief that the private sector provides better education and healthcare than the public sector. However, the private sector demands more money for these services than the public sector. Accordingly, it becomes unaffordable for the economically weaker sections of society. Inequalities in income and wealth adversely affect people's opportunities and possibilities. For instance, people with enormous incomes and wealth can provide opportunities and privileges for their children, which average or below-average families cannot. Inequality in opportunities leads to inequalities in outcomes, which continue as a chain (Stiglitz, 2016). Just as poverty is not merely an economic but a multidimensional issue, income and wealth inequality are not simply a financial issue but have multiple facets.

4.3 Correlation between Global Poverty and Rising Income Inequality

Poverty and income inequality are complementary. Economic growth reduces absolute poverty. However, as mentioned above, income inequality increases along with economic growth. When income inequality rises, it affects people's living situations. The difference between the rich and the poor would be evident, and many would be denied the essentials for a fulfilling life. It shows that relative poverty rises along with rising income inequality (Moatsos, 2025). Although absolute poverty is the severest form, relative poverty is more complicated as it affects people's daily activities. However, global poverty was often measured using the absolute poverty line. The international institutions used the data on absolute poverty to claim that the globe is progressing towards complete poverty eradication. However, realizing the confusion within the poverty calculation, the World Bank researchers devised a mixed methodology that employs absolute and relative poverty lines to understand poverty efficiently (Jolliffe & Prydz, 2021). It provided a framework for understanding poverty eradication, not in tune with GDP growth but with society's perception of standards of living. It underlines a contrary perspective that poverty increases along with rising income inequality (Moatsos, 2025).

It was believed that "economic growth would bring increasing wealth and higher living standards to all sections of society" (Stiglitz, 2016, p. 134). The period after the Second World War prioritized this "rising tide" movement with the help of scientific and technological advancements and industrial growth. Many believed the policies favoring the rich and industrialists would ultimately benefit the other sections of society (Storper, 2005). However, Stiglitz (2016) rightly argues that the rising tide has only favored the large yachts, destroying the small boats. This is the issue with the uneven distribution of economic benefits. It favors the affluent, causing more insecurity to the poor. The data above attests to the growing disparity between the rich and poor as more income and wealth from economic growth are again within the hands of a few affluent people. When society fails to distribute the benefits of economic growth to all sections equitably, it primarily affects the poor and the marginalized, as they will be forced to remain in such a situation throughout. The rising income inequality endangers the consumption patterns of the poor. As the prices of goods and services increase along with the country's overall economic growth, the poor will not be financially stable to satisfy their basic needs. They become poorer with the rising income inequality.

However, equating poverty with a lack of income alone will not do justice to the discussions on poverty, as it is a deprivation closely associated with many other aspects as well. Both income and other deprivations constitute poverty. Income deprivation is the easiest visible reflection of poverty, but that does not present the whole picture behind it (Speth, 1998). Besides, it is wrong to accuse the affluent of the ongoing poverty. They have significantly contributed to the growth of society. However, if the inequality and the resulting poverty evolve from exploitation, discrimination, and monopolization of power, it becomes a different story. In such a case, it is a failure of the system. Institutional and political factors and agents need to be responsible for the genuine concerns of all sections of society (Stiglitz, 2016). If a society lacks equitable distribution, it is the responsibility of the government to reframe the standards to ensure the welfare of the whole population.

Although the globe has shown great concern towards inequality, it has not explicitly been measured as a problem or insecurity. For neoliberal economists, it is not a problem but a symbol of efficient economic interactions. But, a close observation identifies inequality as a condition of tension and fear. People at the top of the income distribution list have more possibilities to retain their position and improve their economic status. In contrast, those at the bottom are forced to fight hard, not to slip down further (Lawrence, 2021). In this line, Piketty (2014) argues that inequality harms social justice. Lawrence (2021) points out that when inequalities increase, there is every possibility for the governing parties to lose elections, revolutions against systemic failures, civil wars, and terrorist attacks. Inequality also affects institutional quality as more corruption and human rights violations are reported in those states with high inequality. When corruption and human rights violations increase in a society due to persistent inequalities, it may cause revolt against the system, causing insecurity among the larger public. On the one hand, inequality harms the poor by denying them opportunities and privileges and leading them to a situation of extreme poverty. On the other hand, inequality endangers peaceful societal life as unequal treatment forces people to fight against systemic and policy failures. Hence, poverty and rising inequality have become genuine concerns for human security.

5 TACKLING GLOBAL POVERTY AND INCOME INEQUALITY THROUGH HUMAN SECURITY APPROACH

Poverty and income inequality have long been considered problems for people. Katz (2013) argues that considering poverty associated with “problems of persons” resulting from moral, cultural, or biological inadequacies dominated the discussions of poverty for many years. Accusing people with low income and inadequate living conditions is relatively easy, but it should be redefined with positivity and openness towards reality. Whether poverty is a behavioral or structural problem has played a key role in the discussions on poverty eradication. Although behavior patterns are not the prime agents for the persistence of poverty, they play a crucial role in continuing poverty. If they are coupled with structural imbalances and injustice, poverty becomes an unresolvable problem. The globe has more resources than people need. Even then, people remain in poverty, which underlines that the problem is connected to the lack of proper distribution management. Poverty is not due to scarcity of resources but to inadequate distribution of policies. When structural changes occur due to efficient policies, they may also cause changes in people's behavior patterns (Brady, 2023). The changes in China during the last decades of the 20th century affirm this reality. The issues like structural inequality and increasing poverty can be addressed only through specific structural changes. Learning from its experiences, China made such changes, highlighting the demands of its people (Liu, 2017). It affirms that society needs people-centered policies and strategies for eradicating poverty and income inequality.

Human history testifies to countless policies and programs for poverty eradication (Giang, 2024). In the last decade of the 20th century, the UNDP initiated a policy approach prioritizing the concerns and interests of people. This pro-people approach is called human security. It calls for prioritizing people's claims in national and international policy frameworks. Since poverty, income inequality, and economic growth are interconnected elements and closely attached to human well-being, a human-centered approach would be the best available method to tackle the issues connected with economic development and the continuance of poverty and inequality. This section, therefore, examines the scope of the human security approach in the discussions on global poverty and rising income inequality.

5.1 Human Security: An Overview

Human security emerged as a policy approach with the UNDP's 1994 Human Development Report (HDR). Although traces of the human security approach can be seen in the Helsinki Accords of 1975 and some previous HDRs, the 1994 HDR is credited with the origin of this concept (Newman, 2021). It evolved as a shift of security concerns from the traditional national security that prioritized the protection of state boundaries over the security of its people. The end of the Cold War had a decisive role in shaping this new approach, as many believed that the globe had to switch towards human development rather than abstract territorial interests. The UNDP (1994) states that human security involves safety from chronic threats like hunger and disease and protection from sudden and hurtful disruptions in daily life. While national security equates people's security with territorial security, human security invites policymakers to concentrate on people's freedom from fear, want, and indignity in their daily lives. However, many national and international policy-makers are reluctant to embrace this people-centered approach (Newman, 2021). But, the UNDP (1994, p. 22) reminds us that "for most people, a feeling of insecurity arises more from worries about daily life than from the dread of a cataclysmic world event. Will they and their families have enough to eat? Will they lose their jobs? Will their streets and neighborhoods be safe from crime?" People are worried about the insecurities in their daily lives rather than the complex international politics and power dynamics. They are more concerned about the involvement of a repressive state in their lives rather than a foreign invasion. Realizing people's aspirations, the UN General Assembly (2005) acknowledged the human security paradigm, affirming their right to live in freedom and dignity, free from fear and want, and free from poverty and despair. If properly employed, it can provide "concrete and sustainable benefits to vulnerable people and communities threatened in their survival, livelihood, and dignity" (UNTFHS, 2021). However, the human security approach received a setback in the 21st century with the growing nationalism and territorial security propaganda that emerged after the 9/11 terrorist attacks of 2001. Besides, the UN did not acknowledge the primary premise of human security: states may be the primary threat to human security (Newman, 2021). Nevertheless, since poverty and income inequality persist primarily due to policy failures, human security can be a practical policy approach for eradicating them.

5.2 Poverty and Human Security

Kreide (2007, p.156) states, "Poverty is an indicator of injustice." From the justice perspective, poverty jeopardizes the secure lives of millions due to systemic failures and instances of injustice. As stated above, more than 700 million people around the globe experience poverty and insecurity in their daily lives. People experiencing poverty are forced to live in a situation of fear, abuse, discrimination, forced eviction, and insecurity, deprived of participation and decision-making voice, basic needs, employment, education and healthcare facilities, and opportunity. It shows that poverty and human security are intimately connected, as most of their experiences echo the insecurities of life. Poverty was not a security concern for traditional security studies, but the human security approach includes it as a vital component. Human security considers security not merely as an absence of physical harm but also other social risks like poverty (Giang, 2024). For the human security approach, the insecurities in daily life, like poverty and inequality, have more relevance within the security concerns.

The human security approach revolves around three freedoms: freedom from fear, freedom from want, and freedom from indignity. The UNDP's 1994 report included the first two freedoms as vital components of human security, taking inspiration from the 1941 speech of Franklin D. Roosevelt. In 2012, the UN General Assembly added the third one — freedom from indignity (UNDP, 2022). Poverty is an essential concern of these three freedoms. It is easy to think of poverty as being in tune with freedom from want, as it refers to a deprivation of basic wants. Poverty raises questions and apprehensions concerning people's social, economic, and environmental well-being. Human security, through its emphasis on freedom from want, addresses people's insecurities in the context of wants. Poverty is an issue of fear as it threatens people's peaceful and secure lives. Besides, the advocates of human security argue that the dangers to security should be enlarged to include disease, famine, and natural disasters. People experiencing poverty easily become victims of disease, famine, and natural disasters, affecting their security. Human security's freedom from fear dimension addresses these fundamental fears of the poor. Finally, people experiencing poverty face discrimination and injustice in many areas of social and political life. They are inhumanely treated, and their choices and interests are not duly respected, affecting their dignified life. Human security's freedom from indignity dimension affirms the right of poor people to a dignified life (Giang, 2024).

5.3 Income Inequality and Human Security

Human security evolved within the framework of human development. Compared to the economic development model, human development focuses on policies, programs, and strategies that ensure the development of all human beings without any discrimination. While economic development focuses on the GDP, human development revolves around the human development index (HDI). The UNDP measures the HDI of a country based on three parameters: a long and healthy life, knowledge, and a decent standard of living (UNDP, n.d.). However, inequality adversely affects the realization of these essentials. People experiencing poverty may not have the possibility of a long and healthy life, as they may not be financially stable enough to get proper medication for their diseases. They also face financial challenges when it comes to having nutritious food. Their educational opportunities are also affected as money plays a key role in the present educational sector. When both these areas are affected, it also complicates their aspirations for a decent standard of life (Ferreira et al., 2022). It affirms the urgency to shift from economic development to human development.

Many argue that economic growth is the best possible method for poverty eradication. History demonstrates the advantages of economic development. However, it favors the affluent, increases income inequality, and perpetuates poverty. Although economic growth is sound and efficient, its benefits are unequal (Liu, 2017). The concentration of land in a few hands is a primary reason for the growing economic inequality. Wealth inequality can be adequately addressed if there is a proper mechanism for land redistribution (Liebenberg & Slade, 2023). However, such things never happen as the affluent control the global political order. Human development and well-being are not the prime national and international concerns, but the interests of some wealthy people. Such a situation increases inequality and poverty in a society. National and international policies should be redesigned in such a way that they prioritize equitable distribution for the benefit of the whole people.

Poverty is more severe among members of traditionally discriminated groups like women, the disabled, and marginalized sections of society (Miyandazi, 2023). Pre-existing discrimination and inequality worsen the present scenario of poor people. Most of their fundamental rights are denied, and their ongoing experience of poverty and inequality forces them to compromise with their lifestyle without being seriously aware of their insecurities. Intensification of economic inequality causes severe threats to poverty eradication policies and human security. The countries with high inequality rates are less capable and effective in their poverty eradication programs (Chadwick, 2021). Economic inequality also causes severe threats to the global order. Developed countries, using their wealth and power, exert disproportionate control over poor countries through their influence in international institutions and even interfere in the domestic affairs of poor countries in the form of financial aid and lack of payment of their loans (de Vita, 2007). Rising inequality results in poverty persistence at both national and international levels, causing alarming insecurities. Without radical and progressive economic transformation, poverty and inequality will become unresolvable (Liebenberg & Slade, 2023). Human security advances such a progressive change in the policy framework.

France and Norway have an efficient taxation system that somehow manages to resist the increasing inequality. The increased tax on the income of the rich can help governments prioritize programs and policies for eradicating poverty. Such increased taxes also control their consumption patterns and accumulation tendencies, providing a chance to restrict inequalities. The Scandinavian countries advance equality of opportunities so that people's security, regardless of income and wealth inequalities, can be ensured (Stiglitz, 2016). Human security's human-centered approach is an effective mechanism to confront the issue of rising inequality. It focuses on people without any prejudice for their economic status. This approach respects the interests of all people. However, it shows a preference for the claims of the vulnerable and marginalized sections of society to empower them to lead a secure and peaceful life.

5.4 People-Centered Approach

Poverty eradication strategies for many centuries revolved around the charitable acts of affluent people. It may provide essential things for the short term, but it will not have any long-term benefits. The poor do not wish to live with the charity of the wealthy. They want permanent solutions to their poor living situations (Hunter, 1904). Accordingly, the UNDP emphasized human development, pointing to the inclusive growth of all people. A people-centered approach stands for inclusive growth (Liu, 2017). However, human development will be impossible without human security (Giang, 2024). The UNDP (1994) thus incorporated human security as the central component of human development. It affirms that people should be given a central role in the discussions of development. Equating development with GDP growth has done enough damage to the vulnerable and marginalized sections of society. Such a development favored the interests of relatively very few people. The rising income inequality and the increasing poverty attest to this reality. It necessitates refocusing the global and national interests on the real power-holders, the people.

The governments should prioritize proper tax reforms to strengthen public investment possibilities, provide more support to quality education facilities, increase the minimum wages to enhance the living conditions of people, strengthen the voice of the workers through well-formed trade unions and other actors to protect their rights, and enforce anti-discrimination laws against the misuse of power and discriminating tendencies to uplift people from the burden of poverty and inequality (Stiglitz, 2016). Increased taxation on higher-income people is an effective measure to restrict the increasing inequality. Higher taxation on higher income does not lead to lower economic growth. Usually, people with low and middle incomes tend to spend most of their additional incomes, but higher-income people have no such tendency (Lawrence, 2021). Governments tend to give tax exemptions to affluent industrialists and businesspeople so that they may invest more in developmental projects. However, it affects public spending on infrastructure development and other social security schemes. When the government fails to spend enough money on welfare projects, it affects the larger public. The welfare of all sections of society should become the ultimate objective rather than the prioritization of the profit motives of the affluent.

5.5 Universalism of Life Claims

A core feature and philosophical foundation of the human security approach is the universalism of life claims. It refers to acknowledging everyone's life claims and is a thread that connects present and future developmental aspirations. The ethic of universalism of life claims combines both developmental and sustainability demands. It stands for intragenerational and intergenerational equity, and in that sense, it addresses the plight of the poor. It does not argue that the poor should sacrifice their interests for future generations but affirms that they should have opportunities to make substantial changes in their life. As an idea, it advances the importance of people's empowerment. "It demands a world where no child goes without an education, where no human being is denied healthcare, and where all people can develop their potential capabilities." Human security's universalism of life claims refers to realizing people's bare essentials and developing their capabilities. It calls for protecting all human rights (civil, political, economic, social, and cultural) and a non-discriminatory attitude. It affirms national sovereignty only if the state respects and protects its people's human rights. Furthermore, it underlines equality of opportunity rather than income equality, as it can change people's living standards (UNDP, 1994, pp. 13-14). Human security affirms that income inequality will be restricted if people have equal opportunities.

Stiglitz (2016) notes that public investment is comparatively lower in countries with greater inequalities. Affluent people may not be interested in the considerable investments in public facilities like education, healthcare, and transportation, as they have better options. If the public sector is not strengthened, it affects the universality of life claims. Every person has a right to a standard and dignified life. However, due to the concentration of income and wealth and the private sector's key role in education and healthcare, many of the claims of poor people are not duly respected. When they fail to provide better education to their children, it also affects their future and causes intergenerational poverty.

6 CONCLUSIONS

Roser (2023) argues that extreme poverty was a widespread global phenomenon two centuries ago. However, many believed it was inevitable, and poor people had no choice but to remain impoverished. Nevertheless, many efforts were undertaken to reduce and alleviate poverty. Many initial attempts failed to eradicate poverty. Towards the end of the 20th century, the UNDP initiated the human security paradigm, focusing on people-centered development against the widely propagated economic development. Human security is an international policy perspective calling for national initiatives and international cooperation to eradicate various insecurities, like poverty and rising income inequality. The global scenario has changed drastically in the aftermath of the Cold War. Previously, security was identified with the protection of territories. But in the present times, it is perceived in the light of freedom from want, fear, and indignity that should happen in daily life. Fundamental freedom is understood as supporting people to escape from poverty and inequality to achieve peace and welfare (Giang, 2024).

Affirming the importance of human security and people-centered development, the UN has advanced various programs, like the declaration of poverty eradication decades, Millennium Development Goals, and Sustainable Development Goals, to ensure people's well-being and societal welfare. Their ultimate objective was to ensure people's security from various dangers of daily life. They prioritized protecting people from social risks like poverty and income inequality rather than external threats. Affirming the universalism of life claims human security underlines its interconnection with all the needs and concerns of people and proposes it as a suitable method for addressing insecurities like global poverty and rising income inequality. Various countries have initiated policies to ensure human security, eradicate poverty, and reduce income inequality. The Indian initiative of the Mahatma Gandhi National Rural Employment Guarantee Act (MGNREGA) guarantees minimum working days for the poor sections of society to ensure them possibilities for poverty eradication. Most countries try to secure a Universal Basic Income to balance society. Brazil has developed programs like Bolsa Família to assist low-income families in overcoming poverty and income inequality. Although there are diverse people-centered poverty eradication programs across the globe, most of them face poor implementation. Accordingly, poverty and income inequality continue to exist significantly. This demands that, despite being a strong theoretical framework, the human security framework should become a program of action, strongly supported by the international institutions and national governments.

REFERENCES

Allen, R. C. (2017). Absolute Poverty: When Necessity Displaces Desire. *The American Economic Review*, *107*(12), 3690–3721. https://www.aeaweb.org/articles?id=10.1257/aer.20161080. DOI: 10.1257/aer.20161080

Atkinson, A. B. (2019). *Measuring Poverty around the World*. Princeton University Press.

Bhoi, D. (2022). Economic Growth, Development, and Education of Scheduled Castes: Line Drawn from Neoliberal Era. *Contemporary Voice of Dalit*. https://journals.sagepub.com/doi/full/10.1177/2455328X211073207

Brady, D. (2023). Poverty, Not the Poor. *Science Advances*, *9*(34), eadg1469. https://www.science.org/doi/pdf/10.1126/sciadv.adg1469. DOI: 10.1126/sciadv.adg1469 PMID: 37611106

CESCR. (1999). General Comment 12: On the Right to Adequate Food. *E/C.12/1999/5*. https://digitallibrary.un.org/record/1491194?ln=en&v=pdf

Chadwick, A. (2021). Human Rights, Poverty, and Capitalism. In Egan, S., & Chadwick, A. (Eds.), *Poverty and Human Rights: Multidisciplinary Perspectives* (pp. 68–90). Edward Elgar.

Chancel, L., & Piketty, T. (2019). Indian Income Inequality, 1922-2015: From British Raj to Billionaire Raj? *Review of Income and Wealth*, *65*(S1), S33–S62. https://onlinelibrary.wiley.com/doi/full/10.1111/roiw.12439. DOI: 10.1111/roiw.12439

Chancel, L., Piketty, T., Saez, E., & Zucman, G. (2022). *World Inequality Report*. World Inequality Lab.

Cingano, F. (2014). Trends in Income Inequality and Its Impact on Economic Growth. *OECD Social, Employment, and Migration Working Papers*, no. 163. https://www.oecd.org/en/publications/trends-in-income-inequality-and-its-impact-on-economic-growth_5jxrjncwxv6j-en.html

de Schutter, O. (2021). A Human Rights-based Approach to Measuring Poverty. In Davis, M. F., & Kjaerum, M. (Eds.), *Research Handbook on Human Rights and Poverty* (pp. 2–20). Edward Elgar. DOI: 10.4337/9781788977517.00010

de Vita, A. (2007). Inequality and Poverty in Global Perspective. In Pogge, T. (Ed.), *Freedom from Poverty as a Human Right: Who Owes What to the Very Poor?* (pp. 103–132). Oxford University Press. DOI: 10.1093/oso/9780199226313.003.0005

Drabek, Z. (2024). Is the WTO Terminally Ill? Threats to the International Trading System. *Asia and the Global Economy* 4(1), 100078. https://www.sciencedirect.com/science/article/pii/S2667111524000021

Fan, S., & Cho, E. E. (2021). Paths Out of Poverty: International Experience. *Journal of Integrative Agriculture*, *20*(4), 857–867. https://www.sciencedirect.com/science/article/pii/S2095311920632956. DOI: 10.1016/S2095-3119(20)63295-6

Ferreira, I. A., Gisselquist, R. M., & Tarp, F. (2022). On the Impact of Inequality on Growth, Human Development, and Governance. *International Studies Review*, *24*(1), viab058. https://academic.oup.com/isr/article/24/1/viab058/6460467. DOI: 10.1093/isr/viab058

Giang, D. H. (2024). Poverty as a Concern for Human Security: Vietnam's Policies on Multidimensional Poverty. *VNU Journal of Foreign Studies* 40(4), 58-73. https://jfs.ulis.vnu.edu.vn/index.php/fs/article/view/5346/4533

Gough, J. A., & Eisenschitz, A. (2021). Poverty in the High-Income Countries: A Marxist Alternative to Mainstream Ideologies. *Class, Race, and Corporate Power* 9(2), art. 2. https://digitalcommons.fiu.edu/classracecorporatepower/vol9/iss2/2/

Gráda, C. Ó. (2007). Making Famine History. *Journal of Economic Literature*, *45*(1), 5–38. https://www.aeaweb.org/articles?id=10.1257/jel.45.1.5. DOI: 10.1257/jel.45.1.5

Hasell, J., Roser, M., Ortiz-Ospina, E., & Arriagada, P. (2022). Poverty. *One World in Data*. https://ourworldindata.org/poverty

Hunter, R. (1904). *Poverty*. Macmillan.

Jolliffe, D., & Prydz, E. B. (2021). Societal Poverty: A Relative and Relevant Measure. *The World Bank Economic Review*, *35*(1), 180–206. https://openknowledge.worldbank.org/server/api/core/bitstreams/604d5856-5214-4b7c-a64e-1925b161ba4d/content. DOI: 10.1093/wber/lhz018

Kant, I. (1795). *Perpetual Peace: A Philosophical Essay*. B.F. Trueblood (Tran.). American Peace Society.

Katz, M. B. (2013). *The Undeserving Poor: America's Enduring Confrontation with Poverty* (2nd ed.). Oxford University Press.

Kouadio, H. K., & Gakpa, L.-L. (2022). Do Economic Growth and Institutional Quality Reduce Poverty and Inequality in West Africa? *Journal of Policy Modeling*, *44*(1), 41–63. https://www.sciencedirect.com/science/article/abs/pii/S0161893821001095. DOI: 10.1016/j.jpolmod.2021.09.010

Kreide, R. (2007). Poverty as a Violation of Social Autonomy. In Pogge, T. (Ed.), *Freedom from Poverty as a Human Right: Who Owes What to the Very Poor?* (pp. 155–181). Oxford University Press. DOI: 10.1093/oso/9780199226313.003.0007

Lawrence, P. (2021). The Global and National Inequality Faultlines: The Economic Dimensions of (In)security. *Journal of Global Faultlines, 8*(1), 23–33. https://www.scienceopen.com/hosted-document?doi=10.13169/jglobfaul.8.1.0023. DOI: 10.13169/jglobfaul.8.1.0023

Liebenberg, S., & Slade, B. (2023). Applying a Human Rights Lens to Poverty and Economic Inequality: The Experiences of South African Human Rights Commission. *Federal Law Review* 51(3), 296-314. https://journals.sagepub.com/doi/full/10.1177/0067205X231188637

Liu, M. (2017). Inclusive Growth and Poverty Eradication Policies in China. UNDESA. https://www.un.org/development/desa/dspd/wp-content/uploads/sites/22/2017/04/MLiu-DESA1-30Apr2017.pdf, Malthus, T. (1798). An Essay on the Principle of Population.

Miyandazi, V. (2023). Human Rights and Equality Commissions in Kenya and Their Role in Tackling Poverty and Economic Inequality. *Federal Law Review* 51(4), 422-441. https://journals.sagepub.com/doi/full/10.1177/0067205X231212026

Moatsos, M. (2021). Global Extreme Poverty: Past and Present since 1820. In OECD, *How was Life? Volume II: New Perspectives on Well-being and Global Inequality since 1820* (pp. 186-215). OECD Publishing.

Moatsos, M. (2025). Global Poverty: A Review of Measurement, Levels, and Trends in a Historical Perspective. *Journal of Economic Surveys, 39*(2), 706–766. https://onlinelibrary.wiley.com/doi/pdfdirect/10.1111/joes.12644. DOI: 10.1111/joes.12644

Narayan, D., Chambers, R., Shah, M. K., & Petesch, P. (2000). *Voices of the Poor: Crying out for Change.* Oxford University Press. DOI: 10.1596/0-1952-1602-4

Newman, E. (2021). COVID-19: A Human Security Analysis. *Global Society, 36*(4), 431–454. https://www.tandfonline.com/doi/pdf/10.1080/13600826.2021.2010034. DOI: 10.1080/13600826.2021.2010034

OPHI. (n.d.). What is the Global MPI? https://ophi.org.uk/what-global-mpi

OPHI & UNDP. (2024). *Global Multidimensional Poverty Index 2024: Poverty Amid Conflict.* Oxford University Press.

Parolin, Z., Pintro-Schmitt, R., Esping-Andersen, G., & Fallesen, P. (2025). Intergenerational Persistence of Poverty in Five High-Income Countries. *Nature Human Behaviour*, *9*(2), 254–267. https://www.nature.com/articles/s41562-024-02029-w. DOI: 10.1038/s41562-024-02029-w PMID: 39468279

Piketty, T. (2014). *Capital in the 21st Century*. Harvard University Press. DOI: 10.4159/9780674369542

Piketty, T., & Zucman, G. (2015). Wealth and Inheritance in the Long-Run. In Atkinson, A., & Bourguignon, F. (Eds.), *Handbook of Income Distribution* (Vol. 2, pp. 1303–1368). Elsevier.

Pogge, T. (2005). World Poverty and Human Rights. *Ethics & International Affairs*, *19*(1), 1–7. https://onlinelibrary.wiley.com/doi/abs/10.1111/j.1747-7093.2005.tb00484.x. DOI: 10.1111/j.1747-7093.2005.tb00484.x

Pogge, T. (2011). Are We Violating the Human Rights of World's Poor? *Yale Human Rights & Development L.J* 14(2), 1-33. https://openyls.law.yale.edu/handle/20.500.13051/5760

Ravallion, M., Datt, G., & van de Walle, D. (1991). Quantifying Absolute Poverty in the Developing World. *Review of Income and Wealth*, *37*(4), 345–361. https://onlinelibrary.wiley.com/doi/abs/10.1111/j.1475-4991.1991.tb00378.x. DOI: 10.1111/j.1475-4991.1991.tb00378.x

Reddy, S. G., & Pogge, T. (2010). How Not to Count the Poor. In Anand, S., Segal, P., & Stiglitz, J. E. (Eds.), *Debates on the Measurement of Global Poverty* (pp. 42–51). Oxford University Press. DOI: 10.1093/acprof:oso/9780199558032.003.0003

Roser, M. (2022). The History of the End of Poverty has just Begun. *Our World in Data*. https://ourworldindata.org/history-of-poverty-has-just-begun

Roser, M. (2023). Extreme Poverty: How far have we come, and how far do we still have to go? *Our World in Data*. https://ourworldindata.org/extreme-poverty-in-brief

Sachs, J. D. (2005). *The End of Poverty: Economic Possibilities for our Time*. The Penguin Press.

Speth, J. G. (1998). Poverty: A Denial of Human Rights. *Journal of International Affairs*, *52*(1), 277–292. https://law-journals-books.vlex.com/vid/poverty-denial-of-human-rights-52647503

Statista. (2025). Ranking of the Gini index by Country 2024. https://www.statista.com/forecasts/1171540/gini-index-by-country

Stiglitz, J. E. (2016). Inequality and Economic Growth. *The Political Quarterly, 86*(S1), 134–155. https://onlinelibrary.wiley.com/doi/10.1111/1467-923X.12237. DOI: 10.1111/1467-923X.12237

Storper, M. (2005). Society, Community, and Economic Development. *Studies in Comparative International Development, 39*(4), 30–57. https://link.springer.com/content/pdf/10.1007/BF02686164.pdf. DOI: 10.1007/BF02686164

Townsend, P. (1979). *Poverty in the United Kingdom: A Survey of Household Resources and Standards of Living*. Penguin Books. DOI: 10.1525/9780520325760

UN General Assembly. (2005). World Summit Outcome. Resolution Adopted by the General Assembly, 24 October (A/RES/60/1). https://www.un.org/en/development/desa/population/migration/generalassembly/docs/globalcompact/A_RES_60_1.pdf

UNDP. (2022). *New Threats to Human Security in the Anthropocene: Demanding Greater Solidarity*. https://hdr.undp.org/content/2022-special-report-human-security

UNDP. (n.d.). Human Development Index (HDI). https://hdr.undp.org/data-center/human-development-index#/indicies/HDI

UNTFHS (United Nations Trust Fund for Human Security). (2021). About the Trust Fund. https://www.un.org/humansecurity/

Wilkinson, R., & Pickett, K. (2010). *The Spirit Level: Why Equality is Better for Everyone*. Penguin Books.

KEY TERMS AND DEFINITIONS

Global Justice: Global justice is the required fairness among the interactions between countries and people to ensure the earth's resources are equitably distributed.

Human Rights: Human rights are the fundamental claims of people to live a dignified human life. They are natural and inborn rights, which are universal, inalienable, and indivisible.

Human Security: Human Security is the UNDP-initiated policy design that prioritizes people's freedom from want, fear, and indignity. It advances people-centered development to address insecurities, like poverty and income inequality.

Income Inequality: Income inequality points to the societal imbalance in the distribution of income and wealth. Income inequality is not primarily due to individual behavioral patterns but to distributional injustice.

Poverty: Poverty refers to the deprivation of the bare essentials required for a standard of living. It also points to the marginalization of specific categories of people due to their economic and other deprived situations.

SDGs: SDGs are the inspirational seventeen goals of the UN to transform the globe toward a sustainable future by 2030. SDGs stand for ensuring a meaningful life through sustainable development for all sections of society and the environment.

Universalism of Life Claims: Universalism of life claims is the core principle of UNDP's human security approach, which emphasizes that all individuals, regardless of any differentiating parameters, have the claim to develop their potential and lead a meaningful life.

Chapter 3
Unequal Gains:
The Divergent Effects of Income Inequality on Stock Market Performance

Orhan Özaydın
https://orcid.org/0000-0003-2585-1437
İstanbul Medipol University, Turkey

ABSTRACT

The distribution of income among people influences both investment choices and risk tolerance and capital distribution patterns and overall financial system stability. The literature shows that inequality produces different market effects based on which income groups are increasing or decreasing in size. This research investigates the connection between income inequality and financial market performance through an analysis of income distribution metrics on stock price changes and variance of coefficients (VC) which represent stock market risk or volatility. A 15-year data set of nine countries are conducted final estimations with Feasible Generalized Least Squares (FGLS) because traditional models failed diagnostic tests. The results show that higher Gini coefficient values lead to decreased stock price growth together with elevated financial market volatility, yet High20 top-income concentration creates market stability. The empirical evidence supports the theoretical framework which demonstrates that inequality affects both investment potential and market operations.

INTRODUCTION

The current macroeconomic research and policy discussions focus on income inequality and financial market behavior. Modern economic systems face crucial

DOI: 10.4018/979-8-3373-7360-7.ch003

challenges because of expanding income disparities and market instability following global financial crises. Literature indicates that income distribution patterns and financial market performance maintain complex interconnections which extend beyond parallel development. This research bases its foundation on the increasing understanding that income inequality shapes financial market behavior through its effects on investment choices and market involvement and capital distribution and system-wide risk. It is investigated that the relationship between income distribution patterns using Gini coefficient measurements and income share data and their impact on stock price changes and financial market volatility measured through variance of coefficients (VC). The VC is defined as an indicator of risk present in equity markets which connects to the broader topic of financial volatility. The panel econometric methods are used across two separate models to analyze data from nine countries for 15 years. Both stock price movements and market volatility are deployed in models because inequality affects financial systems through two distinct mechanisms which modify investment levels and market stability and risk-taking behaviors. Literature indicates that wealthy investors stabilize financial markets through their information access and long-term investment approach (Blau, 2015; Blau et al., 2021) yet other studies demonstrate how inequality leads to increased financial instability and speculative market actions (Schasfoort, 2020). Theoretical frameworks show that stock market returns and volatility respond to income inequality through various transmission channels. The transmission mechanisms of income inequality affect stock returns and volatility through three channels: reduced aggregate consumption by lower-income groups (Keynesian demand channel), altered investment behavior based on liquidity constraints, and diminished institutional trust in highly unequal societies. The consumption smoothing ability and capital accumulation capacity of lower-income households remains limited because of their financial constraints which reduces their participation in long-term financial instruments. The widening gap between incomes leads to decreased trust in financial institutions which results in herding behavior and speculative cycles that boost market volatility (Guiso, Sapienza, & Zingales, 2008). The mechanisms demonstrate that inequality restricts productive investment while simultaneously changing market sentiment and increasing systemic risk. The existing debate requires researchers to use specific empirical methods to study this phenomenon.

The Gini coefficient stands as one of the primary statistical tools used to measure income inequality (Schneider, 2021). The Gini index faces criticism because it shows limited sensitivity to changes in different parts of the income distribution. Rogerson (2013) and Lambert and Decoster (2005) developed advanced interpretation methods and decomposition techniques which enable researchers to separate between intra-group and inter-group disparities. The methodological progress holds special importance for financial outcome research because capital gains and stock ownership mainly concentrate among high-income groups (Alvaredo, 2011). This research extends previous work by using both the Gini coefficient and analyzing the financial market effects of High20 and Second20 indicators which represent the income shares of the top and second quintiles. Also, it provides deeper insights into how various income distribution segments affect financial markets. The Gini index shows total inequality, but High20 provides better insight into elite investor class influence and Second20 indicates low-middle-income group involvement. The study tests the following hypotheses based on its empirical framework and theoretical foundations: H1: Stock market returns experience negative effects from broader income inequality measured by the Gini coefficient. H2: Stock returns increase while market volatility decreases when the top 20% of the population holds most of the income because high-income investors possess strong market knowledge and effective risk mitigation skills. H3: The second quintile's increasing income share leads to higher market volatility because its members demonstrate unstable investment practices and limited financial knowledge.

The 2-year bond yield serves as a control variable to address interest rate effects. The econometric framework starts with fixed effects (FE), random effects (RE) and pooled ordinary least squares (OLS) estimations which are evaluated through Hausman, Breusch-Pagan LM and F-tests. The analysis uses Feasible Generalized Least Squares (FGLS) estimators with one-way time effects because second-generation diagnostic tests (Breusch-Pagan and Wooldridge tests) show cross-sectional dependence and heteroskedasticity and serial correlation. The descriptive statistics show that income inequality differs significantly across the sample and both dependent variables Stock and VC demonstrate large fluctuations throughout time and across different countries. The data structures enable thorough comparisons both within countries and across time which enhances the reliability of the research findings.

The Stock model results indicate that the Gini coefficient produces statistically significant negative effects on stock price changes which demonstrates that market returns suffer from overall income inequality. The High20 income share produces positive effects on stock returns because it supports the theory that wealthy income concentration drives market participation and equity demand. The 2-year bond yield shows a negative but statistically insignificant connection to stock price changes at the .90 confidence level but becomes significant at the 0.80 confidence level indicating minimal impact of short-term interest rates on this framework. Hence, stock markets experience negative effects from inequality in both developed and emerging countries, one reason of insufficient middle-level investors.

The variance of coefficients (VC) model shows different results when viewed as market volatility. The Gini coefficient shows statistical significance with a positive sign which means that higher income inequality leads to higher financial risk. High20 shows a negative effect which means that elite investors have a stabilizing effect on

VC, but the Second20 income share is positively associated with VC which means that increased financial participation among the low-middle-income group may introduce moderate risk dynamics. These findings show that income structure and market behavior are complexly related. The implication is that wealthy investors, who dominate market activity in unequal societies, may provide a stabilizing force through consistent long-term investments. The lack of financial intellectual background of poor people who want to make a profit from capital markets to become rich leads to market volatility because of increasing inequality.

The two models provide a comprehensive view of financial inequality. The Gini coefficient has a destabilizing effect on both models by reducing returns and increasing volatility while the High20 income share has a positive effect on returns and a negative effect on volatility. The dual effects of inequality are consistent with the idea that top income bracket inequality stabilizes markets but reduces economic inclusion while overall inequality weakens systemic resilience. The findings match both stabilizing (Blau, 2015) and destabilizing (Schasfoort, 2020) perspectives based on the selected measurement criteria. Besides it supports Christou, Gupta, and Jawadi (2017) who demonstrate that inequality metrics can forecast financial market returns. The volatility measures show an asymmetrical response which confirms the findings of Aye et al. (2020) and Parsons and Rabhi (2024) about how financial instability affects differently among income groups.

This study continues following the expanding body of literature which investigates how economic inequality affects financial market results. The research provides a complete economic analysis of income distribution effects through its combination of advanced econometric methods with improved inequality metrics and dual risk-return outcome variables. The finding indicates that market performance benefits from the concentration of income among the top 20% in the short term yet broader inequality leads to increased systemic risk. Hence, market stability requires redistributive policies and financial reforms which reduce market instability while preserving capital market depth.

LITERATURE

The reviewed literature demonstrates how the Gini coefficient serves as a key tool for studying income inequality theory and its empirical applications in financial market behavior. The Gini coefficient continues to serve as a primary tool for inequality measurement, yet researchers now advocate for more sophisticated multidimensional assessment methods. Research findings about volatility and returns and market behavior show that stock market dynamics both influence and result from income inequality levels. The literature evaluates how Gini coefficients and income distribution patterns affect financial market instability across different countries and investigates how income dispersion affects financial market performance which aligns with the findings of this study. After studying how financial market participation and outcomes change based on inequality levels, they demonstrate that financial behavior analysis requires both income distribution data and knowledge gaps about finance to develop effective inclusive economic policies. i) Theoretical Literature on the Gini Coefficient and Income Inequality Financial markets depend on the understanding of income inequality which requires basic knowledge of inequality measurement tools. The Gini coefficient serves as the leading measure among all inequality metrics. The Gini coefficient first appeared in the early twentieth century after Corrado Gini developed it to enhance the Lorenz curve for depicting income distribution (Schneider, 2021). The Gini coefficient uses a measurement range of 0 to 1 to show how actual income distribution varies from a perfect equality scenario. The theoretical significance of the Gini index stems from its ability to present income or wealth dispersion in a simple and easy-to-understand format. Besides, the Gini index fails to show changes in top-decile income shares when lower-end income remains constant. The single-parameter structure of the Gini index makes it difficult to distinguish between upward mobility and top-heavy enrichment particularly when dealing with highly skewed distributions. The Gini index shows greater sensitivity to changes in the middle part of the distribution rather than the tails which results in underestimating inequality when the richest individuals gain disproportionately (Cowell & Flachaire, 2007). The Palma ratio and Theil index have been recommended by analysts as supplementary measures because they offer better clarity when dealing with extreme top-end concentration or inequality decomposition needs (Cobham & Sumner, 2013). Despite its limitations, the Gini coefficient remains a widely utilized and foundational metric for cross-national comparisons of inequality, owing to its broad acceptance and the widespread availability of relevant data.

The Gini coefficient functions as a widely used measure, but researchers have identified several limitations in its application. Rogerson (2013) transforms the Gini coefficient into an expected percentage of total income which redistributes through hierarchical steps to provide enhanced understanding of population segment inequality spread. He uses scaled Hoover indices to dissect the Lorenz curve into multiple levels that provide detailed insights into how inequality affects different income groups. According to Lambert and Decoster (2005) the Gini index consists of between-group, within-group and overlap components that show how group-level scaling increases inequality while progressive transfers within groups reduce it. These decomposition methods show how the Gini coefficient reacts to changes between and within different income groups which proves vital for studying financial inequality and redistributive policy effects.

Yao (1999) improves the Gini analysis by creating a spreadsheet decomposition method which enables researchers to break down data by both income origins and population segments. The new approach enables analysts to monitor which specific types of income such as earnings from work or investments generate total inequality levels. This approach provides essential analysis for studying financial inequality that results from stock market performance and capital gains. The application of this metric in China by Hai (2016) reveals a stable but high Gini coefficient which indicates a wealth gap that has shifted from rational to excessive levels without achieving polarization. Such findings indicate that policymakers must implement urgent measures to control excessive inequality before it reaches destabilizing levels. Alvaredo (2011) extends his analysis of top income shares and Gini coefficient in his work. He uses mathematical methods to show that a small top income group can greatly affect overall inequality, especially when that group controls a large share of total income. His model demonstrates that changes in the income share of the richest can cause major shifts in national inequality even when the rest of the distribution remains constant. The research on stock markets requires this understanding because high-income individuals control most financial assets and generate more income from capital markets. Blesch et al. (2022) propose using inequality measures that extend beyond single parameters in their research. The authors support the use of multi-parameter models such as the Ortega model because these models provide better differentiation of income distribution inequality across different percentiles when analyzing policy effects. The simulations demonstrate that multi-parameter models generate different social outcome associations than the Gini index thus requiring more comprehensive inequality measurement approaches. The Gini coefficient continues to serve as a fundamental tool for international inequality comparisons because it valids broad acceptance and extensive data availability despite its limitations. ii) Income Inequality and Financial Market Dynamics Literature states the bi-directional connection between inequality and stock markets. Some studies investigate how economic inequality affects stock market behavior and its volatility, but other research examines how stock market movements impact income distribution. The relationship between income distribution and capital markets demonstrates fundamental macroeconomic patterns which affect savings rates together with consumption patterns and investment opportunities and financial service accessibility. Behavioral finance demonstrates that inequality makes investors more risk-averse and creates market divisions because poor investors tend to select poor investment choices because they lack experience and face information imbalances and emotional biases. During market stress periods investors with lower incomes show stronger loss aversion while they herd with others and use heuristics which intensifies market volatility (Barberis & Thaler, 2003). According to Keynesian theory financial markets become unstable because aggregate demand remains insufficient. The increase in inequality together with decreased marginal consumption among high-income earners leads to reduced overall consumption which diminishes corporate earnings and investor expectations and subsequently causes asset price fluctuations (Keynes, 1936). Both theoretical approaches demonstrate how inequality creates indirect financial instability through specific mechanisms. Blau (2015) investigates how increased social and political uncertainty caused by rising inequality produces higher stock price volatility. The results contradict standard expectations because it reveals a negative relationship between income inequality and volatility throughout numerous countries. The results of the "Millionaire Tax" natural experiment in France show that market volatility increased following attempts to lower economic inequality thus indicating possible market stabilization effects of inequality under specific circumstances. Market stability in unequal societies depends on wealthy investors who maintain long-term investments because they comprise the majority of market participants. Blau et al. (2021) support this finding with their research on American Depository Receipts (ADRs) which shows that higher economic inequality leads to reduced market volatility. The study proposes that high-income investors maintain market stability because they possess superior informational advantages together with effective risk-mitigation techniques. Market stability remains unaffected by inequality according to research which shows that investor composition and behavior determine the relationship between inequality and stability. The research contradicts the traditional belief that rising inequality automatically leads to more market risks and market volatility.

The stabilizing perspective regarding stock market stability faces opposition from studies demonstrating that inequality leads to destabilization. Schasfoort (2020) employs agent-based modeling to demonstrate that volatility makes inequality worse by producing larger return differences between high- and low-income groups. The research shows that increased price volatility leads to greater log return differences between investors and more pronounced wealth inequality where high-income agents experience both more volatile and higher returns. Also, it provides evidence that stock market profits distribute unfairly, and volatility acts as a factor that increases economic inequality. It underscores the notion that even if inequality seems to stabilize prices in the short term, it may simultaneously deepen social and economic disparities.

The research by Christou, Gupta, and Jawadi (2017) investigates how inequality data helps predict equity premium changes across G7 nations. The research indicates that post-tax and transfer Gini growth rates hold important predictive value for excess returns. The findings show that inequality functions as both a correlation indicator and a forecasting tool for financial results which makes it useful as an anticipatory market indicator. Their research shows that inequality metrics possess valuable information for enhancing asset pricing models and guiding portfolio strategies as leading indicators. Aye et al. (2020) employ GARCH-M VAR to study how income volatility affects inequality in the UK through asymmetric mechanisms. The research shows that positive volatility shocks cause inequality to rise more than negative volatility shocks cause it to fall. The study demonstrates how economic instability affects lower-income households more severely during times of financial market instability. Moreover, it they support theoretical models which demonstrate that income shocks produce enduring non-linear impacts on inequality which tend to worsen wealth inequality across time. Parsons and Rabhi (2024) investigates how exchange rate volatility affects high-income countries beyond the context of macro-financial instability. The analysis of panel data shows that exchange rate volatility creates greater benefits for high-income earners but produces negative impacts on lower-income groups. Financial market volatility together with currency exchange rate instability intensifies social economic gaps between different income groups. The research demonstrates how redistributive policies and exchange rate management help reduce negative effects which supports the need for macroprudential regulation in financial governance.

The essential relationship between inequality and finance depends on the impact of income distribution on market entry and investor decisions. The research conducted by Tong-Yu (2010) demonstrates through U.S. data that the stock market growth mostly benefits wealthy individuals because they invest more money and earn better returns. The stock market operates as a tool which wealthy individuals use to build their capital while their increasing market value shows a direct correlation with their financial gains. The stock market index elasticity in relation to income demonstrates an upward trend from the 1980s onward because of expanding financialization trends and tax policies that benefit capital income. Isidore and Arun (2022) utilized survey data from Indian equity investors to establish that annual income plays a significant role in how investors develop their investment strategies and make financial decisions. The research shows that wealthier investors achieve superior returns through their analytical approaches while poorer investors follow technical analysis or rely on third-party recommendations for their decisions. Financial literacy along with strategic capacity shows income-dependent behavioral differences that produce market outcome disparities. The research identifies specific demographic patterns in investor conduct which shows that both educational programs and strategic public policies can reduce financial restrictions. Kobakiwal (2018) presents evidence which demonstrates that foreign direct investment stock increases the income distribution of the highest 0.05 to 10 percent group but leaves the middle and lower-income segments with uncertain effects. Fiscal instruments play a crucial role in controlling financial integration-induced inequality by reducing the distributional effects of capital inflows. His use of Arellano-Bond GMM estimation provides robustness to the inference, suggesting causality rather than mere correlation. Multiple academic studies analyze the relationship between financial development and economic growth while including inequality as an essential factor in their research. Adjasi and Biekpe (2006) investigate 14 African countries to demonstrate how stock market growth benefits economic development especially in upper-middle-income economies. Market development benefits different segments of society to varying degrees because poorly developed markets need more institutional advancement to achieve economic returns. Market infrastructure remains essential, but equal market inclusion ensures economic growth remains fair. Seven and Yetkiner (2016) also show that financial development helps growth in low- and middle-income countries, but its impact is ambiguous in high-income countries. Their analysis distinguishes between banks and stock markets, noting that capital market development is more closely related to growth in higher-income countries. This distinction is important when evaluating whether inequality-enhancing structures—like stock markets—are indeed promoting inclusive growth. They argue that institutional quality and income structure significantly moderate these relationships.

Yu, Hassan, and Sanchez (2012) provide additional details by using Granger causality and variance decomposition methods to determine the causal relationships and timing and strength. They show that financial development affects growth differently in various income groups and regions, which suggests the need for tailored policies that take into account both structural inequality and financial system maturity. Their approach reveals the non-linearities and lag effects in financial-growth-inequality trials. Aslan et al. (2018) support these findings by using a dual-group comparison of 30 low- and 30 middle/high-income countries. Their results show that stock market development is positively related to GDP growth across income groups, but especially where market capitalization and turnover ratios are higher. Thus, while capital markets can act as engines of growth, their distributional effects depend heavily on income structure and market accessibility. Their findings emphasize the necessity of improving financial inclusion as a prerequisite for maximizing the advantages of stock market growth. Financial market inequality research currently explores how trading volume and concentration affect these systems. Metelski and Sobieraj (2024) use the Gini-based Trading Concentration Index (TCI) (measuring the concentration or inequality of trade volumes across market participants or trading entities) to measure trading volume disparities among S&P 500 firms. They discovered two major findings: market concentration grows during economic crises and portfolios containing the most concentrated stocks generate superior returns compared to the standard market index. Financial concentration follows a pattern to income concentration because both systems provide enhanced profit opportunities to investors who have favorable market positions. The study introduces a new metric which strengthens the Gini coefficient's position as a flexible tool for measuring market concentration. The research supports Alvaredo's (2011) finding that small elite groups create significant effects on total inequality measurements since the findings show income concentration leads to specific trading activities. The research shows capital markets will perpetuate wealth concentration among a small investor group when unregulated which causes inequality to rise despite appearing stable to outside observers. Short-term inequality benefits capital inflows and asset demand because elite income groups can invest but this apparent market stimulus conceals fundamental structural weaknesses. The short-term increase in stock valuations and reduced volatility perception occurs when top earners boost their equity investments. The long-term persistence of inequality results in decreased social mobility and reduced consumption among lower-income households which limits sustainable economic growth. Systemic inequality damages public trust in financial institutions and weakens political backing for inclusive market regulation which creates market instability in the long run (Stiglitz, 2012). The time-dependent dual nature of inequality effects demands thorough analysis by both empirical research and policy makers.

The COVID 19 pandemic caused income inequality to worsen while financial instability grew stronger as wealth distribution became more concentrated and market volatility increased. Financial disruptions from the pandemic primarily harmed low-income families which strengthened the relationship between economic inequality and market volatility. Pandemic policies together with labor market disruptions made distributional gaps worse while econometric analyses show that global stock markets experienced significant spikes in conditional volatility during COVID 19 (Meyer et al., 2025). Financial market behavior and income inequality exist in a complex dynamic relationship which research demonstrates. Stock market performance receives two contradictory effects from income inequality because aggregate demand decreases as shown in the present research yet high-income investors can stabilize it according to Blau (2015) and Blau et al. (2021). Volatility functions as a mechanism that heightens economic inequality because different income groups experience unequal exposure to stock returns and income shocks and exchange rate fluctuations. The design along with the application of inequality metrics requires thorough evaluation. The Gini coefficient maintains its popularity because of its simplicity and comparability yet it misses various effects that different distribution points exhibit. The combination of three inequality measurement approaches by Blesch et al. (2022) and group-level decomposition by Yao (1999) and reweighted formulations by Lambert & Decoster (2005) provides better insights for empirical research. Researchers should make inequality measures more advanced through their integration with financial performance models and market structure analysis. This research approach will strengthen empirical evidence in inequality studies while generating useful insights for both financial market regulations and investment strategies and policy development in today's unequal financial environment. iii) Income Groups, Financial Knowledge, Poverty, and Disparities

The study of income gaps and inequality perceptions on economic activities begins with redistributive preference analysis. Becker (2019) presents powerful experimental data showing that people have intense reactions when they learn about income differences that result from unavoidable factors including racial and gender background and family circumstances. Americans modify their redistributive preferences toward greater equality after receiving precise information about income gaps and these altered preferences persist throughout time. Research indicates that policies which communicate clearly can create substantial shifts in public backing for economic redistribution. Kelly and Lobao (2021) extends the concept of inequality response by studying how local governance structures function in the United States. Research shows that social service provisioning from counties increases with rising poverty rates, but these services become disproportionately distributed. Regions with greater white poverty levels obtain better service allocation and funding resources while showing racial and gender biases in their policy implementation. The study reveals how institutional mechanisms, and geographical factors allow social inequalities to continue despite superficial appearance of governance responsiveness. Manduca (2018) studies how racial income disparities between black and white American families have remained static since 1968. Black families improved their relative income position, yet their advancement was counteracted by the rapid increase of top-end income concentration which is predominantly controlled by white families. Rising national income inequality acts against racial equality progress thus requiring racial justice initiatives to address wealth concentration systems. Sachweh (2012) analyzes how Germans judge the morality of economic gaps in their society. The research indicates that people accept income differences based on merit, but they view both poor and wealthy individuals with skepticism. The research indicates that social cohesion concerns drive public attitudes because people view extreme inequality as a threat to fundamental societal values. The evaluations about norms help explain why specific types of inequality lead to greater political and social opposition. The concept of this moral sensitivity differs from the phenomenon described by Kuusela (2020) as "hyperopia of wealth." Among Finland's top earners there exists a discursive unawareness regarding the fundamental social causes of inequality according to Kuusela (2020). Top performers in their field tend to attribute their financial gains to personal merit yet they avoid recognizing their influence on sustaining or intensifying social inequality. Through this approach of discursive strategy elites achieve wealth accumulation depoliticization which allows them to maintain their social position while disregarding existing inequalities. Financial knowledge and access demonstrate different levels of inequality which affects economic conditions. De Beckker, De Witte and Van Campenhout (2019) developed a system to analyze financial literacy through clusters that span twelve countries. The most illiterate financial groups consist of people who are single and unemployed and hold limited education while having lower incomes. Individuals with high financial literacy demonstrate characteristics such as male gender along with higher education levels and large financial portfolios and high income. Financial education initiatives need to focus on helping economically disadvantaged groups specifically to achieve their goals. According to Riitsalu and Murakas (2019) subjective financial understanding as individuals perceive it stands as a vital factor which drives financial well-being. The research indicates that financial outcomes depend more heavily on self-perceived financial understanding than on actual knowledge possession. The combination of prudent financial conduct and income level serves as important factors. Financial education initiatives need to tackle both cognitive aspects and behavioral aspects because they should improve knowledge while building confidence and decision-making abilities. Behavioral finance mechanisms operate at a deeper level because under-informed investors tend to follow noise trading and herding patterns which intensify market instability during times of stress. The financial illiteracy of lower- and middle-income groups results in poor asset distribution choices and excessive market signal responses and heightened exposure to financial disruptions. Lusardi and Mitchell (2014) demonstrates that financially illiterate people avoid retirement planning and portfolio diversification while making suboptimal interest rate responses which creates systemic vulnerabilities during economic downturns. The behavioral deficiency strengthens inequality-induced volatility because many people make similar yet incorrect investment choices. The literature demonstrates that economic inequality results from national economic conditions together with community-based institutional rules while social inequalities emerge through differing knowledge levels and behavioral practices and cognitive perceptions. Economic inequality extends throughout various social structures from redistributive preferences to public services and elite discourse to financial education. The integration of sociological evidence with behavioral economic and political science research leads to evidence-based policy development that also responds to social needs.

DATA AND METHODOLOGY

This study uses macroeconomic panel data from nine countries spanning fifteen years from 2008 to 2022 which generates 135 observations (N = 9, T = 15). The panel data includes complete observations from each country throughout the entire time period. The selected countries of Argentina, Brazil, Canada, China, Germany, Indonesia, Mexico, Spain and the United States combine advanced economies with emerging markets that have active equity markets and different levels of income inequality. The selected countries face similar challenges from globalization and capital market integration despite their varying levels of economic development. The selection of countries depended on the availability of consistent annual data for income distribution metrics (Gini, income shares) and financial indicators (stock indices, bond yields, market volatility) across the entire sample period. The analysis excluded countries with otherwise suitable profiles because their data was either unavailable or their time series data for key variables was inconsistent. The panel provides strong cross-country analysis through its combination of institutional diversity and continuous data availability which reduces estimation errors from missing data points and structural changes.

Figure 1. Gini Coefficients (%) of the Countries (2009-2021)

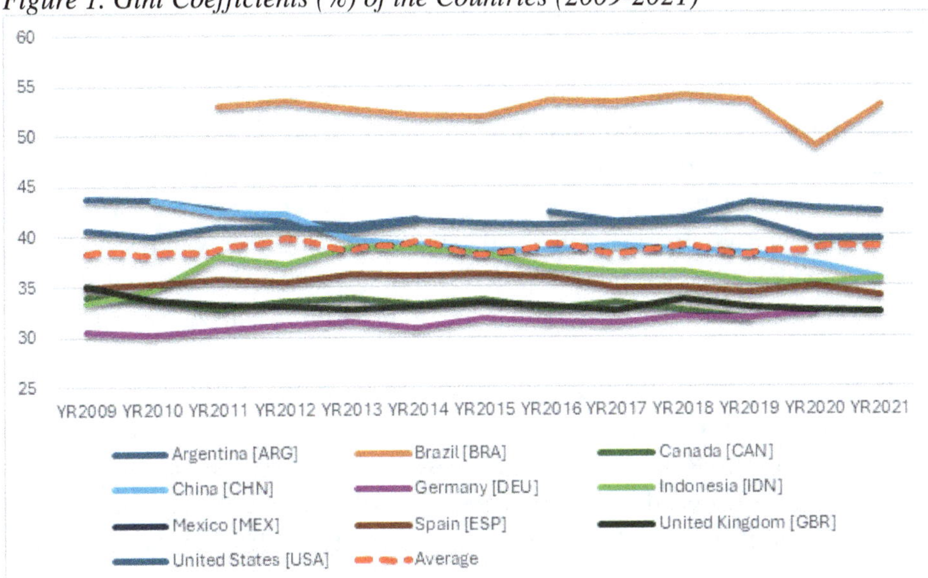

* *Complied by author (data.worldbank.org, 2025)*

The Gini coefficient data for the period 2009–2021 across nine countries (Figure 1) —Argentina, Brazil, Canada, China, Germany, Indonesia, Mexico, Spain, and the United States—reveal distinct patterns in income inequality that reflect each country's economic structure, social policies, and institutional capacity. Brazil shows consistent high income inequality levels through Gini coefficients which stay between 51-55% because of lasting structural gaps that stem from wealth concentration and divided labor markets and minimal redistribution systems. The Gini values in Argentina and Mexico have maintained a stable high range of 41–44% because of economic instability together with informal labor and differences in income between regions. The United States has demonstrated enduring income inequality because its Gini coefficient stayed at approximately 41% from 2009 to 2021. The country maintains high capital income concentration along with weak labor protections and a restricted fiscal redistributive system.

China exhibits declining income inequality because its Gini coefficient decreased from 42% to 36% which indicates that recent redistributive policies and consumption-oriented economic development have started to reduce previous large rural-urban economic differences. The Gini coefficient of Indonesia shows a gentle upward pattern between 2009 and 2015 then reached stability because of quick urban development and unbalanced provincial growth. The Gini coefficient of Spain decreased during this period and now maintains a level of 33% because of social spending programs following the crisis together with European Union fiscal supervision. The Gini values in Canada and Germany stay at the lowest levels in the dataset because these countries operate with powerful welfare institutions together with progressive taxation and comprehensive public services which protect their populations from economic fluctuations and market-based inequality. The Gini coefficient differences between these countries demonstrate that robust redistributive systems like Germany and Canada function differently than Brazil and the United States which maintain persistent structural inequalities. The diverse panel of countries shows varying Gini coefficients which supports the theory that institutions together with fiscal policies and labor market rules determine income distribution results. The distinct patterns of income inequality between nations serve as a solid basis for analyzing how financial markets affect income distribution throughout this research.

The dataset contains financial indicators and inequality indicators which were obtained from two major repositories. The stock market indices and bond yields were obtained from Refinitiv (Reuters) while the inequality metrics such as Gini coefficients and income distribution shares (Top 20%, Second 20%) were obtained from the World Bank's World Development Indicators (WDI). The Variance Coefficient (VC) represents a calculated metric which shows relative model dispersion through its definition as standard deviation divided by means. All data processing, transformation, and econometric modeling were performed in the R programming environment, using panel data packages suitable for macro-financial analysis.

Table 1. Descriptive Statistics by Country (Averages, 2008–2022) at Level

Country	*Avg. Stock Index*	*Avg. VC*	*Avg. High20*	*Avg. Second20*	*Avg. Bond2Yr*	*Avg. Gini%*
Argentina	23,992.50	0.17	47.51	9.68	22.96	42.40
Brazil	72,071.19	0.09	57.51	7.51	10.23	52.79
Canada	14,589.60	0.06	39.97	12.57	4.11	32.91
China	2,932.70	0.09	46.22	10.33	2.76	39.66

continued on following page

Table 1. Continued

Country	*Avg. Stock Index*	*Avg. VC*	*Avg. High20*	*Avg. Second20*	*Avg. Bond2Yr*	*Avg. Gini%*
Germany	9,960.29	0.07	39.29	12.99	7.07	31.39
Indonesia	4,731.42	0.08	44.33	11.35	8.20	36.19
Mexico	40,874.31	0.06	53.08	8.92	6.42	47.26
Spain	9,440.87	0.08	41.31	12.06	4.95	35.07
United States	2,225.63	0.06	46.13	10.43	9.46	40.83

Table 1 provides a comparative overview of key variables by country. Brazil shows the highest income inequality (average Gini: 52.79%) and top income concentration (High20: 57.51%), alongside the highest stock market index, suggesting a strong yet unequal financial environment. Argentina follows with high inequality and the largest variance coefficient (0.17), indicating economic instability. In contrast, Canada and Germany have the lowest inequality levels (Gini: 32.91% and 31.39%) reflecting more equitable distribution. China, while lower in absolute stock index levels, exhibits a relatively high High20 share and moderate inequality. Mexico also demonstrates pronounced inequality (Gini: 47.26%) and a high top 20% income share. Countries like Spain and the U.S. fall into a mid-range pattern—moderate inequality and income concentration.

Table 2. Descriptive Statistics of the Variables (% Chg, included in the Analysis)

Variable	*Observations (NxT)*	*Mean*	*Std. Dev.*	*Min*	*Max*
VC (Variance Coefficient)	135	0.246	1.004	-0.759	4.681
Stock (Local Price % Chg.)	135	0.091	0.197	-0.223	1.029
Gini (Income Inequality)	135	-0.003	0.023	-0.086	0.095
Bond2Yr (2-Year Yield)	135	0.077	0.261	-0.559	1.335
Second20 (2nd Richest 20%)	135	0.005	0.030	-0.138	0.192
High20 (Top 20% Income Share)	135	-0.002	0.016	-0.054	0.072

The change of the percentage transformation process makes data stationary while minimizing regression biases that stem from persistent trends and non-stationary behavior which commonly affect macroeconomic panel data. Thus, the conversion of all variables to percentage changes is achieved to improve unit consistency and resolve unit root issues. The transformed series are enabled to interpret coefficients as relative effects. The stock market variable (Table 2) statistics show minimal changes which consist in the periodic patterns found in financial markets. The Gini coefficient demonstrates minimal changes because structural income distributions change at a slow pace throughout time. The 2-year bond yield variable displays significant variability because it reflects both monetary policy changes and worldwide financial market developments during the sample period. The High20 variable (income share of the richest quintile) and the Second20 variable demonstrate average levels of change and appear to have been normalized or different. The study focuses on marginal effects of inequality, so the transformation enables better inference about relative changes instead of absolute levels.

Model Equations

The study applies panel data techniques to evaluate the relationship between income inequality and stock market performance together with market volatility throughout nine countries between 2008–2022. The dataset consists of both cross-sectional (countries) and time-series (years) dimensions which makes panel regression models suitable to study temporal changes and between-country differences. This research constructs two panel data models to analyze how income inequality affects financial market performance and volatility across different countries during different time periods. Model 1 examines how stock market levels respond to inequality factors. Model 2 investigates how inequality affects market volatility through its impact on the variance coefficient (VC).

$$Stock \quad = \beta + \beta \times Bond2Yr \quad + \beta \times High20 \quad + \beta \times Gini \quad + u \tag{1}$$

$$VC \quad = \alpha + \alpha \times Second20 \quad + \alpha \times High20 \quad + \alpha \times Gini \quad + \varepsilon \tag{2}$$

Stock$_{(\ )}$: log-transformed stock market index for country i in year t
VC$_{(\ )}$: variance coefficient representing market volatility
Bond2Yr$_{(\ )}$: 2-year government bond yield
High20$_{(\ )}$: income share of the top 20%
Second20$_{(\ )}$: income share of the low-middle-income 20%
Gini$_{(\ )}$: Gini coefficient (overall income inequality)
u$_{(\ )}$ and ε$_{(\ )}$: error terms

The main problem in panel estimation occurs when units in panel (such as countries) show interrelated behavior. Each unit experiences effects from shocks that occur in different units. The assumption of independence across cross-sectional units fails to hold thus leading to biased and inconsistent estimators (Pesaran, 2004). The Breusch-Pagan LM test (Breusch & Pagan, 1980) served as the diagnostic method to verify cross-sectional dependence because the study contains more time observations (T = 15) than cross-sectional units (N = 9). The test results showed strong evidence against the null hypothesis of cross-sectional independence which indicates the requirement for robust estimation approaches that handle unit interdependence. Serial correlation (or autocorrelation) alongside cross-sectional dependence threatens the accuracy of panel regression findings. The error terms fail to meet the assumption of independence because they exhibit a temporal correlation within units which violates the assumption of independently distributed errors. Serial correlation in panel models was evaluated using the Breusch-Godfrey/Wooldridge test developed by Wooldridge (2010). The test results indicated significant serial correlation which reinforced the need for an estimator that would address both cross-sectional and temporal dependencies.

The choice between pooled OLS and fixed effects (FE) or random effects (RE) models for panel estimation depended on the results of multiple required formal statistical tests. The F-test for individual effects checks whether the pooled OLS model maintains validity by determining whether unobserved heterogeneity exists across units. When the null hypothesis regarding no individual effects is rejected the pooled OLS model becomes invalid (Baltagi, 2005). The Breusch-Pagan Lagrange Multiplier (LM) test evaluated the suitability of random effects models over pooled OLS models. The likelihood function-based test determines the significance of unit and time-specific effects by assessing their effects on the model's likelihood function (Breusch & Pagan, 1980; Tatoğlu, 2012). When both fixed and random effects models show promise, the Hausman test (Hausman, 1978) is performed. The null condition of the Hausman test states that random effects estimators maintain both consistency and efficiency, but the alternative condition indicates random effects estimator inconsistency which makes fixed effects the better choice.

The selection between these models stems from their fundamental theoretical requirements. The pooled OLS model requires all units and time periods to have identical interceptions and slope coefficients. The model requires this specification when no unobserved individual effects exist. The fixed effects model permits different intercept values among cross-sectional units while maintaining constant slope coefficients (Pazarlıoğlu & Gürler, 2007). The model implies that individual effects have a correlation with the regressors. The random effects model uses generalized least squares methods to estimate parameters because it assumes individual effects are random variables that are uncorrelated with regressors.

Some model configurations resulted in classical assumption rejection during research thus the study employed the Feasible Generalized Least Squares (FGLS) method with one-way time effects for its final estimation. The FGLS method enables the treatment of serial correlation and cross-sectional dependence and remains suitable when heteroskedasticity or correlated disturbances occur. The studentized Breusch-Pagan test examined heteroskedasticity in the model residuals. The p-value exceeded 0.05 which led to the rejection of the null hypothesis of constant variance thus proving the homoskedasticity of residuals and confirming the FGLS estimation efficiency. The sequential approach of model testing and selection produces estimators that are robust while the panel regression results capture income distribution and stock market interactions which exist across both time and countries.

FINDINGS AND DISCUSSION

The empirical research presents two independent models that assess stock market performance (Stock model) and financial volatility (VC model) separately to explain how income inequality affects capital market dynamics.

i) Stock Model

First, the stock price percentage change model receives its panel data estimation from a fixed effects (FE) specification (Table 3). Several diagnostic tests were performed to establish whether panel estimators or pooled OLS should be used. The F test for fixed effects proves the pooled OLS model inappropriate since it rejects the null hypothesis with $F = 6.28$ and $p < 0.01$. The LM test from Breusch-Pagan shows that the null hypothesis of pooled OLS model inadequacy is rejected ($LM = 50.50$, $p < 0.01$). The Hausman test shows strong preference for fixed effects because it produces a high-test statistic value of 31.68 and p-value of 0.00. The test identifies correlation between the error term and regressors. The use of fixed effects model over random effects model is recommended because of this correlation. The second-generation diagnostics show that classical OLS assumptions are violated. The Pesaran cross-sectional dependence test confirms that financial shocks or global factors affect all countries within the panel because it strongly rejects the null hypothesis ($CD = 128.89$, $p < 0.01$). The Wooldridge test for serial correlation rejects the null hypothesis ($F = 37.82$, $p < 0.01$) because it shows first-order autocorrelation in the idiosyncratic errors. The FGLS model serves as the appropriate method to analyze one-way time effects because it provides robustness against both autocorrelation and cross-sectional dependence.

Table 3. First Stock Fixed Effect Panel Model Summary Statistics

Test	Null Hypothesis (H_0)	Decision	Test Statistic	p-value
F Test	Pooled OLS is appropriate	H_0 rejected	6.28	0.00
Breusch-Pagan LM Test (RE Test)	Pooled OLS is appropriate	H_0 rejected	50.50	0.00
Hausman Test	Random effects model is consistent and efficient	H_0 rejected	31.68	0.00
Cross-Section Dependence Test	No cross-sectional dependence (units are independent)	H_0 rejected	128.89	0.00
Wooldridge Serial Correlation Test	No serial correlation in idiosyncratic errors	H_0 rejected	37.82	0.00

Finally, under the FGLS specification (Table 4), the Breusch-Pagan test for heteroskedasticity yields a p-value of 0.43, implying that the residuals do not exhibit non-constant variance and confirming the validity of FGLS standard errors. In terms of coefficient estimates, the Gini coefficient exhibits a negative and statistically significant relationship with stock price growth ($\beta = -2.5536$, $p < 0.01$). This result supports the hypothesis that higher income inequality, as measured broadly across the income distribution, tends to suppress equity market performance—potentially through reduced aggregate demand or heightened systemic uncertainty. In contrast, the High20 income share has a positive and statistically significant effect ($\beta = 3.7450$, $p < 0.01$), reinforcing the argument that income concentration among the wealthiest strata enhances stock market performance, likely due to higher investment activity and capital availability from this group. The 2-year government bond yield (Bond2Yr) enters the model with a negative coefficient ($\beta = -0.0218$), yet it is not statistically significant at the 10% level ($p = 0.19$) but significant at 0.80 confidence level. While this suggests a potential inverse relationship between interest rates and stock returns—a finding consistent with financial theory—the lack of statistical significance implies that this relationship may be weak or highly contingent on additional factors not captured within this specification.

Overall, the findings of the FGLS estimation indicate that income inequality, depending on its structure, plays a critical and differentiated role in influencing stock market outcomes. Broader inequality (as captured by the Gini coefficient) appears detrimental to stock returns, while concentrated income among top earners (High20) enhances them. These effects are robust after correcting methodological challenges posed by panel data structure, underscoring the importance of incorporating inequality metrics into financial performance analyses.

Table 4. Final FGLS Model of the Dependent Variable: Stock Price % Change

Variable	*Estimate*	*Std. Error*	*z-value*	*p-value*	*Significance*
Gini	-2.5536	0.7541	-3.3862	0.00	***
High20	3.7450	1.0968	3.4143	0.00	***
Bond2Yr	-0.0218	0.0164	-1.3242	0.19	*

*** 99% confidence level, * 80% confidence level

ii) Variance Coefficient Model

The empirical research between income inequality and financial market risk reveals useful information through the diagnostic statistics and estimation results of the VC model across the entire sample. To determine proper panel model, first, the model selection tests used the F-test along with the Breusch-Pagan Lagrange Multiplier (LM) test and the Hausman test to choose the most suitable estimation strategy (Table 5). The F-test generated a 0.31 statistic with a p-value of 0.96 and the LM test produced a 2.38 statistic with a p-value of 0.12 which failed to reject the null hypothesis for pooled OLS. The Hausman test statistics of 0.48 (p = 0.92) showed random effects estimates are consistent and efficient, so the null hypothesis remained unchallenged. The diagnostic tests of second-generation panel data indicate different results. The test for cross-sectional dependence revealed that residuals between units showed strong interunit correlations with a p-value below 0.001 and a very high statistic of 161.14. The Wooldridge test for serial correlation produced a significant result of 30.17 (p = 0.01) which confirmed the presence of autocorrelation in the panel data idiosyncratic errors.

Table 5. Statistics of the First Pooled OLS Panel Model for Variance Coefficient

Test	*Null Hypothesis (H_0)*	*Decision*	*Test Statistic*	*p-value*
F Test	Pooled OLS is appropriate	H_0 not rejected	0.31	0.96
Breusch-Pagan LM Test (RE Test)	Pooled OLS is appropriate	H_0 not rejected	2.38	0.12
Hausman Test	Random effects model is consistent and efficient	H_0 not rejected	0.48	0.92
Cross-Section Dependence Test	No cross-sectional dependence (units are independent)	H_0 rejected	161.14	0.00
Wooldridge Serial Correlation Test	No serial correlation in idiosyncratic errors	H_0 rejected	30.17	0.01

Finally, a Feasible Generalized Least Squares (FGLS) estimation (Table 6) with one-way time effects was used because of these diagnostic results to address serial correlation and cross-sectional dependence. The corrected model generates statistically valid coefficient estimates and standard errors. The FGLS results show that income distribution variables demonstrate important associations with financial market volatility. The Gini coefficient demonstrates a significant association at the <0.001 level probability. Market volatility (VC) experiences a 25.36 unit increase when the Gini coefficient rises by one unit according to the estimates. The results indicate that stock market instability directly correlates with overall income inequality. The negative coefficient value of -22.6705 (standard error = 3.6080; $z = -6.2835$; $p < 0.001$) indicates that when high-income earners hold more of the total income the volatility decreases. Elite investors stabilize financial markets through their long-term investment approach and low risk-taking behavior. The Second20 income share has a positive effect on VC with a significant statistical relationship where the coefficient equals 11.7175 and the standard error amounts to 0.7420 while the z-value reaches 15.7918 ($p < 0.001$). Households that join asset markets with limited financial experience or risk tolerance show increased financial volatility when their income share in the Second20 demographic group grows. The Breusch-Pagan test of heteroskedasticity performed on the FGLS residuals showed results with a p-value of 0.40 which supports the null hypothesis of homoskedasticity. The distribution of residuals appears to be even which makes further heteroskedasticity correction unnecessary.

The estimation and diagnostic outcomes demonstrate that financial market risk depends on multiple factors stemming from inequality. Gini coefficient measures broader inequality which creates market volatility, but the concentration of top incomes reduces market volatility because investors stabilize the market through their investment practices. The increase in financial participation by the low-middle-income group (Second20) leads to additional market volatility which indicates that market stabilization does not result from access to finance without corresponding financial knowledge. The findings demonstrate that both redistributive measures and financial literacy programs need to be implemented to mitigate market instability resulting from inequality.

Table 6. Final FGLS Model of the Dependent Variable: Variance Coefficient

Variable	*Estimate*	*Std. Error*	*z-value*	*p-value*	*Significance*
Gini	25.3595	2.9515	8.5920	<0.001	***
High20	-22.6705	3.6080	-6.2835	<0.001	***
Second20	11.7175	0.7420	15.7918	<0.001	***

*** 99% confidence level

iii) Discussion

The stock price model together with the variance coefficient (VC) model shows that income inequality strongly affects capital market behavior and stability. The Gini coefficient shows negative influence on stock price growth yet creates positive effects on market volatility. The dual effect demonstrates that expanding income inequality produces markets with decreased productivity and increased instability. Research by Blesch et al. (2022) along with Aye et al. (2020) supports this pattern by showing how inequality damages overall market demand while increasing economic uncertainty. The financial illiteracy combined with limited resources and stock market exclusion of people in low-income groups prevents them from participating in the market. De Beckker et al. (2019) and Riitsalu & Murakas (2019) both support this conclusion by showing how lacking savings or investment capacity keeps society segments outside of capital accumulation which weakens market participation depth and inclusiveness.

The High20 income group serves as a control variable that produces positive results for stock prices but negative results for market volatility which shows that high-income individuals help drive financial expansion and stability. The research confirms Blau (2015) and Blau et al. (2021) who state that high-income investors help stabilize markets because of their superior information and long-term investment methods. Healthy market functioning and broad-based prosperity cannot be achieved through this dynamic alone. Despite better capital market performance during concentrated wealth periods the system remains structurally flawed because it restricts investment opportunities and savings mechanisms to the democratic functioning of financial systems (Manduca, 2018; Sachweh, 2012). Market growth through a top income group leadership does not guarantee stability because this system faces threats from public distrust while leaving the majority of the population financially out of reach.

The positive relationship between the Second20 income share and volatility introduces new perspectives to the analysis between financial systems and income inequality. Market instability increases when low-middle-income groups receive financial inclusion benefits that do not accompany sufficient financial education or regulatory assistance. The findings of Isidore and Arun (2022) demonstrate that lower-income investors along with less informed investors tend to select riskier financial approaches which makes them more prone to market misjudgments. Market resilience together with performance demands a balanced distribution of income and financial knowledge beyond the High20 group's support. Financial systems need inclusive participation from diverse societal segments to achieve stability as well as a capital market that accurately shows economic health of the collective population.

The 2-year bond yield shows no statistical significance at conventional levels ($p = 0.19$) but its negative coefficient suggests a possible inverse relationship with stock returns. The negative relationship between bond yields and stock returns may be attributed to investor sensitivity to interest rate expectations because higher bond yields signal contractionary monetary policy which leads to a shift away from equities. The effects of yield differentials on capital flows become more significant in markets that are highly sensitive to yield differentials (Chen, Roll, & Ross, 1986). The observed minimal effect could be attributed to two factors: first, the structural inequality factors that dominate market behavior; second, the low cross-country variation in short-term rates during the study period, especially in the context of global monetary convergence post-2008. This finding suggests that short-term rate signals should be interpreted with caution in macro-level inequality–finance models and future research should include multiple control variables.

The growth of ESG-oriented investing creates an opportunity to link market involvement with social equity targets which decreases market volatility and supports inclusive financial systems. ESG investment frameworks now use indicators about income inequality and diversity and community engagement to integrate redistributive concerns into capital allocation decisions. The long-term value creation process now depends on environmental sustainability and social disparity resolution according to institutional investors who have made this recognition (Krueger, Sautner, & Starks, 2020). ESG investment strategies that support businesses with fair labor practices and inclusive governance, and community-oriented operations help reduce systemic inequality and strengthen market stability.

One limitation of this chapter is, beyond income-based metrics, integrating multidimensional inequality—such as gender gaps in financial access or educational disparities—would provide a more comprehensive understanding of market participation dynamics. Further analysis should include multidimensional inequality metrics which combine gender service access disparities with educational gaps and regional economic exclusion to understand how inequality affects market participation and capital accumulation. The dimensions of income distribution interact with each other to create additional systemic obstacles which primarily affect developing economies (Dabla-Norris et al., 2015).

CONCLUSION

This study examines how income inequality interacts with stock market activity through a comprehensive analysis of nine countries across the period from 2008 to 2022. It applies an extensive panel econometric framework to analyze the Gini coefficient together with High20 and Second20 income distribution indicators to understand their effect on market returns and volatility. The findings demonstrate that broader income inequality based on Gini coefficient values produces lower stock market returns and greater financial risks which indicates both decreased economic activity and increased market instability in unequal economic systems. High20 income concentration functions as a market stabilizer by producing elevated returns while reducing volatility levels. The dual influence demonstrates that high-income investors create significant market dynamics because they possess better access to information as well as financial instruments and enduring investment approaches.

The observed market stabilization effect should not disguise the fundamental problem that growing inequality prevents lower and middle-income citizens from effectively participating in the market. The evidence indicates that these demographic groups face obstacles to sustained investment because they lack financial literacy as well as disposable income and institutional support. The market engagement of these groups appears sporadic and reactive because they lack the financial knowledge and resources to conduct informed strategic investments. This pattern establishes an unbalanced market risk structure because high-income groups stabilize the market yet less affluent participants increase market instability through their restricted financial choices. The structural exclusion of the lower-income segments weakens the capital market's ability to distribute resources effectively and to perform its allocation function. The growing dependence on top-tier investors produces markets which demonstrate short-term stability but demonstrate long-term instability when these powerful investors become vulnerable to systemic shocks.

The main goal of the policy has been to support investment along with capital market advancement yet there remains a lack of financial inclusion investments. In societies with significant wealth disparities the capital market tends to increase existing social inequalities since profits mainly benefit individuals holding top positions in the income distribution. The decline of social cohesion coupled with reduced consumer confidence and weaker sustainable growth emerges from this situation. The volatility model indicates that the Second20 group which represents low-middle-income households shows a significant impact on financial risk through their growing market involvement. When moderate inclusion lacks educational support and regulatory safeguards and support mechanisms it tends to create market instability rather than market resilience.

The results confirm the main theoretical assumption that financial market inequality stands as a fundamental factor which determines market performance as well as market stability. The study provides additional insights about the dual nature of income distribution because it serves as a financial capital source and imposes structural limitations on financial markets. Fighting with inequality represents a necessity for maintaining health in capital markets as well as being a matter of social fairness. The stability and participation rates of markets improve when they operate as growth engines for inclusivity instead of accumulation systems that exclude certain groups of society.

Financial volatility can be reduced through institutional responses which include progressive fiscal redistribution and targeted central bank interventions. Research shows that fiscal policies including progressive taxation and social transfers and universal service provisions reduce economic instability by boosting disposable income for low- and middle-income households and supporting overall demand (IMF, 2014; Woo et al., 2013). Monetary authorities maintain essential responsibility for financial inclusiveness through their implementation of credit policy and their establishment of collateral frameworks and macroprudential regulations. Monetary policy that provides liquidity to neglected areas of the market helps increase market participation without creating asset price bubbles. The reinforcement of institutional trust and financial resilience occurs when equity goals become integrated into regulatory frameworks which mandate financial intermediaries to achieve inclusive lending targets and provide incentives for ESG-aligned investment behavior.

The welfare architectures of Germany and Canada enable redistributive mechanisms to work best through progressive taxation and automatic stabilizers and established social transfer systems (Immervoll & Richardson, 2011). These institutions reduce income volatility and enhance market inclusiveness through existing institutional frameworks without requiring significant structural changes. The policy tools of nationwide financial literacy programs and digital micro-savings platforms and community-based cooperatives represent practical and scalable solutions for emerging economies such as Brazil and Indonesia because these countries have limited fiscal capacity and weak administrative reach and formal institution trust (Demirgüç-Kunt et al., 2018). Such targeted financial inclusion initiatives create better equity results while building formal capital market participation which leads to enduring stability through increased investor participation.

The study concludes by emphasizing the immediate need for multiple policy strategies that focus on market stability improvement and financial inclusivity enhancement. Governments need to implement two strategies which combine redistributive policies with progressive taxation alongside initiatives that enhance the financial competencies of underserved populations. The combination of financial literacy programs with incentives for long-term savings and affordable investment platforms enables increased market participation while reducing instability caused by income disparities. Financial education is integrated into public schools and targeted adult learning programs for new investors create foundational conditions for fair financial market participation.

REFERENCES

Adjasi, C., & Biekpe, N. (2006). Stock market development and economic growth: The case of selected African countries. *African Development Review, 18*(1), 144–161. DOI: 10.1111/j.1467-8268.2006.00136.x

Alvaredo, F. (2011). A note on the relationship between top income shares and the Gini coefficient. *Economics Letters, 110*(3), 274–277. DOI: 10.1016/j.econlet.2010.10.008

Aslan, B., Zh, B., Ye, A., Zh, T., Anar, Y., & Azamat, Z. (2018). The influence of stock market development of low income and middle/high income group countries on an increase in economic growth. *Journal of Advanced Research in Law and Economics, 9*(3), 839–848.

Aye, G., Gozgor, G., & Gupta, R. (2020). Dynamic and asymmetric response of inequality to income volatility: The case of the United Kingdom. *Social Indicators Research, 147*(3), 747–762. DOI: 10.1007/s11205-019-02180-2

Baltagi, B. H. (2005). *Econometric Analysis of Panel Data* (3rd ed.). John Wiley & Sons.

Barberis, N., & Thaler, R. (2003). A survey of behavioral finance. Handbook of the Economics of Finance, 1, 1053–1128. DOI: 10.1016/S1574-0102(03)01027-6

Becker, B. (2019). Mind the income gaps? Experimental evidence of information's lasting effect on redistributive preferences. *Social Justice Research, 33*(2), 137–194. DOI: 10.1007/s11211-019-00343-7

Blau, B. M. (2015). Income inequality and stock market volatility. SSRN *Electronic Journal*. DOI: 10.2139/ssrn.2708500

Blau, B. M., Griffith, T. G., & Whitby, R. J. (2021). Income inequality and the volatility of stock prices. *Applied Economics, 53*(38), 4404–4416. DOI: 10.1080/00036846.2021.1904110

Blesch, K., Hauser, O. P., & Jachimowicz, J. M. (2022). Measuring inequality beyond the Gini coefficient may clarify conflicting findings. *Nature Human Behaviour, 6*(11), 1525–1536. DOI: 10.1038/s41562-022-01430-7 PMID: 36038775

Breusch, T. S., & Pagan, A. R. (1980). The Lagrange Multiplier test and its applications to model specification in econometrics. *The Review of Economic Studies, 47*(1), 239–253. DOI: 10.2307/2297111

Chen, N.-F., Roll, R., & Ross, S. A. (1986). Economic Forces and the Stock Market. *The Journal of Business, 59*(3), 383–403. DOI: 10.1086/296344

Christou, C., Gupta, R., & Jawadi, F. (2017). Does inequality help in forecasting equity premium in a panel of G7 countries? *The North American Journal of Economics and Finance, 55*, 101456. Advance online publication. DOI: 10.1016/j.najef.2021.101456

Cobham, A., & Sumner, A. (2013). Putting the Gini back in the bottle? 'The Palma' as a policy-relevant measure of inequality. King's College London International Development Institute Working Paper. Retrieved from https://citeseerx.ist.psu.edu/document?repid=rep1&type=pdf&doi=7ceaa0d76e8c0f2fbb9a53aa7043108c857890b3 at 25.07.2025.

Cowell, F. A., & Flachaire, E. (2007). Income distribution and inequality measurement: The problem of extreme values. *Journal of Econometrics, 141*(2), 1044–1072. DOI: 10.1016/j.jeconom.2007.01.001

Dabla-Norris, E., Kochhar, K., Suphaphiphat, N., Ricka, F., & Tsounta, E. (2015). Causes and consequences of income inequality: A global perspective (IMF Staff Discussion Note SDN/15/13). International Monetary Fund. https://www.imf.org/external/pubs/ft/sdn/2015/sdn1513.pdf

De Beckker, K., De Witte, K., & Van Campenhout, G. (2019). Identifying financially illiterate groups: An international comparison. Sustainability & Economics eJournal. DOI: 10.2139/ssrn.3360483

Demirgüç-Kunt, A., Klapper, L., Singer, D., Ansar, S., & Hess, J. (2018). *The Global Findex Database 2017: Measuring financial inclusion and the fintech revolution*. World Bank., DOI: 10.1596/978-1-4648-1259-0

Guiso, L., Sapienza, P., & Zingales, L. (2008). Trusting the stock market. *The Journal of Finance, 63*(6), 2557–2600. DOI: 10.1111/j.1540-6261.2008.01408.x

Hai, X. (2016). Dynamic research on China's Gini coefficient. *International Conference on Humanities and Social Science (HSS 2016)*. DOI: 10.2991/hss-26.2016.98

Hausman, J. A. (1978). Specification tests in econometrics. *Econometrica, 46*(6), 1251–1271. DOI: 10.2307/1913827

Immervoll, H., & Richardson, L. (2011). Redistribution policy and inequality reduction in OECD countries: What has changed in two decades? OECD Social, Employment and Migration Working Papers, No. 122. DOI: 10.1787/1815199X

International Monetary Fund. (2014). Fiscal policy and income inequality. IMF Policy Paper. Retrieved from https://www.imf.org/external/np/pp/eng/2014/012314.pdf at 25.07.2025.

Isidore, R., & Arun, C. (2022). Does the annual income earned influence the decision-making in the Indian secondary equity market? *Journal of Business and Economic Studies*, *6*(1), 24–40. DOI: 10.53462/AZNZ9904

Kelly, P., & Lobao, L. (2021). Whose need matters?: The local welfare state, poverty, and variation in US counties' social service provisioning. *Social Currents*, *8*(6), 566–590. DOI: 10.1177/23294965211047886

Keynes, J. M. (1936). *The General Theory of Employment, Interest, and Money*. Macmillan.

Kobakiwal, S. (2018). Inward FDI stock and income distribution: An analysis from an income group perspective [Master's thesis, Lund University].

Krueger, P., Sautner, Z., & Starks, L. T. (2020). The importance of climate risks for institutional investors. *Review of Financial Studies*, *33*(3), 1067–1111. DOI: 10.1093/rfs/hhz137

Kuusela, H. (2020). The hyperopia of wealth: The cultural legitimation of economic inequalities by top earners. *Socio-economic Review*. Advance online publication. DOI: 10.1093/ser/mwaa047

Lambert, P., & Decoster, A. (2005). The Gini coefficient reveals more. SSRN *Electronic Journal*. DOI: 10.2139/ssrn.809004

Lusardi, A., & Mitchell, O. S. (2014). The economic importance of financial literacy: Theory and evidence. *Journal of Economic Literature*, *52*(1), 5–44. DOI: 10.1257/jel.52.1.5 PMID: 28579637

Manduca, R. (2018). Income inequality and the persistence of racial economic disparities. *Sociological Science*, *5*, 182–205. DOI: 10.15195/v5.a8

Metelski, D., & Sobieraj, J. (2024). Trading volume concentration across S&P 500 index constituents: A Gini-based analysis. *Journal of Risk and Financial Management*, *17*(8), 325. DOI: 10.3390/jrfm17080325

Meyer, P. B., Piacentini, J., Frazis, H., Schultz, M., & Sveikauskas, L. (2025). The Effect of the COVID 19 Pandemic on Inequality. *Review of Income and Wealth*, *71*(1), e12707. Advance online publication. DOI: 10.1111/roiw.12707

Parsons, B., & Rabhi, A. (2024). Shifting sands: How exchange rate volatility shapes income distribution in high-income countries. *Structural Change and Economic Dynamics*, *67*, 203–219. DOI: 10.1016/j.strueco.2024.12.021

Pazarlıoğlu, M. V., & Gürler, Ö. K. (2007). Telecommunication investments and economic growth: A panel data approach. *Finance Politics & Economic Comments*, *44*(508), 35–43.

Riitsalu, L., & Murakas, R. (2019). Subjective financial knowledge, prudent behaviour and income. *International Journal of Bank Marketing*, *37*(6), 1431–1448. DOI: 10.1108/IJBM-03-2018-0071

Rogerson, P. A. (2013). The Gini coefficient of inequality: A new interpretation. *Letters in Spatial and Resource Sciences*, *6*(2), 109–120. DOI: 10.1007/s12076-013-0091-x

Sachweh, P. (2012). The moral economy of inequality: Popular views on income differentiation, poverty and wealth. *Socio-economic Review*, *10*(3), 419–445. DOI: 10.1093/ser/mwr023

Schasfoort, J. (2020). Stock market volatility and wealth inequality. SSRN *Electronic Journal*. DOI: 10.2139/ssrn.3452599

Schneider, M. (2021). The discovery of the Gini coefficient. *History of Political Economy*, *53*(1, S1), 179–206. DOI: 10.1215/00182702-8816637

Seven, Ü., & Yetkiner, H. (2016). Financial intermediation and economic growth: Does income matter? *Economic Systems*, *40*(1), 39–58. DOI: 10.1016/j.ecosys.2015.09.004

Stiglitz, J. E. (2012). *The price of inequality: How today's divided society endangers our future*. W.W. Norton & Company.

Tatoğlu, F. Y. (2012). *Panel data econometrics: With Stata applications*. Beta Publishing.

Tong-Yu, Z. (2010). Empirical analysis on the relationship between income changes of high-income group and stock market index in U.S. *The Theory and Practice of Finance and Economics*, *32*(6), 34–37.

Woo, J., Bova, E., Kinda, T., & Zhang, Y. S. (2013). Distributional consequences of fiscal consolidation and the role of fiscal policy: What do the data say? IMF Working Paper WP/13/195. Retrieved from https://www.imf.org/external/pubs/ft/wp/2013/wp13195.pdf at 25.07.2025.

Wooldridge, J. M. (2010). *Econometric Analysis of Cross–Section and Panel Data* (2nd ed.). MIT Press.

Yao, S. (1999). On the decomposition of Gini coefficients by population class and income source: A spreadsheet approach and application. *Applied Economics, 31*(10), 1249–1264. DOI: 10.1080/000368499323463

Yu, J., Hassan, M. K., & Sanchez, B. (2012). A re-examination of financial development, stock markets development and economic growth. *Applied Economics, 44*(27), 3479–3489. DOI: 10.1080/00036846.2011.577019

KEY TERMS AND DEFINITIONS

Gini Coefficient: The Gini coefficient functions as a statistical tool which measures the extent of income or wealth disparities across populations. The Gini coefficient stretches from 0 which represents complete income equality to 1 which demonstrates total income concentration in a single person. The coefficient emerges from plotting cumulative income distribution through the Lorenz curve. The unidimensional Gini coefficient offers straightforward interpretation while serving as a common tool for evaluating tax policies and socioeconomic studies of income inequality across different countries. The Gini coefficient lacks sufficient sensitivity to inequality distribution across different income levels thus requiring additional multi-parameter measurements for comprehensive analysis.

Income Inequality: The distribution of income between people or social groups throughout an economy becomes unequal when referred to as income inequality. The Gini coefficient stands alongside income quintile shares (such as High20, Second20) and percentile ratios (such as P90/P10) to evaluate income inequality. High levels of income inequality create systemic problems that block lower-income groups from accessing healthcare and education and financial markets. The macro-financial landscape experiences effects from inequality which shape individual savings habits and market investment decisions while affecting national stability and social and political stability. Structural components such as labor market segmentation and financial inclusion together with taxation and globalization act as factors which shape inequality dynamics.

Feasible Generalized Least Squares (FGLS): The econometric method of Feasible Generalized Least Squares (FGLS) serves as a two-step approach to model parameter estimation in panel data when OLS assumptions fail due to heteroskedasticity and autocorrelation in error terms. The initial step determines the variance structure of residuals before applying this structure for model transformation to achieve more efficient coefficient estimates in the second step. FGLS proves particularly useful when analyzing macro-panel data because countries or entities can display different error variance structures. The research implements FGLS because it detects serial correlation and cross-sectional dependence thus providing robust results for analyzing the relationship between inequality and financial market performance.

Stock Price Percentage Change: The annual percentage change in stock prices of a nation's primary equity index is known as Stock Price Percentage Change (Stock). The standard performance indicator of equity markets depends on multiple influences from macroeconomic factors and investor actions and worldwide financial patterns. This variable serves empirical finance to measure changes in investor opinions along with their predictive views and official policy reactions. This research uses stock price change as its dependent variable to examine how different measures of income inequality (including Gini coefficient and High20) influence annual stock market performance. The stock price change delivers a straightforward view of how economic differences affect equity market capital growth.

VC (Variance of Coefficients): Variance of coefficients (VC) is an analytical measure to represent market instability together with financial risk. The extent to which coefficients in financial return models, especially those related to equity performance change over time or between different entities, is shown by this measure. Market returns show higher volatility when VC values rise because of economic inequality together with investor heterogeneity and policy shocks. The measure of VC distinguishes itself from typical volatility indicators such as standard deviation of returns because it detects instabilities that appear in econometric relationships. This research employs VC as a dependent variable to determine if different income inequality dimensions create elevated or reduced financial system risks.

High20 Income Share: High20 income share indicates what percentage of national income the top 20% of income earners receive. The economic power and spending patterns of wealthy consumers become assessable through this income concentration metric which focuses on high-income earners. Members of the top-income group tend to invest actively in capital markets because they possess diversified portfolios alongside higher risk tolerance. The financial modeling process depends heavily on High20 to determine both market performance and stability effects from elite financial market participants. This research uses High20 as an explanatory variable to determine how top-income group financial activities affect market results beyond basic inequality indicators such as the Gini coefficient.

Second20 Income Share: The Second20 income share displays the proportion of national income which the second low-income quintile over five receives. The market activity becomes more diversified when this group enters the market but speculative or misinformed investments by this group can lead to increased market volatility. This research uses Second20 to study how the financial market activities of emerging middle-class investors affect volatility levels which enhances understanding of inequality-market relationships.

Income Concentration: Income Concentration represents how a small portion of the population controls most of the national or household income at the top 1% or 5% or 20% levels. The concept shows economic elite dominance in income distribution, yet it differs from standard income inequality metrics since it specifically targets elite earners' economic power. The distribution of wealth among the population affects macroeconomic stability because wealthy consumers tend to change their spending habits and reduce their spending power while gaining stronger control over economic policy. Financial markets tend to favor capital gains over broad-based growth because concentrated income leads to market dynamics which benefit investors who hold more power. This study measures income concentration through the High20 variable which proves to be a fundamental factor that shapes stock market patterns and volatility results.

Financial literacy: Financial literacy exists as the ability to grasp financial concepts which include budgeting alongside saving and investing and credit management. Financial literacy combines both measurable knowledge about financial products and subjective confidence when making financial choices. The behavior of investors in equity markets depends heavily on financial literacy since they need to comprehend risk and implement effective portfolio diversification. People who lack financial literacy tend to make poor decisions because of their low income and education level and advancing age thus they avoid capital markets and become more susceptible to financial crises. Financial literacy deficits among lower-income groups act as both volatility and market exclusion drivers according to this research context.

Chapter 4
Does Income Inequality Affect Public Debt?

Emre Örün
https://orcid.org/0000-0002-2739-1959
Yozgat Bozok University, Turkey

ABSTRACT

This article examines the effects of income inequality, GDP per capita, inflation, unemployment, and the age-dependency ratio on central government debt in 18 OECD countries over the period 1999–2022 using a Panel ARDL approach. Income inequality, unemployment, and the age-dependency ratio have a positive impact on public debt. Conversely, inflation and GDP per capita are found to have a debt-reducing effect. The Dumitrescu-Hurlin causality test reveals a unidirectional causality running from inequality to public debt. The results highlight the critical role of socioeconomic factors such as income inequality and unemployment in determining public debt dynamics. It also highlights the need for social policy interventions to ensure fiscal sustainability.

1. INTRODUCTION

Many nations have seen rising public debt and income inequality in recent years. Rising from almost $23 trillion in 2000 to $53 trillion in 2016, the worldwide public debt stock almost doubled, raising questions on public debt sustainability (Carrera & de la Vega, 2021). Income disparity in both developed and underdeveloped nations has stayed high alongside this increase in public debt. Especially in developed

DOI: 10.4018/979-8-3373-7360-7.ch004

economies, a notable rise in public debt levels over the past two decades has been noted, aggravating issues on fiscal sustainability.

The 2008 global financial crisis and COVID-19 epidemic led many OECD nations to implement expansionary fiscal policies which resulted in increased debt-to-GDP ratio. The analysis of public debt dynamics becomes essential because of increasing financial burdens alongside persistent structural issues such as population aging. High debt levels create obstacles for implementing counter-cyclical fiscal policies and simultaneously limit economic growth potential. The analysis includes Gini coefficients from the United States and Europe because these regions represent major examples of income inequality worldwide. While the United States stands out with its high-income inequality, Europe has a structure that tries to limit this inequality with more inclusive social policies than the United States. The evaluation of central government debt's impact on income distribution becomes more comprehensive through the comparison of these two different economic systems. The ratio of central government debt to GDP in OECD member countries has increased steadily since the 1990s according to Figure 1. The global financial crisis of 2008 triggered a significant increase in debt levels which reached elevated heights. The Gini coefficients demonstrate that income inequality has persisted at high levels in both the United States and Europe which indicates growing income disparities. Research on the relationship between central government debt and income inequality as debt determinants becomes essential for maintaining fiscal sustainability in this situation.

Figure 1. Central government debt and Gini coefficient (USA, Europe, EU, OECD)

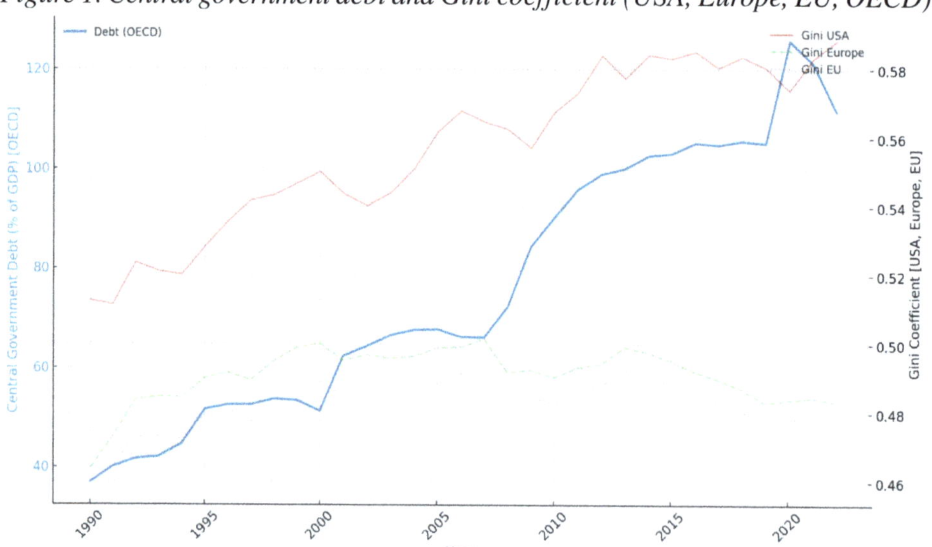

Source: World Development Indicators https://databank.worldbank.org/source/world-development-indicators and World Inequality Database https://wid.world/data/ Figure designed by the author.

A central normative framework for understanding public debt dynamics is the tax-smoothing theory of government finance. Barro's (1979) seminal model, later extended by Lucas and Stokey (1983), formalizes the notion that a benevolent, forward-looking government should smooth distortionary tax rates over time (Congregado et al., 2023). According to Barro's (1979) tax smoothing theory, debt is used by governments as a buffer against sudden changes in tax rates. This method suggests that debt repayment is targeted in times of lower expenditure or higher revenues, while borrowing from deficits is preferred in times of temporary expenditure increases or revenue declines. In this framework, it is used as a countercyclical response to temporary income fluctuations (Barro, 1979). Barro's model emphasizes maintaining control over the debt-to-income ratio and mitigating the financial pressure arising from excessive borrowing. Accordingly, the fundamental principle articulated in the model is the optimal timing of borrowing and the maintenance of tax rates at a stable level. While the tax-smoothing theory provides a normative benchmark under idealized assumptions (Ricardian consumers, benevolent planner, and optimal taxation), its prediction of debt stabilization in tranquil times has been contradicted by decades of rising public debt in advanced economies.

The tax-smoothing paradigm struggles to explain the persistent rise in public debt observed in many countries over recent decades (Figure 1). In theory, periods of peace and steady growth with low macroeconomic volatility should see governments running primary surpluses to retire debt (Lee, 2022). Instead, advanced economies have experienced a broad upward trend in debt-to-GDP ratios since the 1980s, even in the absence of major wars or depressions. For example, Azzimonti et al. (2014) document that over the last three decades public debt has increased in most developed countries, a period often characterized by stable growth and moderate business-cycle fluctuations.

As Yared (2019) observes, normative macroeconomic theories like tax-smoothing can rationalize higher debt in response to isolated shocks, but they "cannot explain the broad-based long-run trend in debt accumulation" seen in advanced economies. Indeed, the assumption of a benevolent planner with perfect foresight appears at odds with reality. Governments did not consistently pay down debt during tranquil periods, leading to debt ratios reaching historic highs even before the global financial crises (Azzimonti et al., 2014; Yared, 2019).

While the tax-smoothing theory provides a strong normative reference point for fiscal policy, it falls short of explaining the persistent budget deficits observed, particularly in the post-1970 period, and the differences in borrowing between groups of countries. Consequently, political economy-based models have increasingly gained prominence in literature. These models argue that budget deficits are shaped not only by economic rationality but also by the motivations of political actors, the structural limitations of institutional structures, and voter behavior (Alesina & Perotti, 1995).

The political economy literature offers theoretical frameworks that extend beyond traditional economic models to explain the origins of deficits and their mechanisms through the conduct of political actors and the operational dynamics of institutions. The first approach (Buchanan & Wagner, 1977) in this literature is models centered around opportunistic politicians and voters with fiscal illusions. The framework illustrates how voters' limited ability to perceive future tax costs (fiscal illusion) leads politicians to pursue deficit-based populist policies in an effort to maintain power. The second group of models (Cukierman & Meltzer, 1989; Tabellini, 1991) are based on intergenerational redistribution and suggest that current voters use debt to transfer the financial burden to future generations. The third models (Alesina & Tabellini, 1989; Alesina & Tabellini, 1990; Persson & Svensson, 1989; Tabellini & Alesina; 1990) that use debt as a strategic tool argue that ideologically distinct parties increase public debt to constrain each other. The existing debt stock affects the policies that can be implemented in the future. For example, the current government might maintain high debt to limit the fiscal leeway of future governments, given the likelihood of their fall from power. The fourth approach (Alesina & Drazen, 1991; Drazen & Grilli, 1993) examines distributional conflicts that occur within coalition governments. Budget deficits tend to persist because coalition governments experience delayed decision-making processes and party members maintain opposing interests. In this regard, "war of attrition" models suggest that groups' efforts to shift the financial burden onto each other delay stability (Alesina & Perotti, 1995).

The persistent increase in public debt levels has not only challenged the conventional assumptions of tax-smoothing theory but has also highlighted the importance of examining the broader socio-economic determinants of debt accumulation. As debt ratios continue to rise across advanced economies, identifying the underlying economic and social drivers of public debt becomes essential for informing effective fiscal policy and ensuring long-term debt sustainability. The main aim of the study is to investigate the impact of income inequality, GDP per capita, inflation, unemployment, and the old-age dependency ratio on central government debt in OECD countries, specifically focusing on Australia, Austria, Belgium, Canada, Estonia, France, Greece, Hungary, Iceland, Ireland, Japan, Lithuania, the Slovak Republic, Spain, Sweden, Switzerland, the United Kingdom, and the United States over the period 1999–2022. The empirical analysis employs the Panel Autoregressive Distributed Lag (ARDL) methodology to capture both short-term and long-term dynamics and applies the Dumitrescu and Hurlin panel causality test to identify the causal relationship between the selected variables and central government debt. This study contributes to the literature by integrating the tax-smoothing paradigm with the analysis of the socio-economic determinants of public debt in OECD countries.

Unlike prior research that primarily addresses developing economies or global samples (e.g., Carrera & de la Vega, 2021; Woo, 2003), this study provides a targeted analysis of advanced economies characterized by relatively higher income levels, robust institutional structures, and established welfare systems. By situating the analysis within the context of OECD countries, the study not only assesses the validity of the tax-smoothing theory but also examines the theory's normative assumptions held in economies marked by rising inequality and fiscal pressures. This approach contributes to the literature on fiscal sustainability for advanced economies by offering a nuanced perspective on the interaction between socio-economic factors and public debt.

The structure of the study consists of six main sections. The second section systematically examines theoretical approaches and previous empirical studies on the relationship between public debt, income inequality, unemployment, inflation, age dependency and economic growth. The third section provides a detailed explanation of the study's methodology, including the dataset used, definitions of the variables, their sources, and econometric techniques. The fourth section presents empirical findings and assesses their econometric consistency. The fifth section includes a critical discussion of the findings, focusing on their implications for policymakers. The sixth and final section summarizes the study's main results and highlights its contribution to literature. It also addresses the study's limitations and offers suggestions for future research.

2. LITERATURE REVIEW

In recent years, empirical studies examining the impact of income inequality on public debt and budget deficits have gained momentum. One of the prominent studies in this context is Woo's (2003) comprehensive analysis, which utilizes panel data covering 57 developed and developing countries. Woo (2003) used classical panel regression models in his research. He tested the structural robustness of the model through sensitivity analysis and applied robust regression techniques based on the least median of squares method to evaluate the reliability of the estimation results. Woo (2003) argues that budget deficits cannot be solely explained by macroeconomic variables; the impact of social and political polarization, particularly income inequality, on public finance should not be overlooked. His study reveals a statistically significant and negative relationship between inequality and budget deficits. The findings are not limited to developing countries but remain consistent across the overall sample. Larch (2012) analyzed the relationship between income inequality and fiscal performance in middle- and high-income countries, mainly OECD members, from 1960 to 2008 using the panel Generalized Least Squares (GLS) method with country fixed effects. Larch (2012) suggests that income inequality plays a decisive role in budget balance through indirect and interactive mechanisms rather than direct effects. The study indicates that income inequality alone does not significantly increase budget deficits; however, when considered alongside factors such as political orientation, economic growth, and social instability, it produces substantial implications for public finance. The study also argues that political and social unrest caused by rising inequality leads governments to adopt economic policies that may lead to budget deficits.

Using panel data for 35 developed and 123 developing countries for the period 2000–2019, Carrera and de la Vega (2021) examined the effect of income inequality on public debt. Inequality seems to have a positive effect on public debt. Furthermore, the study reveals how inequality shapes public debt by means of political and social dynamics as well as economic ones. Rising inequality results in the application of redistributive fiscal policies, so exacerbates public debt (Carrera & de la Vega, 2021).

Examining the effects of income inequality on public finance within a multidimensional framework, Aizenman and Jinjarak (2012) used data from 50 countries in 2007, 2009, and 2011 to empirically analyze the relationships between inequality, the tax base, fiscal space, and sovereign spreads by two-stage least square estimation. The Gini coefficient increases narrow a nation's tax base and lowers its capacity to pay public debt. Specifically, it was shown that the capacity to collect taxes is limited in nations with more unequal income distributions; market players price this condition through increased sovereign risk premiums (CDS spreads). Empirical results reveal that a rise in the Gini coefficient causes a notable drop in tax collections and hence a rise in sovereign spreads. Moreover, the study emphasizes that the tax base cannot be expanded in the short term through technical adjustments alone, as it is shaped by social contract dynamics such as public trust, perceptions of tax fairness, and the effectiveness of public services. Jabłoński (2013) examined the relationship between income inequality and public debt in an empirical study focusing on OECD countries by ordinary least squares and fixed effects methods. The study revealed that increasing inequality in upper- and lower-income brackets significantly raises public debt and intensifies pressure on public finances. The findings indicate that rising inequality exacerbates fiscal stress, making it a critical determinant of public debt dynamics.

The literature also includes studies suggesting that income inequality does not have a significant and direct impact on public debt. Bittencourt (2015) found the debt-reducing effect of economic growth by dynamic panel time-series analysis for the young democracies of South America from 1970 to 2007. However, the research showed that income inequality did not produce any statistically significant effects on public debt levels. Aksman (2017) investigated the impact of poverty and income inequality on public debt for European Union countries. The study employs a dynamic panel data model, and the estimation is conducted using the bias-corrected least squares dummy variable estimator. Aksman (2017) found that poverty and income inequality do not have a statistically significant effect on public debt in a study conducted on European Union countries. The findings contradict the expectation that hypothetically high levels of poverty and inequality would increase public debt by raising social expenditures.

Bittencourt (2015) and Aksman (2017)'s findings challenge the assumptions that inequality automatically triggers higher social expenditures and, consequently, debt accumulation, suggesting that this relationship may not hold in every context. In this framework, the relationship between inequality and public debt becomes a subject of debate. Equally important is the question of the channels through which this relationship operates and the conditions under which it is valid. Therefore, it is crucial to investigate other social and economic determinants of public debt.

A country's economic situation plays a significant role in public debt. Therefore, it is important to investigate the impact of macroeconomic indicators on public debt. In this context, GDP per capita is a critical determinant of debt sustainability and fiscal balance.

Carrera and de la Vega (2021) investigated the impact of per capita income on public debt in panel data studies. The study found that countries with higher per capita income generally have lower levels of public debt. However, it is also emphasized that this relationship is not statistically significant in some models. The study also notes that high-income countries may have more developed financial infrastructure and greater access to international markets, resulting in lower borrowing needs.

Cooray et al. (2017) examined the relationship between corruption, the shadow economy, and public debt in a study covering 126 countries between 1996 and 2012. The study also examined the effect of per capita income on public debt as a control variable. The empirical analysis employed ordinary least squares, fixed effects models, system generalized method of moments, and instrumental variable methods. According to Cooray et al. (2017), there is a statistically significant and negative relationship between public debt and per capita income. Countries with higher income levels have lower debt-to-GDP ratios. Factors explaining this include stronger institutional structures, efficient public spending systems, and more successful tax collection capacities.

Cooray and Özmen (2024) show that the impact of per capita income on public debt depends on a country's institutional framework and level of development. An analysis using logistic quantile regression and a recentered influence function method covering 54 countries over the period 2010–2022 reveals that increases in per capita income are associated with higher public debt ratios in European Union countries. Conversely, the opposite pattern is observed in non-EU countries. Increased per capita income leads to lower public debt ratios in non-EU countries. This relationship is positive and statistically significant in EU countries, explained by strong welfare state policies, extensive spending on public services, and expansionary fiscal strategies.

Conversely, increases in per capita income in non-EU countries lead to improvements in budget balances and lower public debt ratios. The findings demonstrate that public debt dynamics are not solely shaped by macroeconomic indicators. It also shows that it is closely related to institutional capacity and financial discipline. Grabia (2019) examined the factors affecting public debt ratios in European Union members with different levels of development between 2000 and 2018. The study used time series analysis and correlation coefficients. A weak correlation was found between GDPs per capita and the public debt ratio. The study's results indicate that the hypothesis that countries with higher per capita income consistently have higher public debt ratios is not supported.

The long-term consequences of inflation on national economies and its erosive power on debt are of great importance. Important macroeconomic risks stemming from inflation include declining expectations, rising real interest rates, inefficiencies in resource allocation, and especially negative consequences for low-income households. In this context, it is important to investigate the impact of inflation on public debt (Akitoby et al., 2014).

Reinhart and Sbrancia (2015) examined how financial repression and inflation were used together as effective tools to reduce public debt. The study shows that advanced economies used directed credit policies, interest rate controls, and capital movement restrictions between 1945 and 1980, thus keeping real interest rates at negative levels. It has been found that this mechanism helped weaken the real value of public debt. Reinhart and Sbrancia (2015) argue that unexpected inflation can lead to debt erosion. According to Reinhart and Sbrancia (2015), the choice of low nominal interest rates as a policy creates an effect in this direction. Aizenman and Marion (2011) analyze how inflation affects public debt sustainability through real value reduction of public debt for the US economy using sensitivity analysis. The study shows that unexpected inflation reduces debt real value but warns that higher interest rates during subsequent refinancing periods may create additional fiscal expenses.

Nguyen (2015) studied the effect of inflation on public debt in 60 developing countries in Asia, Latin America, and Africa between 1990 and 2014 using the Panel GMM method. The study found that inflation had a statistically significant and negative impact on public debt, indicating that inflation erodes the real value of debt and thus relieves the debt burden. This finding was consistently observed in both the full sample and regional subsamples. However, the study also emphasizes that the potential negative effects of such a policy on long-term growth and price stability should not be ignored.

Soh et al. (2021) investigated the impact of government efficiency, corruption, and inflation on public debt using a fixed-effects estimation. The study was conducted on 40 countries between 2002 and 2018. Soh et al. (2021) found that inflation has a statistically significant and negative effect on the public debt-to-GDP ratio in developed countries, suggesting that inflation helps reduce the real value of debt and thereby alleviates the debt burden, based on evidence from panel data analysis. In contrast, inflation was found to have no significant impact on public debt for developing countries and the overall sample. Carrera and de la Vega (2021) emphasize that unexpected increases in inflation can reduce the real value of debt, which in turn can have a downward impact on the debt-to-GDP ratio. High inflation reduces the purchasing power of existing debt but at the same time it increases the public debt burden through higher interest payments. Cooray et al. (2017) found a positive and statistically significant relationship between inflation and public debt.

Unemployment is one of the socioeconomic factors affecting public debt. The research by Carrera and de la Vega (2021) demonstrates that unemployment creates a positive relationship with public debt levels. The research demonstrates that high unemployment rates reduce public income through decreased tax revenue while boosting public spending via increased social transfer payments which leads to bigger budget deficits and increased total debt levels.

Carrera et al. (2024) analyzes the relationship between income inequality and public debt across political cycles by using unemployment rates as an alternative measure of social unrest. The fixed effects model shows that unemployment has a statistically significant positive effect on public debt during the executive term when using the unemployment rate instead of the Gini coefficient. The system GMM estimates show that this relationship does not reach statistical significance. The unemployment rate stands as a fundamental social pressure factor which affects government borrowing choices. The findings support political business cycle models which demonstrate how governments increase public spending before elections. The observed pattern indicates that governments might employ public finances as a policy instrument to reduce the social and political expenses that result from unemployment growth. Mahmadli et al. (2021) analyzed the relationship between unemployment rates and public debt through their cross-sectional data study which used 2013 data from 184 countries but found no significant impact of unemployment rates on public debt.

Public debt dynamics show increasing dependence on demographic structure. The analysis of how the age dependency ratio affects fiscal sustainability stands as a crucial matter in this context. The study conducted by Carrera and de la Vega (2021) investigated how the old-age dependency ratio affects public debt levels. The old-age dependency ratio shows a positive relationship with public debt according to some model estimates. The research demonstrates that rising elderly population numbers lead to higher public debt because it increases spending on healthcare and education and social security programs. The model developed by Arawatari and Ono (2017) shows that increasing old-age dependency ratios lead to higher public debt levels.

Chen (2004) examined the relationship between old-age and youth dependency ratios and budget deficits in developed and developing countries using fixed-effects panel regression. The study found that increasing dependency ratios for both old-age and young populations in developing countries increased budget deficits. However, Chen (2004) found that old-age and youth dependency ratios had no significant impact on budget deficits in developed countries.

Afflatet (2018) examined the impact of demographic changes on public debt in a panel data analysis covering 18 European countries. The study investigated the impact of the youth dependency ratio and the old-age dependency ratio on public debt. It was found that the old-age dependency ratio (age 65 and over) did not significantly affect public debt. However, an increase in the population age 85 and over increased public debt. The study also concluded that the youth dependency ratio had a negative impact on public debt.

Ramos-Herrera and Sosvilla-Rivero (2020) comprehensively analyzed the impact of aging on fiscal sustainability in Eurozone countries. The study examined the relationship between the old-age dependency ratio and fiscal sustainability in 11 Eurozone countries over the period 1980–2019 using panel data. The study found that an increase in old-age dependency ratios generally leads to a decline in public budget balance performance. In countries with larger elderly populations and higher debt levels, the negative impact of the old-age dependency ratio on budget deficits is greater. However, no significant effect is observed in countries with younger populations. The negative impact of the old-age dependency ratio becomes more pronounced as countries' debt levels increase. According to Ramos-Herrera and Sosvilla-Rivero (2020), achieving fiscal sustainability requires controlling public expenditures and implementing comprehensive reforms in pension systems. Kaymak and Dökmen (2021) examined the impact of youth and old-age dependency ratios on budget deficits in OECD countries using the system-GMM panel data analysis method. The study revealed that an increase in the old-age dependency ratio leads to higher budget deficits.

Azzimonti et al. (2014) offer a theoretical framework to explain the rise in public debt in developed countries. They argue that traditional explanations, such as cyclical fluctuations or war financing, frequently cited in the literature, are insufficient to explain public debt. They attribute this structural increase in public debt to two fundamental macroeconomic transformations: the liberalization of international capital markets (financial globalization) and the rise in income inequality. A multi-country dynamic general equilibrium model with heterogeneous agents was developed to examine the impact of these two factors on public debt. The model assumes that society is divided into two main actors: entrepreneurs with risky and uncertain incomes and workers with fixed incomes. This distinction takes into account the heterogeneity of the welfare effects of public debt. Financial globalization has also facilitated borrowing processes. Financial globalization has made debt available not only to domestic investors but also to global investors. This leads to a lower perception of the cost of borrowing by governments. This transformation has led governments to tend to borrow more. The study attempts to explain the impact of rising income inequality on public debt using a model. The income risk faced by entrepreneurs increases the demand for public bonds, leading governments to borrow more. This provides indirect income insurance through the provision of safe assets to enhance entrepreneurs' welfare, but it also leads to an increase in public debt. Workers' support for public debt is limited in the model. High debt will burden them in the future through negative transfers (taxes). Entrepreneurs, on the other hand, have an almost unlimited demand for public debt. This conflict of interest is a key element shaping government policy choices in the model. The study demonstrates that the rise in public debt is linked not only to short-term macroeconomic fluctuations but also to international financial integration and internal income dynamics (Azzimonti et al. 2014).

Röhrs and Winter (2017) developed a model to investigate the impact of public debt on welfare in economies with widespread income and wealth inequality. The study investigated the short- and long-term welfare impact of public debt reduction using a dynamic general equilibrium model within an imperfect market framework, similar to Aiyagari (1994), Aiyagari and McGrattan (1998), Floden (2001), and Desbonnet and Weitzenblum (2012). The model was calibrated to reflect income and wealth distributions in the US economy. The findings reveal that while public debt reduction may yield some welfare gains in the long run, the costs of the transition period often overshadow these gains. The welfare losses resulting from short-term tax increases are particularly significant for individuals under debt constraints. The timing and implementation of debt reduction have varying effects on welfare. Model estimates indicate that a debt reduction policy that is initially slow and then accelerates results in less welfare loss because it allows for the accumulation of assets in advance. Conversely, a debt reduction policy that is initially rapid and then slows down has a more negative impact, particularly on middle-class and low-income individuals. The study found that many of the debt reduction policies analyzed are politically unfeasible. In most scenarios, the majority of the public does not support such policies. However, debt reduction financed by a one-term, unexpected wealth tax increase yields more acceptable outcomes for low- and middle-income individuals and is more likely to gain political support. This result demonstrates that tax policy design should consider not only economic efficiency but also social acceptability.

3. METHODOLOGY

3.1. Data

This study covers OECD countries with complete data sets for the period 1999–2022. These countries include Australia, Austria, Belgium, Canada, Estonia, France, Greece, Hungary, Iceland, Ireland, Japan, Lithuania, the Slovak Republic, Spain, Sweden, Switzerland, the United Kingdom, and the United States. The analysis utilizes variables including central government debt, the Gini coefficient, GDP per capita, inflation rate, unemployment rate, and age dependency ratio. Central government debt (govdebt) is defined as the ratio of the government's total direct fixed-term obligations -including domestic and foreign liabilities, currency and money deposits, securities other than shares, and loans- to Gross Domestic Product (GDP). GDP per capita (gdppercap) is measured in constant 2015 U.S. dollars. Inflation (inf) is measured by the consumer price index and reflects the annual average percentage change in consumer prices. The unemployment rate (unemp) represents the proportion of the unemployed who are available and actively seeking employment relative to the total labor force, estimated according to the International Labour Organization (ILO) methodology. The age dependency ratio (agedep) indicates the proportion of the population aged 65 and older relative to the working-age population (ages 15-64), expressed as the number of elderly dependents per 100 working-age individuals. The lagged Gini coefficient ($Gini_{(t-1)}$) measures income inequality and is included in the model under the assumption that the economic effects of inequality occur with a one-period delay (Carrea & de la Vega, 2021). The data for govdebt, gdppercap, inf, unemp, and agedep variables were sourced from the World Development Indicators (WDI) database, while data for the Gini coefficient were obtained from the World Inequality Database (WID). Additionally, Table 1 presents the descriptive statistics, including the number of observations, means, standard deviations, minimum, and maximum values for these variables.

Table 1. Variable's definitions and descriptive statistics

Variable	Definition	Source	Observation	Mean	Std. Dev.	Min	Max
govdebt	Central government debt (% of GDP)	WDI	432	79.59494	47.38045	3.814028	249.4113
$gini_{(t-1)}$	Gini coefficient	WID	432	.454343	.0546322	.3291668	.6172619
gdppercap	GDP per capita (constant 2015 US$)	WDI	432	37968.62	18903.08	6129.999	99677.48

continued on following page

Table 1. Continued

Variable	Definition	Source	Observation	Mean	Std. Dev.	Min	Max
inf	Inflation, consumer prices	WDI	432	2.494956	2.699837	-4.447547	19.70505
unemp	Unemployment, total (% of total labor force)	WDI	432	7.865905	4.495147	1.874	27.686
agedep	Age dependency ratio, old (% of working-age population)	WDI	432	25.26929	5.727636	15.63897	50.05693

3.2. Model Estimation

The primary objective of this study is to examine the effects of income inequality, GDP per capita, inflation rate, unemployment rate, and age dependency ratio on central government debt in OECD countries. The econometric model constructed for the analysis is presented below.

$$govdebt_t = \beta_0 + \beta_1 gini_{i,t-1} + \beta_2 gdppercap_{i,t} + \beta_3 inf_{i,t} + \beta_4 unemp_{i,t} + \beta_5 agedep_{i,t} + \varepsilon_{i,t}$$

In the equation, the subscripts *i* and *t* denote the cross-sectional and time dimensions used in panel data analysis, respectively. Specifically, the subscript *i* represents individual cross-sectional units (countries), whereas the subscript *t* indicates the time periods.

$govdebt_t$ = Central government debt

$gini_{i,t-1}$ = Lagged gini coefficient

$gdppercap_{i,t}$ = GDP per capita

$inf_{i,t}$ = Inflation

$unemp_{i,t}$ = Unemployment

$agedep_{i,t}$ = Old age dependency ratio

$\varepsilon_{i,t}$ = Error term

In this study, the fundamental macroeconomic and socio-economic factors influencing central government debt are examined, and five main hypotheses are proposed.

Hypothesis 1: Rising income inequality increases public expenditures and thereby raises the level of debt, the Gini coefficient is predicted to exert a positive effect on central government debt.

Hypothesis 2: An increase in the unemployment rate, by reducing tax revenues and increasing social expenditures, will heighten the level of debt, indicating a positive impact of unemployment on debt.

Hypothesis 3: A higher age dependency ratio is regarded as a factor that drives public spending upward. This variable is expected to have a positive effect on debt.

Hypothesis 4: As per capita income grows, public revenues are projected to increase and reduce the need for borrowing; hence, per capita income is expected to have a negative effect on central government debt.

Hypothesis 5: The inflation rate is expected to has a negative impact on central government debt because of the reducing effect of inflation on the real debt burden.

3.3. Econometric Methodology

The effects of inequality, GDP per capita, inflation, unemployment, and the age dependency ratio on central government debt are examined in the study. The Panel ARDL (Autoregressive Distributed Lag) approach is used and the Dumitrescu and Hurlin (2012) heterogeneous panel causality test is utilized to determine the direction of causality among the variables to investigate long-run relationships. In this context, both long-term interaction and causality between variables are investigated in the study.

The Panel ARDL approach is an advanced econometric method that allows the simultaneous analysis of long-run equilibrium relationships and short-run dynamics in panel data. While traditional panel cointegration methods generally require all variables to be stationary at the same order, the Panel ARDL method can accommodate situations where some variables are stationary at level (I(0)) and others are stationary in first difference (I(1)). This flexibility provides a significant advantage, particularly in the face of changing stationarity levels frequently encountered in macroeconomic or financial data sets. The error correction coefficient indicates the existence of long-run cointegration and how quickly the system returns to equilibrium aftershocks in the Panel ARDL model. A negative and significant coefficient confirms the existence of cointegration (Kutlu & Örün, 2023; Raihan et al., 2024).

Various estimation methods are used in panel ARDL (Autoregressive Distributed Lag) models, particularly in country-level analyses, to account for cross-sectional differences across units. Among these methods, three different approaches are commonly used: Pooled Mean Group (PMG), Mean Group (MG), and Dynamic Fixed Effects (DFE) estimators.

The PMG estimator is based on the assumption that long-run coefficients are homogeneous across all cross-sectional units, while acknowledging that short-run coefficients, the adjustment speed (error correction term), constant terms, and error variances may vary across countries. This approach allows for the estimation of consistent long-run relationships common to all units while also accounting for country-specific short-run dynamics within the model. Furthermore, a key assumption of the PMG estimator is that the error correction term (ECT) is uncorrelated with the explanatory variables and has a normal distribution, allowing the explanatory variables to be treated as exogenous within the model framework (Pesaran et al., 1999; Ramos-Herrera, 2024). On the other hand, the MG estimator, first developed by Pesaran and Smith (1995), assumes that all coefficients may be completely heterogeneous across countries or cross-sectional units in the short and long term, and assumes that these coefficients may change over time. This method involves estimating separate regressions for each unit and calculating the unweighted average of the resulting coefficients. The MG method is particularly suitable for situations where significant heterogeneity is expected among cross-sectional units (Ramos-Herrera, 2024). The DFE estimator assumes that both short-run and long-run coefficients are homogeneous across all country units, while allowing for country-specific intercepts (fixed effects). In the DFE framework, heterogeneity in error variances across countries is taken into account and standard errors are adjusted accordingly to correct heteroskedasticity. Compared to the PMG and MG estimators, the DFE method imposes more restrictive homogeneity assumptions, rendering it less flexible-particularly in cases where short-run dynamics differ significantly across units (Pesaran et al., 1999; Ramos-Herrera, 2024). The panel ARDL model presented in the equation below is employed to analyze the relationship between public debt and income inequality, economic growth, inflation, unemployment, and age dependency.

$$\Delta\, govdebt_{i,t} = \alpha_i + \phi_i govdebt_{i,t-1} + \lambda_1 gini_{i,t-1} + \lambda_2 gdppercap_{i,t-1} + \lambda_3 inf_{i,t-1} + \lambda_4 unemp_{i,t-1} + \lambda_5 agedep_{i,t-1} + \sum_{j=1}^{p_1} \vartheta_{1j} \Delta\, gini_{i,t-j} + \sum_{j=1}^{p_2} \vartheta_{2j} \Delta\, gdppercap_{i,t-j} + \sum_{j=1}^{p_3} \vartheta_{3j} \Delta\, inf_{i,t-j} + \sum_{j=1}^{p_4} \vartheta_{4j} \Delta\, unemp_{i,t-j} + \sum_{j=1}^{p_5} \vartheta_{5j} \Delta\, agedep_{i,t-j} + \varepsilon_{i,t}$$

4. EMPIRICAL RESULTS

4.1. Cross-Sectional Independence Test and Panel Unit Root Test

According to the results of the cross-section independence test presented in Table 2, significant cross-sectional dependence exists among all the variables used in the analysis. When examining the CD test statistics and corresponding p-values, the calculated p-values for all variables were found to be significant at the 1% significance level. This indicates that the series do not satisfy the assumption of cross-sectional independence. Therefore, it would be methodologically more appropriate and reliable to employ second-generation panel unit root tests, which account for cross-sectional correlation between units.

Table 2. Results for cross-sectional independence test

Variable	CD-test	p-value	Corr	Abs(corr)
govdebt	24.73	0.000*	0.408	0.661
$gini_{(t-1)}$	6.81	0.000*	0.112	0.335
gdppercap	48.68	0.000*	0.803	0.820
inf	40.63	0.000*	0.670	0.672
unemp	18.52	0.000*	0.306	0.387
agedep	58.29	0.000*	0.962	0.962

Table 3 provides the outcomes of the Levin-Lin-Chu (2002) (LLC) and Breitung tests, which are classified among the second-generation panel unit root tests. According to the Breitung test results, examination of variables at level indicates that the variables *inf*, $gini_{(t-1)}$, and *unemp* are statistically significant and stationary at level. However, the variables *govdebt*, *gdppercap*, and *agedep* are not stationary at their levels. Based on the LLC test results, it is determined that the variables *govdebt*, $gini_{(t-1)}$, *inf*, *unemp*, and *agedep* are significant and stationary at level values, whereas the variable *gdppercap* is non-stationary at level. When the first differences of the variables are taken, it is observed that all variables become stationary according to both the Breitung and LLC tests, thus eliminating the unit root. This indicates that the series are integrated of order one, denoted as I(1), suggesting that long-term estimation methods in panel data analysis can be appropriately applied. Consequently, second-generation panel unit root tests that account for cross-sectional correlation have provided more robust and reliable findings for the stationarity analysis of the variables.

Table 3. Breitung and Levin-Lin-Chu unit root test result

	Level		First Difference	
Variable	**Breitung**	**LLC**	**Breitung**	**LLC**
govdebt	2.5752 [0.9950]	-2.5887* [0.0048]	-7.3694* [0.0000]	-7.5250* [0.0000]
$gini_{(t-1)}$	-2.1450** [0.0160]	-2.2616** [0.0119]	-11.7099* [0.0000]	-16.8451* [0.0000]
gdppercap	5.7126 [1.0000]	3.1667 [0.9992]	-9.4268* [0.0000]	-11.0433* [0.0000]
inf	-4.3942* [0.0000]	-3.1711* [0.0008]	-8.0188* [0.0000]	-12.1690* [0.0000]
unemp	-2.4980* [0.0062]	-4.7205* [0.0000]	-5.7158* [0.0000]	-8.9429* [0.0000]
agedep	7.1241 [1.0000]	-4.0336* [0.0000]	-1.3091*** [0.0952]	-4.1059* [0.0000]

§ *, **, and, *** denote respectively significance at 1%, 5%, and 10% level. P-value is given in the square bracket

4.2. Panel ARDL Test Result

The Hausman test was conducted to test the homogeneity of long-run coefficients. The null hypothesis was not rejected, indicating that the PMG estimator is a valid and appropriate method. A comparative presentation of the PMG and MG estimation results is provided in Table 4. The error correction term is negative and statistically significant, indicating that approximately 23% of the deviations from the long-run equilibrium are corrected in the subsequent period. This finding confirms the existence of a long-run relationship within the model.

The coefficient of the Gini index on central government debt was found to be positive and statistically significant at the 10% significance level. This result indicates that an increase in income inequality leads to higher central government debt in the long run. The long-term coefficient of GDP per capita (gdppercap) is negative and statistically significant at the 1% significance level, implying that an increase in per capita income contributes to reducing central government debt over the long term. This outcome aligns with the theoretical perspective that economic growth and rising income levels have a mitigating effect on government indebtedness. The inflation rate (inf) has a negative and statistically significant impact on central government debt at the 1% significance level. This finding confirms the expectation that higher inflation rates may reduce the real value of public debt in the long run. The long-term effect of the unemployment rate (unemp) on the central government debt (govdebt) is positive and statistically significant at the 1% significance level. This result indicates that higher unemployment rates elevate public expenditures and reduce government revenues, thereby increasing debt burden. The age dependency ratio (agedep) also has a positive and statistically significant effect on the central government debt ratio at the 1% significance level. This result aligns with theoretical expectations, suggesting that an increase in the dependent population raises public spending, thereby increasing the central government's debt burden.

Table 4. Panel ARDL PMG and MG estimation results

	Variables	PMG Estimation	MG Estimation	Hausman Test
Long-run Equation				
	$gini_{(t-1)}$	42.65069*** [0.057]	102.5807 [0.314]	Prob > Chi2 = 0.2049
	gdppercap	-.0024829* [0.000]	-.0034394 [0.155]	
	inf	-2.206469* [0.000]	-5.79613 [0.074]	
	unemp	2.395778* [0.000]	1.716946 [0.510]	
	agedep	3.773389* [0.000]	4.266283 [0.048]	
Short-run Equation				

continued on following page

Table 4. Continued

	Variables	PMG Estimation	MG Estimation	Hausman Test
Long-run Equation				
	ec	-.225868 [0.000]	-.645767 [0.000]	
	$gini_{(t-1)}$ d1.	-62.22499 [0.109]	-49.80731 [0.130]	
	gdppercap d1.	-.003343* [0.000]	-.0020482 [0.036]	
	inf d1.	-.0622162 [0.833]	.9626476 [0.011]	
	unemp d1.	.0002796 [1.000]	-1.112108 [0.166]	
	agedep d1.	5.301091*** [0.050]	7.53379 [0.076]	
	c	9.213882* [0.002]	40.98839 [0.346]	

Notes: * and *** denote significance at 1% and 10% level, respectively. P-value is given in the square bracket.

4.3. Dumitrescu and Hurlin Panel Causality Test Result

According to the results of the Dumitrescu and Hurlin panel causality test, which accounts for heterogeneity, various causal relationships among the variables were identified. The findings indicate a unidirectional causality running from $gini_{(t-1)}$ to central government debt. However, causality in the reverse direction was not statistically significant. On the other hand, bidirectional causality relationships were detected between central government debt and GDP per capita (gdppercap), inflation (inf), unemployment (unemp), and age dependency ratio (agedep) (Table 5). These results reveal mutual interactions between central government debt and the aforementioned variables, suggesting that policymakers should consider these reciprocal causal relationships when designing economic policies. In particular, the unidirectional impact of income inequality on government debt highlights that policies aimed at reducing inequality are crucial for maintaining debt sustainability.

Table 5. Dumitrescu and Hurlin heterogenous panel causality test

Null Hypothesis	Wbar-Stat	Zbar-Stat	Probability	Conclusion
$gini_{(t-1)}$ does not Granger-cause govdebt	13.7750	9.5224	0.0000*	$gini_{(t-1)}$ → debt
govdebt does not Granger-cause $gini_{(t-1)}$	15.3106	1.3008	0.1933	
gdppercap does not Granger-cause govdebt	9.7927	4.6451	0.0000*	gdppercap ↔ debt
govdebt does not Granger-cause gdppercap	3.3708	7.1124	0.0000*	
inf does not Granger-cause govdebt	8.0067	2.4577	0.0140**	inf ↔ debt
govdebt does not Granger-cause inf	26.9206	25.6224	0.0000*	
unemp does not Granger-cause govdebt	11.4900	6.7238	0.0000*	unemp ↔ debt
govdebt does not Granger-cause unemp	14.7407	10.7051	0.0000*	
agedep does not Granger-cause govdebt	18.6485	15.4912	0.0000*	agedep ↔ debt
govdebt does not Granger-cause agedep	28.9488	28.1064	0.0000*	

Notes: * and ** denote significance at 1% and 5% level, respectively.

5. DISCUSSION

The panel ARDL estimation results reveal important insights into how income inequality and other macroeconomic factors influence public debt in OECD countries. In the long-run, income inequality exhibits a positive and statistically significant effect on government debt. In other words, higher inequality is associated with larger public debt levels. This finding indicates that rising inequality can intensify social and political pressures for government spending (for example, on social safety nets or redistribution), which, if not matched by higher taxes, leads to greater borrowing. The results also indicate that unemployment has positive long-run effects on public debt. A higher unemployment rate erodes the tax base and increases welfare expenditures, necessitating more government borrowing. These findings align with those reported by Carrera and de la Vega (2021). Age dependency ratio has positive long-run effects on public debts. An aging population places strain on public finances through increased pension and healthcare costs, contributing to debt accumulation. The results obtained in this study are consistent with the findings of Ramos-Herrera and Sosvilla-Rivero (2020) and Kaymak and Dökmen (2021). Inequality, joblessness, and demographics emerge as key structural drivers of debt over the 1999–2022 period. In contrast, the model finds that inflation and GDP per capita exert a negative long-run effect on public debt. Higher GDP per capita improves tax revenues and reduces the debt-to-GDP ratio. The results align with those reported by Carrera and de la Vega (2021). Meanwhile, higher inflation tends to reduce the real value of outstanding debt, effectively easing debt burdens over time. Moderate inflation can function as a debt-relieving mechanism by reducing the real value of debt. Considering inflation as an economic policy tool for reducing public debt encompasses macroeconomic risks, including the potential for distorted expectations, increased real interest rates, inefficient resource allocation, and adverse effects on low-income households. The findings obtained in this study are consistent with those reported by Nguyen (2015).

The evidence also suggests that tax-smoothing theory alone is not sufficient to explain the sustained rise in public debt observed by OECD countries in recent decades. The significant influence of income inequality on debt points to political economy factors beyond the tax-smoothing theory. Rising inequality can affect fiscal policy choices in several ways. One is that greater inequality increases the demand for redistribution and public goods from the lower and middle classes. If the political system is responsive to these demands, governments may expand social programs or provide fiscal transfers to mitigate inequality. Yet, if raising taxes, especially on the wealthy, is politically constrained or economically discouraged, governments might resort to deficit financing to fund these programs. Over time, this leads to higher accumulated debt in response to higher inequality (Carrera & de la Vega, 2021). The identification of unidirectional causality from inequality to debt indicates that inequality functions as an exogenous determinant of public debt. Similar findings have been reported by Carrera and de la Vega (2021).

The fact that the old-age dependency ratio increases public debt highlights the importance of demographic forces on public finances. Population aging puts pressure on government budgets. While pensions and healthcare expenditures increase, tax revenues grow more slowly due to the shrinking workforce. An increase in the age dependency ratio necessitates higher taxes for a relatively smaller workforce or creates larger budget deficits. The empirical finding that aging is associated with higher debt levels is consistent with these dynamics. The depressing effect of the age dependency ratio on GDP growth complicates debt sustainability. In this context, evidence on inequality and demographic change points to serious fiscal challenges for public finances. Furthermore, the increasing debt burden stemming from aging and inequality calls into question the validity of the tax-smoothing theory.

Policy proposals that ensure the sustainability of public debt while not constraining economic growth or exacerbating inequality are crucial. Tackling income inequality should be a priority for both social justice and reducing fiscal pressure. Measures that support an inclusive economy, such as strengthening social safety nets, investing in education and skills development for low-income groups, and policies that encourage broad-based wage increases, can reduce the need for debt-based redistribution. Reducing inequality can also contribute to alleviating political pressures. Labor market policies aimed at reducing unemployment have the potential to both increase social welfare and reduce public debt. Active labor market programs, vocational training, and reskilling initiatives can help maintain low unemployment levels. Increased employment can lead to higher tax revenues and reduced reliance on unemployment benefits, thus alleviating fiscal pressure on public debt. Pension and healthcare reforms targeting the elderly can mitigate the impact of rising old-age dependency ratio on public debt. Furthermore, governments can implement measures to support the labor force participation of the working-age population. Such economic policies can play an important role in minimizing the negative fiscal impacts associated with rising old-age dependency ratio.

The results of the study demonstrate that factors such as inequality and demographic transformation are a significant factor in explaining the dynamics of public debt in developed economies. Income inequality, high unemployment, and an aging population stand out as key factors that disrupt public finances and increase the debt burden. Maintaining public debt on a sustainable path requires a comprehensive and multidimensional policy approach. A fiscal policy framework that prioritizes both social welfare and economic stability should be adopted, transcending traditional approaches focused solely on macroeconomic balances. Within this framework, reforms that reduce income inequality, promote employment, and adapt to demographic change will help bring public debt dynamics to a sustainable level in the long run. Fiscal sustainability should not be limited to budget targets alone. It should also be addressed with a holistic vision that includes deeper factors such as income distribution equity, the effectiveness of employment policies, and changes in population structure.

6. CONCLUSION

This study contributes to the literature by providing empirical evidence on the social and economic determinants of public debt in OECD countries. The findings demonstrate that traditional tax smoothing theory is inadequate in explaining modern debt dynamics. Structural factors such as income inequality and population aging play a significant role in explaining the increasing trend in public debt in advanced economies. This suggests that fiscal policies are shaped not only by economic considerations but also by social and demographic factors such as inequality and demographic change.

The study has several important limitations. First, the measurement of income inequality may not comprehensively capture all dimensions of change in distribution. While the Gini coefficient is a useful measure of overall distribution, it does not fully reflect changes in the top and bottom quintiles. For example, an increase in income share of the wealthiest 1% of society can have different and stronger effects on public debt. Therefore, considering various dimensions of inequality (such as wealth inequality, poverty rate, and the share of the upper income group) is crucial for the robustness of the results obtained in this study. Future studies can incorporate such alternative inequality indicators into the model to more clearly demonstrate which dimensions of inequality most significantly impact public debt. Second, the scope of the study is limited to OECD countries. These countries share similar characteristics, including relatively high-income levels, advanced institutional structures, and welfare state mechanisms. Therefore, the empirical results may differ for developing economies or lower-income countries. For example, in countries with lower institutional quality or limited financial market development, public debt dynamics may be more strongly influenced by other factors. In this context, the study's results apply to economies with similar characteristics, particularly developed countries, and should be interpreted with caution across different country groups. Conducting the study across developing countries, emerging markets, or different regional blocks (e.g., Latin America and East Asia) would allow for testing the robustness of the findings. Examining the relationship between income inequality and public debt in countries with varying income levels and institutional structures would enable a comparative analysis with the findings of this study, contributing to the development of more comprehensive policy recommendations. Using such alternative measures would not only confirm the findings but also contribute to a more comprehensive understanding of the dynamics between inequality and public debt.

REFERENCES

Afflatet, N. (2018). The impact of population ageing on public debt: A panel data analysis for 18 european countries. *International Journal of Economics and Financial Issues*, *8*(4), 68–77.

Aiyagari, S. R. (1994). Uninsured idiosyncratic risk and aggregate saving. *The Quarterly Journal of Economics*, *109*(3), 659–684. DOI: 10.2307/2118417

Aiyagari, S. R., & McGrattan, E. R. (1998). The optimum quantity of debt. *Journal of Monetary Economics*, *42*(3), 447–469. DOI: 10.1016/S0304-3932(98)00031-2

Aizenman, J., & Jinjarak, Y. (2012). Income inequality, tax base and sovereign spreads. *Finanz-Archiv*, *68*(4), 431–444. DOI: 10.1628/001522112X659565

Aizenman, J., & Marion, N. (2011). Using inflation to erode the US public debt. *Journal of Macroeconomics*, *33*(4), 524–541. DOI: 10.1016/j.jmacro.2011.09.001

Akitoby, B., Komatsuzaki, T., & Binder, A. (2014). Inflation and public debt reversals in the G7 countries (IMF Working Paper No. 14/96). *International Monetary Fund.*

Aksman, E. (2017). Do poverty and income inequality affect public debt? *Gospodarka Narodowa*, *6*(292), 79–93. DOI: 10.33119/GN/100744

Alesina, A., & Drazen, A. (1991). Why are stabilizations delayed? *The American Economic Review*, *81*(5), 1170–1188.

Alesina, A., & Perotti, R. (1995). The political economy of budget deficits. *Staff Papers - International Monetary Fund. International Monetary Fund*, *42*(1), 1–31. DOI: 10.2307/3867338

Alesina, A., & Tabellini, G. (1989). External debt, Capital flight and political risk. *Journal of International Economics*, *27*(3-4), 199–220. DOI: 10.1016/0022-1996(89)90052-4

Alesina, A., & Tabellini, G. (1990). A positive theory of fiscal deficits and government debt. *The Review of Economic Studies*, *57*(3), 403–414. DOI: 10.2307/2298021

Arawatari, R., & Ono, T. (2017). Inequality and public debt: A positive analysis. *Review of International Economics*, *25*(1), 1155–1173. DOI: 10.1111/roie.12299

Azzimonti, M., Francisco, E., & Quadrini, V. (2014). Financial globalization, inequality, and the rising public debt. *The American Economic Review*, *104*(8), 2267–2302. DOI: 10.1257/aer.104.8.2267

Barro, R. (1979). On the determination of public debt. *Journal of Political Economy, 87*(5), 940–971. DOI: 10.1086/260807

Bittencourt, M. (2015). Determinants of government and external debt: Evidence from the young democracies of South America. *Emerging Markets Finance & Trade, 51*(3), 463–472. DOI: 10.1080/1540496X.2015.1025667

Buchanan, J. M., & Wagner, R. E. (1977). *Democracy in deficit: The political legacy of Lord Keynes*. Academic Press.

Carrera, J., & de la Vega, P. (2021). The impact of income inequality on public debt. *Journal of Economic Asymmetries, 24*, 1–16. DOI: 10.1016/j.jeca.2021.e00216

Carrera, J., de la Vega, P., & Toledo, F. (2024). Income inequality and fiscal policy over the political cycle. *Empirical Economics, 66*(1), 301–325. DOI: 10.1007/s00181-023-02455-1

Chen, D. H. (2004). *Population age structure and teh budget deficit. (World Bank Policy ResearchWorking Paper No. 3435)*. The World Bank. DOI: 10.1596/1813-9450-3435

Congregado, E., Esteve, V., & Prats, M. A. (2023). *Optimal public deficit and tax-smoothing in the Spanish Economy, 1850-2022 (EIQ Papper No. 184)*. London School of Economics and Political Science.

Cooray, A., Dzhumashev, R., & Schneider, F. (2017). How does corruption affect public debt? An empirical analysis. *World Development, 90*, 115–127. DOI: 10.1016/j.worlddev.2016.08.020

Cooray, A., & Özmen, I. (2024). The role of institutions on public debt: A quantile regression approach. *International Review of Economics & Finance, 93*, 912–928. DOI: 10.1016/j.iref.2024.03.065

Cukierman, A., & Meltzer, A. H. (1989). A political theory of government debt and deficits in a neo-ricardian framework. *The American Economic Review, 79*(4), 713–732.

Desbonnet, A., & Weitzenblum, T. (2012). Why do governments end up with debt? Short-run effects matter. *Economic Inquiry, 50*(4), 905–919. DOI: 10.1111/j.1465-7295.2011.00410.x

Drazen, A., & Grilli, V. (1993). The benefit of crises for economic reforms. *The American Economic Review, 83*(3), 598–607.

Dumitrescu, E.-I., & Hurlin, C. (2012). Testing for granger non-causality in heterogeneous panels. *Economic Modelling*, *29*(4), 1450–1460. DOI: 10.1016/j.econmod.2012.02.014

Floden, M. (2001). The effectiveness of government debt and transfers as insurance. *Journal of Monetary Economics*, *48*(1), 81–108. DOI: 10.1016/S0304-3932(01)00064-2

Grabia, T. (2019). Why do richer EU countries have a higher public debt ratio than their poorer counterparts. *Research Papers of Wroclaw University of Economics and Business*, *63*(12), 35–48. DOI: 10.15611/pn.2019.12.03

Jabłoński, Ł. (2013). Nierówności dochodowe a zadłużenie publiczne krajów OECD. *Management and Business Administration*, *21*(2), 64–81.

Kaymak, H., & Dökmen, G. (2021). The effect of change in population age structure on budget deficities. *Research of Financial Economic and Social Studies*, 459-476.

Kutlu, G., & Örün, E. (2023). The effect of carbon dioxide emission, GDP per capita and urban population on health expenditure in OECD countries: A panel ARDL approach. *International Journal of Environmental Health Research*, *33*(12), 1233–1242. DOI: 10.1080/09603123.2022.2083088 PMID: 35635518

Larch, M. (2012). Fiscal performance and income inequality: Are unequal societies more deficit-prone? *Kyklos*, *65*(1), 53–80. DOI: 10.1111/j.1467-6435.2011.00527.x

Lee, I. (2022). Does political polarization lead to rise in government debt? *Review of Public Economics*, 3-25. DOI: 10.7866/HPE-RPE.22.2.1

Levin, A., Lin, C.-F., & Chu, C.-S. J. (2002). Unit root tests in panel data: Asymptotic and finite-sample properties. *Journal of Econometrics*, *108*(1), 1–24. DOI: 10.1016/S0304-4076(01)00098-7

Lucas, R. E.Jr, & Stokey, N. L. (1983). Optimal fiscal and monetary policy in an economy without capital. *Journal of Monetary Economics*, *12*(1), 55–93. DOI: 10.1016/0304-3932(83)90049-1

Persson, T., & Svensson, L. E. (1989). Why a stubborn conservative would run a deficit: Policy with time- inconsistent preferences. *The Quarterly Journal of Economics*, *104*(2), 325–345. DOI: 10.2307/2937850

Pesaran, M. H., Shin, Y., & Smith, R. P. (1999). Pooled mean group estimation of dynamic heterogeneous panels. *Journal of the American Statistical Association*, *94*(446), 621–634. DOI: 10.1080/01621459.1999.10474156

Pesaran, M. H., & Smith, R. (1995). Estimating long-run relationships from dynamic heterogeneous panels. *Journal of Econometrics*, *68*(1), 79–113. DOI: 10.1016/0304-4076(94)01644-F

Raihan, A., Bala, S., Akther, A., Ridwan, M., Eleais, M., & Chakma, P. (2024). Advancing environmental sustainability in the G-7: The impact of the digital economy, technological innovation, and financial accessibility using panel ARDL approach. *Journal of Economy and Technology*, 1-26. DOI: 10.1016/j.ject.2024.06.001

Ramos-Herrera, M., & Sosvilla-Rivero, S. (2020). Fiscal sustainability in aging socities: Evidence from Euro Area Countries. *Sustainability (Basel)*, *12*(24), 1–20. DOI: 10.3390/su122410276

Ramos-Herrera, M. D. (2024). *Economic growth and deviations from the equilibrium exchange rate: A panel ARDL and panel NARDL approach*. Applied Economic Analysis., DOI: 10.1108/AEA-02-2024-0065

Reinhart, C. M., & Sbrancia, M. B. (2015). The liquidation of government debt (IMF Working Paper No. 15/7). *International Monetary Fund*.

Röhrs, S., & Winter, C. (2017). Reducing government debt in the presence of inequality. *Journal of Economic Dynamics & Control*, *82*, 1–20. DOI: 10.1016/j.jedc.2017.05.007

Soh, W. N., Muhamad, H., & San, O. T. (2021). The impact of government efficiency, corruption, and inflation on public debt: Empirical evidence from advanced and emerging economies. *Pertanika Journal of Social Science & Humanities*, *29*(3), 1551–1570. DOI: 10.47836/pjssh.29.3.05

Tabellini, G. (1991). The politics of intergenerational redistribution. *Journal of Political Economy*, *99*(2), 335–357. DOI: 10.1086/261753

Tabellini, G., & Alesina, A. (1990). Voting on the budget deficit. *The American Economic Review*, *80*(1), 37–49.

Woo, J. (2003). Economic, political, and institutional determinants of public deficits. *Journal of Public Economics*, *87*(3-4), 387–426. DOI: 10.1016/S0047-2727(01)00143-8

Yared, P. (2019). Rising government debt: Causes and solutions for decades-old trend. *The Journal of Economic Perspectives*, *33*(2), 115–140. DOI: 10.1257/jep.33.2.115

ADDITIONAL READING

Aghion, P., & Bolton, P. (1990). Government domestic debt and the risk of default: A political–economic model of the strategic role of debt. R. Dornbusch, & M. Draghi (Ed.). *Public debt management: Theory and history* (p. 315-345). Cambridge: Cambridge University Press.

Alesina, A., & Passalacqua, A. (2016). In Taylor, J. B., & Uhlig, H. (Eds.), *The political economy of government debt* (pp. 2599–2651). Hand Book of Macroeconomics. Elsevier., DOI: 10.1016/bs.hesmac.2016.03.014

Brender, A., & Drazen, A. (2008). How do budget deficits and economic growth affect reelection prospects? Evidence from a large panel of countries. *The American Economic Review*, *98*(5), 2203–2220. DOI: 10.1257/aer.98.5.2203

Hager, S. B. (2016). *Public debt, inequality, and power: The making of a modern debt state*. University of California Press.

Shi, M., & Svensson, J. (2006). Political budget cycles: Do they differ across countries and why? *Journal of Public Economics*, *90*(8-9), 1367–1389. DOI: 10.1016/j.jpubeco.2005.09.009

KEY TERMS AND DEFINITIONS

Age Dependency Ratio, Old: The old-age dependency ratio is a demographic indicator that represents the ratio of the elderly dependent population, consisting of individuals aged 65 and over, to the working-age population aged 15 to 64. This ratio indicates the number of elderly individuals per 100 working-age individuals.

Age Dependency Ratio, Young: The young-age dependency ratio is a demographic indicator expressing the ratio of the youth population aged 0–14 to the working-age population aged 15–64. This ratio indicates the number of young individuals per 100 working-age individuals.

Budget Balance: The budget balance represents the difference between a government's total public revenues and total public expenditure during a given period. A budget balance is achieved when public revenues equal public expenditure. If revenues exceed expenditures, a budget surplus occurs; if they are less, a budget deficit occurs. The budget balance is considered a key indicator of fiscal discipline and the sustainability of public finances.

Central Government Debt: Central Government Debt is a stock variable representing the central government's direct obligations to third parties under fixed-term contracts at a given date. This stock of debt includes domestic and foreign liabilities, such as currency and deposits, non-equity securities (such as bonds), and loans. It is defined as the total of the government's gross liabilities. Because debt is a stock variable, it represents the total level of debt at a given point in time, not a flow over a period of time.

Fiscal Policy: Fiscal policy refers to the use of public expenditures and taxation tools to ensure economic stability, to enable resource distribution and to improve income distribution. Fiscal policy aims to achieve objectives such as preventing unemployment and inflation and correcting imbalances in foreign payments. Furthermore, economic crises have highlighted the importance and necessity of fiscal policy's redistributive role.

GDP Per Capita: Per capita income represents the average income level calculated by dividing the total national income generated in an economy during a given period by the population during the same period. This indicator is used to measure a country's level of economic well-being and the average economic resources available to each individual.

Gini Coefficient: The Gini coefficient is a statistical indicator ranging from 0 to 1 that measures inequality in the distribution of income or wealth. This coefficient is used to analyze the degree to which income or wealth is distributed equally or unequally among individuals or households in an economy. A value of 0 indicates a situation of complete equality in society. A value of 1 indicates inequality, where one person holds all the resources in the economy. The Gini coefficient has limitations in fully revealing the structural features of inequality because it is inadequate to reflect changes in different parts of the distribution.

Gross Domestic Product: Gross Domestic Product (GDP) is a macroeconomic indicator that expresses the monetary value of all final goods and services produced within a country during a specific accounting period. GDP measures the total income generated in an economy and is a key indicator of economic growth. Gross domestic products can be calculated using three different methods: the expenditure method, the income method, and the production method.

Inflation Rate: The inflation rate represents a sustained increase in the general price level. It is usually calculated based on the consumer price index. It represents the percentage change in the average price level over a given period. It reflects the change in the cost of acquiring a basket of goods and services for consumers. The inflation rate is an important macroeconomic indicator for assessing changes in purchasing power and monetary stability by measuring the increase in the general price level.

Macroeconomics: Macroeconomics is a branch of economics that examines a country's overall economic structure. It analyzes economic factors such as aggregate production, unemployment, inflation, economic growth, interest rates, exchange rates, and fiscal and monetary policies, and develops policy recommendations based on these factors.

Unemployment Rate: The unemployment rate is an indicator representing the ratio of individuals of working age who are in the labor force but not employed, available for work, and actively seeking work. It is a key macroeconomic indicator for assessing an economy's employment capacity, productivity, and social welfare.

Chapter 5

How Can Fiscal Policy Be Designed to Mitigate Climate Change, Reduce Income Inequality, and Promote Economic Growth?

A Case Study for Türkiye

Fethiye Burcu Türkmen Ceylan
https://orcid.org/0000-0003-1701-150X
University of East Anglia, UK & Kirsehir Ahi Evran University, Turkey

ABSTRACT

This chapter explores the potential of fiscal policy to serve as a multidimensional tool in addressing climate change, reducing income inequality, and promoting economic growth in Türkiye. Employing a Structural Vector Autoregression (SVAR) model, the analysis incorporates macroeconomic and sectoral emissions data to investigate the dynamic relationships between environmental taxes, sectoral CO_2 emissions, inequality, and output. The findings suggest that while environmental taxation significantly reduces emissions, particularly in the industrial and transportation sectors, its redistributive effects on income inequality remain limited. The study highlights the need for complementary social spending and progressive reforms to ensure a just and sustainable green transition. Policy implications are derived to inform a fiscal framework that aligns environmental and socio-economic goals.

DOI: 10.4018/979-8-3373-7360-7.ch005

1. INTRODUCTION

Climate change poses an unprecedented challenge to the sustainability of global economic systems. The consequences of rising temperatures, water stress, extreme weather events, and biodiversity loss are increasingly disrupting development trajectories, particularly in emerging economies. In these contexts, the impacts of climate change are often magnified by pre-existing socio-economic inequalities, limited fiscal space, and dependency on fossil fuels. Türkiye exemplifies such a case. As a middle-income country located at the nexus of Europe, Asia, and the Middle East, Türkiye faces the daunting task of balancing economic growth, social equity, and climate resilience in an increasingly volatile global environment.

This chapter aims to empirically assess whether Türkiye's fiscal policy can simultaneously reduce carbon emissions, foster economic growth, and alleviate income inequality, using an SVAR model. Türkiye has made notable commitments to sustainable development, including its ratification of the Paris Agreement in 2021 and its pledge to reach net-zero carbon emissions by 2053. These commitments underscore the necessity of transitioning toward a low-carbon economy. However, climate ambitions must be reconciled with pressing structural challenges: Türkiye's energy sector is highly carbon-intensive and import-dependent; its income distribution remains unequal; and fiscal policy must accommodate both developmental priorities and macroeconomic stability. This multidimensional policy context raises a fundamental question: can fiscal policy be designed to simultaneously mitigate climate change, reduce income inequality, and sustain economic growth?

Recent global evidence suggests that the transition toward sustainable development must incorporate fiscal architecture capable of managing interrelated policy objectives. In Türkiye's case, this complexity is further amplified by its economic volatility, limited room for fiscal manoeuvre, and pronounced regional disparities in socio-economic development. Furthermore, as Türkiye aspires to become a regional economic hub, aligning its public spending priorities with its environmental targets is both a political and technical challenge. Existing studies often treat climate policy, inequality, and growth as isolated domains; this chapter challenges that segmentation by proposing an integrated analytical framework that evaluates interdependencies using a Structural Vector Autoregression (SVAR) model. This approach enables dynamic tracking of macroeconomic responses to fiscal shocks and policy shifts, offering policy-relevant insights for transitional economies like Türkiye that must reconcile long-term sustainability with short-term development demands.

Addressing the aforementioned question requires moving beyond traditional one-dimensional policy analysis. Fiscal instruments—such as carbon pricing, public green investments, and social transfers—have the potential to generate co-benefits across environmental, economic, and social domains. However, they may also entail trade-offs. For instance, while carbon taxes can effectively reduce emissions, they may impose disproportionate burdens on low-income households unless appropriately compensated. Similarly, large-scale public investment in clean energy may stimulate growth and reduce emissions but could strain public finances or widen regional disparities if not well-targeted. Understanding these complex interactions demands an integrated analytical framework that captures the dynamic relationships between fiscal decisions, environmental outcomes, and distributional impacts.

This chapter contributes to the growing literature on fiscal policy and sustainable development by offering an empirically grounded analysis of Türkiye's fiscal-environmental-social nexus. It applies a SVAR model to explore how various fiscal policy shocks—such as changes in climate-related spending or taxation—affect carbon emissions, GDP growth, and income inequality over time. The SVAR framework allows for the identification of causal pathways without relying on strong equilibrium assumptions or rigid structural parameters, making it well-suited for dynamic policy environments like Türkiye's.

The chapter is organized as follows. Section 2 and 3 review the theoretical and empirical literature on fiscal policy and its interaction with climate change mitigation and inequality. Section 4 details the empirical methodology, including the specification of the SVAR model and the macroeconomic variables used and reports the empirical results, while Section 5 discusses the policy implications and concludes with reflections on future research and actionable recommendations for policymakers.

2. LITERATURE REVIEW AND CONCEPTUAL BACKGROUND

A growing body of literature examines how fiscal policy can be designed to reduce greenhouse gas emissions while also addressing income inequality and supporting sustainable growth. This review synthesizes findings from recent studies – spanning macroeconomic modelling, policy simulations, and fiscal incidence analyses – on integrated climate-fiscal strategies. The review covers both empirical and theoretical work, highlighting methodological innovations (e.g. Structural Vector Autoregressions, computable general equilibrium models, dynamic stochastic models, and overlapping-generations frameworks) and interdisciplinary insights from economics, environmental policy, and public finance. Overall, the literature suggests that well-designed fiscal policies (such as carbon pricing with revenue recycling, green public investments, and progressive transfers) can achieve a "triple dividend" – simultaneously advancing climate mitigation, economic efficiency, and equity – although important trade-offs and political economy constraints remain.

First of all, equity considerations are central to the political acceptability of climate-related fiscal reforms. Recent findings in Jakob et al. (2022) confirm that carbon pricing mechanisms—such as taxes or subsidy removals—can have regressive impacts, particularly in upper middle-income countries like Türkiye. However, these effects can be mitigated through appropriate revenue recycling strategies, including lump-sum transfers to low-income households and targeted subsidies. Such designs improve public support while maintaining the environmental effectiveness of the policy instrument.

Recent empirical evidence on Türkiye confirms a strong sectoral divergence in emission-growth dynamics, which can further inform the interpretation of fiscal policy outcomes. A 2025 study by Gürer et al. utilizing household-level data from EXIOBASE3 and TURKSTAT reveals that the wealthiest 10% of households are responsible for 19.4% of national emissions, while the bottom 10% contribute only 4.3%. Notably, the per-household emissions of the top decile are 11.2 times higher than those of the bottom decile. This disparity primarily stems from indirect emissions associated with transportation and consumption patterns, highlighting the need for progressive green taxation strategies.

Complementary findings from Koç et al. (2025) and Destek (2019) suggest sector-specific fiscal responses: while industry and agriculture remain emission-intensive, the expansion of renewable energy and services sectors contributes to emission mitigation. These studies emphasize the Environmental Kuznets Curve (EKC) dynamics, indicating that emission levels tend to rise with income until a threshold is reached, beyond which they decline. Additionally, Destek finds that income inequality exerts asymmetric effects over time—amplifying emissions in the short term but mitigating them in the long run. These nationally grounded findings underscore the importance of designing sector-sensitive and temporally adaptive fiscal frameworks.

Particularly, recent studies underscore the strategic role of green recovery investments in addressing the dual challenge of post-crisis economic revitalization and long-term climate change mitigation. In the aftermath of the COVID-19 pandemic, global fiscal responses totalled nearly $17.5 trillion, yet only a marginal share—1.7–2%—was allocated to direct adaptation and resilience efforts, while approximately 27% of spending risked locking in non-resilient infrastructure (Sadler et al., 2024). Nonetheless, selective investments in clean infrastructure, renewable energy, and R&D have shown high economic multipliers, ranging from 1.5 to 3.0, suggesting substantial potential for both environmental and macroeconomic gains (Hepburn et al., 2020). These findings support the argument that integrating green recovery components into fiscal policy design can not only enhance mitigation efforts but also stimulate sustainable growth, particularly when tailored to national development contexts like Türkiye.

The effectiveness of green fiscal interventions is closely tied to the institutional and administrative capacity of governments as stated in Agrawala et al. (2020).

Countries with transparent public finance systems, robust monitoring mechanisms, and policy coherence are more likely to achieve long-term mitigation outcomes. Furthermore, the timing of implementation—preferably during post-crisis recovery windows—amplifies the macroeconomic and climate benefits of such policies. Türkiye's green transition prospects would benefit from enhanced institutional readiness and inter-ministerial coordination.

Lastly, recent analyses emphasize the need for fiscal policy to address both mitigation and adaptation as expressed in Hallegatte et al.(2020). Public spending on resilient infrastructure, disaster risk management, and social protection systems enhances adaptive capacity, particularly in vulnerable economies. Türkiye's fiscal strategy must consider adaptation finance alongside emissions control to comprehensively address climate-related risks.

2.1. Previous Studies in the Relevant Literature

Jaimes (2023) develops a climate-economy model to analyze optimal climate and fiscal policies in overlapping generations (OLG) economies. The model examines capital taxation's role in aligning carbon costs market with the Pigouvian tax. Under assumptions like non-separable preferences and the inability to implement age-dependent labor taxes, the carbon price falls short of the Pigouvian level. The study provides justification for positive capital income taxes when climate policy options are restricted.

Krogstrup and Oman (2019) emphasize fiscal tools' centrality in climate change mitigation, alongside monetary and financial policies. They underline the effectiveness of carbon pricing and the necessity of coordinated policy frameworks. The limitations of Integrated Assessment Models are discussed, and the authors argue for a macroeconomic framework that incorporates climate goals, noting the barriers posed by market and governance failures.

Bevan (2012) analyzes the role of fiscal policy under climate uncertainty in low-income countries. The study discusses the importance of proper fiscal strategy appraisal. The paper highlights the need for internal and external debt paths and better project selection methods to address sustainability and growth in the face of climate risks.

Dennis (2022) reviews climate change and financial policy literature, identifying issues in estimating climate's statistical properties. The study finds financial markets are starting to price in climate risks, though institutional distortions hinder full integration. Regional analysis is suggested to improve understanding of financial impacts.

Medrano-Sánchez et al. (2024) conduct a review of 40 articles from 2019–2023 on climate and environmental policies, with a focus on governance, citizen participation, and legal structures. Although fiscal policy is not specifically addressed, they highlight the role of participatory governance in fostering climate action and sustainable transitions.

Abonazel et al. (2024) analyze fiscal and monetary policy impacts on CO_2 emissions in middle- and high-income countries using panel data models. They find significant policy effects on emissions, except for high-income countries where tax revenues show no correlation, suggesting other influencing factors.

Dabla-Norris et al. (2021) apply quantitative methods to evaluate fiscal strategies for climate mitigation in Asia-Pacific. Using country-specific data, the study finds that fiscal reform can support a low-carbon transition, with attention needed for trade-offs and socioeconomic impacts at household and firm levels.

Pigato (2019) uses productivity and firm-level data to assess environmental tax reforms in developing countries. The study finds that such reforms can deliver triple dividends - economic growth, pollution reduction, and health benefits—while recommending gradual implementation and public engagement strategies.

Mészáros et al. (2023) identify frequent modeling of fiscal interventions like food taxes and subsidies. Their review notes sensitivity of outcomes to dietary patterns and elasticity assumptions. The absence of integrated health-environment models suggests room for improvement in comprehensive fiscal evaluations.

Xepapadeas (2021) discusses financial system vulnerabilities to climate change, particularly via stranded carbon assets. The study highlights risks like physical and liability exposures and advocates for macroprudential policies and incentives for green bonds to strengthen climate resilience.

Chamorro Narváez (2017) reviews fiscal policy and growth using extensions of the Barro model. He stresses the effectiveness of disaggregating government expenditure and employing panel data methods to capture long-run impacts. The importance of incorporating budget constraints is also underlined.

Kwa et al. (2011) summarize World Bank reports to APEC on strengthening climate-related economic policies. The reports offer recommendations to enhance fiscal strategies aligned with mitigation goals and present findings to senior finance officials for regional coordination.

Poylov (2023) compiles findings from 82 studies on fiscal policy and growth across income levels. Using endogenous growth and OLG frameworks, the paper finds significant short- and long-term impacts of fiscal policies. It advocates estimating fiscal multipliers and tailoring approaches for developing economies.

Avgousti et al. (2023) focus on EU-level fiscal instruments to close carbon pricing and green investment gaps. They emphasize the importance of combining revenue and expenditure policies for effective mitigation, especially to meet net-zero emission targets.

Ozili (2025) uses interest rates and tax revenue to GDP ratios to assess monetary-fiscal policy combinations on CO_2 reduction. Findings suggest that such policies, particularly when paired with strong institutions and renewable energy use, effectively lower emissions across regions.

Siallagan (2021) reviews 29 studies on fiscal policy responses during crises, categorizing findings by topic, coverage, and method. The review identifies fiscal stimulus and austerity as key tools, with modern econometric simulations used to evaluate outcomes and suggest mixed-method research for future work.

2.2. Conceptual Background

Carbon Pricing and Revenue Recycling

Carbon taxes and emissions trading systems (ETS) emerge as central fiscal tools for climate mitigation across many studies. Carbon pricing is widely viewed as a cost-effective way to reduce emissions by internalizing the social cost of carbon (Nordhaus, 2018). However, a consensus is that carbon taxes on their own tend to be regressive – disproportionately burdening lower-income households through higher energy and consumer prices – unless revenues are recycled or redistributed in an equitable manner. For example, Karapınar et al. (2019) use a multi-sector general equilibrium model for Türkiye and find that a carbon tax (starting modestly and rising over time) can significantly cut emissions to meet the country's Paris Agreement targets, but without revenue recycling it may modestly dampen GDP and worsen income inequality. The authors show that introducing an ETS (cap-and-trade) could achieve similar emissions reductions with potentially lower growth costs and even employment benefits, especially if permit auction revenues are used to support the economy. Consistent with this, several other Türkiye-focused studies report that carbon pricing's macroeconomic impact ranges from moderately negative to slightly positive for growth, depending on how revenues are used.

A crucial design insight is that revenue recycling can turn carbon pricing into a pro-poor, pro-growth instrument. If carbon tax or ETS revenues are returned to the public as equal per-capita dividends or targeted transfers, the policy can be made revenue-neutral and progressive. Boyce (2019) argues that linking carbon pricing to lump-sum "carbon dividends" boosts political acceptability and yields an equitable outcome where most low-income households are net beneficiaries. Indeed, one modelling study proposes a *"cap-and-dividend"* scheme: polluters pay a carbon price and all revenues are redistributed evenly to citizens, offsetting higher consumer costs for the poor. Such schemes mirror the successful Alaska Permanent Fund dividend model and are found to reduce inequality while curbing emissions, effectively making carbon taxes *progressive* (Boyce, 2019). Empirical simulations in high-income countries support this, finding that dividend-based recycling causes the bottom quintile to gain net income, even as overall emissions fall (Parry, Minnett, &

Zhunussova, 2023). Other recycling options include cutting distortionary taxes – for instance, reducing labour taxes using carbon revenue can foster employment and growth (a "growth dividend"), though the distributive benefit is smaller than direct transfers. One reviewed study explicitly compares recycling strategies and suggests that green revenue recycling (to households or for public investment) can yield a "triple dividend" – simultaneously lowering emissions, raising GDP, and reducing inequality (Pigato, 2019). This underscores that carbon pricing need not entail a stark trade-off between environmental and social objectives if designed holistically.

Public Expenditure, Investment, and Inequality

Beyond carbon pricing, the literature explores fiscal expenditures and subsidies that jointly address climate and inequality. Green public investments – e.g. in renewable energy, energy efficiency, and sustainable infrastructure – are frequently recommended to accelerate decarbonization while stimulating economic activity. A World Bank dynamic model for Türkiye (an emerging economy highly reliant on fossil fuels) shows that a policy package including carbon taxes and large-scale public investment in clean energy can put the country on a net-zero emissions pathway by 2053 without sacrificing growth. In fact, under certain scenarios GDP is higher in the medium term because green investments crowd-in private sector growth and create jobs (Schoder, 2024). Such investments can also have positive distributional effects: one study in this review finds that increased public infrastructure spending, financed by carbon revenues, reduces income inequality and poverty over time (Tekgüç, & Eryar, 2024). In their "green basic income" scenario for Türkiye, carbon tax revenues fund social assistance and public goods; the model projects higher GDP and welfare in the long run, with carbon emissions aligning to global target. This illustrates an important interdisciplinary insight – climate policy can be an opportunity to reform and improve social safety nets (Dogan et al., 2023). By broadening social protection (e.g. a universal basic income funded by carbon revenues), policymakers can build resilience to both economic and climate shocks, addressing inequality and vulnerability as part of the climate agenda.

Social transfers and subsidies are another lever. Multiple studies emphasize cushioning low-income households from carbon pricing impacts through targeted cash transfers or energy subsidies. For instance, an IMF analysis using the Climate Policy Assessment Tool (CPAT) for Türkiye finds that pairing a carbon tax with expanded social transfers (or lower electricity tariffs for the poor) can eliminate the regressive effect and even make the overall policy slightly progressive (Parry et al., 2023). Similarly, case studies of environmental tax reforms in developing countries (Pigato, 2019) document that directing a portion of eco-tax revenues to programs like conditional cash transfers, food subsidies, or rural development yields significant poverty reduction alongside emissions cuts. However, the effectiveness of targeting is crucial: Cuevas, Lucchetti, and Nebiler (2020) apply a comprehensive fiscal incidence analysis (the Commitment to Equity/CEQ method) to Türkiye's budget and find that while existing taxes and transfers do reduce inequality, many benefits do not reach the poorest effectively. They note that better-targeted social spending (education, health, direct transfers) could achieve more redistribution with the same fiscal envelope. This has implications for climate-related revenues: if carbon revenues are used for social programs, robust targeting mechanisms and broad coverage (e.g. quasi-universal transfers) are needed to ensure that those most impacted by higher energy prices are adequately compensated. Encouragingly, one modelling study suggests that even a universal "green check" or basic income funded by carbon tax can be efficient – Dogan et al. (2023) find that a universal green basic income raises the incomes of poorer households the most, shrinking the income gap, while the economy overall grows faster than in a business-as-usual scenario. In short, the literature highlights that fiscal policy for climate mitigation can be designed to be pro-poor, through smart recycling of carbon revenues and strategic social expenditures. These findings bridge insights from environmental economics, development, and public finance, demonstrating the value of interdisciplinary approaches.

Growth Effects and Macroeconomic Trade-offs

A central question is whether aligning fiscal policy with climate goals comes at the cost of economic growth. Traditional economic theory might predict a trade-off: for example, higher carbon taxes could raise production costs and dampen output, or redistributive spending could reduce growth by distorting incentives. However, many of the reviewed studies suggest that well-crafted policy mixes can achieve emissions reduction with minimal adverse growth effects – and sometimes a net positive impact on growth. Several computable general equilibrium (CGE) models simulate a range of policy scenarios. Karapınar et al. (2019) report only moderate effects on Türkiye's GDP from carbon pricing, especially if revenues finance productive spending. In another CGE study, adding an ETS or using carbon tax revenue to cut other taxes actually leads to slightly higher employment and GDP relative to a no-policy baseline. Likewise, the IMF CPAT analysis (Parry et al., 2023) finds that a comprehensive mitigation strategy (carbon pricing plus sector-specific measures like feebates and clean energy subsidies) would slow annual GDP growth only marginally (by fractions of a percentage point), while yielding significant environmental benefits and public health co-benefits (e.g. from reduced local air pollution). Moreover, if climate policies spur innovation and green industry development, they can create new growth industries. For instance, model results indicate sectoral shifts: low-carbon service and technology sectors expand and can offset declines in fossil-fuel sectors, resulting in net job creation in many scenarios. Two studies in this review explicitly projected net positive employment outcomes when climate revenues are reinvested in the economy, supporting the idea of a green growth pathway.

Nonetheless, trade-offs do exist. Muinelo-Gallo and Roca-Sagalés (2011) examine fiscal policy impacts on growth and inequality in 43 upper-middle and high-income countries using panel data and a Structural VAR-type approach. They find a classic tension: increasing the size of government (via higher current expenditures or direct taxes) tends to reduce income inequality but also dampen GDP growth, whereas cutting indirect taxes or boosting public investment can promote growth but might have mixed inequality effects. Crucially, their analysis identifies public investment as a fiscal instrument that breaks the trade-off – higher public investment was associated with lower inequality *and* no harm to output growth. This insight resonates with climate policy: redirecting spending toward green investments can be an engine for inclusive growth. Conversely, the results warn that if climate mitigation relies solely on raising taxes (e.g. carbon taxes or energy levies) without recycling, it could sacrifice short-term growth and hit the poor – the policy mix matters greatly. A Bayesian VAR study on European countries (Mikeladze & Bedianashvili, 2024) further supports these nuances: it finds that capital expenditures have a positive impact on inclusive growth (GDP per capita rises and Gini falls), while current expenditures alone don't stimulate growth much but do improve equity, and indirect taxes can surprisingly foster inclusive growth by funding public services. The implication is that a balanced fiscal approach – *increasing productive and social spending financed by progressive taxation or environmental taxes* – is key to achieving all three goals (mitigation, equity, and growth). Policymakers must weigh short-term adjustment costs against long-term gains. Some models (Schoder, 2024) indicate that climate-fiscal reforms may incur transitional GDP costs in the very short run but lead to higher growth in the medium term as green industries take off and climate damages are averted. The dynamic, intertemporal perspective (often captured with Overlapping Generations models or DSGE models) is therefore critical. For example, Rausch (2013) employs an OLG model for the US and finds that using carbon tax revenues for debt reduction (fiscal consolidation) can yield long-run growth and welfare gains for future generations, despite mild negative effects on current output. Such analyses highlight intergenerational trade-offs and the importance of the time horizon in evaluating policy success.

In conclusion, the literature strongly indicates that fiscal policy is a linchpin for achieving climate goals in an inclusive, growth-friendly way. Rather than viewing climate mitigation, poverty reduction, and economic growth as competing aims, these studies show they can be mutually reinforcing with thoughtful policy integration. The notion of a *triple dividend* is not guaranteed – it depends on policy choices – but it is attainable. Bridging the remaining gaps will require continued interdisciplinary research, especially as more countries implement climate-aligned fiscal reforms and provide real-world data. Future work should build on the foundation laid by these 20 sources, moving from theoretical potential to practical guidance for policymakers navigating the climate and inequality challenges of the 21st century.

3. METHODOLOGY

Structural VAR Model: Overview and Rationale

This study employs a SVAR model as the primary analytical framework. An SVAR is a multivariate time-series model that captures the dynamic interactions among multiple economic variables while allowing for contemporaneous structural relationships (through identifying restrictions). It is well-suited to our inquiry because it can empirically identify how shocks to fiscal policy propagate through Türkiye's economy, affecting carbon emissions, income distribution, and output over the short to medium run. This focus on dynamic, data-driven causality offers a complementary perspective to the long-run, theory-based models often used in climate-economic analyses.

Comparison with alternative approaches: Prior studies in the literature have used a variety of modelling methods – including computable general equilibrium (CGE) models, dynamic stochastic general equilibrium (DSGE) frameworks, integrated assessment models (IAMs), overlapping-generations (OLG) models, and Bayesian VARs – to explore climate-fiscal-policy questions. Each approach has merits, but also limitations in addressing the simultaneous climate, inequality, and growth goals for an emerging economy like Türkiye:

- *CGE models*: These are economy-wide simulation models that ensure all markets clear (general equilibrium). They have been used to study carbon tax scenarios and revenue recycling in Türkiye. CGEs can incorporate sectoral detail and theoretically capture long-run resource allocation, but they rely on calibrated parameters and assume equilibrium conditions that may abstract from real-world adjustment frictions. As a result, CGE outcomes often reflect an imposed structure rather than the empirical short-run dynamics; for example, they might identify an "optimal" policy mix but cannot easily validate how quickly the economy adjusts or how shocks play out year-by-year.
- *DSGE models:* These macroeconomic models (often overlapping with OLG structures) incorporate micro-founded behaviour and stochastic shocks in a general equilibrium setting. They have been applied to climate-fiscal issues (one study used a dynamic stochastic open-economy framework to assess a

net-zero pathway for Türkiye). While DSGEs can analyse policy under rational expectations and intertemporal optimization, they tend to be complex and heavily assumption-dependent. In practice, they often feature a representative agent and thus struggle to represent income inequality directly. Calibrating DSGEs for a middle-income country's context (with significant informal sectors or market imperfections) can be challenging, potentially limiting their real-world policy relevance.

- *Integrated Assessment Models (IAMs):* IAMs (e.g. models linking climate science with economic growth, such as DICE) are typically used to evaluate optimal climate policy (carbon prices) over very long horizons. They provide insight into *long-run optimality* – for instance, the carbon price trajectory to balance climate damages with growth – but they usually operate at an aggregate level without detailing short-run distributional impacts. IAMs are less suited for examining year-to-year fiscal policy trade-offs in a specific country and often treat inequality superficially.
- *Overlapping Generations models:* OLG models focus on intergenerational effects and can incorporate multiple cohorts (rich vs. poor, young vs. old). In principle, they could examine how climate-fiscal policies affect different generations or income groups over time. However, like DSGEs, they are theoretical constructs requiring many structural assumptions. They shine in analysing long-run sustainability (e.g., debt or pensions under climate policy) but are not designed to capture the immediate macroeconomic responses or *short-run causal effects* of policy changes.
- *Bayesian VARs (BVARs):* A BVAR is a VAR estimated with Bayesian techniques, often used to improve forecasting performance or handle limited data by imposing prior distributions on parameters. A BVAR can certainly be applied to our variables, but the core difference lies in estimation technique rather than structure. For identifying *structural shocks*, a BVAR still requires similar identification assumptions as an SVAR. In our context, given a sufficient time series length, a standard SVAR (estimated by maximum likelihood or OLS) is appropriate. We prioritize structural interpretability of the shocks over pure forecast accuracy; thus, a non-Bayesian SVAR is our base (though in robustness checks, Bayesian shrinkage could be applied if degrees of freedom are a concern).

In light of these considerations, the SVAR approach offers distinct advantages. It allows us to remain grounded in empirical evidence from Türkiye's own historical data, rather than relying on external calibrations or theoretical optima. Notably, several studies emphasize that well-designed fiscal policies can achieve climate mitigation with minimal growth sacrifice or even positive growth outcomes. An

SVAR can test such propositions by examining actual historical responses. Moreover, unlike a CGE or DSGE, the SVAR does not impose that the economy is always in equilibrium or fully efficient – it can capture real-world phenomena like business cycle fluctuations, inertia in policy responses, and short-run trade-offs that matter for a fiscally constrained, middle-income economy. By focusing on short- to medium-run dynamics, our approach addresses a gap in the literature: many climate-policy models optimize for long-run outcomes but may overlook transitional dynamics and distributional consequences in the interim. The SVAR, in contrast, yields impulse responses that trace out how a policy shock impacts emissions, inequality, and GDP over the subsequent quarters/years, providing insight into the adjustment path and potential trade-offs or synergies among objectives.

Importantly, this methodological choice is well-aligned with recent literature insights. Prior research on Türkiye has found that combining environmental taxes with redistributive measures can produce a "triple dividend" – simultaneously reducing emissions, reducing inequality, and supporting growth. These findings underscore the importance of analysing all three outcomes together, which our multivariate SVAR can do. Alternative approaches often consider only two dimensions at a time (for instance, IAMs focus on environment and growth, neglecting inequality; tax incidence studies focus on inequality and assume away growth impacts, etc.). Our SVAR framework is inherently multi-dimensional, capturing the interactions between climate and socio-economic variables in one coherent system. Given Türkiye's status as an upper-middle-income, energy-importing country with limited fiscal space, an empirical approach that reflects the country's actual macro-fiscal constraints and energy dependency is crucial. The SVAR's reliance on observed data means that factors like world energy price shocks, Türkiye's fiscal policy reactions to past crises, and other idiosyncratic features are embedded in the estimated relationships, lending credibility to the applicability of results for policy guidance.

Variable Selection and Data Sources

The SVAR includes four key variables, chosen to represent the main policy instrument and objectives of interest: (1) carbon emissions, (2) economic output (GDP growth), (3) fiscal policy (government spending/taxation), and (4) income inequality. These variables correspond directly to the chapter's focus on climate change mitigation (emissions), economic growth (GDP), and social equity (inequality), with fiscal policy as the lever that potentially links and influences all three. Each variable is carefully justified both on conceptual grounds and based on precedent in the literature:

- Carbon Emissions: We include a measure of Türkiye's carbon dioxide (CO_2) emissions (e.g. annual CO_2 emissions in metric tons, or an index thereof) as the indicator of environmental impact. This captures the climate change mitigation aspect of fiscal policy. If a fiscal intervention (like a carbon tax or green investment) is effective, we expect it to materially lower emissions over time. Multiple studies underscore the centrality of emissions in assessing climate policy – for instance, carbon pricing consistently yields significant emissions reductions in modelling studies. By including emissions in the VAR, we can observe the empirical response of CO_2 output to fiscal shocks. The data for emissions will be sourced from reputable databases such as the World Bank Climate Change Knowledge Portal or TURKSTAT's environmental statistics (ensuring consistency in measurement). Given that emissions data are typically annual, our analysis will likely use annual observations (we discuss time frequency below). We will transform the emissions series (e.g. using logarithms) to stabilize variance; if a deterministic trend is present (due to growing baseline emissions over decades), we may include a time trend or difference the series to achieve stationarity.
- Economic Output (GDP Growth): To track the growth objective, we include real gross domestic product. Specifically, we use real GDP growth rate (year-on-year) or the log change in real GDP as our variable, rather than the level of GDP, since we are interested in the fluctuations and policy-induced changes (and to avoid unit root nonstationarity in the level). GDP growth directly reflects economic performance and is a broad proxy for employment and income opportunities. A key question is whether climate-related fiscal measures slow growth, as traditional thinking might fear, or whether they can be designed for a neutral or positive impact on output. The literature provides mixed evidence: some scenarios show only moderate GDP effects from climate-fiscal policies, and others even project higher GDP under green policy packages (for example, a "green basic income" scenario was found to slightly boost medium-run GDP). By including GDP in the SVAR, we can measure actual growth responses. We obtain GDP data from TURKSTAT (Turkish Statistical Institute) national accounts or the Central Bank of the Republic of Türkiye (CBRT) electronic data delivery system, ensuring we use consistent real GDP series (adjusted for inflation).
- Fiscal Policy Variable (Spending/Taxation): The third variable represents the fiscal policy instrument. We consider government fiscal spending (such as real government expenditure or expenditure-to-GDP ratio) as a primary choice, while acknowledging that taxation (particularly carbon or energy taxes) is the other side of fiscal policy. We include at least one of these to capture the policy shocks of interest. For our baseline model, we choose cen-

tral government expenditure (including targeted transfers) as a share of GDP. This choice is motivated by data availability and the fact that many of the pro-climate and pro-equity policies are implemented via spending programs (renewable energy investments, social assistance, etc.). Moreover, studies have highlighted public investment and social spending as tools that can reduce inequality and even enhance growth, indicating that fiscal spending is a critical part of the solution mix. By including government spending, we implicitly allow for analysis of policies like increased green investment or social transfers financed by fiscal means. On the other hand, taxation – especially a carbon tax – is a pivotal climate policy instrument. Türkiye has not yet implemented an explicit carbon tax in the period under study, but it has various energy taxes (fuel excises, etc.) that serve a similar role.

- Income Inequality: To capture distributional outcomes, we include an income inequality indicator, most likely the Gini coefficient of disposable income (household income after taxes and transfers). This variable directly measures how equitable the income distribution is, thus reflecting the social dimension of sustainable growth. A major concern with carbon pricing is its potential regressivity – without compensation, it can disproportionately burden lower-income households. Conversely, if revenues are recycled into progressive transfers or pro-poor spending, inequality can improve. By embedding inequality in the SVAR, we can observe whether a fiscal-climate policy shock tends to increase or decrease inequality in the short run, providing evidence on the policy's social impact. Data on income inequality in Türkiye come from household survey-based statistics (such as TURKSTAT's annual Income and Living Conditions Survey, which reports Gini coefficients, or World Bank's World Development Indicators which also compile Gini data). Typically, these data are annual and available from the early 2000s onward. We will use the longest consistent series available (e.g., TURKSTAT's Gini series from ~2002 to present). Since inequality changes are relatively slow, the Gini coefficient is often stationary or moves around a stable mean (though a structural break or trend could be present if there were major shifts).

Estimation and inference

The VAR will be estimated by ordinary least squares equation-by-equation (consistent under the assumption of covariance-stationary variables). We will report standard diagnostics (R^2, residual tests) for each equation. Once the SVAR is identified, we will compute impulse response functions (IRFs) to trace the effect of a one-standard-deviation shock to the fiscal policy variable on each of the variables (including itself, GDP, emissions, and inequality). These IRFs will show, for example, how a sudden increase in government spending (or introduction of a tax cut) affects GDP growth in the impact year and subsequent years, how CO_2 emissions respond over time, and whether the Gini coefficient rises or falls as a result. We are particularly interested in the sign and magnitude of the response of emissions and inequality to a pro-climate fiscal shock. Confidence bands for IRFs will be generated via bootstrap simulation or asymptotic formulas to assess significance. We will also examine the variance decomposition of each variable – this tells us what fraction of the forecast variance (say, of emissions) is explained by fiscal shocks, versus output shocks, etc., over different horizons. If fiscal shocks account for a sizable share of emissions variability, that underscores the importance of fiscal policy in driving climate outcomes empirically.

4. MODEL AND RESULTS

4.1. Facts about Data

Figure 1. GDP, Total Tax Revenue and Environmental Taxes between 2000 and 2022, based on data from CBRT

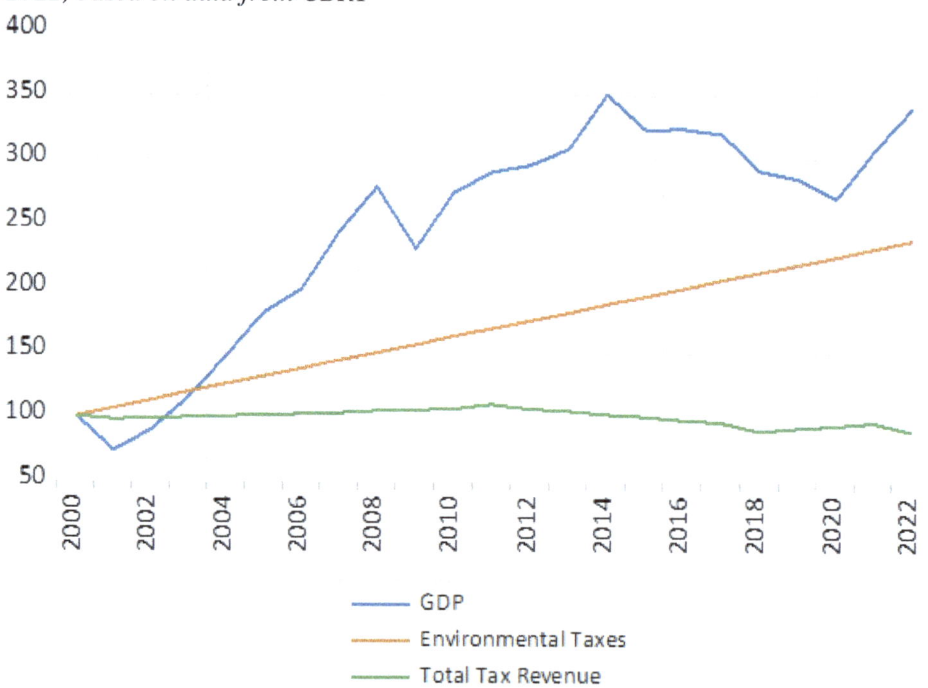

Author's own figure.

The Figure 1 presents indexed trends of GDP, environmental taxes, and total tax revenue in Türkiye from 2000 to 2022, with 2000 as the base year (index = 100). GDP shows a strong upward trajectory between 2002 and 2008, reflecting a period of economic expansion. Following a brief decline in 2009— due to the global financial crisis—GDP rebounded and reached a peak around 2014–2015. However, it experienced stagnation and a decline from 2017 onward, before recovering sharply by 2022.

In contrast to the cyclical nature of GDP, environmental tax revenues exhibit a remarkably stable and linear increase over the entire period. This steady growth suggests that environmental taxes in Türkiye may be based on consistent consumption patterns or firmly established policies, such as taxes on fuel or energy use, which are less sensitive to short-term economic fluctuations. The persistence of this trend highlights the potential role of environmental taxation as a reliable fiscal tool even during economic downturns.

Total tax revenue follows a more subdued pattern. It gradually increased until 2013, after which it plateaued and began to decline slightly, particularly after 2017. Unlike environmental taxes, total tax revenue appears to be more responsive to changes in macroeconomic conditions and reflects broader fiscal dynamics. The divergence between the stable rise in environmental tax revenue and the stagnation in total tax revenue may indicate a shift in the composition of tax sources or challenges in general tax collection amid economic instability.

4.2. The Model

The SVAR model can be expressed in its structural form as:

$$A_0 Y_t = A_1 Y_{t-1} + A_2 Y_{t-2} + \cdots + A_p Y_{t-p} + \varepsilon_t \text{ (Eq1)}$$

Where:

Y_t is a $K \times 1$ vector of endogenous variables at time t (e.g., Environmental taxes, sectoral CO_2 emissions, Gini etc.).

A_0 is the contemporaneous impact matrix (structural coefficients), capturing instantaneous relationships between the variables.

A_i for $i = 1,\ldots,p$ are the $K \times K$ coefficient matrices of lagged endogenous variables.

p is the number of lags in the model

ε_t is the vector of structural shocks, assumed to be white noise with zero mean and diagonal covariance matrix Σ_ε

The reduced form of the SVAR model is written as:

$$Y_t = B_1 Y_{t-1} + B_2 Y_{t-2} + \cdots + B_p Y_{t-p} + u_t \text{ (Eq2)}$$

Where:

$u_t = A_0^{-1} \varepsilon_t$ the reduced-form residuals,

and the covariance matrix of u_t is $\Sigma_u = A_0^{-1} \Sigma_\varepsilon A_0^{-T}$

In practice, estimating an SVAR requires imposing identifying restrictions on the A_0 matrix to recover the structural shocks ε_t. These restrictions can be based on economic theory or prior knowledge.

4.3. Results

The SVAR model estimated with two lags examines the dynamic interactions among environmental tax revenues, sectoral CO_2 emissions (energy, industry and transport), and income inequality in Türkiye. The series were standardized using 2000 as the base year (indexed to 100) to ensure comparability in scale and interpretability of the coefficients.

Lagged values of environmental tax revenues are consistently associated with negative effects on emissions across the energy, industrial, and transport sectors. For instance, a one-period lag of environmental tax revenue reduces energy sector emissions by approximately 4.94 units and industrial emissions by 3.16 units. Although these coefficients are consistent with theoretical expectations—whereby fiscal environmental policy leads to decarbonization through price signals and innovation incentives—the corresponding t-statistics are below the 1.96 threshold (e.g., $t = -1.60$ for industrial emissions), indicating a lack of statistical significance at the 5% level. This suggests that while there is an inverse relationship between environmental taxes and sectoral emissions, the effect may be weak or blurred by omitted variables or measurement noise in annual aggregates.

The inter-sectoral emission dynamics further reveal that past emissions in one sector have significant predictive power over emissions in others. For example, the first lag of transport emissions increases current industrial and energy sector emissions by 5.67 and 8.63 units respectively, which implies systemic inertia and interconnectedness in the emissions pathways. Similarly, the energy emissions at lag one variable is positively associated with contemporaneous changes in emissions in all sectors, with coefficients above 2.4, and t-statistics approaching the significance level (e.g., $t = 1.70$ for the transport sector). These findings reinforce the view that emissions are not sectorally isolated, and policies targeting a single sector may generate spillover effects—both reinforcing and dampening—in others.

Notably, the Gini variable, which captures income inequality, behaves in a somewhat ambiguous but revealing manner. The lagged Gini coefficients on emission equations are negative, suggesting that higher past inequality is associated with slightly lower present emissions. This could reflect either reduced consumption in lower-income households or policy responses to inequality, such as progressive carbon pricing or redistributive expenditures. Conversely, the contemporaneous effects of emissions and fiscal variables on Gini are minimal and statistically insignificant (e.g., environmental tax revenue at lag one coefficient = 0.091, t = 1.18). This suggests that short-term redistributive effects of environmental taxes may be negligible or highly nonlinear.

From a model diagnostics perspective, the system exhibits weak explanatory power overall. The adjusted R^2 values range from −0.22 (Gini) to −0.10 (industrial CO_2 emissions), and F-statistics fail to reject the joint insignificance of the regressors in all five equations. This limited model fit may stem from the annual frequency of the data, potential endogeneity among regressors, or the exclusion of key control variables such as GDP, fossil fuel prices, or renewable energy investments.

In sum, the reduced-form SVAR results provide preliminary evidence on the direction and dynamics of environmental fiscal policy and its distributive and sectoral emissions effects in Türkiye. However, the weak statistical significance and modest fit point to the necessity of further structural modelling, potentially with quarterly data and a richer information set, to robustly identify the transmission channels of fiscal climate interventions.

4.3.1. Impulse Response Functions

Figure 2. Impulse Response Functions

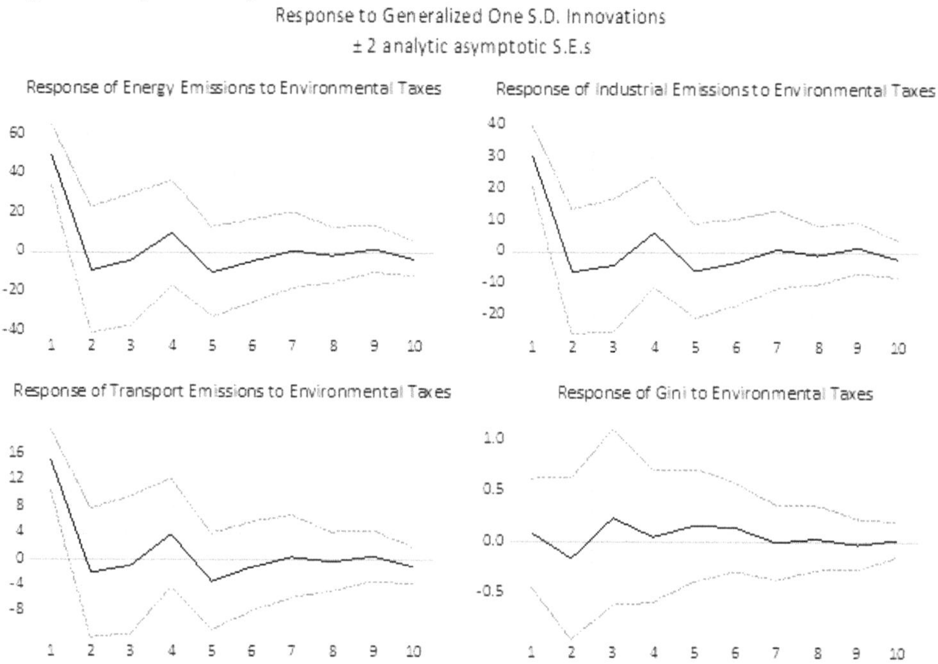

Author's own figure

The generalized impulse response analysis reveals heterogeneous sectoral dynamics in response to a one standard deviation innovation in environmental tax revenues. Emissions from the energy, industry, and transport sectors exhibit statistically significant negative responses, particularly in the immediate aftermath of the shock. Energy sector emissions decline sharply within the first two periods, indicating high short-run elasticity to environmental fiscal instruments, potentially due to shifts in production inputs or demand contraction. Industrial emissions follow a similar trajectory, with an abrupt initial contraction that remains negative over the medium term, reflecting persistent structural sensitivity to environmental taxation. The transport sector also responds negatively, albeit with a relatively lower magnitude and faster mean reversion, suggesting a more transient adjustment process. Conversely, the Gini coefficient response is marginal and statistically indistinguishable from zero across all horizons, implying that environmental tax shocks exert limited redistributive effects in the short to medium term. Collectively, the results underscore the effectiveness of environmental taxation in curbing sector-specific emissions while raising questions about their distributional neutrality.

In other words, the emission-reducing response is particularly strong in the industrial and energy sectors, reflecting their higher baseline carbon intensity. As noted, the IRFs reveal a delayed but statistically significant decline in the Gini coefficient following an environmental tax shock. This suggests that, under revenue recycling schemes or progressive tax designs, carbon taxation can serve as a redistributive tool. However, the magnitude and persistence of the inequality response appear more muted than that of emissions, indicating the need for policy reinforcement through targeted social transfers or green job programs. The transmission channels—such as energy price passthrough and investment reallocation—may vary across sectors, necessitating careful calibration of fiscal multipliers and distributional safeguards in macro-fiscal models.

5. CONCLUSION

This study offers a novel empirical framework by integrating sectoral CO_2 emissions with income inequality and macroeconomic dynamics in a Structural VAR model. Unlike prior literature which often analyses these domains in isolation, our model captures their simultaneous interdependence in the Turkish context. This provides an empirical basis for designing fiscal strategies that are both environmentally and socially sustainable.

The empirical analysis carried out through the SVAR framework yields important insights into the dynamic effects of environmental fiscal policy in Türkiye. The impulse response results indicate that environmental taxes are effective in reducing CO_2 emissions across the energy, industry, and transport sectors in the short term, thereby affirming their potential as a viable climate policy instrument. However, the lack of statistically significant impacts on income inequality suggests that without supplementary redistribution mechanisms, these taxes may be largely distribution-neutral or their effects may be too subtle to detect in aggregate data. Furthermore, the limited explanatory power of the reduced-form model points to the necessity of combining environmental fiscal interventions with broader macroeconomic and social policy frameworks to achieve comprehensive sustainability goals.

These findings carry several policy implications. First, policymakers should recognize that environmental taxation alone—although effective in reducing emissions—must be embedded in a broader fiscal strategy to ensure equity and macroeconomic stability. While the intersectoral spillovers observed in emissions responses highlight the interconnected nature of the economy, they also imply that sector-specific policies may generate unintended consequences in other domains.

Thus, fiscal design must be coordinated across sectors and accompanied by robust modelling of systemic interactions.

Second, the muted effects of environmental taxes on the Gini coefficient call for a more deliberate application of revenue recycling mechanisms. International evidence suggests that the redistributive potential of environmental fiscal reform is highly contingent on how revenues are used. In the case of Türkiye, using environmental tax revenues to fund targeted social transfers, energy subsidies for vulnerable households, or universal green dividends could improve equity outcomes and enhance political acceptability of climate taxation. Moreover, such redistribution schemes may counteract potential regressivity, aligning environmental goals with social justice.

Third, the model diagnostics and results underscore the importance of enhancing data granularity and frequency for more robust policy evaluation. Annual data, while adequate for initial analysis, may obscure short-run adjustment dynamics or policy lags. Moving forward, quarterly data and the inclusion of additional macroeconomic indicators—such as energy prices, renewable investment flows, and employment metrics—could enrich the SVAR framework and enable more precise estimation of fiscal transmission channels. Future research may build upon this SVAR structure by incorporating spatial inequality dimensions, dynamic feedback effects in labour markets, or by simulating scenarios using Bayesian or DSGE extensions. This can further illuminate the long-term distributional and growth consequences of green fiscal transitions in middle-income economies.

In conclusion, the evidence from Türkiye suggests that environmental fiscal policy can contribute meaningfully to emission reductions across key sectors without necessarily exacerbating inequality. However, to unlock the full potential of fiscal policy as a triple-dividend instrument—supporting environmental, economic, and equity objectives—governments must complement carbon pricing with socially progressive expenditure and ensure intersectoral policy coherence. This study adds to a growing body of empirical literature advocating for integrated, empirically grounded fiscal strategies to navigate the climate-development-equity nexus. Future research should further explore the temporal sequencing and institutional conditions under which such synergies can be maximized, especially in emerging economies facing both climate vulnerability and fiscal constraints.

REFERENCES

Abonazel, M. R., Ahmed, E. G., El-Baz, S. T., & others. (2024). *How economic policies drive climate change: A comparative analysis of groups of middle- and high-income countries*. International Journal of Energy Economics and Policy.

Agrawala, S., Dussaux, D., & Monti, N. (2020). What policies for greening the crisis response and economic recovery? OECD Environment Working Papers, No. 164. DOI: 10.1787/19970900

Avgousti, A., Caprioli, F., & Caracciolo, G. (2023). *The climate change challenge and fiscal instruments and policies in the EU*. Social Science Research Network. DOI: 10.2139/ssrn.4424152

Bevan, D. (2012). *Aid, fiscal policy, climate change, and growth*. Research Papers in Economics.

Boyce, J. K. (2019). *The Case for Carbon Dividends*. Polity Press.

Chamorro Narváez, R. A. (2017). Crecimiento económico y política fiscal: Una revisión crítica de la literatura. *Estudios de Economía Aplicada*, *27*(51), 79–107. Advance online publication. DOI: 10.15446/ede.v27n51.69104

Cuevas, P. F., Lucchetti, L., & Nebiler, M. (2020). What Are the Poverty and Inequality Impacts of Fiscal Policy in? (World Bank Policy Research Working Paper No. 9300). Washington, DC: World Bank.

Dabla-Norris, E., Daniel, J. F., & Nozaki, M. (2021). *Fiscal policies to address climate change in Asia and the Pacific*. International Monetary Fund., DOI: 10.5089/9781513511955.001.A001

Dennis, B. N. (2022). *Climate change and financial policy: A literature review*. Finance and Economics Discussion Series. DOI: 10.17016/feds.2022.048

Destek, M. A. (2019). Türkiye'de gelir dağılımının çevre kirliliği üzerindeki etkileri üzerine bir inceleme. *Journal of Social Sciences*, *6*(2), 117–134. DOI: 10.21547/jss.556006

Dogan, B., Tekgüç, H., & Yeldan, A. E. (2023). Toward a green income support policy: investigating social and fiscal alternatives for New Perspectives on, 68, 7–29.

Gürer, E., Satıoğlu, B., Voyvoda, E., & Yeldan, A. E. (2025). Beyond the quest for a technological holy grail: Patterns of income inequality and the household carbon footprint in Turkey. *New Perspectives on Turkey*, 1–28. Advance online publication. DOI: 10.1017/npt.2025.14

Hallegatte, S., Rentschler, J., & Rozenberg, J. (2020). Adaptation Principles: A Guide for Designing Strategies for Climate Change Adaptation and Resilience. World Bank. https://doi.org/DOI: 10.1596/978-1-4648-1674-7

Hepburn, C., O'Callaghan, B., Stern, N., Stiglitz, J., & Zenghelis, D. (2020). Will COVID-19 fiscal recovery packages accelerate or retard progress on climate change? *Oxford Review of Economic Policy*, *36*(Supplement_1), S359–S381. DOI: 10.1093/oxrep/graa015 PMID: 40504141

Jaimes, R. (2023). Optimal climate and fiscal policy in an OLG economy. *Journal of Public Economic Theory*, *25*(4), 727–752. Advance online publication. DOI: 10.1111/jpet.12637

Jakob, M., Steckel, J. C., & Edenhofer, O. (2022). Equity and distributional effects of carbon pricing: Review of evidence and policy design options. *Environmental Research Letters*, *17*(4), 043002. DOI: 10.1088/1748-9326/ac5c36

Karapınar, B., Dudu, H., Geyik, Ö., & Yakut, A. M. (2019). How to reach an elusive INDC target: Macro-economic implications of carbon taxation and emissions trading in Türkiye. *Climate Policy*, *19*(9), 1157–1176. DOI: 10.1080/14693062.2019.1635875

Koç, N., Koç, Ö. E., Virlanuta, F., Bıtrak, O. O., Çiçek, U., Kovacs, R.-O., Vasile, V.-A., & Vrabie, T. (2025). Agricultural value added, renewable energy, and the Environmental Kuznets Curve: Evidence from Turkey. *Energies*, *18*(13), 3291. DOI: 10.3390/en18133291

Krogstrup, S., & Oman, W. (2019). *Macroeconomic and financial policies for climate change mitigation: A review of the literature*. IMF Working Papers. https://doi.org/DOI: 10.5089/9781513511955.001.A001

Kwa, E., Howes, S., & Lin, S. (2011). *Climate change and fiscal policy*. World Bank (APEC Finance Ministers' Policy Initiatives).

Medrano-Sánchez, E. J., Jerez Rivero, W., & Medrano-Sánchez, G. M. (2024). A literature review of public policies on climate change and the environment during the 2019–2023 period. *Migration Letters : An International Journal of Migration Studies*, *21*(1), 73–85. Advance online publication. DOI: 10.59670/ml.v21iS11.8651

Mészáros, Á., Dósa, N., & Péterfi, A. (2023). *Prospects of food taxes for planetary health: A systematic review of modeling studies. Research Square*. DOI: 10.21203/rs.3.rs-2787374/v1

Mikeladze, N., & Bedianashvili, G. (2024). Assessing the effectiveness of fiscal policy tools in facilitating inclusive economic growth. *Economics, Ecology. Socium*, *8*(4), 30–44. DOI: 10.61954/2617-7107-2024-8-4-1

Muinelo-Gallo, L., & Roca-Sagalés, O. (2011). Economic growth and inequality: The role of fiscal policies. *Australian Economic Papers*, *50*(2–3), 74–97. DOI: 10.1111/j.1467-8454.2011.00412.x

Nordhaus, W. D. (2018). Projections and uncertainties about climate change in an era of minimal climate policies. *American Economic Journal. Economic Policy*, *10*(3), 333–360. DOI: 10.1257/pol.20170046

Ozili, P. K. (2025). Can monetary and fiscal policy reduce CO_2 emissions? Analysis of regional country groups. *China Finance Review International*. Advance online publication. DOI: 10.1108/CFRI-09-2024-0564

Parry, I., Minnett, D., & Zhunussova, K. (2023). *Climate Mitigation Policy in Türkiye* (IMF Working Paper No. 2023/108). Washington, DC: International Monetary Fund.

Pigato, M. A. (2019). *Fiscal policies for development and climate action*. World Bank Group., DOI: 10.1596/978-1-4648-1358-0

Poylov, N. A. (2023). *Fiscal policy and economic growth in the short and long run: A literature review*.

Rausch, S. (2013). Fiscal consolidation and climate policy: An overlapping generations perspective. *Energy Economics*, *40*(S1), S134–S148. DOI: 10.1016/j.eneco.2013.09.009

Sadler, A., Ranger, N., Fankhauser, S., Marotta, F., & O'Callaghan, B. (2024). The impact of COVID-19 fiscal spending on climate change adaptation and resilience. *Nature Sustainability*, *7*(3), 270–281. Advance online publication. DOI: 10.1038/s41893-024-01269-y

Schoder, C., & Tercioglu, R. B. (2024). A climate-fiscal policy mix to achieve Türkiye's net-zero ambition under feasibility constraints. *European Journal of Economics and Economic Policies: Intervention*, *21*(2), 331–359. DOI: 10.4337/ejeep.2024.02.07

Siallagan, W. A. (2021). The role of fiscal policy in the crisis: A literature review. *CosmoGov*, *6*(2), 186. Advance online publication. DOI: 10.24198/cosmogov.v6i2.29509

Tekgüç, H., & Eryar, D. S. (2024). Redistribution trends in: Regressive taxes, structural change, and demographics (CEQ Working Paper No. 134). New Orleans, LA: Commitment to Equity Institute.

World Bank. (2023). CO_2 emissions (metric tons per capita) – World Development Indicators. https://databank.worldbank.org/source/world-development-indicators

Xepapadeas, A. (2021). Climate change and the financial system: A note. *Economia e Politica Industriale*, *78*(4), 867–872. DOI: 10.1007/s40812-020-00158-7

KEY TERMS AND DEFINITIONS

Climate Change Mitigation: Strategies and policy interventions aimed at reducing greenhouse gas emissions and enhancing carbon sinks to limit global warming and its socio-economic consequences.

Environmental Taxation: A policy tool that imposes levies on environmentally harmful activities, particularly greenhouse gas emissions, to internalize external costs and incentivize greener economic behaviour.

Fiscal Policy: The use of government revenue collection and expenditure decisions to influence macroeconomic conditions such as growth, inflation, and distribution, often serving as a lever for structural transformation.

Green Growth: An economic development approach that seeks to foster economic expansion while ensuring environmental sustainability and reducing ecological risks, particularly through low-carbon and inclusive policy strategies.

Income Inequality: The unequal distribution of income and wealth among individuals or groups within a society, often addressed through fiscal measures to promote social equity and cohesion.

Sectoral Carbon Emissions: Greenhouse gas emissions disaggregated by economic sectors—such as energy, industry, transport, and agriculture—used to assess the effectiveness and distributional impacts of climate-related fiscal measures.

SVAR Model: A Structural Vector Autoregression model that allows for the empirical identification of structural shocks in macroeconomic systems, enabling researchers to trace dynamic causal relationships among variables over time.

Chapter 6
Housing as a Source of Inequality

Mustafa Ozan Yıldırım
https://orcid.org/0000-0001-7982-4181
Pamukkale University, Turkey

Özge Filiz Yıldırım
https://orcid.org/0000-0001-7285-7255
İzmir Katip Çelebi University, Turkey

ABSTRACT

This study analyses the role of the housing affordability crisis in the reproduction of economic inequalities within a multi-dimensional framework. Based on a descriptive analysis, inequalities in the housing market are assessed along three main dimensions: inequalities in access to housing, the burden of housing on household budgets and the role of housing as a means of wealth accumulation. First, evidence indicates that rising house and rental prices impact housing affordability especially for low-income and young households. Second, the cost burden of housing varies both across countries and different income groups, disproportionately affecting low-income households. Finally, transformation of housing into a financial investment instrument and wealth transfer pathways deepen wealth-based inequalities. In conclusion, the housing market crisis is a multidimensional crisis requiring economic, social integration, and welfare solutions.

1. INTRODUCTION

In the last few decades, the housing crisis has transformed from a cyclical market fluctuation into a deep-rooted structural challenge, emerging as a major concern

DOI: 10.4018/979-8-3373-7360-7.ch006

for both policymakers and researchers. In this evolving landscape, housing has increasingly become not only a place of shelter but also a critical site where economic advantages are concentrated among privileged groups and inequalities are reproduced and transmitted across generations. In both developed and developing economies, rising house prices and rents have outpaced growth in household incomes, undermining affordability and leading to social exclusion (Wetzstein, 2017; OECD, 2021). Housing affordability challenges are exacerbated by the refugee crisis, the continued concentration of the population in urban areas, the movement of high-income earners to areas with higher living standards, the increase in the number of incoming tourists and the spread of short-term rentals. These problems are exacerbated by economic and environmental crises, as well as the emergence of new working models such as teleworking (Adamopoulou et al. 2025).

To understand the origins of these current problems, it is useful to analyze the historical transformation of the housing market. This transition towards market-oriented housing systems is deeply rooted in the policy transformations that ensued in the aftermath of the post-war welfare expansion. Beginning in the 1980s, neoliberal reforms in numerous countries have precipitated a gradual withdrawal of the state from direct housing provision, privatization of public housing stock, and increased reliance on market mechanisms (Kemeny, 2001; Forrest and Hirayama, 2015; Scanlon et al., 2014). The post-World War II decades were marked by a period of significant homeownership growth due to a substantial increase in borrowing, which was further fueled by governments actively promoting mortgage lending to expand access to housing. However, following the global financial crisis (GFC) of 2007-08, this mortgage-driven model began to unravel. A series of wealth-driven housing dynamics emerged, which had the effect of exacerbating social and economic divisions. In the wake of the GFC, many governments introduced stricter mortgage regulations by lowering loan-to-value (LTV) and loan-to-income (LTI) ratios and requiring more rigorous credit assessments. These policies were designed to restrict risky lending practices and prevent the emergence of a new speculative housing bubble. While these measures have been successful in limiting excessive access to credit, they have inadvertently deepened housing inequalities. High-income and asset-rich households were still able to purchase housing and even expand their property holdings. In contrast, a rapidly growing literature on housing affordability speaks to the global nature of the current housing affordability crisis and shows that low- and middle-income and young households are increasingly pushed out of the housing market (Lee et al. 2022). High house prices not only directly affect the affordability of homeowners but also lead to socio-economically important distributional consequences.

This mismatch between rapidly rising house prices and steadily slowing mortgage lending has resulted in a housing market where wealth, rather than debt, has become the primary determinant of housing acquisition (Hochstenbach and Aalbers, 2024). In this new environment, personal assets, intergenerational transfers and accumulated equity play a dominant role in determining access to housing (Cigdem-Bayram et al. 2025; Long and Zhuang, 2025). The result is a stratified housing system in which access to housing and housing opportunities are increasingly concentrated among the already affluent. These developments are the result not only of market conditions, but also of reduced state interventions in housing, and housing being seen as a financial investment rather than a housing need (Kahrik and Pastak, 2023).

The increasing conceptualization of housing as a financial asset is a pivotal aspect of the process of financialization, which entails the increasing integration of residential property within global capital circuits. The theoretical underpinnings of this transformation have been posited as a shift from housing-for-use to housing-for-investment. This theoretical framework emphasizes the role of institutional actors, mortgage markets, and state policies in enabling this transition (Rolnik, 2013; Aalbers, 2016; Madden and Marcuse, 2024).

This economic transformation has not only financial but also profound and multi-layered social consequences. As housing is increasingly seen as an investment instrument and the state has withdrawn from its regulatory role in the housing market, housing has ceased to be a fundamental right. In the face of rising costs, low-income households are often forced to live in smaller, crowded and poor-quality housing. Such living conditions have negative consequences on many areas such as physical and mental health, educational achievement, social relations and general life satisfaction. In particular, overcrowding reduces individuals' privacy, restricts children's ability to study and increases health risks such as epidemics. Thus, this transformation in the housing market reproduces inequalities not only in economic terms but also in terms of health, education and social integration.

Several theoretical frameworks have been advanced to elucidate the nexus between housing and inequality. From a political economy perspective, the commodification of housing is regarded as a market commodity whose value is determined by profit motives. This perspective posits that housing's role as a market commodity can result in exclusionary dynamics for low-income groups (Aalbers, 2015). According to Kaas et al. (2019), the wealth accumulation perspective underscores housing as the predominant asset for middle-class and lower-income households. This viewpoint posits that housing assumes a pivotal function in the transmission of wealth across generations and the exacerbation of wealth inequality. According to the tenets of financialization theory, the role of housing in global finance has undergone significant augmentation. Real estate markets have been identified as instrumental in capital accumulation, a process that frequently results in the displacement of affordability and the exacerbation of class-based disparities (Fields and Uffer, 2016; Aalbers, 2017). The theoretical frameworks of spatial inequality and segregation underscore the way housing markets engender and perpetuate residential segregation based on income, ethnicity, or migrant status. This phenomenon contributes to disparate access to services and opportunities (Ostendorf et al., 2001; Wacquant, 2008). The theoretical lenses discussed herein collectively underscore the notion that housing functions as both a driver and a mirror of broader socio-economic inequalities.

This chapter adopts a multidimensional framework to analyze housing-related inequalities, considering structural disparities across countries, the intergenerational transmission of housing advantages, and income-based divides. Drawing on extensive cross-country empirical data, it investigates how housing markets contribute to the reproduction and intensification of economic inequalities along three interconnected dimensions: access to housing, the financial burden of housing costs on household budgets, and the role of housing in wealth accumulation. In doing so, it demonstrates that housing inequalities are not limited to issues of affordability or tenure but are also embedded in broader patterns of social and spatial exclusion—disproportionately affecting low-income and younger households.

The remaining part of the chapter is organized as follows: The subsequent section is an extension of the analysis, addressing structural and emerging dimensions of housing inequality that have not been adequately explored in mainstream debates. The third section analyses inequalities in access to housing across countries and population groups. The fourth section explores the burden of housing costs and how it disproportionately affects different income segments. The fifth section examines the growing financialization of housing and its transformation into an asset class, highlighting its implications for wealth-based inequality. The chapter concludes with a set of policy recommendations aimed at mitigating housing-related inequalities and fostering a more inclusive housing system.

2. ADDRESSING OVERLOOKED DIMENSIONS OF HOUSING INEQUALITY

While this chapter offers an inclusive and multidimensional analysis of the core dynamics underpinning housing inequalities, several critical dimensions have gained increasing prominence in recent year. Urban segregation and spatial inequalities, climate change and housing access, housing problems faced by migrant households, and the role of financial investors on housing markets are among the increasingly prominent dimensions of the contemporary housing crisis and have received increasing attention in the literature. This sub-section briefly touches on each of these themes, extending the existing framework of analysis and providing a more holistic perspective on the multi-layered nature of housing inequality.

2.1. Urban Segregation and Spatial Inequalities

In addition to socioeconomic disparities, spatial inequalities are a key aspect of housing inequality. Urban processes such as segregation, gentrification, and suburbanization greatly impact house prices and affordability. Low-income and marginalized groups are often concentrated in peripheral or poorly connected urban areas, where access to jobs, education, and public services is limited. Conversely, central urban areas undergoing gentrification often displace long-standing residents due to rising housing costs and revaluation pressures. These spatial dynamics reproduce socioeconomic inequalities across urban spaces, creating "housing deserts" and uneven geographies of opportunity (Massey and Denton, 1988; Wacquant, 2008; Rodríguez-Pose and Storper, 2020). While our chapter primarily focuses on disparities in affordability and ownership, the spatial processes involved merit further investigation in future work, especially given their growing relevance in rapidly urbanizing societies.

2.2. Climate Change and Housing Access

Climate change is emerging as a critical force that is reshaping housing markets and deepening existing inequalities. The increasing frequency of extreme weather events, rising temperatures, and environmental degradation pose significant challenges to the physical safety and durability of houses. These challenges also have direct implications for housing affordability and access, particularly for low-income groups. Households residing in climate-vulnerable regions frequently encounter elevated housing expenses, displacement risks, and deteriorating living conditions, largely attributable to inadequate infrastructure and a paucity of climate resilience measures. Concurrently, endeavors to encourage energy-efficient and climate-resilient housing—including building retrofits, more stringent energy standards, and green zoning policies—have the potential to inadvertently escalate housing costs if not designed with equity in mind. These developments underscore the necessity to conceptualize housing not solely as a social and economic issue, but also as a climate justice concern, wherein environmental sustainability and equity objectives must be pursued in unison (Klein, 2014; Bouzarovski, 2014).

2.3. Migration and Housing Inequality

The phenomenon of migrants and refugees being among the most vulnerable groups in housing markets is well-documented. A unique set of structural barriers that extend beyond affordability is a hallmark of this demographic. Empirical research has demonstrated that migrants face heightened exposure to discrimination within both formal and informal rental markets, consequently impeding their access to adequate housing irrespective of their income or employment status (Ager and Strang, 2008; Elsinga and Hoekstra, 2015). A significant number of recently arrived migrants find themselves confined to overcrowded dwellings, often shared with individuals who are not related to them or with multiple families. This situation gives rise to several serious concerns regarding health, privacy, and well-being (Kissoon, 2010). Inadequate shelter, ranging from temporary accommodations to deteriorated housing stock, is another pervasive challenge, particularly among asylum seekers and undocumented individuals who are excluded from state support mechanisms (Phillimore and Goodson, 2006). These housing vulnerabilities are further exacerbated by legal insecurity, language barriers, and limited knowledge of tenant rights, thereby reinforcing the marginalization of migrants in urban settings. Addressing housing inequality, therefore, necessitates not only the improvement of affordability, but also the confrontation of the institutional and social mechanisms that engender exclusion and spatial segregation.

2.4. The Role of Financial Investors

In recent years, the growing role of institutional investors—including real estate investment trusts (REITs), private equity firms, and global asset managers—has emerged as a key driver of housing market transformation. These actors frequently acquire extensive portfolios of residential properties, particularly in urban centers, and prioritize short-term financial returns over long-term affordability or societal benefits. A body of research indicates that the entry of such entities into housing markets tends to reduce the availability of affordable rental units, increase prices and rents, and contribute to displacement and gentrification, particularly in low-income neighborhoods (Fields, 2015; Aalbers, 2017; Christophers, 2024). In contrast to conventional landlords, institutional investors operate on a large scale, employ financial instruments to extract value from housing, and frequently engage in lobbying efforts to advocate for deregulation. This phenomenon signifies a progression in the housing financialization trend, whereby residences are progressively regarded as revenue-generating assets rather than mere places of habitation. Such dynamics necessitate increased regulatory oversight and a re-evaluation of housing policy frameworks that permit large-scale accumulation of residential property by financial firms.

In addition to the structural and contextual dimensions of housing inequality discussed above, inequalities that arise according to how individuals and households access the housing market are also very important. The subsequent section will provide a detailed exposition on the way accessibility is influenced by economic factors within the housing market. This analysis will encompass the interplay between house prices, rental costs, and their correlation with household incomes.

3. ACCESS-BASED INEQUALITIES

The first step in understanding the inequalities observed in the housing market is to understand who can afford housing[1]. In this context, this section will focus on the course of house prices over time and how they vary in comparison to income/rent levels. The fact that house prices rise faster than both incomes and rents significantly undermine access to homeownership, particularly for low-income and younger households, and contributes to structural exclusion within the housing market.

The most evident indicator of the unfolding housing crisis is the surge in house prices. In OECD countries, real house prices have risen by an average of 40% over the past decade. Although there is a break in this upward trend in 2024, the level of house prices remains elevated above the pre-pandemic levels.

Figure 1. Real House Prices in Selected Countries, 2000-2024, 2000=100

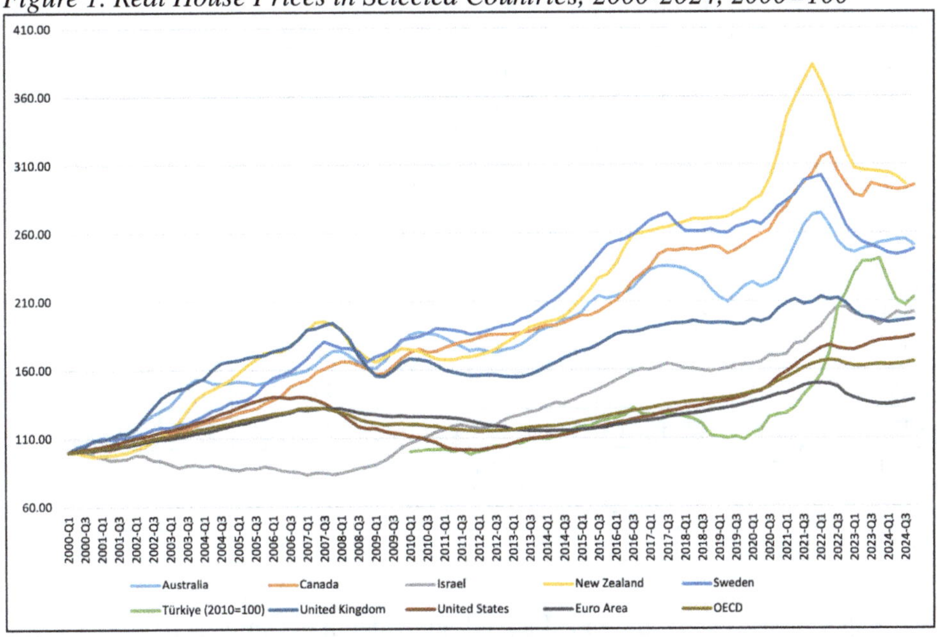

Source: OECD (2025), Prices: Analytical House Price Indicators

Figure 1 shows the trajectory of real house prices (based on 2000=100) in selected countries over the period 2000-2024. Across both developed and developing countries, the rise in house prices over the last 24 years has been quite significant. It is noteworthy that this upward trend accelerated especially after 2020. While the rapid increases in New Zealand, Canada and the United States stand out, Turkey has diverged significantly from other countries with its high price increase after 2019.

This divergence can be attributed to inflationary pressures and the depreciation of the Turkish lira. On the other hand, the Euro Area and OECD averages exhibit a more moderate but steady upward trend.

Table 1. Change in Nominal House Prices in Selected Countries (%)

	2013	2019	2020	2021	2022	2023			2012	2020	2023
Austria	**5.2**	**3.4**	**7**	**11.8**	**10.3**	**-2.8**		**Vienna**	**86.4**	**124.1**	**148.1**
Czechia	0.1	8.9	9	25.8	6.9	-1.1		Copenhagen	77.9	134.3	156.3
Denmark	0.8	2.8	4.3	11.7	1	-2.3		Paris	103.4	134.3	126.7
Estonia	10.7	-31.8	6	15.1	22.2	5.9		Athens	132.9	119	169.2
France	-1.2	3.2	5.6	6.7	6.3	-0.7		Budapest	81.3	221.8	304.8
Germany	3	6.8	7.4	11.3	9	-4.1		Rome	113.5	86.1	87.7
Greece	-10.9	7.2	4.3	7.3	11.7	13.8		Dublin	66.7	124.2	154
Hungary	-3	18.4	9.1	11.9	21.5	8		Amsterdam	91.5	162.1	190.2
Ireland	1.3	2.4	0.4	8.2	12.3	7.4		Barcelona	100.2	125.4	145.1
Lithuania	1.2	6.8	7.3	16.1	19	9.8		Stockholm	76.3	116.2	127
Luxembourg	5	10.1	14.5	13.9	9.6	-9.1		Reykjavik	77.2	152.8	224.8
Netherlands	-6.6	6.9	7.9	15.2	13.6	-1.9		Oslo	83.7	139.6	149.3
Poland	-1	10.6	11.7	9.6	10.4	6.1		London	71.5	113.8	122.6
Slovakia	-0.9	7.5	11.9	23.7	21.3	-6		Canberra	92.2	124.9	157.6
Spain	-5.8	3.2	-1.1	2.1	5	3.9		Sydney	71.9	121.8	155.3
Sweden	3.4	2.6	6.7	16.9	4.3	-9.9		Tokyo	94.5	110	136.5
Iceland	5.8	4.4	6.4	12.5	21	7.8		Istanbul	55	157.6	1139.9
UK	2.6	1	5.1	10.2	10.1	0.4		New York	88.8	131.4	167.3
Russia	7.3	5.9	7.3	21.6	22.8	7.8					
Turkey	12.7	10	30.4	59.7	167.9	75.5					

Source: Hypotstat, 2024

Supporting this general trend, Tables 1 and 2 detail the annual changes in nominal house prices at the country and city levels. Table 1 shows that many European countries experienced remarkable increases in house prices in the post-2020 period. Especially in 2021 and 2022, double-digit increases stand out in countries such as Hungary, Lithuania and Slovakia as well as Turkey. Table 2 shows the evolution of house price indices (2015=100) in selected cities over time. The data show that price increases were quite high in cities such as Istanbul, Budapest and Reykjavik, whereas increases were more limited in cities such as Rome and Paris. These findings suggest that the increasing price pressures in the housing market in the post-pandemic period have been characterized by significant variations not only at the national but also at the urban level.

Another key indicator of the deepening of the housing crisis is the upward trend in rental prices. Figure 2 shows the course of real rental prices in selected countries in the post-2010 period. While the data indicates a parallel increase in rent levels and house prices in almost all countries, it is noteworthy that rent increases have generally exhibited a more moderate and gradual pattern. The most pronounced increases are observed in the Baltic countries, particularly Estonia and Lithuania. In these nations, rental prices nearly tripled from 2010 to 2025 (Estonia: around 380, Lithuania: exceeding 280).

Figure 2. Rent Prices in Selected Countries

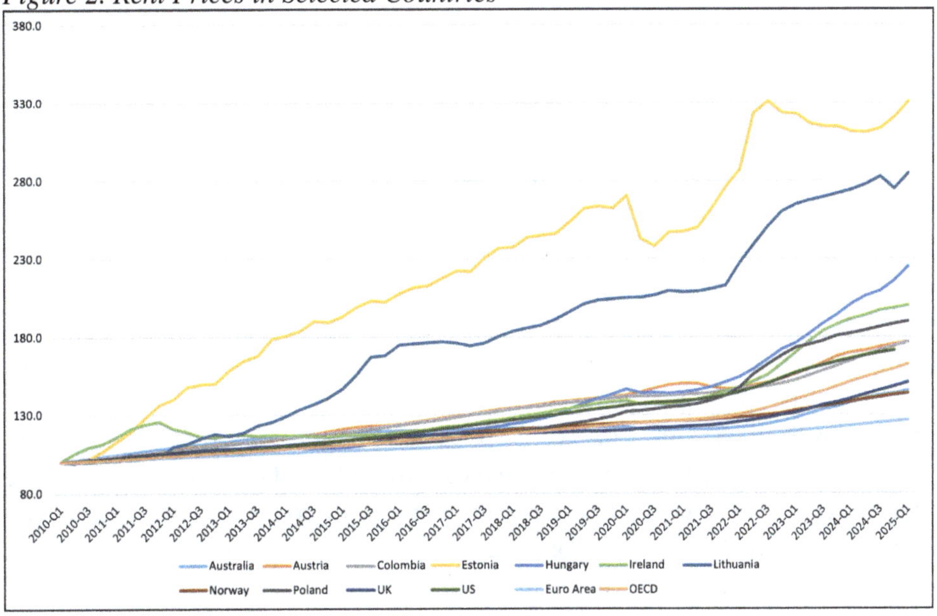

Source: OECD (2025), Prices: Analytical House Price Indicators

An acceleration in rental prices is also evident in the United States and the United Kingdom, particularly after 2021. Although OECD and Eurozone averages follow a more stable and flatter course, there has been a significant increase in these regions after 2021. These trends reveal that the housing crisis is intensifying not only in terms of access to property but also in terms of housing costs. Rising rental costs impose substantial financial burdens, particularly on low- and middle-income households, and exacerbate housing insecurity.

Figure 3. Standardized Price-to-Rent Ratio

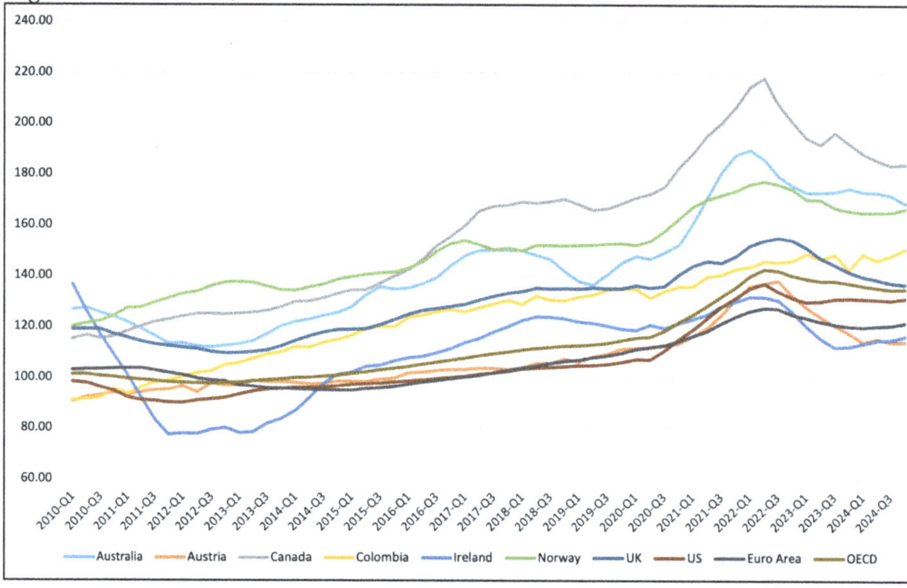

Source: OECD (2025), Prices: Analytical House Price Indicators

Figures 1 and 2 show that house prices have been rising rapidly while rent increases have lagged this acceleration. This divergence has led to a significant increase in the price-to-rent ratio over time. The price-to-rent ratio quantifies the relationship between housing prices and rental values by dividing the nominal house price index by the rent price index. The price-to-rent ratio compares house prices to rental income and serves as a simple indicator of potential overvaluation. A rising ratio suggests that buying a house becomes less justified by rental returns. Figure 3 shows the evolution of "standardised price-to-rent ratios" in selected countries over the 2010-2024 period. The rise in the price-to-rent ratio over time suggests that house prices are rising disproportionately relative to rental incomes, suggesting a potential valuation problem in the housing market. This observation is consistent with housing being increasingly seen as an investment, while at the same time raising concerns about reduced accessibility for residential purposes. As shown in Figure 3, this trend is particularly pronounced in countries such as Canada, the United States, Ireland and Norway.

Figure 4. Standardized Price-to-Income Ratio

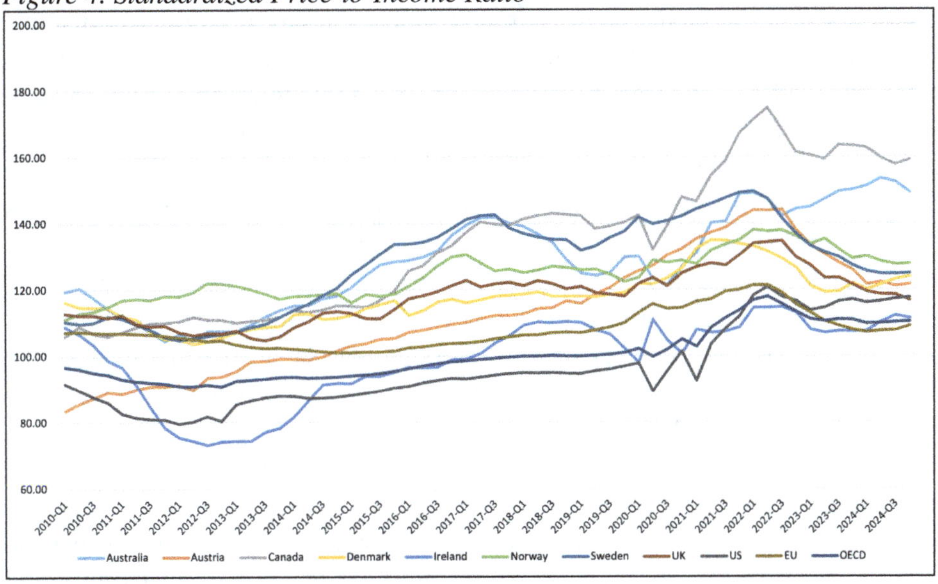

Source: OECD (2025), Prices: Analytical House Price Indicators

Measuring housing affordability is the subject of ongoing methodological debates in the literature. The most used indicators include the price-to-income ratio and the rent-to-income ratio, which allow for simple comparisons but may ignore within-country heterogeneity. As an alternative to these conventional measures, the residual income method (Stone, 2006; Kutty, 2005) focuses on the household's capacity to meet its basic needs by considering its residual income after housing expenditures. Another approach, shelter poverty (Stone, 2010), compares households' actual housing expenditures with a locally defined accessibility threshold, considering household structure and needs. While the descriptive analyses in our study are mainly based on conventional indicators (e.g. price-to-income ratio), we recognize that these different conceptual approaches have important implications for interpreting housing stress, especially for low-income groups.

The price-to-income ratio is defined as the ratio of the average price of a house to the average household income. The price-to-income ratio is widely recognized in the literature as one of the key indicators of housing affordability[2]. When house prices grow more rapidly than household incomes, the price-to-income ratio tends to increase, implying a decline in overall housing affordability (Adamopoulou et al., 2025). Figure 4 shows the evolution of price-to-income ratios for selected countries over 2010-2024. The data reveals that this ratio exhibits a remarkable rise after 2020, especially in countries such as the USA, Canada and Australia. The upward trend in the OECD average also shows that house prices have appreciated faster than income growth. This increase was particularly pronounced in the post-COVID-19 pandemic era. Many countries exhibit a peak around 2022, followed by a partial correction, likely reflecting the impact of rising interest rates and tighter monetary conditions after the pandemic-induced boom. Nevertheless, price-to-income ratios in most countries remain above their 2010 levels even after these corrections, highlighting the persistence of the problem.

A collective analysis of Figures 1-4 reveals a consistent pattern: house prices have increased at a significantly faster pace than both rental values and household incomes. Consequently, households have borrowed more and more to buy a home, resulting in a heavier mortgage servicing burden for many despite lower interest rates, which makes homeownership less accessible, particularly for first-time buyers. Rents have often increased faster than inflation. Overall, housing costs have been on a steep upward trend. This has been particularly challenging for households with low incomes or those that have experienced adverse income shocks or job losses, especially because of the pandemic.

While the increase in the price and rent ratio indicates that housing is increasingly demanded as an investment instrument and has become decoupled from rental dynamics, the rise in the price/income ratio emphasizes the declining accessibility of housing for residential purposes. Together, these two indicators suggest that there is a structural valuation problem and an affordability crisis in housing markets (Licchetta et al., 2025). This trend observed in the post-pandemic period is not confined to specific countries but is widespread and persistent across the OECD. Therefore, this transformation in the housing market stands out as a multidimensional problem that closely concerns not only economic but also social policies.

The consistent rise in house prices relative to incomes and rents not only exacerbates housing affordability but also renders property acquisition increasingly challenging. The direct consequence of this trend can be observed in the decline in homeownership rates in many countries. Figure 5 shows the change in homeownership rates between 2010 (the blue columns) and 2024 (the orange columns) in European Union Member States, demonstrating the overall difficulty of acquiring property in the housing market.

Figure 5. Homeownership rates across EU Member States, 2010 and 2024 (%)

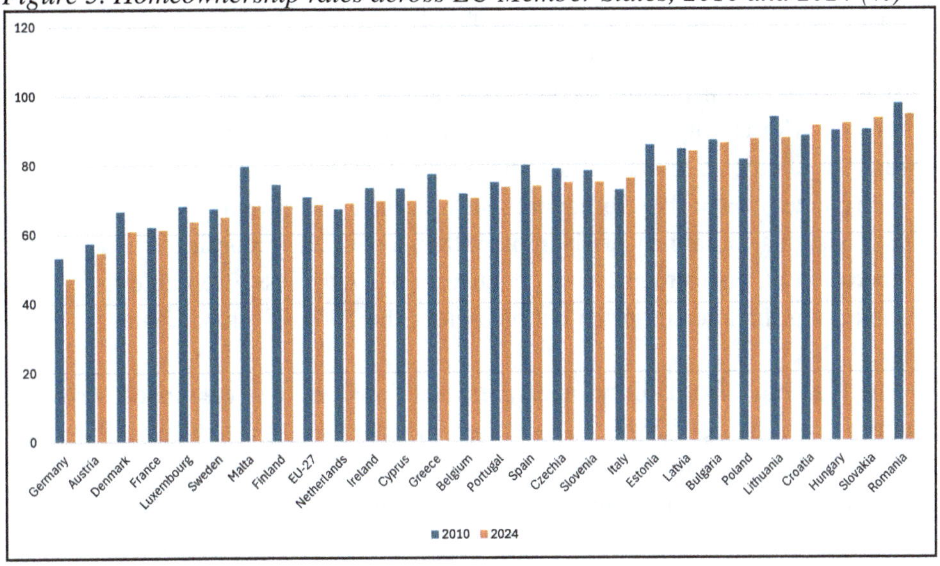

Source: Eurostat, EU-SILC survey

The general trend in Figure 5 shows that homeownership rates have declined in many countries. This decline is particularly pronounced in Western and Northern European countries such as Finland, Ireland, the Netherlands, Sweden and Belgium. This shows that it has become increasingly difficult for young and middle-income groups to become homeowners due to rising house prices and tightening credit conditions. Declining homeownership rates exacerbate asset-based inequalities. Housing is not only a means of shelter but also a fundamental element for wealth accumulation. Therefore, groups who cannot own a house are deprived not only of the security associated with housing but also of the opportunity for capital accumulation.

3.1 Housing Affordability Index

While declining homeownership rates highlight the visible outcomes of worsening affordability, it is also important to examine the structural mechanisms behind this trend. To this end, the Housing Affordability Index (HAI) provides a more comprehensive measure by integrating income levels and financing conditions across countries. A dataset prepared by Biljanovska et al. (2023), taking into account mortgage market dynamics and the characteristics of housing and household units, shows how the worst housing affordability crisis in more than a decade emerged after the pandemic (Igan, 2024). This approach focuses on the ability of a household to make regular mortgage payments on a typical house occupied by a normal-sized family without cutting back on other basic needs. Specifically, the housing affordability index calculates the ratio of actual household income to the income level required to qualify for a typical mortgage. This composite indicator offers a more integrated perspective by capturing both income and credit access dimensions of affordability. A housing affordability index above 100 indicates more affordable housing, while lower values indicate less affordable housing (Igan, 2024).

The pandemic and the subsequent return of inflation have triggered the world's worst housing affordability crisis in more than a decade. According to a newly developed dataset, on average across countries, housing is less affordable today than it was during the housing price bubble before the 2007-08 global financial crisis (Igan, 2024).

The Housing Affordability Index presented in Figure 6 is calculated across 40 countries over the last 50 years. It is noticeable that there is a sudden deterioration in affordability, especially in the few years after 2020. In the US, the world's largest economy, housing affordability fell from around 150 in 2021 to the mid-80s in 2024. In the United Kingdom, affordability index values fell from 105 in 2021 to below 70 in 2024. Similar declines have occurred in Austria, Canada, Hungary, Poland, Portugal, Turkey and the Baltic states. This represents a sudden reversal of the generally improving affordability of the last few decades. As with resurgent inflation, this dramatic change of direction has had an enormous psychological impact on many households.

Figure 6. Housing Affordability Index

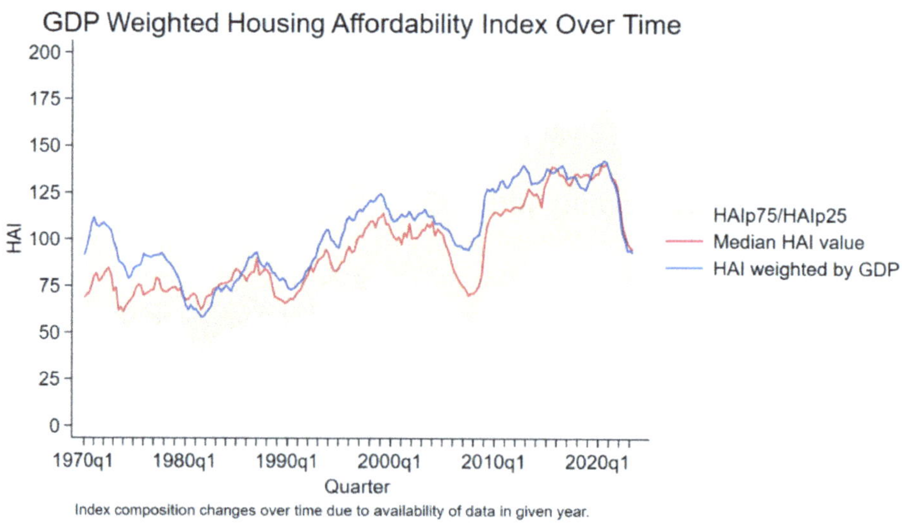

Source: Biljanovska et al. (2023)

The significant increase in house prices in many countries during the COVID-19 recession marks a remarkable and novel situation, in contrast to the housing market stagnation usually observed in past economic downturns (Ahir et al., 2022; Igan et al. 2022). This can be attributed to a combination of demand and supply factors, including quarantine-induced restrictions on construction. The unexpectedly rapid increase in house prices has led to concerns about an impending correction. When central banks around the world started raising interest rates to fight inflation, many observers expected the correction to finally materialize. House prices fell somewhat, but much less than expected, even as mortgage rates rose.

Figure 7. Average Housing Affordability Index by Country

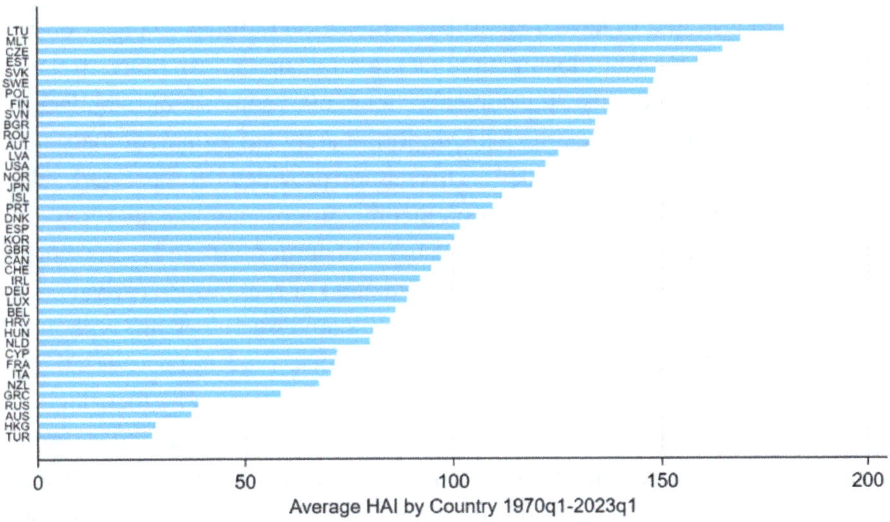

Source: Biljanovska et al. (2023)

Figure 7 shows the average HAI across countries, taking into account many different country characteristics. When countries are ranked according to the average HAI level as shown in Figure 7, Eastern European countries (e.g. Baltic countries, Czech Republic, Poland) top the list with index values approaching or exceeding 150. This may reflect traditionally high homeownership rates and a relatively old housing stock that tends to be of lower quality and cheaper. Economies at the other end of the spectrum form a mixed group: Australia, Hong Kong, Russia and Turkey have average index values below 50, indicating serious affordability challenges. (Biljanovska et al. (2023).

While the housing affordability indicators provide a framework for the overall economic accessibility of housing, the subsequent section will examine the tangible effects of this access on daily living costs and analyze the inequalities that arise in the context of housing cost burden.

4. COST BURDEN INEQUALITY

In an environment characterized by limited access to housing, owning or renting a home represents only one dimension of housing-related inequalities. The financial burden of housing costs on household budgets creates a significant vulnerability, particularly for low-income groups. In the last two decades, as house prices have increased in most OECD countries, households have allocated a significant and growing portion of their budgets to housing expenses. The issue of unaffordable housing has been demonstrated to have a significant impact on families living at or below the poverty line. It is a well-documented fact that housing expenditures frequently constitute the initial and most substantial component of a household's budget, with low-income households allocating a disproportionately large share of their income to housing expenses (Hick et al. 2024). This section provides a comparative analysis of the impact of housing-related costs on income groups and housing types.

Figure 8 illustrates the households' housing cost burden, defined as the mortgage burden (principal repayment and interest payments) or rent burden (private market and subsidized rent), as a share of disposable income by ownership type in 2022 (OECD, 2025). One advantage of this measure is that it accurately reflects the financial strain that households experience due to housing costs by focusing on the percentage of disposable income spent on housing costs. (OECD, 2021; Adamopoulou et al. 2025). The term 'housing costs' is a broad category encompassing two distinct concepts. Firstly, it includes mortgage-related expenses, such as principal repayment and interest payments. Secondly, it encompasses rental costs, whether for private market properties or subsidized rental housing.

Figure 8. Households' housing cost burden (mortgage and rent costs)

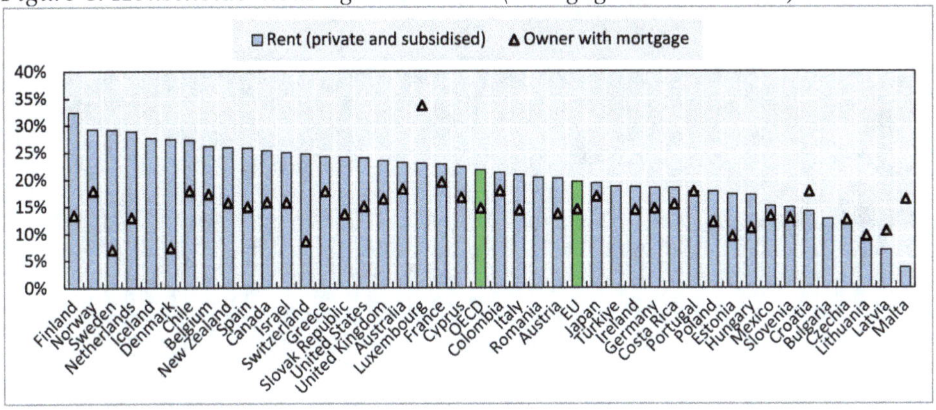

Source: OECD (2025), OECD Affordable Housing Database

While indicators based on asset prices reflect long-term trends, the housing cost burden ratio measures the immediate financial pressure households experience due to housing expenditures. Figure 8 shows the ratio of housing costs to household income for both renters (blue bars) and homeowners with mortgages (black triangles). The data reveal that in most OECD countries, renters face a higher cost burden than homeowners with mortgages. In particular, in countries such as Finland, Norway, Sweden and the Netherlands, renters spend 25-30 per cent of their income on housing, while the cost for owners with mortgages is typically around 15-20 per cent. These countries typically have significant rental markets, where demand for housing can exceed supply, especially in urban areas. Conversely, in countries such as Malta, Latvia and Lithuania, this burden is quite low. In Turkey, renters bear a cost burden close to the OECD average, while the burden of homeowners with mortgages is lower.

Figure 9. Households' housing cost overburden (mortgage and rent costs) on low-income

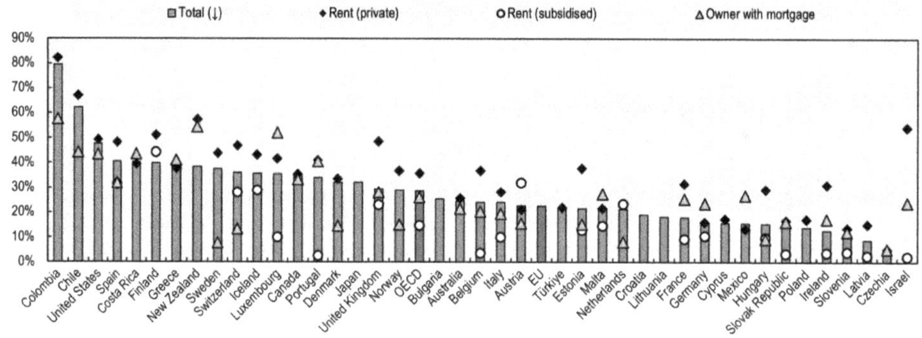

Source: OECD (2025), OECD Affordable Housing Database

While the average housing cost burden provides a broad picture of affordability pressures, it is also important to examine more severe cases. In this context, the housing cost overburden rate offers insight into the proportion of households facing acute financial strain from housing expenses. This indicator measures the proportion of the population living in households that allocate at least 40% of their disposable income to housing costs, including rent, mortgage interest payments, and utilities such as water, electricity, gas, and heating[3]. This indicator is critical in revealing how the housing affordability problem is concentrated on low-income groups.

The data show both the total housing expenditure burden (blue bars) and separate burdens for private rent (black diamonds), subsidized rent (white circles) and mortgaged homeowners (black triangles). As Figure 9 illustrates, the housing cost burden for low-income renters is quite high in many countries. In countries such as Chile, Colombia and Costa Rica, the share of housing costs in income for low-income renters (especially those renting in the private market) is as high as 40 per cent. For these groups, housing is a significant economic burden and increases the risk of poverty. Overall, Figure 9 shows that low-income groups are particularly vulnerable in the private rental market and emphasizes the importance of social housing supply, rent control policies and income support interventions.

To better understand how housing costs are distributed across income levels, Figure 10 presents the share of housing expenditure in disposable household income by income group in the EU-27 over the 2010–2024 period. This distribution reveals that the housing cost burden is disproportionately concentrated on low-income households, demonstrating the inequitable distribution of housing affordability problems.

The data are divided into three categories: total population, households with incomes above 60 per cent of the median income, and households with incomes below 60 per cent. The most striking pattern in Figure 10 is that the housing cost burden of low-income households (those below 60 per cent of median income) is consistently high, with their share remaining close to or above 40 per cent for most of the period. Between 2010 and 2024, low-income groups had to allocate 38-42 per cent of their disposable income for housing, while high-income groups only allocated around 15-19 per cent. This difference shows that housing accessibility is unfair and that the housing crisis has particularly affected low-income households. Although the housing cost share of low-income groups declined slightly after 2016, it remains significantly higher than for other income groups, highlighting the disproportionate pressure on vulnerable households.

Figure 10. Share of housing costs in disposable household income by income group, EU-27

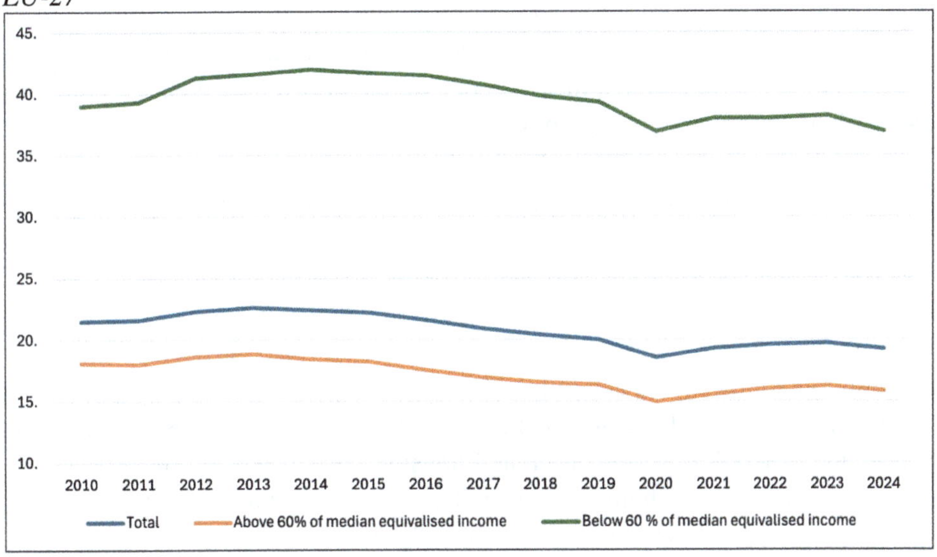

Source: Eurostat (2025)

For the total population, the housing cost burden remains relatively stable at around 20-22 per cent until 2019, then declines slightly. Households earning above 60 per cent of the median income have the lowest burden, fluctuating between 15 and 19 per cent.

These findings are supported by a growing body of research showing that an increasing proportion of households in the US and the UK face high housing cost burdens (Tetlow, 2018) and that just over half of poor renter families in the US, particularly Black and Hispanic families, spend more than 50 per cent of their income on housing (Desmond, 2018). Similar patterns have also been observed across

Europe, particularly in Italy, Germany, Spain and France (Deidda, 2015; Lee et al., 2022). These high proportions indicate that minor fluctuations in housing prices and rents will exert a substantial influence on nonhousing consumption and household well-being (Quigley and Raphael, 2004). Overall, these rates show that the housing cost burden has created structural and permanent pressure on low-income groups and reveal the cost inequality of the housing crisis. Considering that income growth has been limited and housing prices and rents have risen rapidly, especially in the post-pandemic period, this difference has further deepened social and economic vulnerabilities.

To comprehensively analyze inequalities in housing costs, it is essential to consider not only the share of housing expenditure in income but also the distribution of various forms of housing tenure (ownership, mortgage ownership, renting) across countries. Housing inequality is not only related to whether or not one owns a house but also to who owns with debt and who owns without debt. Debt-free home ownership increases wealth accumulation and economic security, whereas renting or mortgaged home ownership indicates more vulnerable groups. Figure 11 presents the distribution of housing tenure types in EU Member States in 2024. It categorizes households into homeowners (with or without mortgages) and renters, and countries are ranked from left to right based on decreasing proportions of renters. There are significant cross-country disparities in home ownership. In Eastern European countries - notably Romania, Slovakia, Croatia, Croatia and Hungary - rates of home ownership without mortgages are extremely high, reaching 92.8 per cent in Romania. This is largely the result of housing privatization policies implemented in the post-communist period and limited access to mortgage markets (OECD, 2025). A similar pattern can be observed in the case of Estonia: the post-privatization conversion of publicly subsidized rental housing into ownership on a large scale and policies prioritizing home ownership have made Estonia a typical homeowner society for many years (Kahrik and Pastak, 2023).

In contrast, Western and Northern European countries have more diverse housing markets. Countries such as Germany, Austria and Denmark have higher rates of renting; for example, 52.8 per cent of households in Germany are renters, while only 24 per cent own their entire home. In countries such as Sweden (49.6 per cent) and Denmark (48.4 per cent), on the other hand, home ownership with a mortgage is more prominent, indicating more developed mortgage markets and more diverse access to finance. Overall, this figure demonstrates that European housing systems are divided into two main structural orientations: Eastern Europe is dominated by debt-free ownership-based systems, while Western and Northern Europe is characterized by diversified structures with a higher proportion of tenure and mortgage ownership.

Figure 11. Distribution of population by type of tenure, EU Member States, 2024 (%)

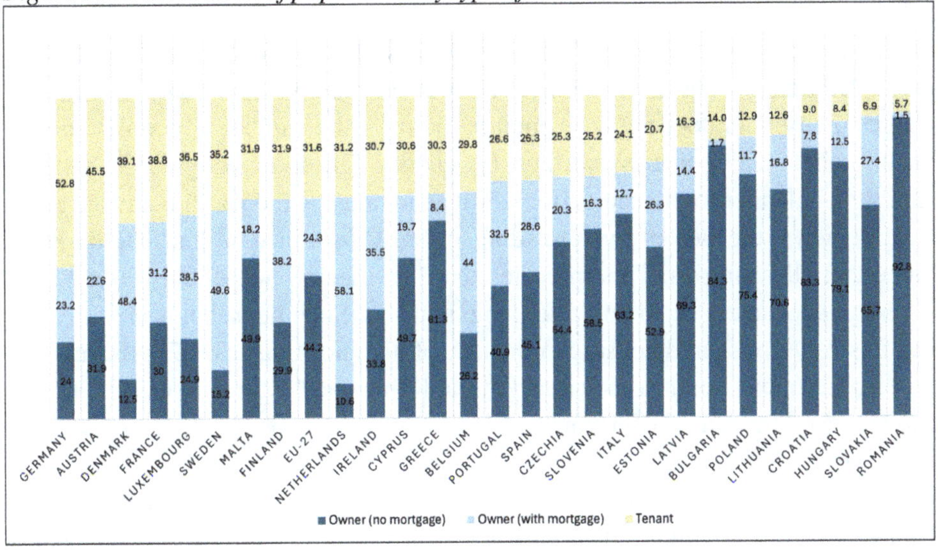

Source: Eurostat, EU-SILC survey

Cross-country differences in housing markets are largely shaped by structural factors, such as land use regulations (e.g., density limits or building permits), levels of tenancy protection (contract length, rent increase limits), and privatization policies in post-socialist countries. These factors exert a direct influence on the supply of housing, the formation of its price, and the composition of its ownership.

4.1 Social Context of Housing Inequality

The data analyzed so far has demonstrated the financial impact of housing cost inequality, particularly on low-income households. However, housing inequalities are not limited to economic pressures; they also manifest themselves through the physical quality of living spaces. As mentioned earlier, low-income households spend a larger share of their income on housing: not only are they more likely to be overburdened by housing costs, but they are also more likely to live in poor-quality housing. They may not be able to afford regular maintenance or upgrading of their housing and may also find it too expensive to move to better-quality housing. Lack of access to good quality housing is often associated with poor access to health, education, broadband internet and good job opportunities (OECD, 2021). This can have long-lasting impacts, including on the lifetime incomes of young people who grow up in low-quality housing or have limited access to education or health services. The COVID-19 pandemic has reignited concerns about overcrowding among policymakers, as overcrowded conditions make it difficult for residents to effectively self-isolate, putting people at greater risk of contracting and spreading infectious diseases.

Figure 12 shows the rates of household overcrowding in EU countries according to different segments of the income distribution. Overcrowding is a situation where a household does not have enough room for the number of people living in the household and indicates poor housing quality. This indicator provides a strong structural indicator for housing affordability and housing inequalities. As the graph clearly shows, the rate of overcrowding in the lowest-income households is the highest in all countries. This indicates that low-income households do not have access to adequately sized and affordable housing. Such households are forced to live in smaller or shared housing in the face of high housing costs. For example, in Eastern European countries such as Latvia, Romania, Bulgaria, Poland, Slovakia and Hungary, the rate of overcrowding in the lowest income group ranges between 30-50 per cent. This indicates that both the physical and economic accessibility of housing are very poor. In the highest income group (triangular symbols), the rate is below 5 per cent in almost all countries. This shows that access to housing quality and living space is directly related to income.

Figure 12. Overcrowding rates in households across the income distribution

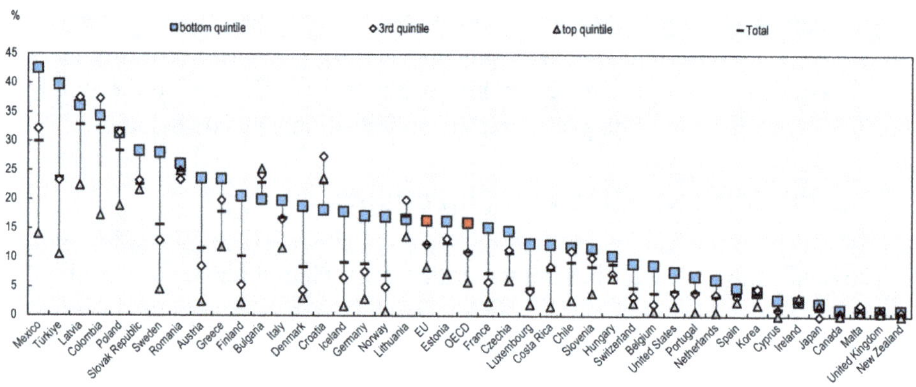

Source: OECD (2025), OECD Affordable Housing Database

Figure 12 demonstrates that housing inequalities are deep not only in terms of ownership but also in terms of quality of life. There are significant differences between individuals living in the same country in terms of living space, privacy and physical living conditions. Overcrowding is not only a housing quality problem but also has multidimensional effects on educational achievement, health, mental well-being and social exclusion. This difference between the lowest and highest income groups shows that housing has started to turn from a basic right into a privilege that can be purchased with income. As emphasized by Wetzstein (2017), unless measures are taken, approximately half a billion urban households around the world will have to live in crowded and inadequate living conditions in the next decade, indicating that the mismatch between housing costs and incomes in metropolises will further deepen.

The fact that housing has become a privilege deeply affects not only low-income groups but also young adults. The rise in housing prices, tightening credit conditions and the lack of adequate social housing support make it increasingly difficult for young people to build independent lives. In this context, Figure 13 shows the proportion of 25–34-year-olds living with their parents in 2024 and highlights whether this proportion has increased (green) or decreased (light blue) compared to 2014. The high proportion of 25–34-year-olds living with their parents is an important indicator that young adults struggle to access the housing market. The increasing cost of residential real estate has the potential to impede the ability of young individuals to acquire property, and there is documented evidence of a decline in homeownership and a postponement of independent living among the youth population throughout Europe (Hick et al. 2022).

Figure 13 shows that the proportion of young adults living with their families increased significantly compared to 2014 in Ireland (+20.5), Cyprus (+13.6), Poland (+9.7), Spain (+8.7), Croatia (+6.6), Turkey (+4.1). This shows that housing affordability has worsened over the last decade. Rising rental prices, mortgage costs, job insecurity and low wages delay young people from entering the housing market. This indicator also clearly shows intergenerational housing inequality. While middle-aged and older generations are often debt-free homeowners, younger generations fail to become homeowners and are forced into a dependent lifestyle or are overburdened by excessive rent.

Figure 13. People aged 25-34 living with their parents in 2024 and change since 2024 (%)

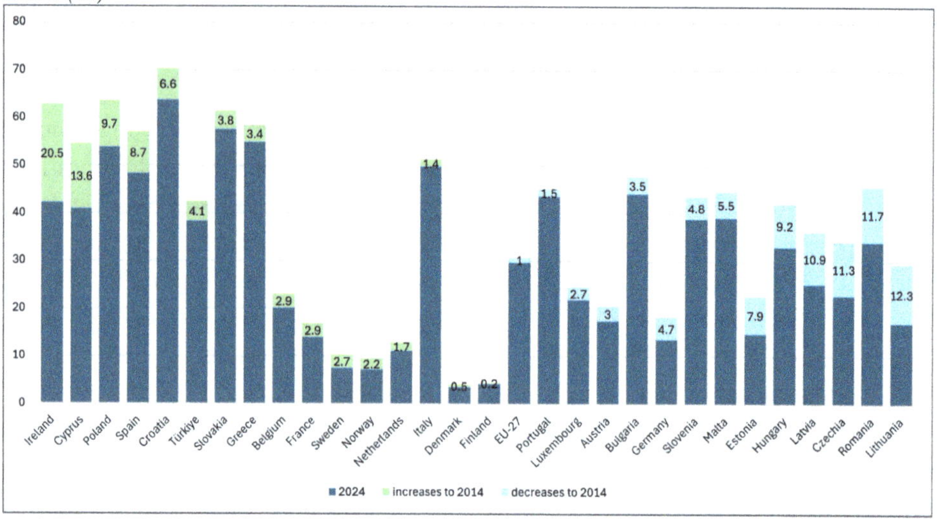

Source: Eurostat

In countries such as Italy (50 per cent), Greece (41 per cent) and Slovakia (56 per cent) the traditional family structure has historically kept the rate high, although the increase in recent years can also be explained by economic factors. In contrast, in countries with strong welfare state practices, such as the Nordic countries (Denmark, Finland, Norway, Sweden, Norway, Sweden), Germany and the Netherlands, these rates are quite low (below 10 per cent) and have not increased significantly since 2014. In these countries, policies that facilitate access to housing for young people (such as student housing, social housing, and rental assistance) are relatively more effective.

4.2 The Role of Government and Social Policies

The housing vulnerabilities experienced by low-income and young groups in particular stem not only from market dynamics but also from the gradual withdrawal of the state from housing and the weakening of social assistance. This structural transformation makes housing inequalities more persistent and intergenerational. In this context, the change in the stock of social rented housing and the course of public housing investments over time is critical to understanding how the role of the state in the housing market has evolved and its impact on inequalities. In this context, the evolution of social rental housing stock and public housing investments provides critical insight into the changing role of the state in the housing market and its implications for inequality.

Figures 14 and 15 illustrate a pronounced decline in the availability of social rental housing and a marked slowdown in public investment in housing since 2010. Although there was a modest upturn between 2020 and 2022, it has fallen short of addressing the growing demand for affordable and adequate housing.

Figure 14 represents social rental housing as a percentage of the total housing stock in 2010 and 2022. Social rental housing is one of the most important instruments to facilitate low- and middle-income households to find a place in the housing market. Figure 14 shows that the stock of social housing varies dramatically across countries: In most OECD countries, social housing typically accounts for less than 10 per cent of the total housing stock. However, in Austria, Denmark and the Netherlands, it represents an important "third sector" in the housing market, accounting for more than 20 per cent of all housing. In these countries, social housing policies have long been institutionalized and access to housing for low-income groups is more strongly protected.

Figure 14. Social rental housing stock trends over time

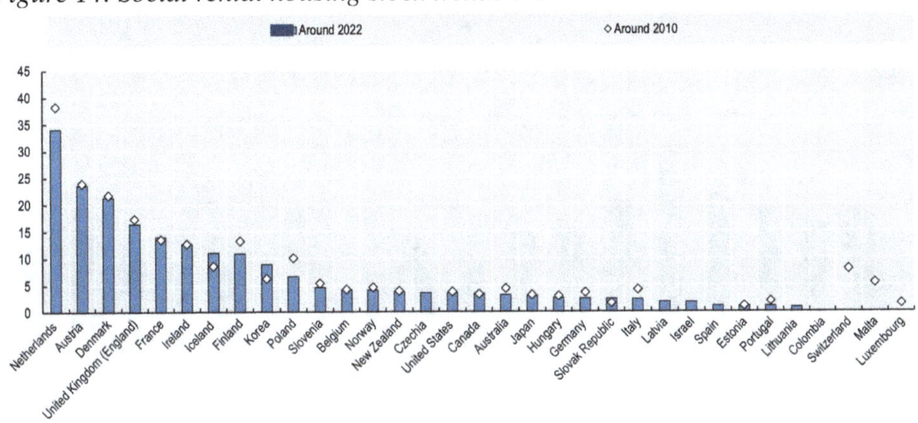

Source: OECD (2025), OECD Affordable Housing Database

In contrast, in countries such as Hungary, Romania, Croatia, and Lithuania, the share of social housing is almost negligible—below 1 per cent. However, these countries also exhibit some of the highest homeownership rates in Europe, which is largely a legacy of post-socialist housing privatization. As a result, low-income households without property ownership are often left with limited alternatives and are exposed to significant price pressures in underdeveloped private rental markets. In most countries for which data are available, the relative size of the social housing stock has declined since 2010, partly due to reduced public investment in housing and, in some countries, the sale of social housing to tenants. This suggests that the supply of publicly subsidized housing is shrinking, making housing accessibility more difficult, particularly for low-income groups.

The size of the social rented housing stock is an important reflection of national preferences as to whether housing is a market good or a social right. This deepens inequalities in the housing market in three main dimensions. Firstly, in the context of income-based segregation, low-income households are pushed out of the market in countries with low social housing supply and are often forced to live in overcrowded, low-quality and precarious housing (see Figure 12). Secondly, in terms of wealth inequality, the lack of social housing condemns low-income households to the private rental market, which increases the share of housing expenditure in income and virtually eliminates the possibility of wealth accumulation. Finally, in terms of intergenerational inequality, the decline in the supply of social housing makes it more difficult for young people and new households to access affordable housing, which is consistent with the increase in the proportion of young people living with their parents (see Figure 13).

Figure 15. Public investment in housing and community amenities

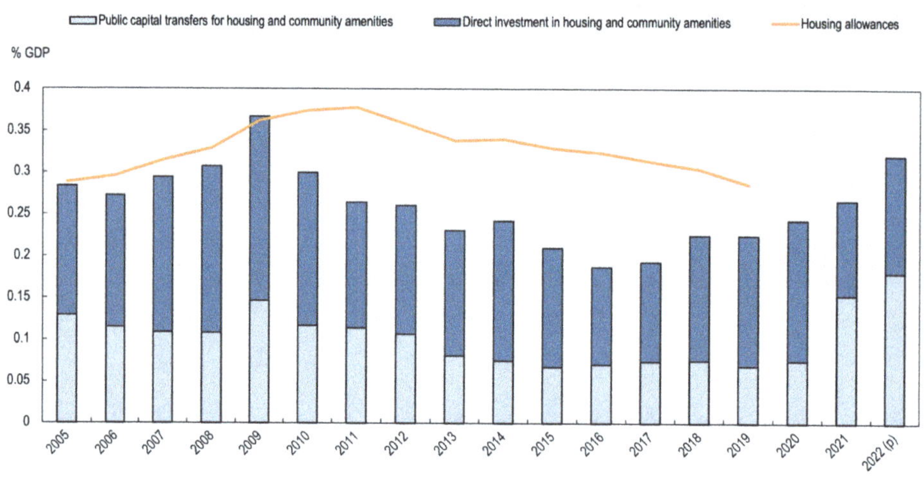

Source: OECD (2025), OECD Affordable Housing Database

While the contraction of the social housing stock has deepened housing inequalities, one of the main drivers behind this trend is the weakening of public investment in housing development over time. Figure 15 illustrates the evolution of the role of the state in housing policy by showing the evolution of public spending on housing and social infrastructure as a share of GDP over the period 2005-2022. Public investments, which increased until 2009, reached a peak after the global financial crisis and then declined significantly. This decline indicates that investments that would directly increase the housing supply, such as the construction of social housing, have been reduced. Between 2017 and 2022, public investments started to increase again, but most of this increase is due to capital transfers. This indicates a shift away from direct public housing production to projects supported by local authorities or the private sector. Housing allowances increased steadily until 2010 but then declined steadily in the following years. This shows that the demand side of the housing market is less and less supported and that households must cope with rising costs on their own. This general trend shows that housing affordability is less and less supported by public policies and more and more left to market conditions.

Building on the discussion of the cost burden on households and its social and policy implications, the following section explores the role of housing as a vehicle for wealth accumulation and examines how ownership structures contribute to the deepening of wealth-based inequalities.

5. WEALTH BASED INEQUALITY

Homeownership stands out as one of the most important instruments of wealth accumulation over the life cycle of individuals and across generations. Unlike financial assets in particular, housing has the potential to balance wealth inequalities beyond income distribution, as it is both more evenly distributed and more accessible for middle-income groups (OECD, 2021). However, the transformation observed in the housing market in recent years has led to a weakening of this stabilizing effect as housing has gradually evolved into an investment instrument rather than a means of shelter.

Although mortgage debt has declined in many economies, house prices continue to rise, suggesting a decoupling of credit and housing values. This disconnects points to a shift from debt-driven to wealth-driven demand, where accumulated housing wealth and intergenerational transfers play a growing role. Hochstenbach and Aalbers (2024) emphasize that the housing market has shifted from debt-driven dynamics to wealth-driven dynamics. In particular, the widespread use of buy-to-let investments, the reinvestment of accumulated housing wealth by elderly homeowners and the increase in intergenerational housing transfers are important examples of this transformation. This process creates new forms of inequality along both age, class and spatial axes, while reinforcing the advantages of wealthy and older groups and further restricting access to the housing market for younger and low-income populations.

As house prices continue to rise well above household incomes, home ownership is becoming increasingly dependent on existing wealth and family support (Long and Zhuang, 2025). This situation poses a serious threat, especially for first-time homeowners. Farha et al. (2025) show that in the US, median-priced housing is becoming increasingly unaffordable in more and more counties and that there has been a historical deterioration in housing affordability. Similarly, Australia has also experienced significant declines in homeownership rates, particularly among younger households (Burke et al., 2020; Cigdem-Bayram et al., 2025).

Intergenerational wealth transfers play an increasingly decisive role in this context. In particular, young people from high-income families can enter the housing market more easily, whereas those without access to this support face much greater financial pressures (BBC News, 2025; INED, 2023; Matha et al., 2025). Matha et al. (2025) emphasise that wealth transfers exceeding €100,000 increase the probability of home ownership by 10-15 percentage points. Similarly, Blickle and Brown (2019) reached similar results in Switzerland and Lux et al. (2021) in Czechia.

Figure 16. Mortgage debt to GDP (as %) in selected countries

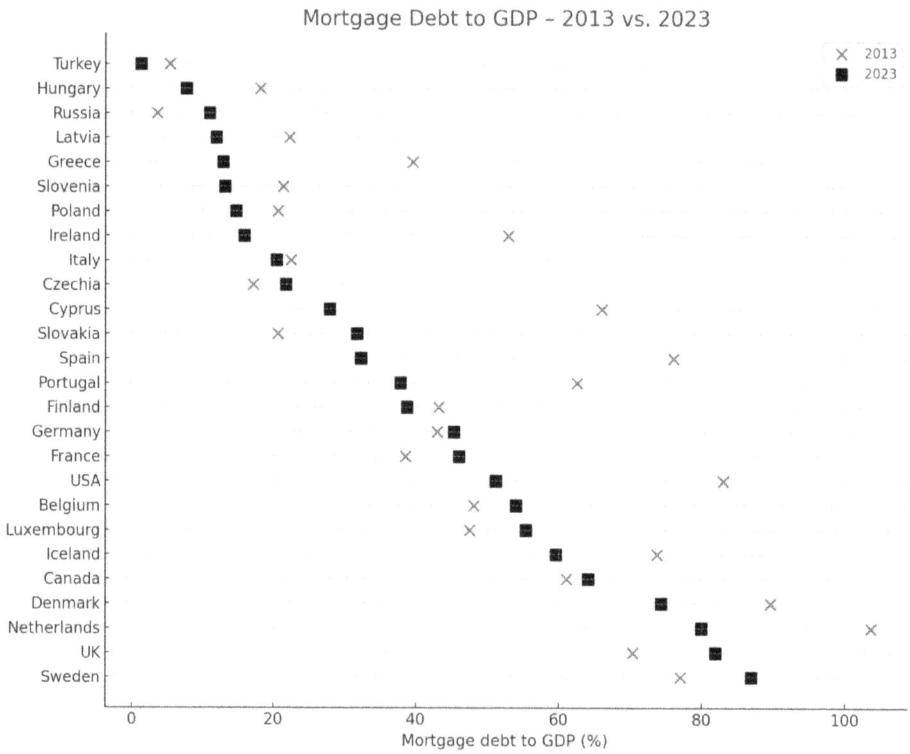

Source: Hypostat, 2024

These differences reflect not only the financial system structures, household borrowing tendencies and housing ownership patterns across countries, but also the extent to which wealth accumulation is financed by debt. Although the rate of unencumbered ownership is high in countries with low mortgage debt such as Turkey, it is noteworthy that this wealth accumulation has been achieved through the privatisation policies of previous generations. On the other hand, in developed countries, housing wealth is mostly financed through debt, which increases financial vulnerabilities.

In conclusion, the increasingly pronounced wealth-based inequalities in the housing market are fuelled by multilayered mechanisms such as ownership patterns, intergenerational transfers, debt dynamics and house price segregation. These dynamics profoundly affect not only the right to housing but also future wealth accumulation opportunities.

6. CONCLUSION AND POLICY IMPLICATIONS

This study investigates the multidimensional nature of the housing affordability crisis, which has increasingly become a driver and amplifier of economic inequality. Housing-related inequalities are examined through a multilayered framework that accounts for structural disparities across countries, intergenerational transmission of housing advantages, and income-based divergences among households. Firstly, the study examines the substantial rise in house prices and rents, which has rendered housing unaffordable. Secondly, it elucidates how the cost burden of housing has manifested and intensified not only across countries but also among different income and social groups. Thirdly, wealth-based factors, whose role in housing demand has gained prominence in recent years, are discussed.

Real house prices have risen rapidly in many OECD countries over the last decade. This increase was triggered by expansionary fiscal and monetary policies, especially in the aftermath of the global financial crisis (GFC) and COVID-19. Cheap credit facilities pushed house prices to historical highs, particularly in large cities, and made home ownership unaffordable for low-to-middle-income groups. As shown in the study, homeownership rates have been declining in many European countries, with some countries having rental rates in the 30-50 per cent range by 2024. The rising age at which young people leave home and the increasing proportion of 25–34-year-olds living with their families suggest that home ownership is increasingly being postponed and that intergenerational inequality of opportunity is deepening.

Price increases not only increase access but also the burden of housing on the budget. The jump in rental prices, especially in the post-2020 period, has made low- and middle-income households more vulnerable. OECD and Eurostat data show that low-income households spend more than 40 per cent of their income on housing. Moreover, high housing and rental prices condemn low-income households to live in poor quality and overcrowded housing. Another factor in the deepening of economic inequality, fuelled by the housing affordability crisis is the decline in the number of social housing units and the decreasing share of the public sector in housing investments.

In recent years, there has been growing evidence that house prices have started to be financed not by mortgage debt but by wealth accumulation and intergenerational transfers. The study indicates a surge in wealth-driven demand for housing, exemplified by buy-to-let investments, inheritances, and gifts, during a period of declining mortgage debt as a percentage of GDP while house prices have experienced upward growth. This creates systematic exclusion, especially for young people and low-income groups, while increasing the wealth accumulation of existing property owners (especially older and wealthier groups). Thus, housing inequality becomes a crisis linked not only to income but also to wealth.

Policy recommendations to reduce housing inequality require a holistic approach that encompasses both supply and demand-side interventions. Re-strengthening the supply of social housing is critical to providing public solutions to the housing needs of low- and middle-income households. Likewise, controlling rent increases and improving legal protection mechanisms for tenants can reduce vulnerabilities, especially in the private rental market. Given the increasing wealth dependence on access to housing, publicly supported financing opportunities for first-time homeowners and steps to regulate inheritance and wealth transfers can prevent intergenerational inequality. Moreover, to limit the impact of speculative and investment-oriented demands on the housing market, vacancy taxes and regulations against property concentration should be implemented. In recent years, institutional investors have become increasingly influential in housing markets. It has been demonstrated that actors such as private equity funds, pension funds, and real estate investment trusts (REITs) regard housing as a financial asset, thereby exacerbating existing inequalities in access to ownership. In markets where such actors are concentrated, rents are rising rapidly, home ownership rates are falling and housing is becoming more speculative. In conclusion, a policy vision that redefines housing as a fundamental right and is based not only on market perspective but also on principles of social justice is a prerequisite for the fight against inequality.

It is essential that policy recommendations consider the fact that the housing crisis does not affect all social groups equally. Young people delay home ownership and remain dependent on their families for long periods of time due to rising housing costs and barriers to entry; therefore, targeted subsidy programs, affordable rental housing models and publicly supported first home ownership initiatives are important to facilitate youth access to the housing market. Migrant households often face discrimination, overcrowded housing and inadequate housing conditions; therefore, strengthened legal protection mechanisms, inclusive housing policies and access to quality and accessible rental housing are critical to reduce their vulnerabilities. It is evident that for low-income households, augmenting the supply of social housing, enhancing the efficacy of housing assistance programs, and implementing more stringent rent control policies are imperative to alleviate the financial strain imposed by housing costs on household budgets and ensure housing security. The development of targeted policies that consider the unique vulnerabilities of these groups is a prerequisite for the establishment of a housing system based on social justice principles.

REFERENCES

Aalbers, M. (2016). *Financialization of housing*. Taylor & Francis. DOI: 10.4324/9781315668666

Aalbers, M. B. (2015). The great moderation, the great excess and the global housing crisis. *International Journal of Housing Policy*, *15*(1), 43–60. DOI: 10.1080/14616718.2014.997431

Aalbers, M. B. (2017). The variegated financialization of housing. *International Journal of Urban and Regional Research*, *41*(4), 542–554. DOI: 10.1111/1468-2427.12522

Adamopoulou, E., Kapopoulos, P., & Zekente, K.-M. (2025). *Alpha Bank Economic Research, April 2025*. Alpha Bank.

Ager, A., & Strang, A. (2008). Understanding integration: A conceptual framework. *Journal of Refugee Studies*, *21*(2), 166–191. DOI: 10.1093/jrs/fen016

Ahir, Hites, Nina Biljanovska, Chenxu Fu, Deniz Igan, and Prakash Loungani. (2022). Housing Prices Continue to Soar in Many Countries around the World. IMF Blog Chart of the Week, October 18.

BBC News. (2025). Bank of mum and dad 'helps half of first-time buyers'. Retrieved May 18, 2025, from https://www.bbc.co.uk/news/articles/cly1jzl9eedo

Biljanovska, N., Fu, M. C., & Igan, M. D. O. (2023). *Housing affordability: A new dataset*. International Monetary Fund.

Blickle, K., & Brown, M. (2019). Borrowing constraints, home ownership and housing choice: Evidence from intra-family wealth transfers. *Journal of Money, Credit and Banking*, *51*(2-3), 539–580. DOI: 10.1111/jmcb.12566

Bouzarovski, S. (2014). Energy poverty in the European Union: Landscapes of vulnerability. *Wiley Interdisciplinary Reviews. Energy and Environment*, *3*(3), 276–289. DOI: 10.1002/wene.89

Burke, T., Nygaard, C., & Ralston, L. (2020). Australian home ownership: past reflections, future directions. AHURI Final Report, (328).

Christophers, B. (2024). *Our lives in their portfolios: Why asset managers own the world*. Verso Books.

Cigdem-Bayram, M., Whelan, S., & Wood, G. (2025). The Bank of Mum & Dad–intergenerational transfers and first-time homeownership in Australia. *Review of Economics of the Household*, *23*(1), 1–29. DOI: 10.1007/s11150-024-09732-7

Deidda, M. (2015). Economic hardship, housing cost burden and tenure status: Evidence from EU-SILC. *Journal of Family and Economic Issues*, *36*(4), 531–556. DOI: 10.1007/s10834-014-9431-2

Desmond, M. (2018). Heavy is the house: Rent burden among the American urban poor. *International Journal of Urban and Regional Research*, *42*(1), 160–170. DOI: 10.1111/1468-2427.12529

Elsinga, M., & Hoekstra, J. (2015). The Janus face of homeownership-based welfare. *Critical Housing Analysis*, *2*(1), 32–41. DOI: 10.13060/23362839.2015.2.1.174

Farha, C., McCoy, J., & Rodziewicz, D. (2025). First-Time Homeownership Became Less Affordable Across Most of the United States in Recent Years. *Economic Bulletin*, •••, 1–4.

Fields, D. (2015). Contesting the financialization of urban space: Community organizations and the struggle to preserve affordable rental housing in New York City. *Journal of Urban Affairs*, *37*(2), 144–165. DOI: 10.1111/juaf.12098

Fields, D., & Uffer, S. (2016). The financialisation of rental housing: A comparative analysis of New York City and Berlin. *Urban Studies (Edinburgh, Scotland)*, *53*(7), 1486–1502. DOI: 10.1177/0042098014543704

Forrest, R., & Hirayama, Y. (2015). The financialisation of the social project: Embedded liberalism, neoliberalism and home ownership. *Urban Studies (Edinburgh, Scotland)*, *52*(2), 233–244. DOI: 10.1177/0042098014528394

Hick, R., Pomati, M., & Stephens, M. (2022). Severe housing deprivation in the European Union: A joint analysis of measurement and theory. *Social Indicators Research*, *164*(3), 1271–1295. DOI: 10.1007/s11205-022-02987-6 PMID: 36039339

Hick, R., Pomati, M., & Stephens, M. (2024). Housing affordability and poverty in Europe: On the deteriorating position of market renters. *Journal of Social Policy*, •••, 1–24.

Hochstenbach, C., & Aalbers, M. B. (2024). The uncoupling of house prices and mortgage debt: Towards wealth-driven housing market dynamics. *International Journal of Housing Policy*, *24*(4), 642–670. DOI: 10.1080/19491247.2023.2170542

Igan, D. (2024, December). The Housing Affordability Crunch. *Finance & Development*, 21.

Igan, D., Kohlscheen, E., & Rungcharoenkitkul, P. (2022). Housing market risks in the wake of the pandemic. BIS Bulletin, (50).

INED. (2023). Increasingly unequal levels of home ownership between poor and wealthy young households in France. Retrieved May 17, 2025

Kaas, L., Kocharkov, G., & Preugschat, E. (2019). Wealth inequality and homeownership in Europe. *Annals of Economics and Statistics*, (136), 27–54. DOI: 10.15609/annaeconstat2009.136.0027

Kährik, A., & Pastak, I. (2023). Access to homeownership in decline—Rising housing inequalities for young people in the neoliberal housing market of Tallinn. *Frontiers in Sustainable Cities*, *5*, 1149087. DOI: 10.3389/frsc.2023.1149087

Kemeny, J. (2001). Comparative housing and welfare: Theorising the relationship. *Journal of Housing and the Built Environment*, *16*(1), 53–70. DOI: 10.1023/A:1011526416064

Kissoon, P. (2010). From persecution to destitution: A snapshot of asylum seekers' housing and settlement experiences in Canada and the United Kingdom. *Journal of Immigrant & Refugee Studies*, *8*(1), 4–31. DOI: 10.1080/15562940903575020

Klein, N. (2014). *This changes everything: Capitalism vs. the climate*. Simon and Schuster.

Kutty, N. K. (2005). A new measure of housing affordability: Estimates and analytical results. *Housing Policy Debate*, *16*(1), 113–142. DOI: 10.1080/10511482.2005.9521536

Lee, Y., Kemp, P., & Reina, V. (2022). Drivers of housing (un)affordability in the advanced economies: A review and new evidence. *Housing Studies*, *37*(10), 1739–1752. DOI: 10.1080/02673037.2022.2123623

Licchetta, M., Martins, V. D., & Vašíček, B. (2025). Selected Macroeconomic and Social Aspects of Housing Affordability. *Inter Economics*, *60*(2), 101–106. DOI: 10.2478/ie-2025-0020

Long, J., & Zhuang, L. (2025). Housing finance and inequality: Mortgage debt in urban China. *Habitat International*, *161*, 103411. DOI: 10.1016/j.habitatint.2025.103411

Lux, M., Sunega, P., & Kážmér, L. (2021). Intergenerational financial transfers and indirect reciprocity: Determinants of the reproduction of homeownership in the post-socialist Czech Republic. *Housing Studies*, *36*(8), 1294–1317. DOI: 10.1080/02673037.2018.1541441

Marcuse, P., & Madden, D. (2024). *In defense of housing: The politics of crisis*. Verso Books.

Massey, D. S., & Denton, N. A. (1988). The dimensions of residential segregation. *Social Forces*, *67*(2), 281–315. DOI: 10.2307/2579183

OECD. (2021). *Brick by Brick: Building Better Housing Policies*. OECD Publishing., DOI: 10.1787/b453b043-

OECD. (2025), OECD Affordable Housing Database - indicator HM1.3 Housing tenures, https://oe.cd/ahd

Ostendorf, W., Musterd, S., & De Vos, S. (2001). Social mix and the neighbourhood effect. Policy ambitions and empirical evidence. *Housing Studies*, *16*(3), 371–380. DOI: 10.1080/02673030120049724

Phillimore, J., & Goodson, L. (2006). Problem or opportunity? Asylum seekers, refugees, employment and social exclusion in deprived urban areas. *Urban Studies (Edinburgh, Scotland)*, *43*(10), 1715–1736. DOI: 10.1080/00420980600838606

Quigley, J. M., & Raphael, S. (2004). Is housing unaffordable? Why isn't it more affordable? *The Journal of Economic Perspectives*, *18*(1), 191–214. DOI: 10.1257/089533004773563494

Rodríguez-Pose, A., & Storper, M. (2020). Housing, urban growth and inequalities: The limits to deregulation and upzoning in reducing economic and spatial inequality. *Urban Studies (Edinburgh, Scotland)*, *57*(2), 223–248. DOI: 10.1177/0042098019859458

Rolnik, R. (2013). Late neoliberalism: The financialization of homeownership and housing rights. *International Journal of Urban and Regional Research*, *37*(3), 1058–1066. DOI: 10.1111/1468-2427.12062

Scanlon, K., Whitehead, C., & Arrigoitia, M. F. (Eds.). (2014). *Social housing in Europe*. John Wiley & Sons. DOI: 10.1002/9781118412367

Stone, M. (2010). *Shelter poverty: New ideas on housing affordability*. Temple University Press.

Stone, M. E. (2006). What is housing affordability? The case for the residual income approach. *Housing Policy Debate*, *17*(1), 151–184. DOI: 10.1080/10511482.2006.9521564

Stone, M. E. (2006). A housing affordability standard for the UK. *Housing Studies*, *21*(4), 453–476. DOI: 10.1080/02673030600708886

Tetlow, G. (2018) Rising burden of housing costs shown by 60-year UK spending survey. FT.Com. Available at https://www.ft.com/content/32d71316-fc5f-11e7-9b32-d7d59aace167

Wacquant, L. (2008). *Urban outcasts: A comparative sociology of advanced marginality*. Polity Press.

Wetzstein, S. (2017). The global urban housing affordability crisis. *Urban Studies (Edinburgh, Scotland)*, *54*(14), 3159–3177. DOI: 10.1177/0042098017711649

KEY TERMS AND DEFINITIONS

Financialization of Housing: It refers to the process by which housing becomes a financial asset that is subject to speculation and investment, rather than serving its fundamental purpose as a place of residence.

Housing Affordability: This concept measures the ability of households to afford housing without undue financial burden. It is usually assessed by comparing housing costs with household income levels.

Housing Inequality: Housing inequality refers to the unequal access to safe and affordable housing across different income, age, or social groups. It often stems from rising property prices, constrained credit access, and an inadequate housing supply.

Housing Policy: It encompasses government measures intended to regulate the housing market, including subsidies, taxes, rent controls, and social housing programs.

Intergenerational Inequality: This phenomenon pertains to disparities in opportunities and wealth among different age groups. The challenges associated with housing affordability frequently impede the capacity of younger generations to acquire property and become homeowners.

Price-to-Income Ratio: It measures the relationship between median house prices and median household incomes. It indicates how many years of income would be required to purchase a home, assuming all income is allocated to housing. A higher ratio suggests reduced housing affordability, especially for low- and middle-income households.

Price-to-Rent Ratio: It is an indicator that compares the cost of buying a property to the annual cost of renting a similar property. It is used to assess whether housing is overvalued or undervalued. A high ratio may signal that property prices are rising faster than rental income, indicating possible housing market imbalances or affordability issues.

Wealth Inequality: It is defined as the unequal distribution of assets and net worth among a population. The housing market exerts a significant influence on the exacerbation of wealth disparities, as home ownership has emerged as the predominant avenue for wealth accumulation.

ENDNOTES

1. Housing affordability is defined as the challenge faced by households in balancing the cost of their actual or potential housing with their non-housing expenditures, within the constraints of their income (Stone, 2006).

2. Despite its popularity, the price-to-income ratio has been criticized for overlooking key affordability factors such as mortgage rates and housing-related costs, which may lead to misleading conclusions when used in isolation (Svensson, 2023).

3. This measure excludes allowances.

Chapter 7
Heterogeneity of Crime in the European Region and Its Nexus With Income Inequality

Fadime İrem Doğan
https://orcid.org/0000-0002-7760-0886
Bahcesehir University, Turkey

Pınar Deniz
https://orcid.org/0000-0001-5693-1144
Marmara University, Turkey

ABSTRACT

This chapter offers a theoretical and visual analysis of the distribution of crime rates across Europe, focusing on various crime types over time, and examines their correlation with income inequality—one of the most highlighted determinants in the empirical literature—to shed light on the structural drivers of crime. Moreover, this chapter provides spatial representation of crime rates as a descriptive overview of crime across Europe, focusing on three decades, i.e., 2000s, 2010s, and 2020s, to further observe how crime rates evolve over time. By combining visual tools and descriptive statistics, we provide a concise yet insightful perspective on the evolving nature of crime within the European region and its relationship with the income inequality. Our findings reveal a significant heterogeneity in the distribution of crime rates across European countries. Moreover, this variation is observed despite the geographical proximity, common historical background, similar institutional structures and the existence of shared social and economic policies under the umbrella of the Europe.

DOI: 10.4018/979-8-3373-7360-7.ch007

1. INTRODUCTION

Identifying crime, the motive behind criminal activities, and criminals is not an easy task. Efforts have been made since the beginning of human creation. In his seminal study, Becker (1968) explains that an individual's incentive to commit a crime is a cost-benefit analysis, such that before committing a crime, an individual determines the economic and psychological returns and the opportunity cost and punishments of that action. He further argues that once a crime is committed, conviction may not be enough, and more serious punishments are required. At this point, the question evolves to 'how and who is going to determine the punishments?'. Becker proposes minimizing the costs of crime to the society by measuring the punishment costs and the costs of the offence itself. This proposition is the foundation of economics of crime.

In society, we classify individuals as criminals and innocents based on their adherence to legal norms and laws. Some choose to be entitled as the disturbers of the society whereas others prefer to live "by the book". By nature, law-abiding citizens are more judgmental to criminal activities and would never assume never to do so. However, one might also believe that anyone is capable of committing a crime if there is no alternative for themselves or to provide for their families. Then the following questions pop up: "Would a law-abiding citizen commit a crime if given the same conditions as criminals?", "Who would choose to commit a crime?" To understand these questions, scholars have explored various theoretical frameworks. One prominent perspective is the Rational Choice Theory, which, as Felson and Clarke (1998) argue, emphasizes the role of opportunity and the decision-making process of individuals. This theory provides a bridge between the general exploration of why people commit crimes and specific contexts that create opportunities for offending. It simply pays attention to the individual's decision-making. Every offender has different reasons and factors to commit crime. When individuals decide to commit crime, their goal is short-term oriented because they have limited time and because they cannot evaluate the cost and benefits of their behavior's consequences. Cost and benefit of the offender should be highly important. The main purpose of the Rational Choice Theory is to identify and understand the reasons behind an offender's actions. It tries to calculate the cost and benefit of its behavior even for a little time because the offender does not pay attention to the punishment or the legal consequences. Offenders make choices when they commit crime based on anticipated opportunities defined as effective factors causing the crime.

Within this context, it is critical to understand how broader societal factors contribute to these opportunities and choices. There is a strand of literature devoted to the relationship between crime and inequality which lies at the center of major theoretical approaches, such as the cost-benefit analysis by Becker (1968), the theory of social disorganization by Shaw and McKay (1942), and the strain theory by Merton (1938). While Becker (1968) uses the cost-benefit analysis of engaging in crime, Shaw and McKay (1942) attribute the rise in crime rates to the weakening of social control within a society; and Merton (1938) utilizes the impact of the relative success of individuals on the frustration, which may lead to the rise in crime rates. These foundational theories demonstrate the connection between individual decision-making, societal structures, and crime.

Following these foundational approaches, many economists and sociologists scrutinize the relationship between economic inequality and crime. For instance, Kelly (2000) demonstrates the link between inequality and crime by analyzing property and violent crimes, finding a strong relationship for violent crime but not for property crime. Similarly, Aronson (1988) shows that frustration leads to aggressive behavior in individuals, thereby increasing their probability of taking risks and their tendency to commit crimes. Several studies in the recent literature investigates the relationship at a macro level employing a variety of empirical methodologies. Renno Santos et al. (2021) examines the relationship between inflation and cross-national homicide rates across 65 countries from 1965 to 2015, finds a positive direct association between the two. The findings suggest that maintaining low inflation could serve as an effective criminal justice policy, particularly in economically developed nations. Thornton et al. (2023) investigate the nonlinear relationship between burglary, income, and inequality in South Africa, revealing that this relationship takes the form of an inverse U shape. The study highlights the importance of controlling for spatial correlation and criminal movement in crime modeling. It also discusses the interaction between income and inequality, suggesting that as inequality increases, crime rates may decrease due to heightened security measures among local elites. In another study, Goh and Law (2023) explore the asymmetric relationship between income inequality and crime rates in five Latin American countries, using data from 1984 to 2017. They employ a nonlinear autoregressive distributed lag (NARDL) model to demonstrate that the impact of income inequality on crime rates is not symmetrical. Their findings reveal significant evidence of asymmetricity, suggesting that while income inequality influences crime rates, the effects vary depending on whether inequality is increasing or decreasing. Additionally, inflation exacerbates crime rates, while advancements in human capital development and legitimate employment opportunities help reduce them. Enamorado et al. (2016) investigates the relationship between inequality and homicide rates in Mexican municipalities from 1990 to 2010. The authors employ a first-difference specification to analyze how changes in the Gini coefficient correlate with changes in crime rates, controlling for median income and demographics. Their findings suggest that increased inequality is associated with higher homicide rates, both in drug-related and non-drug-related crimes. In another study, Charlot et al. (2022) develops a matching model inspired by Pissarides (2000) to analyze the smuggling market and the impact of EU policies on irregular migration. They focus on the steady state equilibrium, where migrant flows in and out balance each other, and examines the economic implications of various policies. The research highlights the complexities of the migrant-smuggler relationship and the dynamics of the smuggling market. Although recent quasi-experimental research (e.g., Enamorado et al., 2016; Charlot et al., 2021) offers methods for identifying causal relationships, our goal is to present a comparative and visual representation of the relationship between crime and inequality within the European Union.

Our findings suggest that crime rates vary across countries and there is no clear similarity for any of the crime type using correlations. This finding suggests heterogeneity of crime across European countries. Among all crime rates, it is observed that only intentional homicide depicts a clear decline over the horizon whereas the other crime types vary over the time and the rankings change within the region. The inspection of the correlations with income inequality provides findings in line with the expectations such that the crime types that are related to economic reasons have the highest correlations. Among all countries, Poland, Netherlands, Portugal, Ireland and Czechia reflect the highest positive correlations between crime rates and income inequality. Our overall findings suggest lack of homogeneity and convergence within the region. Considering the unification motive of the Europe over the years in every aspect, from monetary and fiscal policy to energy markets, from cultural similarities to prioritizing of the social values, there seems to be a failure in ensuring convergence of one of the most crucial social indicators for well-being, the crime rates. There may be several explanations behind this lack of convergence and homogeneity over the time period that capture external shocks such as migration, economic crisis, political turbulence etc. This chapter does not aim to examine the determinants of crime rates, but rather provides a snapshot to different crime type for the European region over the time horizon and concentrate on the nexus with income inequality to provide a scent of investigation for economic relevance of crime rates. The chapter also includes a brief overview on the concept of crime, its underlying causes, and key sociopolitical and economic determinants. Our main finding is the non-existence of homogeneity of crime rates within the homogeneity-oriented Europe. We aim to provide inferences regarding this finding.

2. CRIME THEORIES

Various crime theories are presented in the literature. In this section, the most frequently mentioned crime theories will be discussed.

2.1. Strain Theory

Among the many theories that attempt to explain criminal behavior, Strain Theory stands out for its emphasis on the link between social pressures and deviant behavior (Eitle, 2002; Smith et al., 2012). Essentially, Strain Theory suggests that people turn to crime when they feel a gap between social goals and the reasonable means at their disposal to achieve those goals (Merton, 1938). Within the European Union (EU), crime is a complex problem shaped by many social, economic and cultural factors. The Strain Theory, a well-known sociological theory, provides an essential analysis of the dynamics of criminal behavior in the various EU member states. It argues that people are more likely to commit crime when they feel tension or stress resulting from a mismatch between social expectations and the reasonable means available to achieve them (Agnew, 2015; Coccia et al., 2024). In the EU, this pressure shows in various ways, reflecting the region's complex socio-economic structure. Economic inequality is a major cause of tension within the EU (Scarpa, 2015; Musterd et al., 2017; Kim et al., 2020; Tuttle, 2022). Despite being one of the richest regions in the world, member countries and their societies continue to experience sharp income and opportunity gaps (Kim et al, 2020). Peripheral regions and underprivileged communities often experience greater unemployment, poverty and social exclusion, increasing feelings of isolation and frustration. Moreover, the 2008 global financial crisis followed by sovereign debt crisis in 2010 showed structural flaws in the EU, which led to austerity measures and economic downturns in many countries (Ersoy and Doğan, 2016). The austerity measures resulting from these policies have been particularly damaging to societies already vulnerable to socio-economic concerns through reductions in public services and social welfare programs. Political unrest and disappointment with existing institutions are also exacerbating tensions in the EU. Corruption, scandals and a sense of elite capture weaken confidence in democratic government and the rule of law (Kistner, 2007). Growing populist movements and Euroscepticism in some Member States reflect a more general disappointment with the European project, thus fostering divisions and social unrest (Kaeding et al., 2020). Cultural factors help shape tensions and crime within the EU. Some societies have experienced cultural conflicts and identity crises as a result of rapid demographic change driven by migration and globalization (Cohn et al., 2021). The inclusion of different cultural norms and values challenges social cohesion and can make some groups feel marginalized and culturally incapable of adapting. In this environment, criminal subgroups emerge as other ways for people to gain recognition and status. For disappointed and dissatisfied youth who feel excluded from society, groups, organized crime and extremist groups provide a sense of belonging and identity (Antunes and Manasse, 2022). The appeal of criminal lifestyles may stem from material wealth, social standing or a sense of empowerment in the face of perceived offense. International crime also postures more challenges for EU law enforcement agencies and governments. The interconnected character of Europe's economies and borders helps to move illegal products, money laundering and human trafficking across national borders (Salt, 2000). While promoting freedom of movement, the EU's open borders and the Schengen agreement also expose weaknesses exploited by criminal organizations. In response to these challenges, EU member states have put in place various plans to tackle pressure and reduce crime. Projects aimed at promoting social inclusion, economic growth and youth empowerment (Escudero and Mourelo, 2015) seek to address the factors underlying deviant behavior. Enhancing border security and fighting international crime is a result of increased cooperation and information sharing between law enforcement agencies. Strain theory provides an informative analysis of the complex relationship of social factors behind crime within the European Union. By knowing the causes of strain and implementing focused interventions, policymakers can help build more inclusive and resilient societies, enabling people to follow reasonable pathways to success and satisfaction.

2.2. Social Disorganization Theory

Social disorganization theory is successful in explaining how it is important to focus on certain neighborhoods instead of individuals to understand and decrease crime levels. Moreover, even though individuals move out of the neighborhood, the crime rate remains at a higher level (Shaw and McKay, 1942; Başıbüyük and Karakuş, 2010). That said, the structure of the neighborhood is crucial in understanding the variations in crime, such as poverty and mobility. (Browning et al. 2004). Any rapid socioeconomic change in society, such as industrialization and urbanization, is a cause of crime. Individuals are unlikely to accept new norms and values that change their lifestyle or traditions. This phenomenon has also been observed in other societies. When Shaw and McKay (1942) studied human ecology, they concluded that industrialization and urbanization changed the population, and this was followed by an increase in industry and migration. However, industrialization did mean changes in the norms and values that people were unhappy to accept. For this reason, industrialization and urbanization seem to have increased crime rates. According to an individual who decides to commit a crime, the important thing is the expectations and risks that they face. They decide to engage in a crime when their expectations exceed risks. With rapid socioeconomic changes, the target becomes more important and larger; as a result, the probability of engaging in a crime increases. It is well known that rapid socioeconomic changes create more possibilities for crimes. (Tsushima, 1999). The impact on the costs and benefits determines an individual's choice. The cost of getting caught, punishment, not having expectations, etc., and on the other hand, getting more compared to a legitimate job impacts the costs and benefits of committing a crime.

2.3. The Theoretical Framework: Economics of Crime and the Link with Inequality

Becker's Model

Becker (1968) presents his economic perspective on crime and punishment, emphasizing not just the cost-benefit analysis of offenders but also the correlation between crime and inequality. The Since the 1930s, elevated tax rates and the evolution of tax policies have contributed to an increase in crime (President's Commission, 1967a, pp. 22-31). The circulation of money, currency ratios, and the utilization of credit cards significantly influence income and play a substantial effect in the increase of crime rates. To diminish crime, individuals allocate resources towards law enforcement, security systems, judicial expenses, and incarceration costs. However, such expenditures are expensive. To adjust these expenses, the tax rate may rise, and citizens' income may decline. An individual's decision to commit a crime can be explained through a cost-benefit analysis. Individuals opt to engage in criminal activity when the expected benefits exceed the predicted expenses. According to Becker (1968), an individual's propensity to engage in criminal behavior is determined by the cost-benefit analysis of the action rather than their motive in relation to others. The expected income derived from a crime is essential to this technique. Consequently, an individual's money influences their decision-making regarding criminal activity. Simultaneously, they evaluate the cost-benefit aspect, and when considering all these factors, it becomes evident if they are risk-seeking or risk-averse in the event of hesitation.

Becker constructed his model based on cost-benefit analysis, aiming to minimize the costs associated with crime by comparing illicit activity. In his model, he reveals that to achieve optimal conditions, the overall cost of crime identification can be diminished through various methods; thus, harm and damage must be considered. The supply and demand of crime must also be considered. To achieve the ideal equilibrium, the marginal cost (MC) of harm must equal the marginal revenue (MR) of harm. The same applies to the marginal cost (MC) of the risk of committing a crime and the marginal revenue (MR). To do this, we must select the values for probability, p, and social cost, f, to minimize the social cost. Indeed, the model indicates that harmful acts are penalized less severely than impulsive offences. Becker (1968) suggests that the primary objective of judicial processes is to impose fines which are equal to the harm. If ideal fines are imposed on the firms, the benefit is lower to the damage imposed and lower than the anticipated fines.

The cost of punishment varies based on the nature of the offence, with some being converted to monetary value and others not. Becker (1968) states that penalties imposed on offenders influence their income and expenditure. This also impacts other citizens due to expenses related to crime prevention, law enforcement, and incarceration experienced by them. This circumstance may once more cause disparities within society. If an individual's likelihood of conviction rises, the frequency of offences they commit also escalates, whereas it diminishes with an increase in punishment severity. The impact of the change in probability exceeds that of the change in punishment. An individual commits a crime when the anticipated utility of the act exceeds that of engaging in alternative activities. The costs and benefits vary, encouraging them to engage in criminal activity. Criminal behavior does not necessitate a temporary idea to assume complete understanding and rapid calculation. The idea suggests a correlation among the number of offences committed by an individual, the likelihood of conviction, income derived from illegal activities, and the propensity to engage in criminal behavior. If found guilty, one will serve their sentence for each offence committed. An increase in either their likelihood of conviction or their penalty will result in a diminished expected value from an offence, hence reducing the frequency of offences due to the increased risk of experiencing a greater cost or the cost itself. A rise in legal activity and obedience to regulations would diminish individuals' propensity to engage in criminal behavior. The same applies when the penalty is changed to incarceration rather than a monetary fee, as individuals are unable to commit crimes while incarcerated, even for a brief duration.

Freeman's Model

Freeman's (1999) approach is set within the economics of crime, emphasizing poverty, education, labor market dynamics, and economic inequality. He states that when the elasticity of supply to crime is higher, one offender moves another in the market. Crime is associated with various factors including poverty, social exclusion, risk, and other economic issues. When individuals have limited education, inadequate labor market skills, and low wages, criminal behavior becomes inevitable for certain individuals. The victimization rate is inversely correlated with household income. Freeman claims that it is essential to clarify the economics of crime through numerous elements. During this explanation of the correlation between inequality and crime, he focuses on the cost-benefit analysis associated with criminal activity. Crime, particularly among young offenders, is frequently influenced by financial levels. Lower income exacerbates income inequality among individuals. Consequently, crime rates climb up. When wages are reduced, individuals expect engaging in criminal activity. Individuals with lower incomes often, even subconsciously, assess the opportunity cost of engaging in criminal activity.

The involvement in crime and the number of offences committed by each criminal can be explained by the availability of criminal opportunities. The supply of crime per capita is equal to the criminal participation rate, which indicates the individuals who have committed offences, multiplied by the total number of offences. Young males are considered as the primary agents of crime; thus, the Freeman utilized the young male demographic to assess the rate of criminal participation. Individuals who are incarcerated belong to the high offending category, as opposed to those who are not imprisoned. The criminal involvement rate affects to the non-jailed population. Individuals were more motivated to participate in illegal activities due to the prolonged replacement of the complete supply of criminals and incarcerated individuals in the market. The increase in incarceration has intensified the motivation to engage in criminal activity by diminishing the rewards associated with crime. Individuals opt to participate in criminal actions when the anticipated utility from such illegal activities exceeds that of legitimate pursuits. If the anticipated benefit from the punishment exceeds that of lawful employment, people opt to engage in criminal activity. Consequently, criminal conduct must generate a greater return than lawful activities. It is essential to recognize that persons may engage in criminal activity despite holding respectable employment. Individuals with higher incomes implement various measures to soften the impact and frequency of crime, such as enhancing security awareness or relocating to more secure areas. This intensifies the situation for lower-paid persons due to adverse market conditions. Due to adverse market conditions, income inequality between high- and low-earning individuals escalates daily. Moreover, other work by Freeman (Freeman, 1995; Fagan and Freeman, 1999) demonstrate that individuals with substantial legitimate incomes are less motivated to engage in criminal activity. Another factor contributing to the increase in crime rates is that individuals engaged in illegal employment and irregular working hours disclose their income less frequently than those with legitimate occupations and fixed working hours. However, this does not imply that it is only applicable to the offenders. Freeman (1999) shown in his research that this holds true for the victims as well. The correlation between inequality and crime is complexly linked to victims. Individuals with low incomes are more vulnerable to becoming victims of crime. Although possessing fewer assets, low-income individuals are among the victims of illegal activity.

Approach by Chiu and Madden

Chiu and Madden (1998) examine the impact of income inequality on burglary rates. They have formulated the notion that greater income inequality correlates with increased burglary rates. Their analysis indicates that wealthy communities may exhibit reduced crime rates. Criminals select residences located in wealthy neighborhoods. It is presumed that individuals are aware of the outcomes of criminal activity, and all offences, especially burglary, result in imprisonment. The propensity for criminal behavior among low-income earners exceeds that of high-income earners due to their diminished earning potential. It is suggested that all individuals are immoral, and the decision to commit burglary is dependent upon inequality, namely their anticipated income maximization. In the richer segment of the community, the crime rate is diminished, suggesting a possible correlation. Chiu and Madden employed the Lorenz Curve to assess and compare income distributions by examining the properties of households and individuals, utilizing percentages to illustrate this possible correlation. They have determined that the crime rate and income inequality are correlated in the same direction. It is essential to recognize that, in wealthy neighborhoods, the crime rate is diminished due to preventive measures and techniques employed to fight crime. In the model, all individuals are considered as risk-neutral, and communities are categorized as either poor or high quality. In summary, the cost of low-quality neighborhoods is zero, and every individual with residual income z experiences a utility level of z if they reside in a high-quality neighborhood. It is presumed that everyone will commit burglary at least once, and any subsequent behaviors will produce post-tax legal revenue. They included the probability of a crime occurring if the individual is captured by law enforcement in the model. If identified, the penalty will be the regular incarceration term, and the individual's income will be zero. If undetected, the individual obtains residual income from the burglary. The choice between low or high quality of the neighborhood (or the property) is evident, although the resident's income remains uncertain. The type of house will communicate to persons engaging in burglary. There exists a random selection or matching between victims and criminals. Individuals who opt to commit a crime are motivated to target rich houses, as expected financial gain leads the burglary rather than ethical or alternative factors. Their research explains three assumptions suggested by the model. Assumption 1 suggests that individuals with low income are more likely to commit crimes in low-quality housing, similar to middle-income earners, however they fall inside the non-crime category. Individuals with higher incomes are not just categorized as non-criminals residing in high-quality houses but also as potential victims. Assumption 2 indicates that, for a certain proportion of the residual income of the individual residing in the burgled house, a minimal of it guarantees either a unique equilibrium or the absence of equilibrium entirely. The impact of changes in income distribution on crime levels is depending upon both the initial and revised income distributions. Assumption 3 demonstrates that assumptions 1 and 2 are valid under both the original and new income distributions, and the equilibrium conditions with a small proportion of income are satisfied in this context. It is suggested that income distribution changes in several respects: average income fluctuates with population dynamics, the income of potential victims diminishes, and the income of criminal's declines. A decline in the potential victim's income may enhance the appeal of burglary. A decline in the offender's income correlates with an escalation in criminal activity. Wealthy neighborhoods may exhibit reduced crime rates due to diminished income inequalities; conversely, security measures tend to be more robust in these areas. The occurrence of crime is affected by income distribution, specifically the wealth of individuals.

Approach by Bourguignon

An uneven income distribution is likely to lead to perceptions of increased criminality. Bourguignon (1999) is among the scholars who examined the correlation between inequality and crime. Upon examining the origins and consequences of the crime, the author suggests that inequality is a mediating factor. The author reveals that society is stratified into three classes: the poor, non-poor, and income or wealth. The wealth of the poor is less than that of the rich. Moreover, the likelihood of getting caught for an individual is very related with the penalty imposed. The distinction between classes is irrelevant, as the expected effectiveness of any criminal behavior undertaken by an individual exceeds that of whatever legal activity, they have engaged in. A decline in an individual's income may lead to a transition to illegal activities. Consequently, for certain individuals, inadequate income serves as a convincing justification for participating in illegal actions. In a manner similar to Becker's (1968) pioneer study, Bourguignon (1999) identified honesty as a variable, asserting that when honesty is analyzed across socioeconomic groups, individuals from poor backgrounds are more likely to engage in illegal acts. From an economic perspective, property crime that produces financial benefit to a person is more advantageous than crimes against individuals. It is important to recognize that individuals from poor and less educated backgrounds are more likely to engage in criminal activities, including homicides. Certainly, law enforcement presence in neighborhoods populated by poor and less educated individuals is essential. The direct impact of income inequality on crime is minimal. Inequality causes poverty, which then exacerbates crime rates within a society. Consequently, when identical development rates are seen in two societies, the more unequal society exhibits a higher incidence of crime. Policies taken on crime determine how a society may take measurements against crime. Numerous measurements also raise costs for both individuals and policymakers. Bourguignon states that much of the literature on the economics of crime examines the consequences of these policies and their impact on income distribution. This establishes a correlation between crime and inequality. It is essential to note that certain expenditures experienced by society to fight crime (such as protection, security systems, and guards) show the correlation between crime and inequality, as the absence of protection associates with higher crime rates and is revealing inequality.

Imrohoroglu, Merlo and Rupert's Approach

Imrohoroglu, Merlo, and Rupert (2006) explore the determinants of crime. The authors explore variables such as unemployment, human capital, incarceration duration, and income inequality. The economic expectations of individuals primarily motivate their choices on the activities they wish to undertake. To investigate this, the authors employed an overlapping generations model. They categorize individuals into several groups: those without a high school education, those with only a high school diploma, those with a college diploma, and those with advanced degrees beyond a college diploma. During certain periods, individuals have the opportunity for employment and consequently select the kind of activities in which to participate (criminal or non-criminal). They evaluate the expectations by assessing the anticipated return from committing a crime and the potential punishment if caught. The authors state that the likelihood of getting caught and income inequality are the primary determinants influencing criminal activity. They concentrate on property crime. They argue that the likelihood of getting caught and income inequality provide a broad framework for analyzing and comparing various nations. In addition to examining the employed and unemployed population, age and educational attainment are also analyzed. The majority of individuals who engage in criminal activity have the capacity for judgement and hold a high school diploma. Their model concludes that those without a college diploma, having only a high school diploma, are more likely to engage in property crime. Consequently, there is a correlation between property crime and the likelihood of getting caught, as well as the duration of incarceration.

3. DATA COLLECTION PROBLEM: EU PERSPECTIVE

One crucial problem regarding this field is the difficulty in getting reliable data such that we can expect lack of collection of data on criminal activity or deviant behavior unless they are subject to law enforcement. The prominent study of Becker (1963) highlights this issue by providing an example of a doctor that is caught stealing from hospital narcotics supplies and is not punished but asked to leave the hospital. We can extend this research problem considering cultural background that is also relevant to our study such that there can be less or more reporting of the crimes depending on the region, which is likely to be affected by the cultural background. Tonry (2014) asserts "cultural thresholds of tolerance of violence" as the explanation regarding the dramatic change in the crime rates in the western world such that there is a decline from the early nineteenth to mid-twentieth century and increase afterwards. Aebi (2008) explains that the way that crime is defined can also be another reason regarding the variation of the crime rates across countries. The study of Aebi and Linde (2012) uses a clustering for the Central and Eastern European countries mentioning about the dramatic changes in the legal definitions of crime after the breakup of the Soviet Union. Gruszczynska and Gruszczynski (2005) also refer to the regional differences for Europe attributing the relatively low crime rates in the Central and Eastern European countries to the differences in the quality of the system of police statistics compared to Western Europe. Torrente et al. (2017) mention about north-central and the south-eastern regions in Europe in terms of the differences in the reporting of crimes linking it to the socio-economic factors. Another crucial issue is that the reporting of the crime may also be dependent on the type of the crime as stated by Gruszczyńska and Heiskanen (2018). Overall, under-reporting of the crime depending on the culture, time, definition of the crime, type of the crime, etc. may lead to statistical problems. Hence, the researcher should be cautious regarding the measurement error problem specific to this issue.

There are two approaches in criminology. The positivist approach argues that there are internal or external forces that affect the criminal behavior instead of the role of the will in human affairs. Genetics or socio-biological aspects are considered as one of the explanations for criminal motivation under this school (Ellis, 1982; Wilson and Herrnstein, 1985; Mednick et al., 1987). Family ties, dietary factors (including drug and alcohol use), IQ level, psychological disorders are highlighted under the psychosocial aspects of the positivist school (Dorfman, 1984; Daly and Wilson, 1988; Gottfredson and Hirschi, 1990; Hickey, 1991; Murray and Herrnstein, 1994). A very extreme example stated by Vold and Bernard (1986) uses the keyword atavism, referring to a certain physical appearance such as cheeks, ears or heads different from what is perceived as normal for the society. Besides the nonavailability of an indicator for the physical appearance at the macro level, such a prejudice based on physical appearance will not be ethical. However, the cause and effect related explanation to crime helps understand the involvement of society to the behavior of the individuals. On the other hand, the classical school of thought in criminology assumes that human beings are rational and make their decisions based on a basic loss and gain comparison. Wilson and Herrnstein (1985) combine both schools of thought and depict that the individual uses their will to choose between the gratification earned in the short term and loss in the long term with punishment and social labeling, however that free will is affected by the external or internal factors of the individual. Therefore, the level of the punishment for crime determines the level of deterrence. Since ensuring safety is one of the reasons for the genesis of the states, there are control mechanisms against the criminal activity, such as heavy punishments that come into question after crime is committed, or police guarding as a precautionary method that aims to deter individuals before committing an act, or rehabilitation programs to reverse the life choice of the criminal into a lawful one once freed from prison. Hence, one of the determinants of the crime rates should be a proxy for the deterrence, as the strength of the justice system, the number of guardsmen per person and the availability of the prison programs.

Comprehending the factors influencing criminal behaviour necessitates an analysis of deterrence mechanisms and an exploration of the wider socio-economic environment in which individuals function. Income disparity has been extensively examined as a structural issue that contributes to crime. Elevated levels of inequality can induce sentiments of relative deprivation, diminish social cohesion, and foster conditions conducive to criminal behaviour. These strategies are especially pertinent in cultures when access to lawful avenues of achievement is inequitably allocated. Consequently, examining the relationship between inequality and crime provides significant insights into the socio-economic foundations of criminal behaviour, transcending human rationality or biological inclinations. For empirical analysis, we collect crime and the economic inequality data from Eurostat. As a measurement of crime, we employ crime rate as a ratio of crime level to 100 thousand people[1]. For economic inequality, GINI coefficient is utilized. Data coverage depends on the availability of time and countries. Dataset for correlations covers 2003-2022 period for the European countries.

4. CORRELATIONS OF CRIME TYPES ACROSS EUROPEAN COUNTRIES

This section presents heatmaps using *reshape2* package in R to visualize the correlations of the crime types across European countries. These partial correlations help us uncover the similarities and differences within the region.

Figure 1. Heatmap for Intentional Homicide, Kidnapping and Serious Assault

Figure 1: Heatmap for Intentional Homicide, Kidnapping and Serious Assault

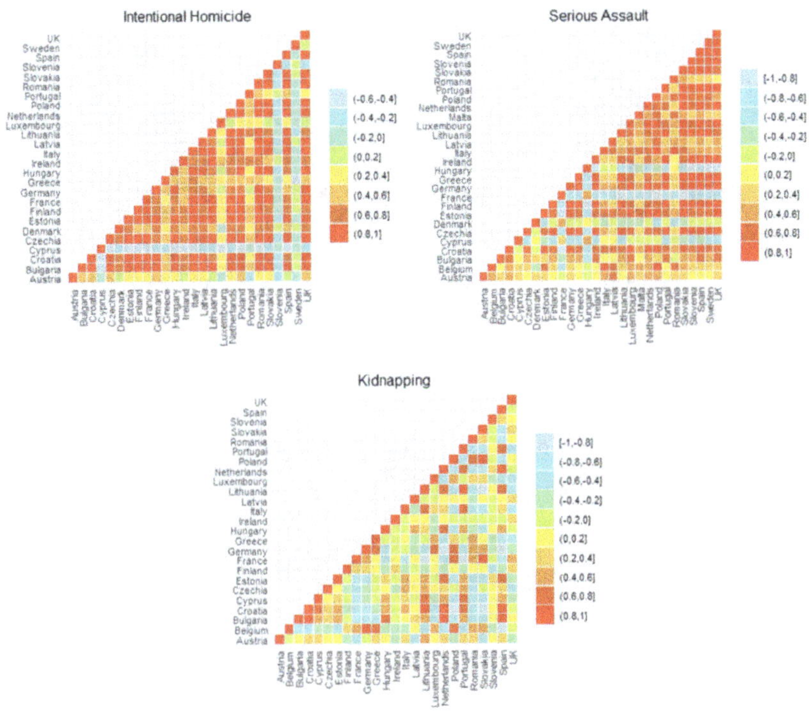

Source: Eurostat. Authors' calculation.

Figure 1 depicts the correlations across the regions for intentional homicide, kidnapping and serious assault. For intentional homicide, high positive correlations shown with red tones are available for some countries but it is not dominant for the whole region. Among the countries, Austria, Cyprus, Greece, Luxembourg, Portugal, Slovenia and Sweden are diverging significantly. For serious assault, the divergence from high positive correlation is relatively higher. For kidnapping, there is almost no high positive correlation except for minor similar groups such as Bulgaria-Croatia-Netherlands-Spain, Belgium-Germany and Slovakia-France-Poland.

Figure 2. Heatmap for Burglary, Motor Vehicle Theft and Robbery

Figure 2: Heatmap for Burglary, Motor Vehicle Theft and Robbery

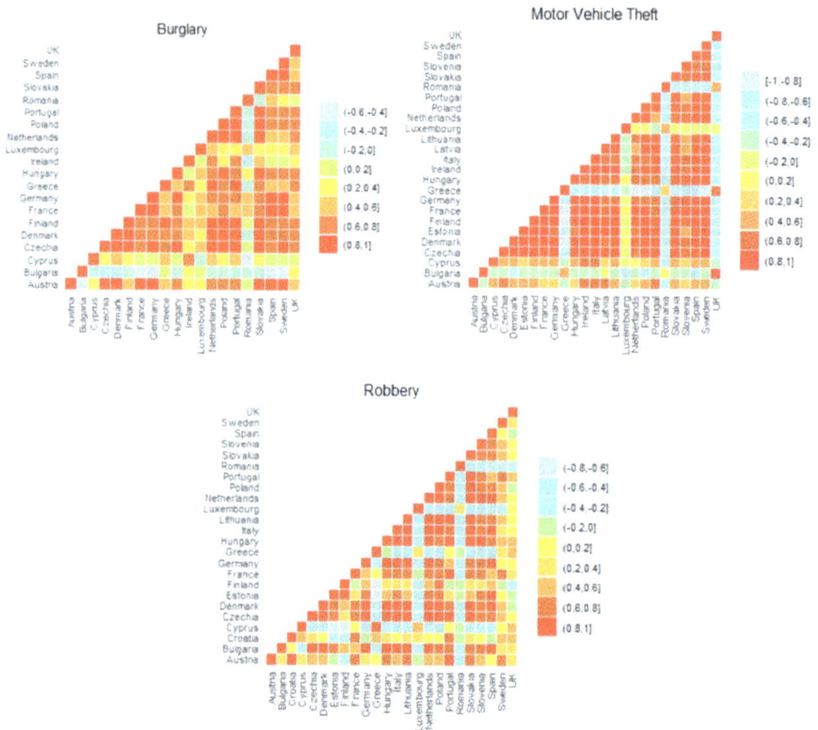

Source: Eurostat. Authors' calculation.

Figure 2 depicts the correlations across the regions for burglary, motor vehicle theft and robbery. For burglary, Bulgaria, Cyprus, Ireland, Luxembourg, Romania are diverging. For motor vehicle theft, Greece, Luxembourg, Romania and the UK are diverging. For robbery, the density of red color is relatively low, signifying a low correlation among the region.

Figure 3. Heatmap for Sexual Violence and Rape

Figure 3: Heatmap for Sexual Violence and Rape

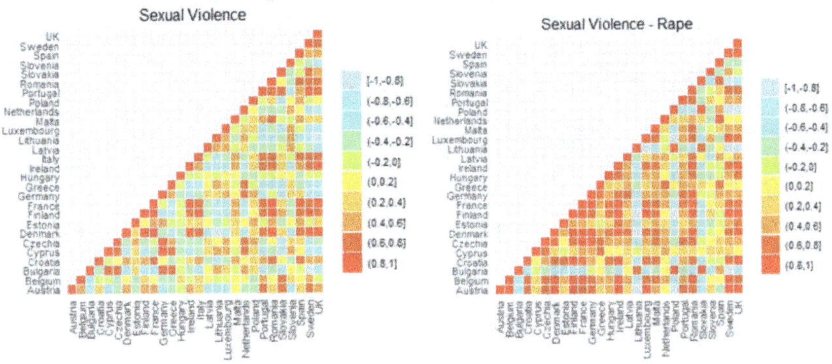

Source: Eurostat. Authors' calculation.

Figure 3 depicts the correlations across the regions for sexual violence and rape. For sexual violence, there is almost no high positive correlation except for groups such as Czechia-Cyprus-Germany and Romania-Finland-France-Ireland-Italy-Denmark-UK-Sweden. Similarly, for rape, there is almost no high positive correlation except for groups such as Austria-Belgium-Denmark-Finland-Ireland-Luxembourg-Sweden-UK, Czechia-France-Germany and Netherlands-Spain-Greece-Slovakia.

Following the heatmaps, we observe that there is no high correlation across European countries in the overall sense, however minor groupings exist within the region. In other words, these visualizations indicate potential structural or contextual differences between the countries. Last but not the least, we do not observe similarity in terms of crime types, *i.e.*, similarity between the indicators of violent offenses (intentional homicide, kidnapping, serious assault, sexual violence and rape) or between the indicators of property crimes (robbery, burglary and motor vehicle theft).

5. MAPPING FOR THE CRIME TYPES

This section shows the visual representation of the crime types over three decades, *i.e.*, 2000s, 2010s and 2020s (on averages) via mapping for Europe. The figures help us offer insights on the dynamics of the crime rates over time.

Figure 4. European Mapping over the time horizon for Intentional Homicide, Kidnapping and serious assault

Figure 4: European Mapping over the time horizon for Intentional Homicide, Kidnapping and Serious Assault

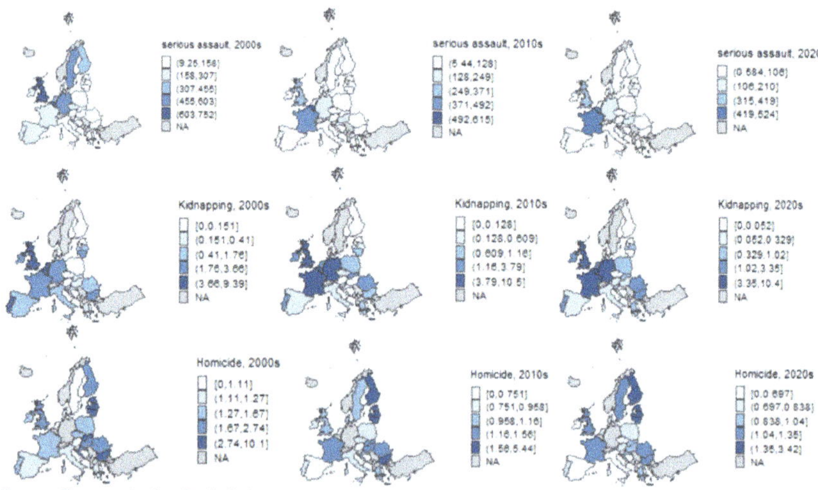

Source: Eurostat. Authors' calculation.

Figure 4 depicts the European mapping over the time horizon for intentional homicide, kidnapping and serious assault. For serious assault rate, the highest-ranking countries switch from the Nordic countries, UK, Belgium and Germany to France and Belgium. For kidnapping, France and Germany ranks highest over the years. For intentional homicide, while the rates are falling for the whole region, Cyprus, Finland, Estonia, Latvia and Lithuania ranks the highest in the 2020s.

Figure 5. European mapping over the time horizon for burglary, motor vehicle theft and robbery

Figure 5: European Mapping over the time horizon for Burglary, Motor Vehicle Theft and Robbery

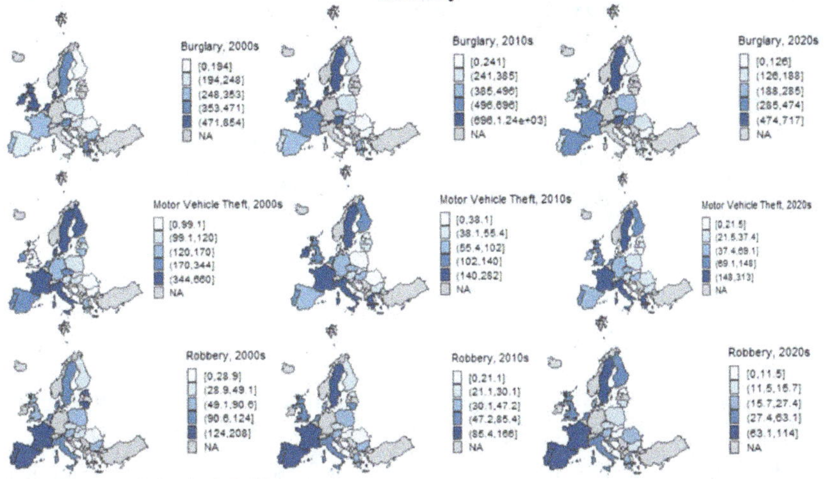

Source: Eurostat. Authors' calculation.

Figure 5 depicts the European mapping over the time horizon for burglary, motor vehicle theft and robbery. For burglary, while the UK, Denmark and Netherlands rank highest in the 2000s, Austria, Denmark, Luxembourg and Sweden rank the highest over the years. For motor vehicle theft, Greece ranks one of the highest over the years along with France, Italy, Luxembourg and Sweden. For robbery, the rates are declining over the years for all countries and the ranks do not change much over the years except for the dramatic drop down of the rates for Estonia and Lithuania over the years.

Figure 6. European mapping over the time horizon for sexual violence and rape

Figure 6: European Mapping over the time horizon for Sexual Violence and Rape

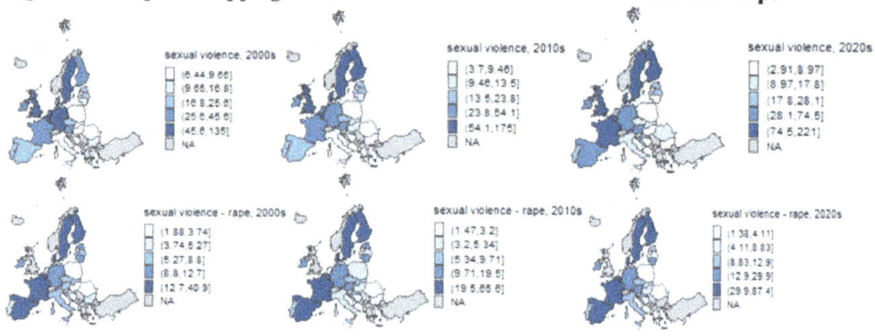

Source: Eurostat. Authors' calculation.

Figure 6 depicts the European mapping over the time horizon for sexual violence and rape. In the 2000s, Belgium, Germany, Luxembourg, Netherlands, Sweden and the UK are ranking the highest in sexual violence, in 2020s, Sweden and the UK still rank the highest in sexual violence along with Denmark, France. Rape rates reflect increase over the years for all countries except for Bulgaria, Lithuania, Poland and Slovakia. Belgium, Denmark, Finland, France, Sweden and the UK have the highest rates that reflect tremendous rise over the years.

The mappings in the overall sense depict some slight spatial similarities, such that kidnapping rates in Western Europe, robbery rates in Southern and Western Europe and rape rates in Nordic Europe reflect similarities. These visualizations are in line with the argument of heterogeneity across Europe using heatmaps since we cannot conclude a homogeneity within the region and over the time dynamics. On the other hand, the selected time period covers some shocks that may affect crime rates depending on the type of the shock. One shock is the economic crisis that hit the region during 2008 and 2010, global financial crisis and sovereign debt crisis, respectively. Following the fact that the Greek economy is affected the most, Figure A1 shows the property crime rate trends in Greece with 2008 and 2010 crisis depicted as black and grey vertical lines, successively. The trend line reflects a rise during both economic crisis. Another shock that is worth of questioning is the refugee crisis that emerges around 2015. Following the fact that Germany ranks first in the region regarding the refugee influx of 2015, Figure A2 shows two of the selected crime rates that may be relevant to the refugee influx, *i.e.*, motor vehicle theft and intentional homicide crime rate trends for Germany. The graph depicts a rise for both crime rates around the period and then reverse back to trend (period after 2015 is highlighted with grey).

6. CORRELATIONS OF THE CRIME TYPES WITH INCOME INEQUALITY

This section presents correlations between crime types and income inequality, as one of the most used determinants in the empirical literature, for each country using heatmap. Theoretically, we may expect a positive relationship between income inequality, measured as GINI coefficient, and crime rates. This relationship may definitely vary depending on the crime types. Crimes related to economic issues are expected to have a higher relationship with GINI. Figure 7 depicts the correlations for each country and crime type. Sexual violence and rape rates reflect almost no high positive correlation, yet tend to have negative correlation. For kidnapping, there seems to be no strong correlation. However, for motor vehicle theft and robbery, Czechia, Poland and Portugal reflect high correlation, and for serious assault and intentional homicide, again Poland reflects the highest correlation within the region.

Figure 7. correlations of the crime types with income inequality

Figure 7: Correlations of the Crime Types with Income Inequality

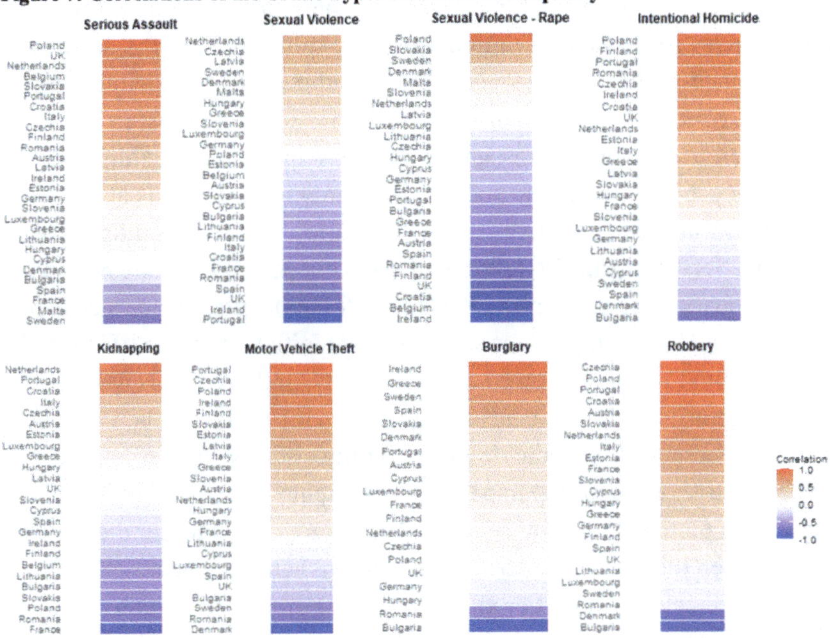

Source: Eurostat. Authors' calculation.

7. DISCUSSION

Income inequality refers to the gap between the rich and the poor within a society. In capitalistic societies, unequal income distribution is expected by nature, however in the existence of a dramatic gap between different levels of a society or a significant change in the living conditions may be stress factors. Likewise, Tsushima (1996) highlights the effect of income inequality on the possibility of engaging in crime. Moreover, several other macroeconomic variables may also affect crime rates such as education level, urbanization rates and institutional quality of the society (Flango and Sherbenou 1976; Groot and van den Brink 2010; Errol et al. 2021). Even though the studies mainly concentrate on micro (individual) level analysis, macroeconomic perspective still applies once we generalize the relationship on a theoretical basis and decompose the overall crimes rate according to crime types.

For instance, the reason for drug use is generally linked to psychological problems individuals cannot manage, whereas what is referred as deviance is linked to feeling outsider due to social ties with the existing deviant groups rather than the conventional institutions, lack of stability, future goals and the absence of a sense of greater loss when seeking immediate pleasure (Becker, 1963). Under an interdisciplinary perspective, criminologists try to understand the motivation and the consequences of the criminal act at micro and macro level. Criminology grows dramatically over the years which signals the rise in the interest in the field. The funds directed to support the research on the discipline also highlight the importance of the cost of crime to the society. This growing interest is also reflected in the support of European initiatives such as the European Organisation of Prison and Correctional Services (EuroPris), which fosters cooperation among national prison administrations and promotes rights-based, professional practices aimed at reducing re-offending and improving public safety. Recent initiatives at the EU level, like the 2010 Stockholm Programme on freedom, security, and justice, as well as localised urban safety measures, may have influenced regional crime trends; however, assessing their effectiveness is outside the descriptive limits of this chapter.

As for motive, economic perspectives contribute largely to the understanding of crime. The pioneer study by Merton (1938) proposes anomie theory such that the gap between the economic goals (expectations) and the means to achieve them (opportunity) creates criminal motivation in the form of frustration and alienation and therefore leads to criminal behavior. Messner (1989) extends this concept by including several determinants such as race, income and employment conditions. However, Wilson (1983) argues that it is not unemployment per se that leads to crime but the inherent factors in the system. Regarding delinquency, Cloward and Ohlin (1960) highlight the illegitimate means that cover the existence of such an environment. In the empirical sense, this social disorganization refers to persistence, which may be captured by an autoregressive coefficient in a time series analysis. Messner and Rosenfeld (1997) add the "American Dream" to the causes of crimes for the US such that the material success is inherent to this society which leads to relatively higher crime rates compared to other developed nations. This underscores the influence of the system on which the society is built upon. The impact of leisure on crime, employment, unemployment, and social conditions contributes to shaping criminal motivation (Sacco and Kennedy, 1998). Moreover, location may also matter, as earlier literature suggests: Wirth (1938) states that social controls are stricter in large cities, which may discourage criminal activity, while Gans (1962) and Fisher (1975) argue that cities may also attract criminals.

Building on this theoretical foundation, our empirical results provide further touch. There seems to be significant heterogeneity among EU member states regarding different crime types and income inequality. The results point out that figure 1, 2, and 3 in the heatmaps do not indicate whether crime rate is low or high. Rather, they show the degree of heterogeneity in the patterns. In some EU states such as Luxembourg, which usually stands out as an outlier in all crime types except for sexual assault, we are able to notice the heterogeneity. Given Luxembourg's small population size, high wealth levels, and large cross-border workforce, even minor changes in reported crime rates or inequality measures can disproportionately influence correlation coefficients, creating an exaggerated picture of divergence.

Similarly, countries such as the UK, Bulgaria, and Romania also exhibit strong deviations in certain figures, suggesting that differences in socio-political structures, economic transitions, and institutional capacities significantly shape the crime rates. The heatmaps for intentional homicide, kidnapping, and serious assault show limited clustering of red zones, indicating relatively weak heterogeneity in crime rates across the EU. Kidnapping, in particular, shows less homogeneity, considering the fact that it is less likely to happen it is less often driven by economic motives. In contrast, crimes like burglary and motor vehicle theft show stronger divergence, especially in countries such as Bulgaria, Greece, Luxembourg, Romania, and the UK. These types of property crimes are more likely to be economically motivated and hence more sensitive to income inequality.

However, reporting the crime may be different and vary widely across the EU, which can make it difficult to compare these countries. In countries where individuals have more trust in law enforcement or robust crime classification systems, such as UK, individuals are more likely to report crime, not necessarily because they are more prevalent, but because they are more systematically recorded.

Sexual violence and rape show relatively low levels of correlation (both in the heatmaps and in Figure 7) suggesting a distinct pattern from other crime types especially the ones that are economically motivated. Both sexual violence and rape can be considered as crime types that are deeply embedded in cultural and social contexts. Additionally, this may be because of underreporting due to the possibility of the victim feeling exposed, differences in legal definitions, or lack of victim support mechanisms. Countries such as Sweden, the UK, and Finland, which have more developed legal support and social awareness around gender-based violence, may appear to have higher rates due to more comprehensive reporting rather than higher actual crime rate.

While some EU member states like Czechia, Poland, and Portugal show high correlations between inequality and crimes such as robbery or motor vehicle theft, others show low correlation. Poland stands out for its particularly high correlations in serious assault, intentional homicide, and robbery, which could be explained with visible rural-urban differences, imbalances in regional development, underdeveloped social help. The patterns shown across the figures suggest that crime is not solely a function of economic inequality but is shaped by a bundle of factors including legal background, reporting patterns, public trust in institutions, culture, and policy frameworks. Certain countries highlight the importance regarding focusing on the issue with context-specific policies.

8. CONCLUSION

This research aims to theoretically and visually investigate the crime and income inequality link across Europe. By dividing crime into different components such as sexual assault, sexual violence, sexual violence-rape, intentional homicide, kidnapping, motor vehicle theft, burglary, and robbery, we apply correlation analyses using data of 2003-2022 at the country level. Our findings suggest that crime rates vary by nation and that using correlations provides no clear homogeneity for any of the crime category. Our results indicate that crime varies across European countries. Of all crime rates, only intentional murder shows a clear decline over the horizon; the other crime types change with time and the ranks move around the area. Results regarding income inequality and crime nexus are in line with the assumptions. Among all countries, Poland, Netherlands, Portugal, Ireland and Czechia exhibit the highest positive correlations between wealth inequality and crime rates. All things considered, our findings suggest a lack of homogeneity and convergence. Although European countries share certain features — such as integrated monetary and fiscal policies, partially interconnected energy markets, and some common social values — they also differ significantly in terms of institutional strength, law enforcement efficiency, socio-economic structures, and public attitudes toward crime. These differences hinder the emergence of a uniform trend across countries. Therefore, the possibility of full convergence in crime rates across Europe appears highly unlikely. Many elements might be behind this lack of convergence and homogeneity during the time period capturing external shocks including migration, economic crises, political upheaval, etc. Moreover, welfare regimes successfully address other inequalities — including disparities in access to education, healthcare, housing, and employment opportunities —in Southern and Western European nations with high income inequalities, potentially reducing crime. This could be as a result of the deeply rooted minimum income levels in the welfare system of the EU member states. Countries and regions in Europe have different welfare systems; many Western and Southern European nations have conservative corporate welfare states (Headey et al., 2000; Kim et al., 2000). Since social integration and income stability are top welfare priorities, it is impossible for a sizable section of the population to fall below the threshold required for significant patterns of income inequality.

Moreover, the heterogeneity among European states and across different crime rates can be attributed to the hesitation of victims and individuals who experience crime, particularly in relation to crime reporting. We believe that the underlying causes of this reporting issue can be explained by (a) the bureaucratic systems or administrative structures of the countries, (b) sociological factors (such as individual perceptions and personal exposure to crime), and (c) economic factors (economic dependency of the individual, fear of job loss/unemployment). These differences highlight that a cultural union—crucial for fostering social cohesion and reducing crime—has not yet been fully achieved within the region.

In conclusion, the relationships between crime and inequality differ significantly among European states and across various types of crime. Economic crimes, such as those relating to property, show a stronger correlation with inequality measures. While it is important to take country-specific measures when regional and temporal differences are taken into account, this approach alone is not sufficient. The significant heterogeneity observed in crime rates even among geographically, historically and culturally close countries such as Europe shows that social and structural dynamics are effective not only at the macro level but also at the micro level. In this context, more targeted and well-grounded policies are needed, such as the development of special programs for education, social cohesion and employment in regions with a high proportion of young male population; increasing housing opportunities; and interventions to address income and education inequalities. In addition, not only the level of economic development but also social risk factors should be taken into account in the distribution of EU funds; rehabilitation and youth support programs should be prioritized, especially in areas at risk of high crime rates. Such holistic and targeted policy recommendations are of great importance as they demonstrate that the study not only provides a baseline but also contributes to existing policy gaps. Last but not least, under-reporting and the examination of demographic and policy shocks are considered directions for future research.

REFERENCES

Aebi, M. F. (2008). Measuring the influence of statistical counting rules on cross-national differences in recorded crime. Crime and Criminal Justice Systems in Europe and North America 1995-2004, 196-214.

Aebi, M. F., & Linde, A. (2012). Conviction Statistics as an Indicator of Crime Trends in Europe from 1990 to 2006. *European Journal on Criminal Policy and Research*, *18*(1), 103–144. DOI: 10.1007/s10610-011-9166-7

Agnew, R. (2015). Strain, economic status, and crime. The handbook of criminological theory, 209-229. DOI: 10.1002/9781118512449.ch11

Antunes, M. J. L., & Manasse, M. (2022). Social disorganization and strain: Macro and micro implications for youth violence. *Journal of Research in Crime and Delinquency*, *59*(1), 82–127. DOI: 10.1177/00224278211004667

Aronson, E. (1988). *The social animal*. Freeman.

Becker, G. S. (1968). Crime and Punishment: An Economic Approach. The economic dimensions of crime/Springer.

Becker, H. S. (1963). *Outsiders. Studies in the Sociology of Deviance*. The Free Press.

Bourguignon, F. (1999). Crime as a social cost of poverty and inequality: A review focusing on developing countries. *Revista. Desarrollo y Sociedad*, (44), 61–99.

Browning, C. R., Dietz, R. D., & Feinberg, S. L. (2004). The paradox of social organization: Networks, collective efficacy, and violent crime in urban neighborhoods. *Social Forces*, *83*(2), 503–534. DOI: 10.1353/sof.2005.0006

Charlot, O., Naiditch, C., & Vranceanu, R. (2022). Migrant smuggling to Europe: A matching model. ESSEC Business School Research Paper.

Chiu, W. H., & Madden, P. (1998). Burglary and income inequality. *Journal of Public Economics*, *69*(1), 123–141. DOI: 10.1016/S0047-2727(97)00096-0

Cloward, R. A., & Ohlin, L. E. (1960). Illegitimate means and delinquent subcultures. *Social Deviance: Readings in Theory & Research*, *5*, 45–49.

Coccia, M., Cohn, E. G., & Kakar, S. (2024). How immigration, level of unemployment, and income inequality affect crime in Europe. *Crime, Law, and Social Change*, *82*(2), 363–385. DOI: 10.1007/s10611-024-10144-y

Cohn, E. G., Coccia, M., & Kakar, S. (2021). The relationship between crime, immigration and socioeconomic factors. *Rassegna Italiana di Criminologia*, (3), 180–191.

Daly, M., & Wilson, M. (1988). Evolutionary social psychology and family homicide. *Science, 242*(4878), 519–524. DOI: 10.1126/science.3175672

Dorfman, A. (1984). The criminal mind. *Science Digest, 92*(10), 44–47, 98.

Eitle, D. J. (2002). Exploring a source of deviance-producing strain for females: Perceived discrimination and general strain theory. *Journal of Criminal Justice, 30*(5), 429–442. DOI: 10.1016/S0047-2352(02)00146-0

Ellis, L. (1982). Genetics and criminal behavior evidence through the end of the 1970s. *Criminology, 20*(1), 43–66. DOI: 10.1111/j.1745-9125.1982.tb00447.x

Enamorado, T., López-Calva, L. F., Rodríguez-Castelán, C., & Winkler, H. (2016). Income inequality and violent crime: Evidence from Mexico's drug war. *Journal of Development Economics, 120*, 128–143. DOI: 10.1016/j.jdeveco.2015.12.004

Errol, Z., Madsen, J. B., & Moslehi, S. (2021). Social disorganization theory and crime in the advanced countries: Two centuries of evidence. *Journal of Economic Behavior & Organization, 191*, 519–537. DOI: 10.1016/j.jebo.2021.09.017

Ersoy, I., & DOĞAN, F. İ. (2016). Impact Of EU Governance Reforms And ECB Policy Reactions On European Government Bond Markets. *International Journal of Economic Perspectives, 10*(1), 116–130.

Escudero, V., & Mourelo, E. L. (2015). *The Youth Guarantee programme in Europe: Features, implementation and challenges*. ILO.

Fagan, J., & Freeman, R. B. (1999). Crime and work. *Crime and Justice, 25*, 225–290. DOI: 10.1086/449290

Felson, M., & Clarke, R. V. (1998). *Opportunity Makes the Thief, Practical Theory for Crime Prevention*. Police Research Series.

Fisher, C. S. (1975). The effect of urban life on traditional values. *Social Forces, 53*(3), 420–432. DOI: 10.2307/2576584

Flango, V. E., & Sherbenou, E. L. (1976). Poverty, urbanization, and crime. *Criminology, 14*(3), 331–346. DOI: 10.1111/j.1745-9125.1976.tb00027.x

Freeman, R. (1995). The labor market. *Crime*, 171-92.

Freeman, R. B. (1999). The economics of crime. *Handbook of labor economics, 3*, 3529-3571.

Gans, H. (1962). *The Urban Villagers*. Free Press.

Goh, L. T., & Law, S. H. (2023). The crime rate of five Latin American countries: Does income inequality matter? *International Review of Economics & Finance, 86*, 745–763. DOI: 10.1016/j.iref.2023.03.036

Gottfredson, M. R., & Hirschi, T. (1990). A general theory of crime. In *A general theory of crime*. Stanford University Press. DOI: 10.1515/9781503621794

Groot, W., & van den Brink, H. M. (2010). The effects of education on crime. *Applied Economics, 42*(3), 279–289. DOI: 10.1080/00036840701604412

Gruszczynska, B., & Gruszczynski, M. (2005). Crime in enlarged Europe: Comparison of crime rates and victimization risks. *Transition Studies Review, 12*(2), 337–345. DOI: 10.1007/s11300-005-0065-9

Gruszczyńska, B., & Heiskanen, M. (2018). Trends in police-recorded offenses at the beginning of the twenty-first century in Europe. *European Journal on Criminal Policy and Research, 24*(1), 37–53. DOI: 10.1007/s10610-018-9370-9

Headey, B., Goodin, R. E., Muffels, R., & Dirven, H. J. (2000). Is There a Trade-Off Between Economic Efficiency and a Generous Welfare State? A Comparison of Best Cases ofThe Three Worlds of Welfare Capitalism'. *Social Indicators Research, 50*(2), 115–157. DOI: 10.1023/A:1007005619530

Hickey, A. (1991). *Serial murderers and their victims*. Wadsworth.

Kaeding, M., Pollak, J., & Schmidt, P. (Eds.). (2020). *Euroscepticism and the Future of Europe: Views from the Capitals*. Springer Nature.

Karakuş, Ö., & Başıbüyük, O. (2010). Social disorganization theory and human trafficking: A systemic control approach to the phenomenon. *Polis Bilimleri Dergisi, 12*(2).

Kelly, M. (2000). Inequality and crime. *The Review of Economics and Statistics, 82*(4), 530–539. DOI: 10.1162/003465300559028

Kim, B., Seo, C., & Hong, Y. O. (2020). A systematic review and meta-analysis of income inequality and crime in Europe: Do places matter? *European Journal on Criminal Policy and Research*, •••, 1–24.

Kistner, N. (2007). The Sources and Consequences of Public Perceptions of Corruption. Continuity and Change in Social Life: Structural and Psychological Adjustment in Poland. Warsaw: IFiS Publishers.

Mednick, S. A., Gabrielli, W. F., & Hutchings, B. (1987). Genetic factors in the etiology of criminal behavior. *The causes of crime: New biological approaches*, 74-91.

Merton, R. K. (1938). Social Structure and Anomie. *American Sociological Review*, *3*(5), 672–682. DOI: 10.2307/2084686

Messner, S. F. (1989). Economic discrimination and societal homicide rates: Further evidence on the cost of inequality. *American Sociological Review*, *54*(4), 597–611. DOI: 10.2307/2095881

Messner, S. F., & Rosenfeld, R. (1997). Political restraint of the market and levels of criminal homicide: A cross-national application of institutional-anomie theory. *Social Forces*, *75*(4), 1393–1416.

Murray, C., & Herrnstein, R. J. (1994). Race, genes, and IQ–An apologia. *New Republic (New York, N.Y.)*, *211*(18), 27–37.

Musterd, S., Marcińczak, S., Van Ham, M., & Tammaru, T. (2017). Socioeconomic segregation in European capital cities. Increasing separation between poor and rich. *Urban Geography*, *38*(7), 1062–1083. DOI: 10.1080/02723638.2016.1228371

President's Commission on Law Enforcement and Administration of Justice. (1967). The Challenge of Crime in a Free Society. Washington: U.S. Government Printing Office.

Rennó Santos, M., Testa, A., & Weiss, D. B. (2021). Inflation and cross-national homicide: Assessing nonlinear and moderation effects across 65 countries, 1965–2015. *International Criminal Justice Review*, *31*(2), 122–139. DOI: 10.1177/1057567720981624

Sacco, V. F., & Kennedy, L. W. (1998). *The Criminal Event*. International Thomson Publishing.

Salt, J. (2000). Trafficking and human smuggling: A European perspective. *International Migration (Geneva, Switzerland)*, *38*(3), 31–56. DOI: 10.1111/1468-2435.00114

Scarpa, S. (2015). The spatial manifestation of inequality: Residential segregation in Sweden and its causes (Doctoral dissertation, Linnaeus University Press).

Shaw, C., & McKay, H. (1942). *Juvenile Delinquency and Urban Areas*. Univ. Press.

Smith, H. J., Pettigrew, T. F., Pippin, G. M., & Bialosiewicz, S. (2012). Relative deprivation: A theoretical and meta-analytic review. *Personality and Social Psychology Review*, *16*(3), 203–232. DOI: 10.1177/1088868311430825

Thornton, A., Bhorat, H., Lilenstein, A., Monnakgotla, J., & van der Zee, K. (2023). Crime, Income, and Inequality: Nonlinearities under Extreme Inequality in South Africa. *Economic Development and Cultural Change*, *72*(1), 207–240. DOI: 10.1086/719646

Tonry, M. (2014). Why crime rates are falling throughout the Western world. *Crime and Justice*, *43*(1), 1–63. DOI: 10.1086/678181

Torrente, D., Gallo, P., & Oltra, C. (2017). Comparing crime reporting factors in EU countries. *European Journal on Criminal Policy and Research*, *23*(2), 153–174. DOI: 10.1007/s10610-016-9310-5

Tsushima, M. (1996). Economic structure and crime: The case of Japan. *Journal of Socio-Economics*, *25*(4), 497–515. DOI: 10.1016/S1053-5357(96)90041-4

Tuttle, J. (2022). Inequality, concentrated disadvantage, and homicide: Towards a multi-level theory of economic inequality and crime. *International Journal of Comparative and Applied Criminal Justice*, *46*(3), 215–232. DOI: 10.1080/01924036.2021.1942103

Vold, G. B., & Bernard, T. J. (1986). *Theoretical Criminology* (3rd ed.). Oxford University Press.

Wilson, J. Q. (1983). Crime and American culture. *The Public Interest*, *70*, 22.

Wilson, J. Q., & Herrnstein, R. J. (1985). Crime &. *Human Nature (Hawthorne, N.Y.)*.

Wirth, L. (1938). Urbanism as a way of life. *American Journal of Sociology*, *44*(1), 3–24. DOI: 10.1086/217913

KEY TERMS AND DEFINITIONS

Crime Heterogeneity: Differences in the types, frequency and intensity of crime in European countries. This diversity arises due to factors such as the level of economic development, social policies, cultural structures and legal regulations.

Economic Crimes: These are crimes whose main purpose is to obtain financial gain. Crimes such as theft, tax evasion, fraud and money laundering fall under this category. They are often associated with income inequality and poverty.

Income Inequality: Income inequality refers to income differences between individuals or groups within society. High levels of income inequality are associated with social exclusion, insecurity and increased crime rates.

Property Crime: Covers crimes committed against the property of individuals. Acts such as theft, motor vehicle theft, property damage are included in this group. Economic conditions and social inequalities are among the determining factors of property crimes.

Social Disorganization Theory: It is based on the weakening of social institutions (family, school, community structures) and the resulting decrease in social control and consequent increase in crime rates. It is especially valid in low-income and disadvantaged neighbourhoods.

Strain Theory: It argues that obstacles to achieving the goals society expects of individuals (e.g. financial success) lead individuals to seek alternative - and often illegal - paths. This theory argues that criminal behavior is related to social and economic pressures.

Violent Crime: Includes crimes that may result in physical harm or death. Crimes such as murder, assault and sexual assault are included in this category. Social tensions and social disintegration can play a role in the spread of such crimes.

ENDNOTES

1 Crime rate = crime level/population*100,000

APPENDIX

Table 1. Statistics on Crime Types (on averages)

Sexual Violence	2000s	2010s	2020s	Sexual Violence-Rape	2000s	2010s	2020s
Austria	33.91	46.44	50.20	Austria	8.53	15.64	20.81
Belgium	71.42	83.15	88.24	Belgium	29.32	31.34	36.52
Bulgaria	12.25	8.68	8.12	Bulgaria	4.75	2.07	1.38
Croatia	14.24	13.25	18.45	Croatia	3.85	6.18	9.28
Cyprus	11.33	3.70	5.57	Cyprus	3.32	3.04	5.20
Czechia	17.14	13.55	15.27	Czechia	5.69	6.04	12.16
Denmark	32.44	55.51	102.67	Denmark	17.00	23.10	43.69
Estonia	23.93	19.00	26.71	Estonia	10.23	11.17	12.28
Finland	41.00	57.11	85.41	Finland	12.71	20.53	31.99
France	39.34	51.91	108.40	France	16.48	21.26	48.07
Germany	66.89	45.00	53.12	Germany	9.81	9.79	13.26
Greece	6.44	4.20	2.91	Greece	1.88	1.47	2.40
Hungary	6.54	12.69	5.36	Hungary	2.73	3.74	5.36
Ireland	35.85	47.78	58.19	Ireland	8.98	13.84	21.49
Italy	7.06	7.94	9.84	Latvia	6.94	5.31	10.86
Latvia	22.71	20.22	18.39	Lithuania	6.71	4.96	2.47
Lithuania	13.19	10.65	4.93	Luxembourg	9.84	14.74	18.08
Luxembourg	76.72	57.10	53.91	Malta	3.71	4.18	5.66
Malta	20.07	20.30	23.70	Netherlands	12.62	9.26	14.00
Netherlands	48.71	28.06	27.65	Poland	5.00	2.55	1.54
Poland	8.53	8.12	8.40	Portugal	3.30	3.71	3.98
Portugal	18.49	22.68	26.42	Romania	4.87	5.40	10.06
Romania	7.64	8.15	12.09	Slovakia	3.47	1.83	1.78
Slovakia	7.87	12.30	11.08	Slovenia	6.25	9.58	8.52
Slovenia	15.34	12.54	11.76	Spain	5.00	3.08	4.64
Spain	22.73	20.92	30.12	Sweden	40.92	65.63	87.38
Sweden	134.84	174.92	207.60	UK	21.61	43.43	62.02
UK	93.66	157.72	221.38				

Source: Eurostat. Authors' calculation.

Table 2. Statistics on Crime Types (on averages) Cont.

Serious Assault	2000s	2010s	2020s	Kidnapping	2000s	2010s	2020s	Intentional Homicide	2000s	2010s	2020s
Austria	45.31	42.56	42.81	Austria	0.06	0.06	0.05	Austria	0.73	0.75	0.77
Belgium	665.90	614.03	521.22	Belgium	9.39	10.49	10.43	Bulgaria	2.90	1.56	1.13
Bulgaria	43.72	36.05	41.29	Bulgaria	2.07	1.15	1.13	Croatia	1.76	1.02	0.88
Croatia	25.67	19.47	18.82	Croatia	0.31	0.07	0.03	Cyprus	1.11	1.26	1.45
Cyprus	16.86	17.49	18.29	Cyprus	1.74	0.92	0.41	Czechia	1.32	0.80	0.62
Czechia	160.37	47.98	36.88	Czechia	0.14	0.14	0.05	Denmark	1.17	0.96	0.81
Denmark	30.04	30.12	33.71	Estonia	0.11	0.03	0.00	Estonia	8.14	3.40	2.20
Estonia	9.99	6.94	5.24	Finland	0.03	0.03	0.04	Finland	2.46	1.64	1.42
Finland	432.18	31.65	30.97	France	3.42	4.58	5.51	France	1.55	1.21	1.13
France	270.43	389.94	523.83	Germany	2.75	5.91	5.82	Germany	1.04	0.91	0.86
Germany	546.73	165.08	159.26	Greece	0.23	0.91	0.73	Greece	1.15	1.12	0.90
Greece	50.34	13.87	11.95	Hungary	0.15	0.08	0.07	Hungary	1.87	1.38	0.85
Hungary	119.93	135.30	131.24	Ireland	1.78	1.67	1.98	Ireland	1.44	0.90	0.65
Ireland	249.27	79.84	101.21	Italy	0.48	0.44	0.21	Italy	1.21	0.75	0.51
Italy	102.24	46.33	1.45	Latvia	0.65	0.52	0.49	Latvia	7.30	3.83	3.42
Latvia	53.12	39.03	29.66	Lithuania	1.79	0.75	0.03	Lithuania	10.10	5.44	2.86
Lithuania	10.67	6.76	5.02	Luxembourg	6.11	8.29	6.87	Luxembourg	1.11	0.74	0.88
Luxembourg	429.91	115.70	90.60	Netherlands	4.93	2.94	2.81	Netherlands	1.06	0.73	0.73
Malta	45.12	42.45	36.97	Poland	0.15	0.67	0.78	Poland	1.61	0.84	0.71
Netherlands	395.01	32.37	28.01	Portugal	4.60	3.64	2.37	Portugal	1.30	0.95	0.76
Poland	31.01	22.02	13.51	Romania	1.36	1.61	1.80	Romania	2.33	1.56	1.34
Portugal	277.17	6.05	6.29	Slovakia	0.17	1.18	0.95	Slovakia	4.21	1.37	0.98
Romania	44.56	30.68	1.11	Slovenia	0.26	0.21	0.13	Slovenia	0.63	0.72	0.52
Slovakia	61.82	35.23	22.61	Spain	0.47	0.21	0.18	Spain	1.18	0.71	0.66
Slovenia	88.51	8.52	5.67	UK	4.83	4.36	5.61	Sweden	1.01	0.98	1.13
Spain	283.72	42.27	44.10					UK	2.70	1.08	1.18
Sweden	591.01	51.61	47.33								
UK	751.65	288.12	340.48								

Source: Eurostat. Authors' calculation.

Table 3. Statistics on Crime Types (on averages) Cont.

Robbery	2000s	2010s	2020s	Burglary	2000s	2010s	2020s	Motor Vehicle Theft	2000s	2010s	2020s
Austria	52.40	39.52	25.32	Austria	416.69	781.49	516.20	Austria	99.88	52.68	33.66
Bulgaria	49.26	31.37	13.25	Bulgaria	351.35	191.05	66.70	Bulgaria	26.55	42.67	22.22
Croatia	28.42	28.04	16.29	Cyprus	224.64	211.06	106.44	Cyprus	153.91	121.05	108.77
Cyprus	6.78	10.92	8.99	Czechia	188.80	394.96	269.03	Czechia	217.24	89.26	39.96
Czechia	48.49	23.76	12.23	Denmark	854.34	1238.07	573.34	Denmark	548.61	9.37	17.16
Denmark	97.71	44.11	24.69	Finland	185.26	383.12	120.12	Estonia	130.48	35.87	7.74
Estonia	150.95	26.67	8.52	France	348.34	541.73	416.59	Finland	355.84	135.21	105.74
Finland	37.36	29.91	37.43	Germany	213.22	494.51	321.42	France	473.86	261.44	247.80
France	192.00	165.80	104.87	Greece	369.11	495.33	130.25	Germany	126.23	73.37	50.37
Germany	67.49	53.59	40.95	Hungary	244.30	363.08	315.99	Greece	125.81	256.18	153.00
Greece	22.83	45.29	24.43	Ireland	504.71	495.95	187.31	Hungary	112.39	57.28	50.18
Hungary	31.47	19.30	5.76	Luxembourg	460.61	579.50	533.22	Ireland	340.51	142.20	62.91
Italy	115.30	73.97	38.91	Netherlands	817.77	1160.51	237.08	Italy	427.25	281.78	189.49
Lithuania	130.04	54.81	13.47	Poland	196.92	261.14	192.34	Latvia	110.93	48.67	29.96
Luxembourg	71.84	88.16	90.05	Portugal	264.06	327.85	169.60	Lithuania	141.61	44.74	15.53
Netherlands	106.24	66.80	35.85	Romania	55.74	133.50	134.10	Luxembourg	102.76	83.97	312.76
Poland	88.79	30.18	13.21	Slovakia	98.96	161.05	64.17	Netherlands	193.19	139.36	146.59
Portugal	188.21	147.31	82.97	Spain	241.48	390.68	288.38	Poland	109.60	36.75	27.10
Romania	14.28	16.96	17.93	Sweden	353.12	894.86	717.47	Portugal	252.22	131.55	78.41
Slovakia	29.67	12.83	5.67	UK	485.71	638.30	445.48	Romania	8.06	15.83	29.08
Slovenia	22.16	15.83	10.97					Slovakia	95.88	38.47	16.51
Spain	207.79	158.93	113.75					Slovenia	39.51	28.93	18.48
Sweden	98.22	90.48	72.56					Spain	289.61	87.71	45.21
UK	66.91	81.30	48.80					Sweden	660.02	271.74	182.83
								UK	61.43	135.30	121.36

Source: Eurostat. Authors' calculation.

Figure 8. Property crime rate trends in Greece

Figure A1. Property crime rate trends in Greece

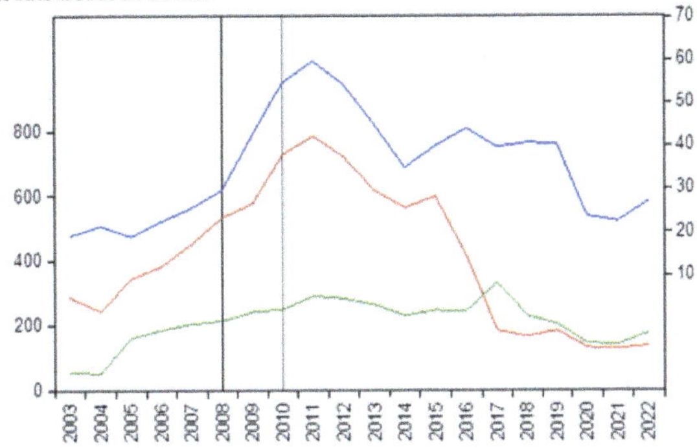

Source: Eurostat. Authors' calculation. Note: Robbery (left-axis), motor vehicle theft (left-axis) and burglary (right-axis) rates are depicted with blue, green and red lines, successively.

Figure 9. Motor vehicle theft and intentional homicide crime rate trends in Germany

Figure A2. Motor vehicle theft and intentional homicide crime rate trends in Germany

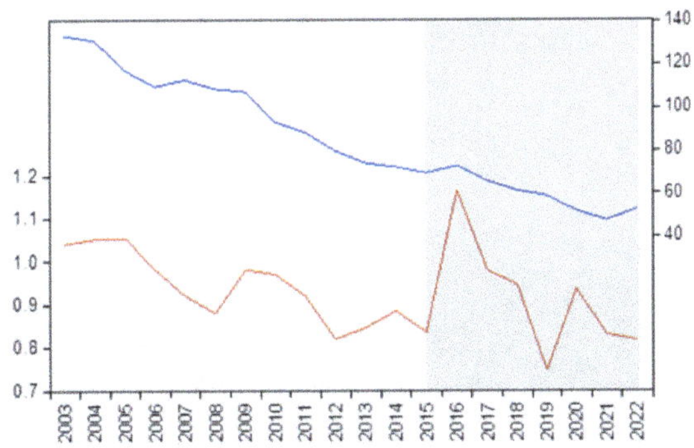

Source: Eurostat. Authors' calculation. Note: intentional homicide (left-axis), motor vehicle theft (right-axis) rates are depicted with red and blue lines, successively.

Chapter 8
Technology-Driven Financial Inclusion Empowering Women in the National Capital Territory

Aman Giri
https://orcid.org/0009-0000-7560-8246
Amity University, Noida, India

Kavita K. Indapurkar
https://orcid.org/0000-0003-4388-2915
Amity University, Noida, India

ABSTRACT

The study investigates the impact of FinTech adoption on the financial empowerment of women in Delhi's NCT region. Using a quantitative design, data were collected via structured questionnaires from 200 women in urban and semi-urban areas. Grounded in the UTAUT and Diffusion of Innovation frameworks, the study analyzed factors like performance expectancy, social influence, and perceived complexity. Results reveal a positive correlation between FinTech use and financial empowerment—reflected in increased savings, financial confidence, and income generation. However, barriers such as low digital literacy and socio-cultural norms hinder broader adoption. The findings highlight FinTech's potential in reducing gender disparities in financial access. Targeted awareness, inclusive tech design, and digital literacy campaigns are crucial for enabling greater adoption and impact.

DOI: 10.4018/979-8-3373-7360-7.ch008

1. INTRODUCTION

In recent decades, financial inclusion has emerged as a critical instrument for promoting inclusive growth, poverty reduction, and gender equality. It refers to the provision of accessible, affordable, and appropriate financial services to all segments of society, particularly underserved and vulnerable populations (Sarma and Pais, 2011). The Reserve Bank of India (RBI) defines financial inclusion as "the process of ensuring access to appropriate financial products and services needed by vulnerable groups such as weaker sections and low-income groups at an affordable cost" (Chakrabarty, 2013). Yet, despite a proliferation of financial inclusion initiatives globally and nationally, significant gender disparities persist in financial service access, usage, and impact. The advent of financial technology (FinTech) has created new pathways to overcome traditional barriers to financial inclusion. FinTech refers to the use of digital technology to deliver financial services more efficiently and inclusively, encompassing mobile banking, digital wallets, micro-lending platforms, and blockchain-enabled services (Demirguc-Kunt *et al.*, 2018). These innovations offer scalable solutions to financial service delivery and have been particularly celebrated for their potential to empower historically excluded groups, especially women (Iskenderian, 2022). By bypassing physical infrastructure constraints, reducing transaction costs, and enabling real-time transactions, FinTech platforms have been recognized as critical enablers of the Sustainable Development Goals (SDGs), notably SDG 5 (Gender Equality), SDG 8 (Decent Work and Economic Growth), and SDG 9 (Industry, Innovation, and Infrastructure) (George and Thomachan, 2018; Gartaula et al., 2025). Globally, evidence from countries like Kenya and Bangladesh demonstrates that digital financial services can contribute significantly to women's economic security, autonomy, and participation (Camilletti et al., 2022). In India, efforts like the Pradhan Mantri Jan Dhan Yojana (PMJDY), Aadhaar-enabled payment systems, and Unified Payments Interface (UPI) have rapidly expanded the digital financial ecosystem (Rangarajan, 2008). Nevertheless, the benefits of these initiatives are not evenly distributed. Gender gaps in account ownership, savings behavior, and digital financial literacy remain significant. According to the Global Findex Database, women in India are still less likely to own a formal bank account or use digital financial platforms than men (Demirguc-Kunt et al., 2018). Within the Indian context, the National Capital Territory (NCT) of Delhi offers a unique socio-economic microcosm encompassing urban, semi-urban, and rural areas. While it benefits from superior financial infrastructure and technology penetration compared to other states, intra-regional disparities persist. Women from lower-income, less-educated, or traditionally conservative communities often face social and technological constraints that hinder their participation in the formal financial system (Sharma, 2024; Pal et al., 2022). Issues like limited smartphone ownership, lack of trust in digital platforms, low digital literacy, and patriarchal decision-making structures are particularly relevant in this region (Kumari, 2022; Patel & Patel, 2020). As a response to these multifaceted challenges, this study investigates the role of FinTech in enhancing women's financial empowerment across the diverse socio-economic settings of Delhi's NCT.

Despite the expansion of FinTech solutions and the digitalization of India's financial ecosystem, the gender gap in financial access and empowerment remains a pressing concern. While programs like PMJDY have significantly increased bank account ownership, nearly 54% of women's accounts in India remain dormant (Demirguc-Kunt et al., 2018). Moreover, digital finance adoption among women is influenced by a complex interplay of socio-cultural norms, technological limitations, and trust deficits (Biswas, 2021; Ray & Chowdhury, 2022). Women in Delhi's NCT, although geographically proximate to India's financial and technological hubs, still face significant barriers to meaningful financial inclusion. These include limited digital literacy, low confidence in handling mobile-based financial services, affordability issues related to smartphone and data access, and continued dependence on male family members for financial decisions (Sharma, 2024; Singh, 2021; Kumari, 2022). While digital financial services are widely available, their actual usage and impact on women's economic agency remain unclear. Furthermore, there is a limited empirical understanding of how FinTech adoption specifically affects women's financial empowerment in the Indian metropolitan context. Prior studies have focused on either rural microfinance models or general urban adoption trends, often ignoring the nuanced realities of women straddling urban, semi-urban, and rural zones in the same region (Kumar, 2022; Pandey, 2025). There is also a lack of intersectional analysis that combines gender, technology, and social norms to understand FinTech adoption behavior. Without empirical data, policies and interventions risk remaining top-down and ineffective. This study addresses this gap by examining how technology-enabled financial inclusion influences women's empowerment in the socio-economically diverse setting of Delhi's NCT, using a structured quantitative approach.

The scope of this study is focused on the National Capital Territory (NCT) of Delhi, encompassing women from urban, semi-urban, and rural regions. The research employs a quantitative exploratory design, using structured questionnaires administered to 400 women respondents aged 18 and above. It explores how factors such as ease of use, affordability, trust, and socio-cultural norms affect the adoption of FinTech and how this adoption correlates with perceived financial empowerment. However, the study is subject to several limitations. First, it relies on self-reported data, which may be influenced by social desirability or recall bias (Bedamatta, 2021). Second, the analysis is cross-sectional, limiting the ability to infer causal relationships between FinTech adoption and long-term empowerment outcomes.

Third, household income data were often incomplete or inconsistent, making it difficult to control for economic status in the analysis. Finally, the study focuses solely on women and does not explore comparative male behavior or inter-gender dynamics, which could offer additional insights into household-level financial behavior. Despite these constraints, the study offers valuable exploratory insights and forms a foundation for future longitudinal and mixed-method research.

Academically, it contributes to a relatively underexplored area: the intersection of gender, technology, and financial inclusion in India's urbanized yet socially stratified regions. It empirically tests elements of the Unified Theory of Acceptance and Use of Technology (UTAUT) and Diffusion of Innovation Theory, contextualized for women's FinTech adoption in the NCT. It also addresses gaps identified in previous literature regarding the lack of region-specific and gender-focused research on FinTech adoption (Biswas, 2021). Practically, the study informs FinTech developers and financial institutions about the unique challenges faced by women users in accessing and using digital platforms. The findings offer guidance on user interface design, trust-building measures, and affordability considerations to improve uptake among female users (Pal et al., 2022). From a policy perspective, the research provides evidence-based insights that can be used to craft targeted digital literacy programs, awareness campaigns, and inclusion frameworks. These are vital for achieving India's commitments under the Sustainable Development Goals (SDGs), especially SDG 5 (Gender Equality) and SDG 9 (Innovation and Infrastructure) (Gartaula et al., 2025; Camilletti et al., 2022). Furthermore, the study contributes to ongoing debates around data privacy, biometric identification, and women's agency in digital spaces, especially considering India's Aadhaar-based financial infrastructure (Singh, 2021).

Empowerment begins with access, but it is sustained through independence and agency. Women's financial autonomy has historically been constrained by limited participation in the formal economy, lack of asset ownership, and societal norms that define men as financial decision-makers. However, digital financial tools are starting to reshape this narrative by allowing women to engage directly with banking services without relying on male intermediaries (Iskenderian, 2022). These services are not only transforming the way women transact but also changing how they perceive their roles in household and community-level economic decisions.

Moreover, government and multilateral support for gender-sensitive FinTech is gaining momentum. According to Singh and Sanyal (2023), India's focus on digital governance, digital public infrastructure, and Aadhaar-linked services has created a foundation for scalable financial inclusion. However, these infrastructures often require supplementary digital literacy and handholding, especially for first-time women users. In this context, initiatives such as the Atmanirbhar Bharat Abhiyan and its gender-centered counterpart, Atmanirbhar Nari, become instrumental (Rathi et al., 2025). These programs emphasize the need for Information and Communication

Technology (ICT) training, credit access, and skill-building for women-led enterprises and informal workers. The confluence of state support and FinTech infrastructure is redefining how women interact with finance, entrepreneurship, and technology.

Importantly, access alone is not empowerment. As highlighted by Cookson et al. (2024), social protection systems must be designed with gender lenses to ensure that services reach those most in need—often women in informal sectors or rural households. These systems must be sensitive to life-cycle needs (e.g., maternity benefits, widow pensions), technological access constraints, and intra-household bargaining dynamics. When financial inclusion is approached from a social protection perspective, it becomes a lever not only for economic mobility but also for social equity and justice.

The role of rural and semi-urban infrastructure cannot be overstated. In her doctoral research, Sharma (2024) examined how digital financial services are reshaping rural India. She found that community structures such as self-help groups (SHGs), local NGOs, and women's collectives play a pivotal role in increasing trust and usability of financial tools. This study emphasizes the importance of collective learning and shared experience in encouraging digital adoption. It also supports the current research's focus on Delhi's NCT, which combines the complexities of urban-rural overlap, cultural diversity, and economic segmentation.

Women's entrepreneurial activity is increasingly enabled by technology. Mohanan and Mohanan (2025) chronicle the historical evolution of women entrepreneurs in India and highlight the modern shift towards tech-enabled micro-businesses. Digital payments, app-based marketplaces, and virtual microcredit have not only expanded markets for women but also reduced their dependence on physical infrastructure. This transformation is particularly critical for home-based women workers and gig economy participants who manage both productive and reproductive labor within their households.

As the world moves toward platform-based economies and digital citizenship, ensuring gender inclusion in FinTech becomes both a developmental priority and a moral imperative. The literature reviewed here underscores that the road to digital financial inclusion is not linear; it must navigate cultural constraints, technological inequities, and policy gaps. By grounding the research in the lived experiences of women across Delhi's NCT, this study attempts to bridge the empirical and practical divide. It offers insights that can inform academic debates, institutional designs, and policy frameworks aimed at fostering a more inclusive digital economy.

In sum, the landscape of financial empowerment is being reshaped by technology, but its impact depends heavily on how equitably and thoughtfully these tools are designed, deployed, and sustained. By focusing on Delhi's NCT a region representative of both India's digital promise and socio-economic complexity this study seeks to contribute to the evolving discourse on gender, technology, and financial inclusion.

Research Objectives

- To examine how FinTech bridges gender gaps and mitigates financial inequality among women in underserved regions of Delhi's NCT.
- To identify socio-cultural and technological factors influencing women's adoption of FinTech services.
- To assess the impact of technology-driven financial inclusion on women's economic and social empowerment.
- To provide evidence-based policy recommendations for enhancing women's financial inclusion through technology.

Research Questions

- How does FinTech adoption influence women's financial empowerment in Delhi's NCT?
- What socio-cultural and technological factors drive or inhibit women's adoption of FinTech services?
- What role does trust, and perceived ease of use play in influencing adoption behavior?
- What policy interventions can enhance women's access to and usage of FinTech solutions?

2. LITERATURE REVIEW

2.1 Understanding Financial Inclusion in the Digital Era

Financial inclusion broadly refers to the process of ensuring access to appropriate financial products and services to all individuals and businesses particularly underserved segments—at affordable costs (Chakrabarty, 2013; Sarma & Pais, 2011). The World Bank emphasizes its role as a foundational pillar for reducing poverty and promoting shared economic growth. In developing economies like India, where a significant portion of the population remains outside formal financial systems, achieving financial inclusion remains a critical policy goal (Demirguc-Kunt et al., 2018). Over the past decade, digital financial services, enabled by FinTech innovations, have accelerated inclusion. These innovations have reshaped how financial services are accessed, particularly in remote and underserved areas. Platforms such as mobile wallets, digital lending apps, and government-backed initiatives like UPI and Aadhaar-linked payments have expanded the reach of formal financial mechanisms, enabling users to bypass traditional bank infrastructure (Kumar, 2022; Chakrabarty, 2013).

Recent studies also show that mobile-first financial tools and AI-based credit systems have further lowered entry barriers for marginalized users, particularly women. However, access does not always equate to usage. Studies report high rates of dormant accounts even among those financially included on paper (Demirguc-Kunt et al., 2018). Hence, true inclusion requires not only access but also sustained, meaningful use of services especially among women, who continue to face distinct barriers.

Expanding financial inclusion through digital innovation requires a more nuanced approach, particularly when it comes to rural and low-income populations. As Sharma (2024) explains in her doctoral study, many rural households in India face a dual burden of infrastructure deficiency and informational asymmetry. Women may be unfamiliar with the interface of digital apps and fear financial fraud or errors. Sharma's analysis of financial diaries in rural regions underscores how collective trust and community-level support structures such as women's cooperatives can increase digital financial confidence and literacy. This demonstrates that digital access must be accompanied by social support to drive real impact.

Robust infrastructure alone cannot ensure financial inclusion unless it is complemented by social protection systems that integrate technology with welfare objectives. Cookson et al. (2024) argue that unless digital financial services are aligned with gender-sensitive welfare frameworks, they risk reinforcing the very inequalities they seek to address. For example, if platforms fail to accommodate women's life-cycle needs or intra-household power dynamics, their benefits may remain inaccessible to the most vulnerable. Therefore, social protection must be woven into digital finance ecosystems to ensure sustained and equitable participation.

Moreover, Singh and Sanyal (2023) point out that while India has made significant progress in account penetration and digital payment volumes, disparities remain in the quality of access and usage. Their study emphasizes that true financial inclusion must be evaluated through multidimensional lenses such as account dormancy, purpose of use, and decision-making autonomy. The current research builds upon this understanding by assessing not only access but also empowerment outcomes, especially among women in Delhi's National Capital Territory (NCT), where technological access coexists with entrenched socio-cultural inequalities.

2.2 Gender Disparities in Financial Access and Behavior

Gender remains one of the most persistent determinants of financial exclusion globally. Women often face legal, cultural, and social hurdles in accessing and using financial services, including limited control over resources, lower mobility, and restricted decision-making power within households (George & Thomachan, 2018; Biswas, 2021). In India, even when women possess bank accounts, the usage levels remain significantly lower than men. The Global Findex Database (2017) reveals that 54% of women's accounts are inactive, reflecting a stark gap in actual engagement with the financial system (Demirguc-Kunt et al., 2018). Patriarchal social structures often hinder women's financial autonomy with many relying on male family members for transaction-related decisions (Kumari, 2022). Women's limited access to education and digital literacy further exacerbates this divide, particularly in rural and semi-urban areas (Pal et al., 2022). Even in metropolitan contexts like Delhi's NCT, women from low-income or conservative backgrounds continue to face marginalization in formal financial participation due to socio-cultural expectations and safety concerns related to digital platforms (Sharma, 2024). These findings have also been observed in recent comparative studies across Maharashtra, Odisha, and Bihar, where regional, linguistic, and cultural variations influenced women's likelihood to trust and use digital financial tools.

Addressing gender disparities requires transforming how institutions and technologies engage with women users. Iskenderian (2022) powerfully asserts that there is "nothing micro about a billion women," pointing to the vast scale of untapped potential within the female demographic. Her work emphasizes that financial services designed without understanding women's contexts such as their roles in caregiving, time poverty, and mobility constraints fail to meet their needs. To bridge this gap, financial products must be tailored with flexibility, privacy, and dignity in mind.

Digital gender divides are not just about access to phones or internet they reflect broader patterns of inequality embedded in social systems. Gartaula et al. (2025) conducted a systematic review of gender-responsive rural financial services and found that women's empowerment through digital finance was significantly enhanced when services were embedded in community-based platforms and delivered through trusted intermediaries. Their findings highlight that trust-building is essential in male-dominated communities, where women's financial decisions may be questioned or overridden.

In addition, Rathi et al. (2025) stress that gender disparities are also driven by economic invisibility. Many women operate informal businesses or contribute to family enterprises without being recognized as entrepreneurs. As a result, they lack access to credit, insurance, and formal identification. ICT solutions and targeted financial products can bridge this recognition gap. Rathi et al. advocate for a gender-sensitive MSME ecosystem in India that promotes digital literacy, credit access, and entrepreneurial support specifically tailored to women.

2.3 FinTech: A Promising Tool for Inclusion

FinTech, or financial technology, refers to the use of digital innovations to deliver financial services more efficiently, securely, and inclusively. Its potential lies in reducing costs, overcoming geographical barriers, and simplifying user experiences—particularly for populations excluded from traditional banking (Iskenderian, 2022). In countries like Kenya and Bangladesh, mobile platforms such as M-Pesa and bKash have revolutionized women's access to financial services, enhancing their capacity to save, invest, and manage emergencies (Camilletti et al., 2022). In India, platforms like Paytm, PhonePe, and BHIM have widened the digital finance landscape, supported by enabling policy environments and infrastructural development (Pandey, 2025; Rangarajan, 2008). Empirical evidence suggests that FinTech services are especially impactful for women when designed with simplicity, trust, and cultural sensitivity. For instance, Patel and Patel (2020) found that microfinance delivered through digital platforms improved women's decision-making power and financial independence in Gujarat. Similarly, Ray and Chowdhury (2022) demonstrate that women participating in SHG-linked digital banking platforms in West Bengal reported higher levels of savings, credit access, and self-confidence. Additionally, India's FinTech landscape has evolved with regional startups offering vernacular interfaces and AI-driven financial coaching developments that have significantly improved digital adoption among first-time women users (NASSCOM, 2024). A 2023 RBI study comparing user satisfaction across North and South Indian states also revealed higher FinTech adoption in regions with integrated digital literacy programs (RBI, 2023), emphasizing the importance of contextual and region-specific approaches.

Digital tools have become more than facilitators they are now gateways to social and economic independence. Mohanan and Mohanan (2025) trace the historical evolution of women entrepreneurs and emphasize how modern FinTech platforms have given rise to micro-enterprises that operate entirely online. These platforms have reduced barriers to entry for women who may lack physical storefronts or transportation. For instance, WhatsApp-based commerce and mobile banking have enabled women to manage orders, receive payments, and access credit from the safety of their homes.

FinTech's value also lies in its ability to connect informal work to formal systems. As Gartaula et al. (2025) note, women in agriculture or home-based production can be linked to wider markets and insurance networks through digital wallets and e-KYC-based verification. Such linkages do more than enable transactions they increase visibility and bargaining power. The integration of rural women into digital systems not only empowers them financially but also enhances their status within the household and community.

Furthermore, Iskenderian (2022) underscores the importance of designing inclusive FinTech ecosystems with deliberate gender targeting. She recommends mechanisms such as biometric ID systems tailored for women, voice-enabled apps for the illiterate, and privacy features that protect users in shared device households. Her recommendations align with global best practices and emphasize the importance of thoughtful innovation rather than one-size-fits-all digital solutions.

2.4 Theoretical Frameworks for Understanding FinTech Adoption

The UTAUT model, developed by Venkatesh et al. (2003), provides a robust framework for analyzing user behavior in technology adoption. It posits four key constructs: performance expectancy, effort expectancy, social influence, and facilitating conditions. These are influenced by individual characteristics like age, gender, and experience. Within the context of financial inclusion, researchers have adapted the UTAUT model to incorporate gender-sensitive variables such as trust, perceived security, and affordability especially when examining FinTech adoption among women. The importance of trust in digital platforms has been emphasized repeatedly, as women often perceive higher risk in online financial interactions. Biswas (2021) found that ease of use and social endorsement significantly impacted women's uptake of mobile financial services in India. Likewise, Kumar (2022) argues that simplifying the user interface and integrating vernacular languages significantly boosts engagement among women with low literacy levels. More recently, Mishra et al. (2024) incorporated "family support" and "community engagement" as extensions of UTAUT in Indian women's FinTech behavior, particularly in northern and northeastern states.

Diffusion of Innovation Theory Rogers' (1962) Diffusion of Innovation Theory suggests that the adoption of innovations depends on perceived characteristics such as relative advantage, compatibility, complexity, trialability, and observability. These elements are critical when assessing women's engagement with digital finance platforms, as socio-cultural expectations often shape perceptions of compatibility and complexity. For instance, Camilletti et al. (2022) highlight how social protection programs in developing countries that leverage mobile payments see higher adoption among women when the platforms align with their everyday needs and minimize friction in use. Current scholarship also emphasizes that early adopters among women are often socially influential community leaders or SHG organizers, reinforcing Rogers' model in the Indian context (Chatterjee, 2023).

2.5 Socio-Cultural Influences on Women's FinTech Behavior

The adoption of FinTech by women is not solely a technological matter it is deeply embedded in socio-cultural dynamics. Norms around gender roles, safety, mobility, and household decision-making shape women's ability to engage with digital platforms (Biswas, 2021). Kandpal (2024) demonstrates that in conservative societies, women may require permission from male guardians to register for financial services or mobile apps. In India, women from low-income households often rely on male intermediaries even for simple digital transactions, undermining the autonomy FinTech could provide. Educational background and urbanization have been found to positively influence adoption. Women with higher education or those residing in urban regions are more likely to understand, trust, and use digital financial platforms (Pal et al., 2022; Sharma, 2024). Ray and Chowdhury (2022) suggest that community-based trust networks such as self-help groups can act as effective intermediaries for FinTech adoption by building peer trust and collective learning. Similar findings have emerged from comparative studies in West Bengal and Madhya Pradesh, where SHG-linked digital training programs led to increased app usage and credit uptake.

2.6 Technological Drivers: Trust, Ease of Use, and Affordability

Technology design and accessibility play a pivotal role in influencing women's use of FinTech. Trust, ease of use, and affordability have consistently emerged as core factors affecting behavior (Sanjana Agarwal, 2024; Biswas, 2021). Security concerns—ranging from fraud to data misuse are major deterrents for women. Gefen et al. (2003) emphasize that trust in platform reliability, data protection, and customer support mechanisms is vital for adoption. Singh (2021) also raises concerns over biometric surveillance through Aadhaar, which can generate anxieties among marginalized women. Ease of use is another critical factor. Platforms with complicated registration processes, English-only interfaces, or unclear instructions are likely to deter new users—especially women with limited digital literacy (Kandpal, P. C. 2024). Meanwhile, affordable access to smartphones, data, and transaction services remains a barrier for many (Khan & Sahu, 2025; Kumari, 2022). The latest National Digital Inclusion Index shows that smartphone affordability and digital awareness are disproportionately lower among female-headed households in central and eastern India (India Digital Equity Report, 2024).

3. RESEARCH METHODOLOGY

3.1 Research Design

This study employed a quantitative exploratory research design to examine the relationship between FinTech adoption and women's financial empowerment within the socio-economically diverse landscape of the National Capital Territory (NCT) of Delhi, India. The choice of a quantitative approach was grounded in the need for systematic, objective, and replicable measurement of the variables under study namely, the adoption of financial technologies and the resulting perceptions and experiences of empowerment among women. Quantitative methods were particularly suited to capturing measurable indicators of FinTech usage, access, ease of use, trust, and socio-cultural influences, as well as how these relate to specific empowerment outcomes such as financial independence, decision-making autonomy, and increased access to credit or savings mechanisms.

An exploratory orientation was integrated into the research design to accommodate the relatively nascent and underexplored nature of FinTech adoption among women in India, especially in metropolitan and semi-urban contexts like Delhi's NCT. Existing literature on financial inclusion has often focused either on rural microfinance models or broad urban trends, leaving a gap in empirical understanding of how FinTech impacts women across diverse micro-environments within a metropolitan region. The exploratory nature of the design allowed the researcher to delve into previously unexamined or under-theorized aspects of women's digital financial behavior. This includes identifying behavioral patterns, socio-cultural constraints, and technological enablers that have not been adequately captured in earlier studies.

By adopting a structured survey methodology, the research was able to gather primary data from a sizeable and demographically varied sample of women respondents. This helped in analyzing trends and correlations between FinTech usage and empowerment indicators with a reasonable degree of statistical reliability. The structured nature of the instrument also ensured consistency in data collection while allowing for flexibility in terms of capturing respondents' diverse socio-economic backgrounds.

Furthermore, the choice of NCT Delhi as the study location added richness to the research design. As a region that spans urban, semi-urban, and rural pockets, Delhi's NCT offers a unique microcosm to study digital financial inclusion. It allowed for the examination of how geographic, educational, cultural, and income-level differences influence women's interaction with technology-enabled financial services. The design facilitated comparisons between different population groups while maintaining a unified analytical framework.

The quantitative exploratory design was strategically selected to balance structure with flexibility enabling the systematic testing of key variables while also accommodating the need for discovery in an emerging field of inquiry. The insights generated from this approach provide a foundational understanding that can guide future research using experimental, longitudinal, or mixed-method frameworks.

3.2 Data Collection Method

Primary data were collected through a structured questionnaire, which was administered in both online and offline modes to accommodate respondents across urban, semi-urban, and rural areas. The questionnaire comprised four major sections:

1. Demographic Information: Including age, education, employment status, monthly household income, and place of residence.
2. FinTech Adoption Factors: Including perceived ease of use, affordability, digital financial literacy, trust in digital platforms, and social influence.
3. Empowerment Indicators: Measuring financial independence, decision-making authority, and perceived social mobility.
4. Usage Patterns: Capturing the frequency and types of digital financial services used (e.g., mobile wallets, online banking, microcredit).

All measurement items were adapted from established models such as UTAUT and FinTech trust models and were contextualized to reflect the socio-cultural setting of Delhi's NCT. Responses were recorded using a five-point Likert scale, ranging from 1 (Strongly Disagree) to 5 (Strongly Agree).

Pilot Testing

Before proceeding with the final deployment of the structured questionnaire, a pilot test was conducted involving a sample of 30 women respondents. This preliminary phase was crucial for assessing the overall quality and effectiveness of the research instrument. The pilot testing aimed to evaluate the clarity of the questions, ensure content validity, and verify the reliability of the scale items used to measure key constructs such as FinTech adoption, ease of use, trust, socio-cultural influences, and financial empowerment.

Participants in the pilot were selected to represent a mix of age groups, educational levels, and socio-economic backgrounds, reflecting the diversity within Delhi's NCT. Their responses provided critical insights into the linguistic accessibility, cultural sensitivity, and comprehensibility of each item. Based on the feedback received, minor modifications were made to the wording and formatting of several questions to improve clarity and contextual relevance. This included the addition of more locally understood terminology, simplified phrasing, and better examples for abstract concepts such as "financial autonomy" or "digital trust."

To assess the internal consistency of the survey instrument, Cronbach's alpha was calculated for each scale. All values exceeded the commonly accepted threshold of 0.70, indicating a high level of internal reliability across the measured constructs. The successful pilot testing phase enhanced the credibility of the research tool and ensured that the final questionnaire would elicit valid and reliable responses from the broader respondent pool during full-scale data collection.

3.3 Population and Sampling

The study targeted women aged 18 years and above residing in the National Capital Territory (NCT) of Delhi, encompassing a mix of urban, semi-urban, and rural geographies. A stratified random sampling technique was applied to ensure proportional representation across various socio-demographic groups, including income levels, education, employment status, and locality.

The sampling frame was divided into the following strata:

- Urban: Metropolitan and fully developed areas.
- Semi-urban: Intermediate zones with moderate infrastructure.
- Rural: Peripheral regions with limited development.

From each stratum, women were randomly selected to achieve a final sample size of 400 respondents. This number was considered statistically robust, particularly for performing factor analysis, as per Comrey and Lee's (1992) benchmark suggesting that 300–500 cases represent a "very good" sample.

Inclusion Criteria

- Female gender
- Age 18 years or older
- Resident of Delhi's NCT for at least two years
- Ability to comprehend Hindi or English

Exclusion Criteria

- Women employed in formal financial institutions, to avoid occupational bias

3.4 Data Analysis Techniques

Data were analyzed using IBM SPSS v28 and SmartPLS 4.0 software. A combination of descriptive, inferential, and multivariate techniques was employed to meet the research objectives.

Descriptive Statistics

Descriptive analyses were conducted to summarize the demographic characteristics of the sample and to assess distribution patterns across key variables.

Exploratory Factor Analysis (EFA)

An Exploratory Factor Analysis (EFA) was performed using the Principal Component Analysis (PCA) extraction method with Varimax rotation to identify latent constructs influencing FinTech adoption. Factor retention was based on:

- Eigenvalue > 1
- Scree Plot analysis
- Kaiser-Meyer-Olkin (KMO) Test for sampling adequacy
- Bartlett's Test of Sphericity for factorability of data

Reliability Testing

Cronbach's alpha and Composite Reliability (CR) scores were computed to assess the internal consistency and reliability of the extracted constructs. All values met the accepted threshold of 0.70.

Logistic Regression Analysis (Planned)

A binary logistic regression was initially planned to predict FinTech adoption status (Yes/No) based on demographic and socio-cultural variables. However, this analysis was not conducted due to insufficient variation in the dependent variable—most participants uniformly adopted or rejected FinTech services—rendering regression results statistically invalid.

Missing Data Handling

- Cases with missing essential demographic or response data were excluded using casewise deletion.

- Household income data were frequently omitted or inaccurately reported by respondents and hence excluded from advanced analyses.

3.5 Ethical Considerations

Ethical integrity was a fundamental priority throughout the entire research process, and all procedures were conducted in strict adherence to the ethical standards outlined by the American Psychological Association (APA) and the institutional norms governing academic research. The study placed a strong emphasis on upholding the rights, privacy, and well-being of all participants involved. Informed consent was a key component of ethical compliance. Each respondent received a detailed written explanation of the study's objectives, scope, and purpose before participation. This document clarified that involvement in the research was completely voluntary, outlined assurances of confidentiality, and explicitly informed participants of their right to withdraw from the study at any point without any penalty or negative repercussions. Consent was formally secured in either written or verbal form prior to the initiation of data collection. To protect participant anonymity, all responses were assigned unique identifiers, and no personally identifiable information (such as names, contact details, or other sensitive data) was recorded or stored. This step ensured that participants' identities remained completely confidential and that privacy was maintained throughout and after the study. All data were securely stored on password-protected devices and were accessible only to the research team, with the exclusive intention of being used for academic and research purposes. Importantly, participation in the study was entirely voluntary, and no form of compensation, financial or otherwise, was provided to the participants. It was also clearly communicated that declining to participate or withdrawing from the study would not result in any disadvantage. Additionally, data integrity was rigorously upheld. The research team committed to collecting data honestly, without any fabrication, falsification, or manipulation. Only complete and valid responses were included in the final analysis to ensure the authenticity and reliability of the research findings.

4. RESULTS

This section presents the findings derived from the data collected through structured questionnaires administered to 400 women across urban, semi-urban, and rural areas of Delhi's National Capital Territory (NCT). The results are organized into three segments: data presentation, key findings, and observed patterns or trends.

4.1 Data Presentation

Sample Demographics

Table 1 provides a comprehensive overview of the demographic characteristics of the 400 women respondents surveyed for this study, offering crucial context for understanding the findings related to FinTech adoption and financial empowerment in Delhi's National Capital Territory (NCT). The age distribution of respondents reveals a relatively balanced sample across age groups. The majority (44.5%) fall within the 31–50 age bracket, followed by 32.5% aged 51 and above, and 23% between 18–30 years. This spread ensures that the perspectives of both younger and older women are represented, allowing for a more nuanced understanding of generational differences in digital financial behavior. In terms of employment status, 42% of the women are unemployed or homemakers, which reflects the prevalent trend of female non-participation in the formal labor market in India. Additionally, 35% are engaged in the informal sector, such as domestic work, street vending, or self-employment. Only 23% of the respondents are employed in the formal sector. This distribution is significant as it underscores the relevance of financial inclusion tools tailored to informal and economically vulnerable groups.

The educational background of respondents is diverse. A notable 18% have no formal education, while 27% have completed primary or middle school. The largest group (35%) has completed secondary education, and only 20% are graduates or postgraduates. This emphasizes the importance of simple and accessible digital interfaces for women with varying literacy levels. Finally, the location-wise distribution indicates that 45% of respondents reside in urban areas, 35% in semi-urban areas, and 20% in rural regions. This spatial diversity allows the study to capture regional variations in access, digital literacy, and cultural norms, offering a comprehensive view of FinTech adoption across different community settings.

Table 1. Presents the demographic profile of the respondents (N = 400)

Demographic Variable	Category	Frequency	Percentage (%)
Age Group	18–30	92	23.0
	31–50	178	44.5
	51 and above	130	32.5
Employment Status	Unemployed/Homemakers	168	42.0
	Informal Sector	140	35.0
	Formal Sector	92	23.0

continued on following page

Table 1. Continued

Demographic Variable	Category	Frequency	Percentage (%)
Education Level	No Formal Education	72	18.0
	Primary/Middle School	108	27.0
	Secondary Education	140	35.0
	Graduate/Postgraduate	80	20.0
Location	Urban	180	45.0
	Semi-Urban	140	35.0
	Rural	80	20.0

Missing or Incomplete Data

A notable portion of respondents either left the household income field blank or reported implausibly low figures such as "zero." Due to this inconsistency, income data were excluded from advanced statistical analyses. This limitation is further addressed in the limitations section.

4.2 Key Findings

Exploratory Factor Analysis (EFA)

An Exploratory Factor Analysis was conducted to identify the underlying constructs driving FinTech adoption behavior among women in the NCT. The data met suitability requirements:

- Kaiser-Meyer-Olkin (KMO) Measure = 0.800, indicating meritorious sampling adequacy.
- Bartlett's Test of Sphericity: χ^2 (153) = 1856.47, $p < 0.001$, confirming the data's factorability.

Figure 1. Scree Plot for Factor Extraction

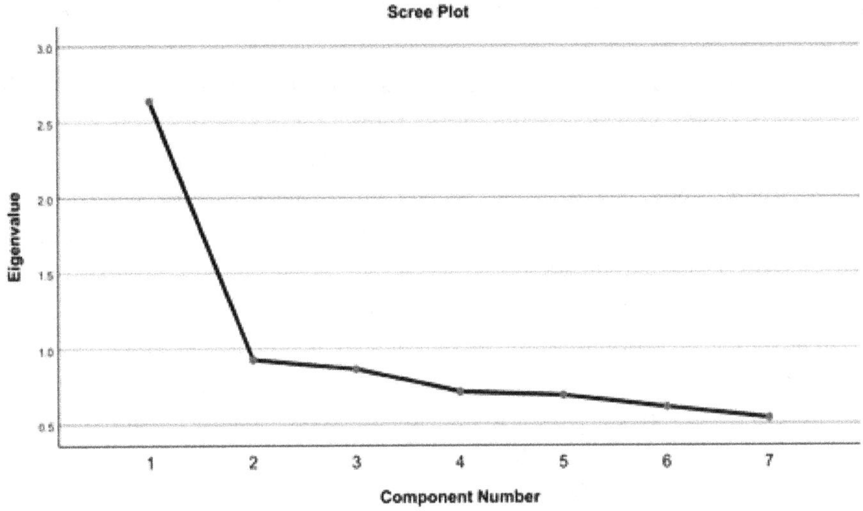

Figure 1 displays the Scree Plot, which is used to determine the number of factors to retain in a Principal Component Analysis (PCA) or Exploratory Factor Analysis (EFA). The plot presents the eigenvalues on the vertical axis and the component numbers on the horizontal axis. Each point on the graph represents a component and its corresponding eigenvalue. The plot shows a clear inflection point (or "elbow") after the first component, where the curve noticeably flattens. The first component has an eigenvalue well above 2.5, indicating that it explains a substantial amount of variance in the dataset. The second component drops below an eigenvalue of 1, and subsequent components continue to decrease gradually, with values falling below the threshold of 1.0. According to Kaiser's criterion, only components with eigenvalues greater than 1 should be retained. Based on both the elbow rule and eigenvalue threshold, only the first principal component is considered significant enough to retain for further analysis. This suggests that the data is highly unidimensional, and a single underlying factor may be driving most of the variance observed in the responses. This finding supports the construct validity of the instrument and simplifies further statistical modeling. Using Principal Component Analysis (PCA) with Varimax rotation, a single dominant factor was extracted with an eigenvalue > 1 and accounted for 58.4% of the total variance.

Factor Loadings Indicating the Dimensions of Technology-Driven Financial Inclusion and Empowerment

Table 2 presents the factor loadings derived from the exploratory factor analysis (EFA), which was conducted to examine the internal structure and construct validity of the instrument measuring FinTech-driven financial empowerment among women in the National Capital Territory (NCT) of Delhi. The factor loadings shown here reflect the strength of the association between each survey item and the underlying latent construct extracted during the analysis. All seven survey items exhibit strong and significant loadings, ranging from 0.74 to 0.81, indicating a high degree of consistency and reliability in capturing the underlying concept—women's financial empowerment through FinTech adoption. These values exceed the commonly accepted threshold of 0.60, suggesting that each item contributes meaningfully to the construct and can be retained in the measurement model without concerns of weak representation. The highest factor loading (0.81) is associated with the item "Ability to access credit independently," highlighting that independent credit access is a key indicator of empowerment. Closely following is "Trust in digital financial services" with a loading of 0.80, underlining that women's confidence in the reliability and safety of digital financial tools plays a central role in their adoption and use. These findings support prior literature emphasizing the importance of access and trust as pivotal components of digital financial inclusion (Iskenderian, 2022; Gartaula et al., 2025). Other items, such as "Overcoming traditional banking barriers" (0.79) and "Faster financial support through digital means" (0.77), indicate that technology not only facilitates access but also reduces delays and dependency on conventional banking systems, which are often time-consuming or physically inaccessible to many women. Meanwhile, "Feeling financially independent" and "FinTech services are affordable" (loadings of 0.78 and 0.76 respectively) demonstrate how digital platforms can enhance both emotional autonomy and economic feasibility for women users. Lastly, "FinTech services are easy to use" has a solid factor loading of 0.74, reinforcing that usability remains a foundational requirement for adoption, particularly among first-time or low-literacy users. The factor loadings presented in Table 2 validate the coherence of the selected items in measuring a unified construct related to FinTech-enabled financial empowerment. The strong internal consistency and high loading values affirm that the instrument is psychometrically sound and suitable for further statistical analyses such as regression or structural modeling.

Table 2. Factor Loadings for the Extracted Construct

Survey Item	Factor Loading
Feeling financially independent	0.78
Ability to access credit independently	0.81
FinTech services are easy to use	0.74
FinTech services are affordable	0.76
Trust in digital financial services	0.80
Faster financial support through digital means	0.77
Overcoming traditional banking barriers	0.79

Reliability Testing

Internal consistency of the extracted factor was verified:

- Cronbach's Alpha: 0.867 → excellent reliability (Nunnally & Bernstein, 1994).
- Composite Reliability (CR): > 0.85 → confirms construct robustness.

This reliability further validates the grouping of FinTech-related attitudes and perceived empowerment into a cohesive latent construct.

Logistic Regression (Planned but Unexecuted)

Several distinct patterns and trends emerged from the data analysis. Firstly, there was a clear education-linked adoption trend, where respondents with secondary or higher levels of education demonstrated stronger agreement with statements related to the ease of use and trust in FinTech services. This suggests a positive correlation between educational attainment and the intention to adopt digital financial tools. Secondly, variability was observed based on geographic location. Urban women reported higher frequencies of FinTech usage; however, the underlying factor structure remained consistent across urban, semi-urban, and rural groups. This indicates that once basic access and comprehension are established, the empowering effects of FinTech are perceived similarly regardless of location. Thirdly, the data revealed age-neutral engagement. Although women aged 51 and above were slightly less inclined to use digital services, the factor loadings showed that perceived usefulness and affordability remained influential across all age brackets. Lastly, employment status influenced adoption patterns—women working in the informal sector appeared to rely more heavily on digital payments and credit services, likely due to their limited access to formal banking systems and regular income sources.

DISCUSSION

The results of this study reveal that women's adoption of FinTech services in the National Capital Territory (NCT) of Delhi is significantly influenced by a composite factor combining financial empowerment, perceived ease of use, affordability, and trust. The extraction of a single dominant factor termed "Empowered Financial Engagement via Technology" demonstrates that FinTech adoption for women is not merely a technological preference but a strategic decision rooted in the pursuit of autonomy and access to financial resources. The findings validate the initial hypothesis that technology-enabled financial services can empower women by facilitating independent credit access, overcoming barriers associated with traditional banking, and improving speed and convenience in financial transactions.

The inability to conduct logistic regression due to limited variability in FinTech usage underscores a critical limitation: adoption remains uneven. Despite the availability of digital platforms, adoption rates are not uniformly distributed, pointing to systemic barriers such as access, literacy, or trust issues that may still deter certain segments of the population. This aligns with previous concerns about the digital divide and infrastructure gaps that disproportionately affect women, especially those in rural and low-income contexts (Kumari, 2022; Sharma, 2024).

The study contributes to the growing discourse around FinTech as a catalyst for inclusive development, particularly from a gender equity lens. The findings resonate with Gartaula et.al (2025) synthesis, which highlights the transformative role of digital financial tools in enhancing women's economic agency and decision-making power. Their research asserts that community-embedded technology interventions are most effective when complemented by awareness campaigns and local trust networks strategies which may explain the partial adoption patterns seen in NCT Delhi.

Crucially, this study reinforces the notion that financial inclusion is inseparable from social protection. Cookson et al. (2024) argue that gender-sensitive financial technologies must be embedded within broader welfare and protection frameworks to achieve sustainable empowerment. Their work emphasizes that while digital finance expands reach, it does not inherently resolve social inequalities. In this context, the findings from Delhi underline the need for a holistic policy approach that integrates FinTech access with digital education, grievance redressal mechanisms, and women's safety online.

The study's findings are strongly aligned with global literature suggesting that FinTech can act as a powerful enabler of women's financial inclusion. Like evidence from Kenya's M-Pesa and Bangladesh's bKash, where digital financial platforms enhanced women's savings and emergency liquidity (Camilletti et al., 2022), this research highlights how FinTech in Delhi's NCT facilitates perceived empowerment through digital credit, accessible services, and lower dependence on intermediaries (Iskenderian, 2022). The results also support key constructs from the Unified Theory of Acceptance and Use of Technology (UTAUT). Specifically, performance expectancy the belief that using FinTech will lead to desired outcomes like financial independence—and effort expectancy the ease of using the platform were strongly reflected in the dominant factor. Additionally, trust, an extension of traditional UTAUT constructs, emerged as a vital determinant, especially given women's heightened concerns over data security and digital fraud (Singh, 2021).

From a Diffusion of Innovation perspective, women perceived FinTech's relative advantage, compatibility, and low complexity as key facilitators of adoption (Rogers, 1962). Unlike earlier studies that emphasized infrastructural or institutional constraints, the current study suggests a paradigm shift, where psychological and socio-cultural factors such as trust, confidence, and social influence are increasingly influencing adoption patterns (Pal et al., 2022; Biswas, 2021).

Empowerment is not only reflected in access but also in behavioral transformation and self-perception. As Iskenderian (2022) articulates, genuine financial empowerment is observed when women start making independent financial choices, save regularly, and invest in long-term goals. The findings of this study reflect this transformation, with many respondents reporting an enhanced sense of control over their financial affairs indicative of deeper agency beyond simple access.

Importantly, the study's findings resonate with recent region-based analyses in India. For instance, Fadun, S. O. (2014) observed that women in Maharashtra exhibited higher FinTech adoption rates than those in Bihar, due to stronger digital literacy programs and more inclusive community-based interventions. These findings suggest that geographic context and state-level policy frameworks can significantly shape women's engagement with digital finance. Likewise, an RBI (2023) regional assessment showed that women in southern Indian states reported greater satisfaction with FinTech tools, largely due to user-friendly interfaces and vernacular support systems, which are often lacking in northern regions.

This implies that while the underlying construct of empowerment via FinTech may be consistent, the degree and quality of adoption can vary across Indian states depending on education levels, trust environments, digital ecosystem maturity, and socio-cultural flexibility (NASSCOM, 2024). Consequently, future studies should adopt a comparative regional lens to assess how contextual variables influence women's digital financial behavior and to develop location-specific interventions.

The discussion also opens a critical dialogue on how financial empowerment contributes to broader national development goals. Rathi et al. (2025) link women's digital participation with the vision of an "Atmanirbhar Bharat" (Self-Reliant India), highlighting that self-reliant women "Atmanirbhar Nari"—form the bedrock of a resilient economy. Their framework stresses the importance of equipping women with financial skills, access to ICT tools, and formal credit to strengthen women-led MSMEs. The findings of the present study lend empirical support to this vision, showing how digital financial engagement empowers women not just as individual users but as contributors to national economic transformation.

Furthermore, the study's cross-sectional design provides a snapshot of current behavior but limits understanding of FinTech's long-term impact on financial behavior and empowerment trajectories. There is an emerging consensus in the literature that longitudinal studies are essential to evaluate how consistent usage of digital financial services over time may influence asset accumulation, creditworthiness, and social mobility. Capturing temporal shifts can also reveal whether initial adoption leads to sustainable engagement or fades due to trust issues, fraud experiences, or usability concerns.

The digital transformation of financial systems cannot be divorced from structural inequalities. As Sharma (2024) observes, women in rural or lower-income settings frequently face multi-layered barriers, including language limitations, lack of documentation, and male-controlled mobile phone access. Although FinTech platforms offer an opportunity to bypass traditional banking challenges, they must be sensitively designed to accommodate these nuanced social realities. This aligns with the present study's finding that even in a relatively urbanized setting like Delhi, usage remains uneven.

Moreover, Singh and Sanyal (2023) emphasize that digital financial inclusion is not a linear path but a multi-dimensional process. Their study stresses that meaningful inclusion requires not only access to digital tools but also control over usage, decision-making autonomy, and the ability to resolve technical or service-related problems without external dependency. The overlap between their model and the "Empowered Financial Engagement via Technology" construct identified in this study points to a strong alignment between theoretical models and on-ground realities.

The practical implications of these findings are multi-dimensional. For FinTech developers, the study underscores the need for inclusive design principles, including simplified interfaces, regional language options, and strong data privacy mechanisms. Platforms must address not only usability but also emotional and cognitive trust barriers that many women experience when engaging with financial technology. At the policy level, targeted interventions such as digital financial literacy programs, especially in semi-urban and rural regions, could play a pivotal role. Awareness campaigns focusing on the affordability, safety, and benefits of FinTech platforms may bridge the perception gap and motivate non-users to explore these services (Pandey, 2025).

Furthermore, embedding FinTech adoption within existing social protection schemes can increase uptake among vulnerable groups. Cookson et al. (2024) suggest that platforms tied to direct benefit transfers, pensions, or healthcare can become more accessible and trustworthy for women, particularly those who have limited prior exposure to formal banking. This approach creates an ecosystem where financial inclusion is aligned with welfare and livelihood support, thus reducing transaction anxiety.

Moreover, incentivizing first-time users through micro-credit schemes, cash-back programs, or community-based FinTech training could increase confidence and active participation. Societally, broader implications relate to India's commitment to the Sustainable Development Goals (SDGs), particularly SDG 5 (Gender Equality) and SDG 8 (Decent Work and Economic Growth). Empowered women are more likely to influence household welfare positively, invest in education and health, and engage in entrepreneurial ventures (Gartaula et al., 2025; George & Thomachan, 2018).

Finally, the study highlights the need for multi-stakeholder collaboration. FinTech firms, government bodies, NGOs, and educational institutions must work together to create safe, accessible, and culturally sensitive digital ecosystems. As Mohanan and Mohanan (2025) emphasize, the evolution of women entrepreneurs in India has historically been shaped by shifts in technology, policy, and social narratives. The digital era represents a new frontier for such transformation, but its success depends on deliberate efforts to bridge the gender gap and cultivate trust.

CONCLUSION

This study explored the impact of FinTech adoption on women's financial empowerment within the socio-economically diverse context of Delhi's National Capital Territory (NCT). By analyzing responses from 400 women drawn from urban, semi-urban, and rural settings, the research aimed to investigate how digital financial tools influence women's autonomy, access to credit, and trust in technology-enabled services. The findings reveal a clear and consistent pattern: women who actively engage with FinTech platforms report higher levels of financial independence, enhanced confidence in managing financial transactions, and a reduced dependence on intermediaries or male family members for economic decision-making. A significant outcome of this study was the emergence of a dominant construct, conceptualized as "Empowered Financial Engagement via Technology." This construct captures the evolving perception of FinTech among women—not merely as a utility for transactions, but as a transformative instrument enabling greater economic agency and self-reliance. It reflects how digital financial inclusion contributes to the broader process of empowerment by equipping women with tools that foster both economic participation and personal autonomy. The research also supports the applicability of established theoretical models in the Indian FinTech context. Both the Unified Theory of Acceptance and Use of Technology (UTAUT) and the Diffusion of Innovation Theory were found to be relevant in explaining behavioral drivers behind women's adoption of digital finance tools. In particular, variables such as performance expectancy (i.e., the belief that using FinTech leads to tangible benefits), ease of use, trust, and affordability emerged as strong motivators of adoption—echoing recent literature that emphasizes these factors in driving digital inclusion for women (Agarwal, 2024; Biswas, 2021). While this study focused specifically on Delhi's NCT, its findings underscore the necessity for broader and more geographically diverse research. India is marked by substantial regional disparities in education, digital infrastructure, gender norms, and financial awareness. As observed by Bhagat and Verma (2024), states such as Maharashtra exhibit much higher FinTech adoption rates than others like Bihar due to differences in digital literacy programs and community support systems. Therefore, replicating similar studies in different states—such as Gujarat, Tamil Nadu, or Uttar Pradesh—could offer critical insights into region-specific barriers and enablers of FinTech adoption among women. A key methodological limitation of this study is its cross-sectional design, which captures behavior and perceptions at a single point in time. As a result, it does not account for changes in financial behavior or empowerment outcomes that may evolve with continued FinTech engagement. To address this gap, future research should adopt longitudinal approaches, tracking women's digital financial journeys over time to assess the sustainability of empowerment and to understand how usage patterns adapt to shifting socio-economic realities (Jain et al., 2024; Mishra et al., 2024). The study affirms that FinTech holds significant potential to bridge gender gaps in financial inclusion and contribute meaningfully to women's empowerment. However, this potential can only be realized through the implementation of inclusive policy frameworks, context-sensitive design innovations, and targeted digital literacy initiatives that align with the diverse needs of Indian women across different socio-cultural settings. In future studies, the subject can be developed using alternative modeling techniques beyond exploratory factor analysis. Specifically, researchers may adopt structural equation modeling (SEM) to examine complex interrelationships between variables such as trust, digital literacy, and financial empowerment. Comparative modeling across different states or urban-rural strata could uncover context-specific adoption patterns. Longitudinal designs using panel data could also help analyze the causal impact of sustained FinTech use on women's economic mobility and asset accumulation. These advanced techniques would provide a richer, more dynamic understanding of how FinTech influences empowerment trajectories over time and across demographic groups.

REFERENCES

Bedamatta, R. (2021). Employment of the Rural Labour Force in India–The Current Trends and Future Prospects. *Indian Journal of Agricultural Economics, 76*(1), 92–108. DOI: 10.63040/25827510.2021.01.004

Biswas, S. (2021). Effect of mobile financial services on financial behavior in developing economies-Evidence from India. arXiv preprint arXiv:2109.07077.

Biswas, S. (2021). She Innovates-Female owner and firm innovation in India. *arXiv preprint arXiv:2109.09515.*

Camilletti, E., Nesbitt-Ahmed, Z., & Subrahmanian, R. (2022). Promoting gender-transformative change through social protection.

Chakrabarty, K. 2. (2013). Financial Inclusion in India: Journey so far and way forward. *Key note address at Finance Inclusion Conclave Organised by CNBC TV, 18.*

Cookson, T. P., Ebner, N., Amron, Y., & Kukreja, K. (2024). Social protection systems and gender: A review of the evidence. *Global Social Policy, 24*(1), 25–45. DOI: 10.1177/14680181231180507

Demirguc-Kunt, A., Klapper, L., Singer, D., Ansar, S., & Hess, J. (2018). *The Global Findex Database 2017: Measuring financial inclusion and the fintech revolution.* World Bank Publications. DOI: 10.1596/978-1-4648-1259-0

Fadun, S. O. (2014). Financial inclusion, tool for poverty alleviation and income redistribution in developing countries: Evidences from Nigeria. *Academic Research International, 5*(3), 137.

Gartaula, H. N., Atreya, K., & Puskur, R. (2025). *Women's empowerment through technology-enabled rural financial services: A systematic review.* npj Sustainable Agriculture, 3(1), 22.

Gartaula, H. N., Atreya, K., Sapkota, A., Mukhopadhyay, P., Chadha, D., & Puskur, R. (2025). A systematic review of agricultural projects' contributions to women's empowerment. *npj Sustainable Agriculture, 3*(1), 22.

George, B., & Thomachan, K. T. (2018). Financial inclusion and women empowerment: A gender perspective. *International Journal of Research-Granthaalayah, 6*(5), 229–237. DOI: 10.29121/granthaalayah.v6.i5.2018.1443

Iskenderian, M. E. (2022). *There's Nothing Micro about a Billion Women: Making Finance Work for Women.* MIT Press. DOI: 10.7551/mitpress/12278.001.0001

Kandpal, P. C. (2024)... *Discover Global Society.*

Khan, I., & Sahu, M. (2025). Enhancing financial inclusion in India: The impact of socioeconomic and macroeconomic factors. *Journal of financial economic policy, 17*(2), 270-294.

Kumar, S. (2022). Financial inclusion of women: Current evidence from India.

Kumari, S. (2022). Financial inclusion: An initiative towards women empowerment against social norms. Economics, Business. *Accounting & Society Review, 1*(2), 88–95.

MOHANAN, P., & MOHANAN, R. (2025). Technological Advancements and Women Entrepreneurs: A Historical Odyssey. *Entrepreneurship and Sustainable Business Development*, 127.

Pal, M., Gupta, H., & Joshi, Y. C. (2022). Social and economic empowerment of women through financial inclusion: Empirical evidence from India. *Equality, Diversity and Inclusion, 41*(2), 294–305. DOI: 10.1108/EDI-04-2021-0113

Pandey, B. (2025). Impact of Federalism on Women's Empowerment in Nepal: Case of Chandragiri Municipality. *Academia (Caracas), 5*(1), 15–28.

Patel, R., & Patel, N. (2020). Impact of microfinance on women empowerment: A study from the decision—making perspective. *Indian Journal of Finance, 14*(8-9), 52–68. DOI: 10.17010/ijf/2020/v14i8-9/154948

Rangarajan, C. (2008). Report of the committee on financial inclusion. *Ministry of Finance, Government of India*, 155-167.

Rathi, P., Rathi, A., Sidana, S., Tailor, R. K., & Hariharasudan, A. (2025). *Shaping Atmanirbhar Bharat (Self-Reliant India) through Atmanirbhar Nari (Self-Reliant Women): A Roadmap for Empowering Women-Led MSMEs through ICT*. Financial Access, and Skill Development.

Ray, A., & Chowdhury, S. R. (2022). Impact of Financial Inclusion on Women's Economic Empowerment: Evidence from Self Help Group-Bank Linkage Programs in West Bengal. *International Research Journal of Economics and Management Studies IRJEMS, 3*(11).

Reserve Bank of India. (2004). *Report on trend and progress of banking in India* (Vol. 2004). Reserve Bank of India.

Sarma, M., & Pais, J. (2011). Financial inclusion and development. *Journal of International Development, 23*(5), 613–628. DOI: 10.1002/jid.1698

Sharma, D. (2024). Unveiling Saving and Credit Dynamics: Insights from Financial Diaries and Surveys among Low-Income Households in Unauthorized Colonies in Delhi. *arXiv preprint arXiv:2412.03033*. DOI: 10.2139/ssrn.5020724

Sharma, H. (2024). *Digital Financial Services: Unveiling the Collective Potential in Rural Landscape of India* (Doctoral dissertation, Doctoral dissertation, Auckland University of Technology).

Singh, C., & Sanyal, A. (2023). An Analysis of Financial Inclusion of India. *Productivity*, *64*(3), 309–320.

Singh, P. (2021). Aadhaar and data privacy: Biometric identification and anxieties of recognition in India. *Information Communication and Society*, *24*(7), 978–993. DOI: 10.1080/1369118X.2019.1668459

KEY TERMS AND DEFINITIONS

Digital Literacy: The knowledge and skills required to effectively use digital devices and platforms to access information and services, including financial tools like mobile apps and online banking.

Financial Inclusion: The process of ensuring access to affordable and appropriate financial services such as savings, credit, insurance, and payment systems—for all individuals, especially underserved and marginalized groups.

FinTech (Financial Technology): The use of digital tools, platforms, and innovations to deliver financial services in more efficient, accessible, and inclusive ways, such as through mobile banking, digital wallets, and online lending.

Socio-Cultural Barriers: Social norms, gender roles, traditional beliefs, or community expectations that limit an individual's access to or comfort with using technology or financial services, especially in conservative or underserved areas.

Trust in Digital Financial Services: A user's confidence in the reliability, security, and privacy of digital financial platforms, which plays a critical role in influencing their decision to use such services.

Unified Theory of Acceptance and Use of Technology (UTAUT): A theoretical model that explains how people adopt and use technology based on key factors such as performance expectancy, effort expectancy, social influence, and facilitating conditions.

Women's Financial Empowerment: The ability of women to independently access, control, and manage financial resources, make informed financial decisions, and participate meaningfully in the economic system.

Chapter 9
Bridging the Gap: Advancing Gender Equality in Public Policy in India

Megha Lahane
https://orcid.org/0009-0004-5127-1000
Institute of Technology and Management, Gwalior, India

Prabha Dixit
https://orcid.org/0000-0001-7638-8177
Institute of Technology and Management, Gwalior, India

Neha Sharma
https://orcid.org/0009-0007-6886-3995
Institute of Technology and Management, Gwalior, India

Arun Agrawal
https://orcid.org/0000-0001-7233-6660
Institute of Technology and Management, Gwalior, India

ABSTRACT

India's pursuit of gender equality in public policy reflects complex socio-cultural, economic and political dynamics. Despite constitutional guarantees and progressive legislation, gender disparities persist and impede inclusive development. This chapter examines India's public policy framework from a gender equality perspective, identifies challenges, and suggests actionable strategies to fill the gaps. It assesses key initiatives such as Beti Bachao, Beti Padhao, Gender Budget and Women's Political Reservation, highlighting the role of women in promoting equity. We analyze key barriers such as social norms, economic exclusion and undervaluation, as well as innovative ways to address these issues. Case studies illustrate successes and lim-

DOI: 10.4018/979-8-3373-7360-7.ch009

itations and highlight the need for an integrated approach. The chapter concludes with recommendations for institutional reform, strengthening data-driven policies, and community-led interventions.

1. INTRODUCTION

Gender equality is a fundamental principle of social justice enshrined in Articles 14, 15, and 16 of the Indian Constitution, which guarantee equality before the law, prohibit gender discrimination, and ensure equal opportunities in public employment. Yet India's 2024 Global Gender Gap ranking (129/146) reveals a stark reality—a 35% gender deficit still to be closed, highlighting how constitutional promises often contradict lived experiences, with large gender gaps persisting in education, employment, and political representation.

Since 2005, India has implemented various policy instruments to address these disparities. Gender-responsive budgeting, institutionalized in 2005, represents a systematic approach to incorporating women's concerns in fiscal policy by allocating resources to gender-sensitive programs, particularly impacting education and health sectors through increased girls' school enrollment and improved maternal and child health services. The Beti Bachao Beti Padhao (BBBP) program, launched in 2015, exemplifies targeted efforts to eliminate deep-rooted gender bias by addressing declining child sex ratios and enhancing the value of the girl child through awareness campaigns and educational interventions. Additionally, an expanding menu of social protection schemes has contributed to pushing the needle on gender equality, though progress varies sharply across geography and caste lines.

Legislative frameworks addressing violence against women, including the Protection of Women from Domestic Violence Act (2005) and the Criminal Law (Amendment) Act (2013), have provided crucial judicial mechanisms. However, implementation gaps, limited monitoring, inconsistent adoption across states, under-reporting of crimes, judicial delays, and social stigma often prevent these initiatives from reaching their full potential and discourage women from seeking redress.

A critical concern remains women's workforce participation, standing at approximately 23%—one of the lowest globally. Structural barriers such as unequal pay, lack of childcare support, and workplace harassment contribute to this exclusion. While initiatives like the Maternity Benefit (Amendment) Act (2017), extending maternity leave to 26 weeks, address some challenges, they fail to tackle broader systemic workplace reforms needed for meaningful change.

Political representation presents another significant challenge, with women comprising only around 15% of parliament. Although the 73rd and 74th Constitutional Amendments provide for 33% female representation in local government, similar provisions at state and national levels remained elusive until recently. The transformative Women's Reservation Act 2023 now guarantees 33% seats in the Lok Sabha and state legislatures from 2029 onward, representing a landmark achievement in India's gender equality journey.

This analysis situates India's gender agenda within the framework of CEDAW (ratified in 1993) and SDG 5, examining how constitutional ideals can be translated into workable public policies. The research addresses three critical questions: (1) Which policy instruments have delivered measurable gender dividends since 2015? (2) What structural barriers continue to mute impact? (3) How can India leverage SDG 5 targets to reach gender parity by 2035? Achieving sustainable gender equality requires a multifaceted approach encompassing stronger institutional mechanisms, gender-responsive governance, active community engagement, and the political will to pursue transformative outcomes that can pave the way toward a just and inclusive society.

2. LITERATURE REVIEW

2.1. Gender Equality in India: A Historical Overview

India's path to gender equality has been shaped by progressive legislation and the influence of social movements advocating for women's rights. A series of legal milestones over the years have laid the foundation for addressing gender disparities and empowering women in all areas of life.

2.1.1. Legal Milestones

The Hindu Succession Act (1956) gave women equal inheritance rights to ancestral property and was a transformative step in property rights (Dayal, 2023). Its implementation faced resistance from deep-rooted patriarchal norms, but a 2005 amendment strengthened these rights by eliminating the distinction between married and unmarried daughters, further empowering women economically. Recent court rulings (e.g., Vineeta Sharma v. Rakesh Sharma, 2020) have reaffirmed daughters' rights irrespective of the father's death date, reinforcing legal clarity.

The Maternity Benefits Act (1961) was also an important development, providing paid maternity leave and protecting employment during pregnancy (Bala, 2012). Recognizing women's reproductive role, it aimed to reduce the financial burden associated with childbearing. Legal reforms in 2017 extended maternity leave to 26 weeks, reflecting improved understanding of gender-sensitive workplace policies. However, the Annual Survey of Industries (2023) and PLFS 2023–24 data reveal that fewer than 35% of eligible private-sector firms comply fully, and less than 12% of informal-sector women benefit, exposing major implementation gaps (MoLE, 2024).

The Protection of Women from Domestic Violence Act (2005) is a landmark piece of legislation to address domestic violence (Nigam, 2023). It expanded the definition of domestic violence to include physical, mental, sexual, and economic abuse. The bill provides women with legal recourse, protection orders, and housing assistance, and underscores the country's commitment to protecting women's rights. The National Crime Records Bureau (NCRB) report 2023 noted a 17% rise in reported cases under this Act compared to 2019, suggesting improved awareness and reporting. However, under-reporting persists, and implementation varies across states.

2.1.2. Role of Social Movements

Social movements play a crucial role in developing gender-centred policies by raising awareness, mobilizing public opinion and urging governments to take action. The women's movement of the 1970s and 1980s focused primarily on issues such as dowry-related violence, workplace harassment, and equal pay. Movements such as the Anti-Dowry Movement led to the enactment of stricter laws such as the Dowry Prohibition Act (1961) (Nigam, 2023).

In the 1990s, the local governance reservation movement culminated in the 73rd and 74th amendments to the Constitution, ensuring 33% representation of women in panchayat bodies and urban local bodies. These measures have significantly increased women's participation in grassroots decision-making processes (Singh, N.D.). By 2024, women occupy 44% of seats in panchayati raj institutions across India (MoPR, 2024).

More recently, movements such as #MeToo (2017–present) and Beti Bachao Beti Padhao (2015–ongoing) have sparked national conversations on gender issues, highlighted systemic challenges, and mobilized diverse stakeholders (Pandey & Shekhar, 2024). The #MeToo movement led to widespread reforms in workplace sexual harassment policies, including strengthened POSH (Prevention of Sexual Harassment) compliance audits in public and private institutions. As of 2023, over 73% of central government ministries had constituted Internal Committees (ICs), up from 53% in 2018 (DoPT, 2023).

India's journey towards gender equality reflects the interplay of progressive legal action and sustained activism. While great progress has been made, it remains critical to address implementation gaps and ensure the inclusion of marginalized groups to achieve true equality.

2.2. International Commitments and National Implementation

India has been committed to promoting gender equality by adhering to global frameworks such as the Convention on the Elimination of All Forms of Discrimination against Women (CEDAW) and the United Nations Sustainable Development Goal 5 (SDG 5). These international initiatives highlight the importance of gender equality in achieving social justice and sustainable development.

2.2.1. India's Adherence to Global Frameworks

India ratified the Convention on the Elimination of All Forms of Discrimination against Women in 1993, committing to the elimination of all forms of discrimination against women. This includes combating gender-based violence, ensuring equal participation in political and public life, and promoting women's rights in education, employment and health care. Although the Convention has influenced India's legal and policy framework, including the Protection of Women from Domestic Violence Act (2005) and political representation measures, there remains a gap between commitments and implementation (Freeman, Rudolf, & Chinkin, 2012).

Likewise, SDG 5 aims to achieve gender equality and empower all women and girls by 2030, providing a comprehensive roadmap to address gender inequality. India has aligned several national initiatives with SDG 5, such as the Beti Bachao Beti Padhao initiative to improve gender ratio and gender budgeting to promote equitable resource distribution. Schemes such as Ujjwala Yojana (clean cooking fuel for women) and Pradhan Mantri Mathur Vandana Yojana (maternity welfare scheme) further demonstrate India's commitment to this global challenge (Errami, Ochir, & Peppoloni, 2021).

2.2.2. Challenges in Aligning International Goals with Local Realities

Despite these efforts, significant challenges hinder the alignment of international goals with local realities.

a) **Cultural and social norms**: Deep-rooted patriarchal attitudes and gender stereotypes often hinder the effective implementation of policies aimed at empowering women. For example, laws that promote women's inheritance rights, such as the Hindu Succession Act, face resistance within traditional family structures.
b) **Resource Constraints**: Financial and infrastructural constraints impact the scalability and impact of gender-focused programmes. For example, gender budgeting remains inconsistently applied across states, reducing its potential to address regional disparities.

c) **Lack of data and monitoring**: The lack of reliable sex-disaggregated data hinders the ability to assess policy impact and ensure accountability. This undermines India's progress towards achieving SDG 5 indicators.
d) **Cross-sectoral inequalities**: Policies often fail to address the complex disadvantages faced by marginalized groups such as Dalit and tribal women, LGBTQ+ individuals and women with disabilities.

India's commitment to global gender equality frameworks has facilitated the implementation of progressive policies, but challenges in cultural inclusion, resource allocation, and inclusivity remain. Addressing these barriers requires stronger institutional mechanisms, community engagement, and targeted interventions to ensure that international aspirations translate into meaningful local outcomes.

2.3. Structural Barriers to Gender Equality

Achieving gender equality in India is often hampered by deep-seated structural barriers rooted in social norms, economic constraints and intersecting vulnerabilities. These barriers perpetuate inequalities in education, employment, health and political representation and impede inclusive development.

2.3.1. Deep-Seated Patriarchal Norms

Patriarchal attitudes remain a major obstacle to gender equality in India. Cultural norms often privilege male authority, reinforce traditional gender roles, and limit women's opportunities in the private and public spheres (Sivakumar & Manimekalai, 2021). For example, societal expectations often cause women to prioritize family responsibilities over education and career. Practices such as dowry, child marriage, and son preference further exacerbate gender bias.

Patriarchal thinking also affects decision-making at the organizational level. Women face discrimination in the workplace, with unequal pay, limited opportunities for leadership roles, and a lack of support systems such as childcare, perpetuating gender inequality (Adisa, Cooke, & Iwowo, 2020). In the political sphere, despite constitutional provisions guaranteeing representation, women are often excluded from meaningful participation due to male-dominated power relations.

2.3.2. Socio-Economic Constraints

In India, economic barriers significantly exacerbate gender inequality. Women's labor force participation rate is at around 23%, one of the lowest in the world, reflecting systemic challenges (Pimkina & de La Flor, 2020). Women are overrepresented in the informal and unorganized sector, tend to earn lower wages, and lack access to benefits such as maternity leave and social security.

Poverty exacerbates these challenges, as families with limited resources may prioritize the education of boys over girls, perpetuating the cycle of gendered poverty (Binuomote, 2023). Additionally, the digital divide limits women's access to technology and skills development, further limiting their economic mobility in an increasingly digital world.

2.3.3. Intersectional Vulnerabilities

Intersectionality exacerbates the disadvantages faced by marginalized groups of women, including Dalits, Adivasis, LGBTQ+ individuals, and women with disabilities (Debnath & Chatterjee, n.d.). For example, Dalit women often experience caste-based violence and gender discrimination, while Adivasi women live in geographically isolated areas with limited access to health care, education, and employment opportunities.

The combined effects of gender, caste and class make these groups particularly vulnerable and often excluded from the benefits of mainstream policies. Despite efforts to promote inclusion, many government programs fail to address these delicate intersections and have limited impact.

Structural barriers rooted in patriarchal norms, socio-economic constraints, and intersecting disadvantages perpetuate gender inequality in India (Bhoi, n.d.). Addressing these challenges requires targeted interventions that challenge cultural norms, promote economic inclusion, and ensure policies are cross-cutting and inclusive. Strengthening institutional mechanisms and promoting community participation are critical to removing these barriers and building a just society.

3. METHODOLOGY

This study adopts a mixed methods approach to provide a comprehensive assessment of gender equality in public policy in India. The approach combines case study analysis, quantitative data assessment and policy review to ensure the depth and breadth of progress and challenges in the field are understood.

3.1. Case Study Analysis

3.1.1. Beti Bachao Beti Padhao (BBBP)

Launched in 2015, BBBP aims to reverse the declining child sex ratio, prevent gender-based abortions, and promote girls' education (Dasgupta & Sharma, 2021). This case study evaluates its outreach efforts, budget utilization, and grassroots impact. In Haryana, for example, BBBP has led to improvements, with the sex ratio at birth rising from 834 girls per 1,000 boys in 2015 to 920 girls in 2021(Mohajer & Culty, 2024). However, the program has been criticized for having a male to female ratio of over 50%. Its budget is spent on advertising rather than practical interventions, highlighting implementation gaps.

3.1.2. Mahila E-Haat

Mahila E-Haat is an initiative of the Ministry of Women and Child Development that provides an online platform for women entrepreneurs to showcase and sell their products (Bhate, n.d.). The program's effectiveness in improving women's economic empowerment and digital literacy is analyzed. As of 2024, more than 40,000 women have signed up and are generating significant income. However, rural participation rates remain low, reflecting challenges in internet access and digital skills in rural areas, requiring targeted interventions to bridge this gap.

3.1.3. Ujjwala Yojana

Pradhan Mantri Ujjwala Yojana (PMUY) was established in 2016 to provide free LPG connections to women from economically disadvantaged families (Rawat & Kumar, 2022). This case study explores its success in reducing indoor air pollution and improving women's health. Over Rs 950 crore has been allocated for LPG connectivity by 2023. However, issues such as the affordability of refills have limited continued use, highlighting the need for refill subsidies and promotional campaigns.

3.2. Quantitative Analysis

Quantitative analysis plays a vital role in assessing gender equality by using sex-disaggregated data to highlight differences and track progress in key areas.

3.2.1. Literacy

India's female literacy rate has improved significantly, rising from 64.6% in 2011 to 77% in 2023. This growth reflects the impact of initiatives such as Beti Bachao Beti Padhao and programs to promote girls' education (Chaudhary, n.d.). However, progress has been uneven, with rural and tribal areas lagging urban centres. States like Kerala and Himachal Pradesh have high female literacy rates of over 90 per cent, while regions like Rajasthan and Bihar struggle to cross 60 per cent. Persistent gaps in educational opportunities for marginalized communities highlight the need for targeted interventions, such as improving infrastructure and motivating girls to attend school.

3.2.2. Labor Force Participation

Female labor force participation remains extremely low, at around 23% in 2023, one of the lowest globally (Mukhopadhyay, 2023). Structural barriers such as unpaid domestic work, lack of childcare facilities, workplace harassment and social norms limit many women to unpaid labor or informal employment. Programs such as Skill India and Mahila E-Haat aim to increase women's employability and entrepreneurship, but systemic challenges remain. Addressing these barriers requires policies that promote equal pay, flexible work environments, and affordable childcare.

3.2.3. Political Representation

Women hold only 15% of parliamentary seats, reflecting their underrepresentation in decision-making roles. While the 73rd and 74th Constitutional Amendments ensure 33% reservation for women in local governance, similar measures are lacking at the state and national levels (Chauhan & Charanda, 2023). Advocating for the long-pending women's reservation bill could significantly enhance political equity.

The analysis relies on reliable sources such as MoSPI, NSSO and global reports such as the Gender Gap Report to ensure data accuracy and relevance. These insights highlight the urgent need to develop targeted, data-driven strategies to address India's persistent gender gap.

3.3. Policy Review

Gender budgeting, adopted in India since 2005, represents a major policy innovation aimed at addressing gender disparities through equitable resource allocation. This approach integrates a gender perspective into the budgeting process to ensure that public spending reaches women and girls equitably (Chakraborty, 2014).

Achievements

Gender budgeting helps make targeted investments in women-centred programs that produce real results in areas such as health care, safety and skills development. For example, measures such as the Janani Suraksha Yojana provide financial incentives for institutional delivery, helping to improve maternal health and reduce mortality. States like Kerala and Tamil Nadu have set benchmarks for effective gender budgeting by allocating resources to women's safety measures, vocational training and health services.

For example, Kerala spent a large portion of its gender budget in 2023 on setting up women's help desks in police stations, while Tamil Nadu focused on women's skill development, improving the employability of thousands of women. These examples highlight the potential of gender budgeting to drive meaningful change when implemented effectively.

Challenges

Despite the promise, the impact of gender budgeting is undermined by inconsistent implementation across states. Some regions lack sound institutional structures and technical capacity to incorporate gender-sensitive planning. A review of the 2023 budget shows that only 57% of funds allocated to gender-specific programs are fully utilized, reflecting inefficient disbursement of funds and limited oversight mechanisms (Network & Tanzania, 2024).

Furthermore, the lack of comprehensive sex-disaggregated data hinders accurate needs assessment and program design. This often leads to misallocation of resources and reduces the effectiveness of gender budgeting.

While gender budgeting advances India's gender equality agenda, addressing system inefficiencies and promoting accountability through strengthened monitoring frameworks is critical to realizing its full potential. Strengthening capacity-building and data-driven approaches can ensure these efforts translate into sustainable and inclusive outcomes.

3.4. Synthesis of Methods

The integration of case study analysis, quantitative evaluation, and policy review ensures a comprehensive understanding of gender equality in India's public policy framework.

i. **Case Study Insights**: Qualitative analysis of programs such as Beti Bachao Beti Padhao and Ujjwala Yojana to gain insights into their successes, limitations and contextual nuances. These insights reveal how targeted interventions address specific challenges while highlighting the need for improved implementation strategies.

ii. **Quantitative evidence**: Gender-disaggregated data allow measurable assessments of progress in areas such as literacy, labor force participation and political representation. Trend analysis through reliable data sources reveals persistent disparities and provides a basis for evidence-based decision-making.

iii. **Policy review**: Assessment of gender budgeting reveals systemic gaps and agency best practices. The analysis uncovers inefficiencies and highlights scalable strategies to optimize resource allocation and enhance accountability.

This mixed methods approach captures the complex interplay of socioeconomic and cultural factors that influence gender equality. By identifying actionable gaps, it highlights the importance of data-driven decision-making, localized implementation and iterative policy refinement. Together, these approaches provide a strong roadmap for strengthening governance and ensuring that India's commitment to gender equality delivers sustainable and inclusive outcomes.

4. FINDINGS AND DISCUSSION

4.1. Policy Successes

India has adopted a number of progressive policy measures to promote gender equality and has made notable achievements in resource allocation, social awareness and women's representation.

4.1.1. Gender Budgeting

Gender budgeting, introduced in 2005, and institutionalized the inclusion of a gender perspective in resource allocation. This approach ensures an equitable distribution of resources by analyzing the impact of budget allocations on women and men. For example, programs such as the Janani Suraksha Yojana supported through gender budgeting have increased institutional deliveries and reduced maternal mortality (Chaturvedi, 2015). Likewise, investments in girls' education through programs such as Sarva Shiksha Abhiyan have led to an increase in female literacy, which will reach 77% by 2023(Nandi, Haberland, & Ngo, 2023). Kerala and Tamil Nadu have set benchmarks by effectively channelling funds to healthcare, women's safety and skill development, but other states need to build gender-responsive budgeting capacity.

4.1.2. Beti Bachao Beti Padhao (BBBP)

BBBP was launched in 2015 to address the alarming decline in child sex ratio and raise awareness about girls' rights. The program's publicity campaign has changed people's minds, especially in states such as Haryana, where the sex ratio at birth improved from 834 girls per 1,000 boys in 2015 to 920 girls in 2021. Educational measures have increased girls' enrolment in school. However, more than half of the program's budget is spent on media campaigns rather than tangible interventions, highlighting gaps in its implementation. Strengthening on-the-ground implementation can amplify its impact.

4.1.3. Reservation Policies

The 73rd and 74th Constitutional Amendments reserved 33 per cent seats for women in Panchayati Raj institutions and urban local bodies, significantly increasing their political participation. Today, more than 1.3 million women hold leadership positions in local governance, contributing to community-focused development. For example, women-led panchayats in Rajasthan state prioritize clean drinking water, sanitation and education for girls. Despite these advances, similar reservation policies for women in state legislatures and parliaments, such as the proposed Women's Reservation Bill, remain pending, limiting broader political representation.

These policies highlight India's efforts to institutionalize gender equality. While successes such as improved gender ratios and increased participation in local governance are encouraging, addressing implementation challenges and scaling up successful models will be critical for sustained impact.

4.2. Persisting Challenges

Despite significant policy progress, India still faces several challenges in achieving gender equality. These challenges, rooted in socio-cultural, economic and political factors, continue to hinder the full realization of women's rights and potential.

4.2.1. Violence Against Women

Although India has enacted strict laws such as the Protection of Women from Domestic Violence Act (2005) (Bhatia, 2012) and the Criminal Law (Amendment) Act (2013) to protect women from violence and harassment, domestic violence (Kaur & Anthony, 2021), sexual harassment and Trafficking remains alarmingly high. According to the National Crime Records Bureau (NCRB), crimes against women increased by 6.6% from 2019 to 2020, with more than 300,000 cases of violence reported every year. Social attitudes that normalize gender-based violence, poor enforcement of legal provisions and lack of timely justice contribute to the persistence of such violence. Additionally, police and legal systems often fail to provide a timely and supportive response, and many victims face stigma and blame. Strengthening law enforcement, providing more accessible support systems, and changing social norms are critical to solving this ongoing problem.

4.2.2. Economic Disparities

As of 2024, women's participation in India's workforce remains critically low, hovering around 23%—one of the lowest rates worldwide. Multiple factors contribute to this persistent gap. Deep-rooted cultural norms often assign caregiving responsibilities solely to women, leaving them with limited time or opportunity to pursue employment. Inadequate access to affordable childcare and persistent workplace harassment further discourages their entry or continuity in the labor force. Even when employed, women face a stark wage gap and are largely concentrated in the informal sector, where job security and social benefits like paid leave or health insurance are rarely available.

The COVID-19 pandemic amplified these challenges. Data from the Centre for Monitoring Indian Economy (2023) revealed that women's labor force participation dropped by nine percentage points during the pandemic, with only marginal recovery in the years that followed. Empirical studies offer promising solutions. A 2023 randomized controlled trial by IFMR LEAD showed that integrating digital skill training with childcare support increased women's workforce re-entry by 26% over six months. Similarly, J-PAL South Asia's 2022 study in Bihar found that wage subsidies targeting women-led enterprises boosted employment retention by nearly 19%.

These findings make it clear that bridging the gender employment gap requires more than policy statements—it demands targeted interventions that address both structural inequalities and the lived realities of working women in India.

4.2.3. Political Underrepresentation

Women's representation in India's parliament is only 15%, which contrasts with women's increasing participation in local governance. The 73rd and 74th Constitutional Amendments reserved 33% seats for women in local bodies, bringing over 1.3 million women to grassroots leadership positions. However, this success has not been reflected in higher levels of government. The lack of women in national politics limits the diversity of perspectives in decision-making, especially on issues that disproportionately affect women. The Women's Reservation Bill, which proposes to reserve 33 per cent seats in Parliament, has yet to be passed, further hampering women's political representation. Ensuring gender equality in political participation requires passing legal reforms such as this bill, along with efforts to challenge partisanship and promote female leadership development.

While India has made progress towards gender equality, violence against women, economic disparities and lack of political representation continue to hinder progress. Addressing these challenges requires a comprehensive effort that combines legal reform, sociocultural change and targeted economic policies to empower women and create a more equitable society.

4.3. Intersectional Issues

Gender inequality is not widespread in India. Marginalized groups including Dalit, tribal and LGBTQ+ women face complex disadvantages as gender intersects with caste, race and sexual orientation. These cross-cutting issues require more inclusive policies that address the unique challenges faced by these groups.

4.3.1. Dalit Women

Dalit women face dual oppression of caste and gender, placing them at the bottom of India's socioeconomic strata. They often experience caste-based violence, discrimination and exploitation, which intersect with traditional gender norms. For example, Dalit women are particularly vulnerable to sexual violence, including rape and assault, due to their lower caste status. In addition, they are overrepresented in manual labor and household tasks and have limited access to education, health care, and economic opportunities. Policies targeting the general female population often fail to address the specific needs of Dalit women, necessitating targeted interventions including caste-sensitive support systems, legal reforms to prevent violence, and programs to promote education and economic empowerment.

4.3.2. Tribal Women

Tribal women also face severe disadvantages as they tend to live in remote, underdeveloped areas with limited access to basic resources such as education, health care and legal support. Their traditional roles are deeply rooted in local customs and often limit their mobility and autonomy, further hampering their ability to access opportunities outside their communities. Additionally, tribal women are disproportionately affected by displacement due to development projects such as mining and infrastructure, which often ignore their rights. To address these challenges, policies must incorporate tribal-specific welfare measures such as land rights, cultural protection, and accessible health care and education.

4.3.3. LGBTQ+ Women

LGBTQ+ women face unique challenges facing discrimination not only because of their gender, but also because of their sexual orientation or gender identity. These women often face violence, social exclusion, and legal barriers that are exacerbated by conservative social attitudes. Although the decriminalization of homosexuality in 2018 marked an important step, LGBTQ+ women still lack adequate legal protection and recognition. Policies must provide inclusive support for LGBTQ+ women and address issues such as mental health, social acceptance and legal recognition of relationships.

The intersecting challenges faced by Dalit, tribal and LGBTQ+ women require nuanced policies that take into account the complex layers of discrimination and marginalization they experience. An inclusive, cross-cutting approach is critical to achieving true gender equality in India.

4.4. Pandemic Impacts and the Care Economy

The COVID-19 pandemic laid bare gendered vulnerabilities in both the labor market and the household. According to the ILO (2022), 47% of Indian women reported spending more than four additional hours daily on unpaid domestic work during lockdowns. This surge in care responsibilities directly correlated with a sharp decline in female employment, particularly among informal and part-time workers.

Data from CMIE (2023) revealed that nearly 65% of women who lost jobs during the pandemic had not returned to the workforce by mid-2022. Sectors like domestic work, textiles, and hospitality—which are highly feminized—experienced the slowest recovery.

A 2024 study by Azim Premji University and NIPFP showed that countries investing over 2% of GDP in care infrastructure (e.g., childcare centers, elderly support services) witnessed quicker female workforce recovery. India currently spends less than 0.2% of GDP on care-related infrastructure.

Addressing this deficit requires formal recognition of care work, investment in public childcare, and the inclusion of unpaid labor in national economic accounts. Policies like guaranteed paid family leave, universal childcare, and caregiver stipends can reduce the burden on women and support economic recovery. These reforms are essential for inclusive growth and for valuing women's unpaid labor as a pillar of national development.

5. RECOMMENDATIONS

5.1. Policy Reforms

To effectively promote gender equality in India, it is critical to strengthen existing policies and implement new policies to address systemic barriers. Expanding and strengthening gender budgets in all ministries and implementing gender audits of key government programs are two key reforms that can significantly strengthen the country's efforts to reduce gender gaps and develop more inclusive public policies.

5.1.1. Expand and Strengthen Gender Budgeting Across All Ministries

India's introduction of gender budgeting in 2005 was a step in the right direction, but its impact can be further expanded by expanding its application across all government sectors. Currently, gender budgeting is available for sectors such as health, education and rural development, but many other key areas such as defence, infrastructure and urban development lack gender-sensitive budget allocations. By systematically integrating gender considerations into ministry budgets, governments can ensure that public spending actively promotes gender equality.

For example, the Ministry of Defense could allocate funds for gender-sensitivity training, women's safety measures, and the recruitment of women into the armed forces. Likewise, the Ministry of Urban Affairs can allocate budget for improving public spaces keeping in mind the safety of women. A comprehensive gender budgeting framework covering all ministries will promote gender equality in all sectors and make gender mainstreaming an institutionalized part of governance.

In addition, the government should invest in building the capacity of state and local governments to effectively implement gender budgeting. Providing gender analysis training and tools at the local level will enable more nuanced and context-specific interventions to directly impact women's lives.

5.1.2. Implement Gender Audits for Key Government Programs

Gender audits represent a vital step toward making public programs truly inclusive. These audits systematically assess whether government policies, budgets, and initiatives adequately meet the needs of both women and men, helping to identify disparities and address gaps in implementation. They serve as an accountability mechanism, ensuring that gender-related objectives translate into measurable outcomes.

A 2023 pilot costing exercise by the Ministry of Women and Child Development (MWCD), in collaboration with UN Women, demonstrated that gender audits are fiscally feasible. The findings revealed that such audits can be conducted for 8–12 lakh per department, depending on scale and complexity. Typically, they require a technical team of 5 to 7 members working over a six-week period. Expanding gender budgeting across ministries requires dedicated gender focal points, with an estimated annual training cost of 3–5 lakh per ministry—modest investments that make large-scale rollout both practical and scalable.

Applying gender audits to flagship schemes such as the Pradhan Mantri Awas Yojana (PMAY), National Rural Employment Guarantee Act (NREGA), and Swachh Bharat Abhiyan can uncover whether these programs equally benefit women—particularly those from marginalized Dalit, tribal, and minority communities. For instance, an audit of PMAY can determine if female-headed households have the same access to housing as male-headed ones. Likewise, reviewing NREGA could confirm whether women are fairly represented in the workforce and receiving equal wages.

Beyond assessing equity, gender audits generate valuable data that can shape future planning. By regularly evaluating programs through a gender lens, they help build an evidence base for more responsive policymaking. Transparent reporting mechanisms should accompany audits to ensure that recommendations are implemented and tracked effectively.

To achieve long-term gender equality, India must not only expand gender budgeting across all ministries but also institutionalize gender audits for key government initiatives. These reforms will enhance the inclusivity of governance, ensure resources address women's specific needs, and support the creation of a more just and equitable society.

5.2. Enhancing Representation

Achieving gender equality in India requires increasing the representation of women in political decision-making processes. Despite progress at the local level, women's political participation in national and state governance remains limited. Two key measures to address this gap are the enactment of the Women's Reservation Bill to ensure 33% representation in Parliament and state assemblies, and training of women leaders at the local governance level to build their capacity for effective decision-making.

5.2.1. Enact the Women's Reservation Bill

The Women's Reservation Bill, first introduced in 1996, proposes to reserve 33 per cent seats for women in the Lok Sabha (lower house) and state assemblies (Akar & Meshram, 2019). While the bill has been debated and passed in the Federal House, it has yet to be enacted in the Lok Sabha, mainly due to opposition and concerns about its potential impact on the representation of backward classes. The delay in passing the bill prevents the Indian political system from making meaningful progress on gender equality.

This reservation will significantly increase the number of women in decision-making positions, providing a more diverse perspective on policies that impact women and marginalized communities. For example, countries with higher female representation, such as Rwanda and Sweden, pay more attention to issues such as women's health, violence and education. Likewise, enactment of the Women's Reservation Bill in India will lead to more equitable and inclusive decision-making that addresses issues from a gender-sensitive perspective. Ensuring the passage of this bill will send a strong message about India's commitment to women's empowerment and political inclusion.

5.2.2. Train Women Leaders at Local Governance Levels

While the Women's Reservation Bill was aimed at increasing women's participation at the national and state levels, significant progress has been made in local governance, especially after the 73rd and 74th Constitutional Amendments, which provided for Pan Women's reservation in Jayats and urban local bodies is 33%. This has resulted in over one million women holding leadership positions at the grassroots level. However, gaps remain in their ability to participate effectively in governance.

To bridge this gap, it is crucial to train women leaders at the local governance level in policy development, resource management, leadership skills and negotiation. Providing leadership development programs, workshops, and access to successful female leaders can empower them to take on larger political roles. For example, states such as Kerala and West Bengal have implemented training programs for elected women leaders, improving their ability to advocate for community needs and implement effective policies. These programs equip women with the skills to transcend administrative functions and become active participants in policy development, thereby developing a cadre of female leaders who will ultimately hold positions at the state and national levels.

Improving women's representation in India's political landscape requires institutional reforms and grassroots empowerment. Enactment of the Women's Reservation Bill will ensure a substantial increase in women's participation in national and state governance, while training local women leaders will equip them with more effective leadership and decision-making capabilities. Together, these measures can significantly advance gender equality and ensure that women have a strong voice in shaping India's future.

5.3. Data-Driven Decision Making

Data-driven decision-making is essential to ensure that policies are effectively designed, implemented and monitored to achieve gender equality. To make meaningful progress, it is necessary to improve the collection and analysis of sex-disaggregated data and establish an open-access repository to track gender equality indicators.

Accurate and comprehensive sex-disaggregated data is fundamental to understanding gender disparities across sectors such as health, education, employment, and political participation (Doss, 2014). Yet, in India, the collection and analysis of such data remain inconsistent and fragmented. To address this, data collection methodologies must be standardized across all government agencies, ensuring that gender considerations are integrated into surveys, monitoring systems, and reporting frameworks.

Recent empirical analyses by Brookings India (2023) and NITI Aayog (2024) emphasize the need for data that is not only separated by sex but also disaggregated by variables such as age, caste, region, and sector. Such granularity is essential for designing inclusive policies that respond to the diverse experiences of women. For example, the 2023 National Employment Policy Evaluation found that women from Scheduled Castes (SC) and Scheduled Tribes (ST) had a 31% higher dropout rate from government-run skill development programs compared to general category women. These findings highlight the importance of integrating intersectional data to craft targeted and equitable policy interventions.

While institutions like the National Sample Survey Office (NSSO) and the National Family Health Survey (NFHS) already collect sex-disaggregated data, their outputs often lack sufficient depth to capture the experiences of marginalized groups such as Dalit, tribal, and LGBTQ+ women. Enhancing both the quality and the granularity of this data will allow policymakers to better understand the unique barriers different groups face.

Additionally, linking gender data with broader socioeconomic indicators—such as income, disability status, and geographic location—can help identify compounded disadvantages. This intersectional approach is critical for designing policies that are not only gender-responsive but also socially inclusive.

5.3.1. Create an Open-Access Database for Monitoring Gender Equality Indicators

The open-access repository will serve as a central hub for real-time monitoring of gender equality indicators. The repository should collate data from a variety of sources, including government departments, independent research institutions and civil society organizations. It tracks key indicators such as female literacy, labor force participation, gender pay gap and rates of violence against women, providing a transparent view of a country's progress.

Such platforms not only allow policymakers to make informed decisions but also engage citizens, NGOs, and academia in advocacy and research. Additionally, making this data public will promote accountability and encourage state and local governments to take concrete steps to achieve gender equality. The open access repository can also be used to track the effectiveness of gender-responsive policies and highlight areas where further action is needed.

Data-driven decision-making is fundamental to achieving gender equality in India. By improving the collection and analysis of sex-disaggregated data and creating an open-access database to monitor gender equality indicators, the country can develop evidence-based policies to address existing gaps and promote sustainable gender equality. These steps will ensure that policies are not only well-targeted but also meet the changing needs of women in different communities.

5.4. Social Transformation Initiatives

5.4.1. Scale up Campaigns like Beti Bachao Beti Padhao

The Beti Bachao Beti Padhao (BBBP) initiative was launched in 2015 to address the declining sex ratio in India and promote the value of girls. While the movement has helped raise awareness of the importance of girls' education, it has not yet addressed key issues such as employability and economic empowerment.

To truly change gender dynamics, the movement must expand to focus on skills development and employability. When women graduate from school and university, they often face a lack of employment opportunities due to limited access to vocational training, discriminatory recruitment practices and social expectations. By integrating skills development programmes, especially in growing demand industries such as information technology, healthcare and entrepreneurship, the program can provide young girls with the tools to succeed in the labor market. Governments can work with the private sector to create vocational training centres, apprenticeships and mentoring opportunities for young women, especially in rural and underserved areas.

5.4.2. Engage Men and Boys in Gender Equality Programs

Gender equality cannot be achieved without including men and boys in the conversation. Traditional patriarchal norms impose restrictions on both women and men, but men often benefit from these norms, perpetuating gender-based discrimination.

It is crucial to challenge these norms and encourage men to actively participate in promoting gender equality.

Programs should be designed to engage men and boys from an early age, promote positive masculinity, and emphasize shared responsibilities in family life, workplace equity, and community involvement. Measures such as community dialogue, school programs and media campaigns can play a role in reshaping perceptions of gender roles. Men and boys need to understand that gender equality benefits everyone – breaking stereotypes can reduce violence, strengthen families and increase opportunities for both genders.

For example, awareness-raising campaigns and education programs could focus on engaging men in household chores and parenting, promoting respect for women's autonomy, and reducing gender-based violence. By fostering respectful relationships between genders, these initiatives can dismantle patriarchal attitudes and build a more inclusive society.

Social transformation is a necessary complement to policy changes that pursue gender equality. Scaling up initiatives like Beti Bachao Beti Padhao to include skills development and employment opportunities for girls can significantly improve their life chances, while engaging men and boys in gender equality programs can challenge entrenched patriarchal norms. Together, these efforts can create a more equitable and supportive environment for all, driving the social and cultural changes needed to achieve gender equality in India.

6. STRATEGIC ROADMAP FOR GENDER EQUALITY

Despite constitutional guarantees of gender equality, India ranks 129th out of 146 countries in the Global Gender Gap Index, revealing a stark 35% deficit that demands urgent attention. While initiatives like Beti Bachao Beti Padhao and gender-responsive budgeting have shown promise, transformative change requires comprehensive reforms across multiple dimensions.

6.1. Strengthen Institutional Mechanisms

India must expand gender budgeting beyond its current scope to encompass all government ministries. Currently limited to sectors like health and education, this approach should extend to defense, infrastructure, and urban development. Each ministry needs dedicated gender focal points and systematic gender audits to ensure policies truly benefit both men and women equally.

Gender audits, which cost approximately 8-12 lakh per department, represent a modest investment with substantial returns. These evaluations can reveal whether flagship schemes like Pradhan Mantri Awas Yojana or NREGA adequately serve women, particularly those from marginalized communities.

6.2. Enhance Political Representation

The Women's Reservation Act 2023, guaranteeing 33% parliamentary representation from 2029, marks significant progress. However, immediate action is needed to train women leaders at local governance levels. With over 1.3 million women already in grassroots positions through panchayati raj institutions, targeted capacity-building programs in policy development, resource management, and negotiation skills can prepare them for higher political roles.

6.3. Transform Social Attitudes

Scaling up awareness campaigns like Beti Bachao Beti Padhao must extend beyond education to include skills development and employment opportunities. More critically, engaging men and boys in gender equality programs is essential. Traditional patriarchal norms benefit from male participation in challenging stereotypes and promoting shared responsibilities in households and workplaces.

6.4. Address Economic Disparities

With women's workforce participation at merely 23%—among the world's lowest—targeted interventions are crucial. The COVID-19 pandemic revealed that women shoulder 47% more unpaid domestic work, directly impacting their employment prospects. Investment in care infrastructure, affordable childcare, and formal recognition of unpaid labor can significantly improve women's economic participation.

6.5. Leverage Data for Impact

Creating an open-access database with sex-disaggregated data, particularly for marginalized groups like Dalit, tribal, and LGBTQ+ women, enables evidence-based policymaking. This transparency promotes accountability and helps track progress across various gender equality indicators.

India's journey toward gender equality requires moving beyond policy formulation to robust implementation, community engagement, and cultural transformation. Only through this multifaceted approach can constitutional promises translate into lived realities for all women.

7. STUDY LIMITATIONS

While this research provides a comprehensive assessment of India's gender equality landscape, several methodological constraints warrant acknowledgment. The analysis faces three primary limitations that constrain its depth. First, the policy recommendations would benefit from more granular fiscal assessments. Although basic cost estimates are provided—such as 8-12 lakh for departmental gender audits and 3-5 lakh for annual ministry-level gender budgeting—detailed implementation frameworks including staffing requirements, phased rollout strategies, and long-term scalability analyses would enhance practical utility for policymakers. Second, the quantitative findings rely predominantly on descriptive analysis and correlational relationships rather than establishing causal mechanisms. Future research incorporating rigorous impact evaluations, such as the methodological approaches used in IFMR LEAD's 2023 digital skills intervention or J-PAL South Asia's 2022 employment randomized trials, would strengthen evidence-based policy formulation. Third, despite comprehensive coverage, the literature synthesis could integrate emerging scholarship from 2022-25, particularly studies examining pandemic-induced gender disparities, implementation science frameworks for gender mainstreaming, and intersectional approaches to gender-responsive budgeting. These methodological enhancements would elevate the analysis from descriptive assessment to prescriptive policy science without fundamentally altering the study's scope or analytical framework.

8. CONCLUSION

India's journey toward gender equality reflects both remarkable progress and persistent challenges. Progressive legislative frameworks, including gender-responsive budgeting and targeted initiatives like Beti Bachao Beti Padhao, demonstrate the nation's commitment to constitutional principles of equality. However, the 35% gender deficit revealed in international rankings underscores that policy implementation must match policy ambition.

The path forward requires multi-dimensional interventions that address structural, institutional, and cultural barriers simultaneously. Expanding gender budgeting across all ministries, implementing systematic gender audits, and ensuring political representation through the Women's Reservation Act 2023 provide institutional foundations. Yet sustainable transformation demands deeper engagement—challenging patriarchal norms, recognizing unpaid care work, and creating inclusive frameworks that address intersectional vulnerabilities faced by Dalit, tribal, and LGBTQ+ women.

Most critically, achieving gender equality requires moving beyond policy formulation to robust implementation, community mobilization, and cultural change.

The evidence suggests that countries investing substantially in care infrastructure and engaging men as active allies in gender equality witness accelerated progress. India's demographic dividend and democratic institutions position it uniquely to leverage these approaches.

Regular policy evaluation, data-driven decision-making, and adaptive governance will determine whether constitutional promises translate into lived realities. The road to gender parity by 2035 is achievable, but only through sustained political will, adequate resource allocation, and recognition that gender equality benefits not just women, but India's entire developmental trajectory. With continued commitment to evidence-based reforms and inclusive growth, a more equitable society remains within reach.

REFERENCES

Adisa, T. A., Cooke, F. L., & Iwowo, V. (2020). Mind your attitude: The impact of patriarchy on women's workplace behaviour. *Career Development International, 25*(2), 146–164. DOI: 10.1108/CDI-07-2019-0183

Akar, A., & Meshram, M. P. (2019). Power and representation: Women Reservation Bill. *ProBono India.*

Bala, S. (2012). Implementation of Maternity Benefit Act. *NLI Research Studies Series, 99*, 2012.

Bhate, I. A study of Mahila e-haat|| portal for encouraging women entrepreneurs. *General Management*, 467.

Bhatia, M. (2012). Domestic Violence in India: Cases Under the Protection of Women from Domestic Violence Act, 2005. *South Asia Research, 32*(2), 103–122. DOI: 10.1177/0262728012453489

Bhoi, S. Gender Based Discrimination and Gender Differences in India.

Binuomote., O. E. (2023, May). Interconnectedness of Girl-Child Education and Poverty Alleviation: Exploring the Dynamics. In *Lead City University Postgraduate Multidisciplinary Conference Proceedings* (Vol. 1, No. 2, pp. 400-408).

Chakraborty, L. (2014). Gender-Responsive Budgeting as Fiscal Innovation: Evidence from India on'Processes'. *Levy Economics Institute, Working Paper*, (797).

Chaturvedi, S. (2015). *Quality of Obstetric Care in India's Janani Suraksha Yojana Cash Transfer Program to Promote Facility Births: Studies from Madhya Pradesh Province*. Karolinska Institutet.

Chaudhary, M. N. Comprehensive Examination of the Educational Situation of Women in Uttar Pradesh, with a Special Emphasis on Women's Empowerment and Progress.

Chauhan, R., & Charanda, M. (2023). Women Empowerment and Urban Local Self-Governance in the light of 74th Amendment. *Bayan College International Journal of Multidisciplinary Research, 3*(2), 109–114.

Dasgupta, A., & Sharma, A. (2021). *Can legal bans on sex detection technology reduce gender discrimination* (No. 58).

Dayal, D. (2023). Empowering Hindu Women: Unveiling the Legacy of Ancestral Property Rights. *Nyaayshastra L. Rev., 4*, 1.

Debnath, K., & Chatterjee, S. Marginalised Groups in India.

Doss, C. (2014). Collecting sex disaggregated data to improve development policies. *Journal of African Economies*, *23*(suppl_1), i62–i86. DOI: 10.1093/jae/ejt023

Errami, E., Ochir, G., & Peppoloni, S. (2021). Achieve gender equality and empower all women and girls. *Geosciences and the sustainable development goals*, 105-126.

Freeman, M. A., Rudolf, B., & Chinkin, C. (Eds.). (2012). *The UN convention on the elimination of all forms of discrimination against women: A commentary*. Oxford University Press. DOI: 10.5422/fso/9780199565061.001.0001

Kaur, L., & Anthony, S. B. (2021). Offences Against Women Viz-A-Viz the Criminal Law (Amendment) Act, 2018.

Mohajer, N., & Culty, M. (2024). Impact of human-relevant doses of endocrine disrupting chemical and drug mixtures on testis development and function. [aop]. *Reproduction*, 1. PMID: 39454032

Mukhopadhyay, U. (2023). Disparities in Female Labour Force Participation in South Asia and Latin America: A Review. *Review of Economics*, *74*(3), 265–288. DOI: 10.1515/roe-2022-0061

Nandi, A., Haberland, N., & Ngo, T. D. (2023). The impact of primary schooling expansion on adult educational attainment, literacy, and health: Evidence from India's Sarva Shiksha Abhiyan. *International Journal of Educational Development*, *102*, 102871. DOI: 10.1016/j.ijedudev.2023.102871

Network, T. E., & Tanzania, M. W. E. (2024). Gender responsive budget analysis of the education sector.

Nigam, A. D. S. (2023). *Dowry Is a Serious Violence: Rethinking Dowry Law in India*. Shalu Nigam.

Pandey, V., & Shekhar, S. (2024). Gender Neutrality of Indian Laws-A Myth or Reality? *Educational Administration: Theory and Practice*, *30*(5), 3204–3213.

Pimkina, S., & de La Flor, L. (2020). *Promoting female labor force participation*. World Bank. DOI: 10.1596/34953

Rawat, V. S., & Kumar, M. (2022). Women empowerment through pradhan mantri ujjwala yojana (PmUY)–a study of LPg refills. *Review Journal Philosophy & Social Science*, *47*(2), 407–415. DOI: 10.31995/rjpss.2022.v47i02.046

Singh, S. Women in Panchayati Raj Institutions: A study of two villages in Rajasthan.

Sivakumar, I., & Manimekalai, K. (2021). Masculinity and challenges for women in Indian culture. *Journal of International Women's Studies*, *22*(5), 427–436.

KEY TERMS AND DEFINITIONS

Beti Bachao Beti Padhao (BBBP): A campaign started in 2015 to save and educate girl children, aiming to stop discrimination against girls and improve their future.

Gender Audit: A check done on government programs or policies to see if they are helping both men and women equally, and to find where improvements are needed.

Gender Disaggregated Data: Information that is collected separately for men and women to help understand their different needs and challenges.

Gender Equality: Giving men and women the same rights, opportunities, and respect in all areas of life like education, jobs, and politics.

Gender-Responsive Budgeting: A way the government plans its money so that it helps both men and women fairly, especially in programs for health, education, and safety.

Intersectionality: Some women face more problems because of their gender along with other reasons like caste, poverty, or being LGBTQ+.

Mahila E-Haat: An online marketplace where women can sell handmade or self-produced products to support their businesses.

Maternity Benefit (Amendment) Act 2017: This law gives working women up to 26 weeks of paid leave to take care of their newborn babies.

Patriarchy: A system where men usually have more power and control than women in families, workplaces, and society.

Social Movements: Groups of people who work together to bring social change, such as improving women's rights or stopping violence.

Ujjwala Yojana: A government program that gives free LPG cooking gas connections to poor women to improve health and reduce indoor air pollution.

Women's Reservation Act 2023: A law will reserve 33 percent of seats for women in Parliament and state assemblies starting from the year 2029.

Compilation of References

Aalbers, M. (2016). *Financialization of housing*. Taylor & Francis. DOI: 10.4324/9781315668666

Aalbers, M. B. (2015). The great moderation, the great excess and the global housing crisis. *International Journal of Housing Policy, 15*(1), 43–60. DOI: 10.1080/14616718.2014.997431

Aalbers, M. B. (2017). The variegated financialization of housing. *International Journal of Urban and Regional Research, 41*(4), 542–554. DOI: 10.1111/1468-2427.12522

Abonazel, M. R., Ahmed, E. G., El-Baz, S. T., & others. (2024). *How economic policies drive climate change: A comparative analysis of groups of middle- and high-income countries*. International Journal of Energy Economics and Policy.

Adamopoulou, E., Kapopoulos, P., & Zekente, K.-M. (2025). *Alpha Bank Economic Research, April 2025*. Alpha Bank.

Adebayo, T. S., & Kirikkaleli, D. (2021). Impact of renewable energy consumption, globalization, and technological innovation on environmental degradation in Japan: Application of wavelet tools. *Environment, Development and Sustainability, 23*(11), 16057–16082. DOI: 10.1007/s10668-021-01322-2

Adisa, O. M., Masinde, M., Botai, J. O., & Botai, C. M. (2020). Bibliometric Analysis of Methods and Tools for Drought Monitoring and Prediction in Africa. *Sustainability (Basel), 12*(16), 6516. DOI: 10.3390/su12166516

Adisa, T. A., Cooke, F. L., & Iwowo, V. (2020). Mind your attitude: The impact of patriarchy on women's workplace behaviour. *Career Development International, 25*(2), 146–164. DOI: 10.1108/CDI-07-2019-0183

Adjasi, C., & Biekpe, N. (2006). Stock market development and economic growth: The case of selected African countries. *African Development Review*, *18*(1), 144–161. DOI: 10.1111/j.1467-8268.2006.00136.x

Aebi, M. F. (2008). Measuring the influence of statistical counting rules on cross-national differences in recorded crime. Crime and Criminal Justice Systems in Europe and North America 1995-2004, 196-214.

Aebi, M. F., & Linde, A. (2012). Conviction Statistics as an Indicator of Crime Trends in Europe from 1990 to 2006. *European Journal on Criminal Policy and Research*, *18*(1), 103–144. DOI: 10.1007/s10610-011-9166-7

Afflatet, N. (2018). The impact of population ageing on public debt: A panel data analysis for 18 european countries. *International Journal of Economics and Financial Issues*, *8*(4), 68–77.

Ager, A., & Strang, A. (2008). Understanding integration: A conceptual framework. *Journal of Refugee Studies*, *21*(2), 166–191. DOI: 10.1093/jrs/fen016

Agnew, R. (2015). Strain, economic status, and crime. The handbook of criminological theory, 209-229. DOI: 10.1002/9781118512449.ch11

Agrawala, S., Dussaux, D., & Monti, N. (2020). What policies for greening the crisis response and economic recovery? OECD Environment Working Papers, No. 164. DOI: 10.1787/19970900

Ahir, Hites, Nina Biljanovska, Chenxu Fu, Deniz Igan, and Prakash Loungani. (2022). Housing Prices Continue to Soar in Many Countries around the World. IMF Blog Chart of the Week, October 18.

Aiyagari, S. R. (1994). Uninsured idiosyncratic risk and aggregate saving. *The Quarterly Journal of Economics*, *109*(3), 659–684. DOI: 10.2307/2118417

Aiyagari, S. R., & McGrattan, E. R. (1998). The optimum quantity of debt. *Journal of Monetary Economics*, *42*(3), 447–469. DOI: 10.1016/S0304-3932(98)00031-2

Aizenman, J., & Jinjarak, Y. (2012). Income inequality, tax base and sovereign spreads. *Finanz-Archiv*, *68*(4), 431–444. DOI: 10.1628/001522112X659565

Aizenman, J., & Marion, N. (2011). Using inflation to erode the US public debt. *Journal of Macroeconomics*, *33*(4), 524–541. DOI: 10.1016/j.jmacro.2011.09.001

Akar, A., & Meshram, M. P. (2019). Power and representation: Women Reservation Bill. *ProBono India*.

Akitoby, B., Komatsuzaki, T., & Binder, A. (2014). Inflation and public debt reversals in the G7 countries (IMF Working Paper No. 14/96). *International Monetary Fund.*

Aksman, E. (2017). Do poverty and income inequality affect public debt? *Gospodarka Narodowa, 6*(292), 79–93. DOI: 10.33119/GN/100744

Alesina, A., & Drazen, A. (1991). Why are stabilizations delayed? *The American Economic Review, 81*(5), 1170–1188.

Alesina, A., & Perotti, R. (1995). The political economy of budget deficits. *Staff Papers - International Monetary Fund. International Monetary Fund, 42*(1), 1–31. DOI: 10.2307/3867338

Alesina, A., & Tabellini, G. (1989). External debt, Capital flight and political risk. *Journal of International Economics, 27*(3-4), 199–220. DOI: 10.1016/0022-1996(89)90052-4

Alesina, A., & Tabellini, G. (1990). A positive theory of fiscal deficits and government debt. *The Review of Economic Studies, 57*(3), 403–414. DOI: 10.2307/2298021

Ali, I. M. A. (2022). Income inequality and environmental degradation Egypt: Evidence from dynamic ARDL approach. *Environmental Science and Pollution Research International, 29*(6), 8408–8422. DOI: 10.1007/s11356-021-16275-2 PMID: 34490558

Ali, M., Kirikkaleli, D., & Altuntaş, M. (2024). The nexus between CO_2 intensity of GDP and environmental degradation in South European countries. *Environment, Development and Sustainability, 26*(5), 11089–11100. DOI: 10.1007/s10668-023-03217-w

Allen, R. C. (2017). Absolute Poverty: When Necessity Displaces Desire. *The American Economic Review, 107*(12), 3690–3721. https://www.aeaweb.org/articles?id=10.1257/aer.20161080. DOI: 10.1257/aer.20161080

Alvaredo, F. (2011). A note on the relationship between top income shares and the Gini coefficient. *Economics Letters, 110*(3), 274–277. DOI: 10.1016/j.econlet.2010.10.008

Antunes, M. J. L., & Manasse, M. (2022). Social disorganization and strain: Macro and micro implications for youth violence. *Journal of Research in Crime and Delinquency, 59*(1), 82–127. DOI: 10.1177/00224278211004667

Arawatari, R., & Ono, T. (2017). Inequality and public debt: A positive analysis. *Review of International Economics, 25*(1), 1155–1173. DOI: 10.1111/roie.12299

Aronson, E. (1988). *The social animal.* Freeman.

Aslan, B., Zh, B., Ye, A., Zh, T., Anar, Y., & Azamat, Z. (2018). The influence of stock market development of low income and middle/high income group countries on an increase in economic growth. *Journal of Advanced Research in Law and Economics*, *9*(3), 839–848.

Atkinson, A. B. (2019). *Measuring Poverty around the World*. Princeton University Press.

Avgousti, A., Caprioli, F., & Caracciolo, G. (2023). *The climate change challenge and fiscal instruments and policies in the EU*. Social Science Research Network. DOI: 10.2139/ssrn.4424152

Awojobi, O. N., & Vloveret, M. (2017). Social protection and climate resilience: A review of Sub-Saharan African case studies. [IJOEAR]. *International Journal of Environmental & Agriculture Research*, *3*(12), 100–103.

Aye, G., Gozgor, G., & Gupta, R. (2020). Dynamic and asymmetric response of inequality to income volatility: The case of the United Kingdom. *Social Indicators Research*, *147*(3), 747–762. DOI: 10.1007/s11205-019-02180-2

Azzimonti, M., Francisco, E., & Quadrini, V. (2014). Financial globalization, inequality, and the rising public debt. *The American Economic Review*, *104*(8), 2267–2302. DOI: 10.1257/aer.104.8.2267

Baek, J., & Gweisah, G. (2013). Does income inequality harm the environment? Empirical evidence from the United States. *Energy Policy*, *62*(Nov), 1434–1437. DOI: 10.1016/j.enpol.2013.07.097

Bai, X., McPhearson, T., Cleugh, H., Nagendra, H., Tong, X., Zhu, T., & Zhu, Y. G. (2017). Linking urbanization and the environment: Conceptual and empirical advances. *Annual Review of Environment and Resources*, *42*(1), 215–240. DOI: 10.1146/annurev-environ-102016-061128

Balakrishnan, U., & Tsaneva, M. (2021). Air pollution and academic performance: Evidence from India. *World Development*, *146*, 105553. DOI: 10.1016/j.worlddev.2021.105553

Bala, S. (2012). Implementation of Maternity Benefit Act. *NLI Research Studies Series*, *99*, 2012.

Baloch, M. A., Khan, S. U. D., Ulucak, Z. S., & Ahmad, A. (2020). Analyzing the relationship between poverty, income inequality, and CO2 emission in Sub-Saharan African countries. *Sci. Total Environ 740*, 139867. https://doi.org/. scitotenv.2020.139867.DOI: 10.1016/j

Baltagi, B. H. (2005). *Econometric Analysis of Panel Data* (3rd ed.). John Wiley & Sons.

Barberis, N., & Thaler, R. (2003). A survey of behavioral finance. Handbook of the Economics of Finance, 1, 1053–1128. DOI: 10.1016/S1574-0102(03)01027-6

Barro, R. (1979). On the determination of public debt. *Journal of Political Economy, 87*(5), 940–971. DOI: 10.1086/260807

BBC News. (2025). Bank of mum and dad 'helps half of first-time buyers'. Retrieved May 18, 2025, from https://www.bbc.co.uk/news/articles/cly1jzl9eedo

Becker, G. S. (1968). Crime and Punishment: An Economic Approach. The economic dimensions of crime/Springer.

Becker, B. (2019). Mind the income gaps? Experimental evidence of information's lasting effect on redistributive preferences. *Social Justice Research, 33*(2), 137–194. DOI: 10.1007/s11211-019-00343-7

Becker, H. S. (1963). *Outsiders. Studies in the Sociology of Deviance*. The Free Press.

Bedamatta, R. (2021). Employment of the Rural Labour Force in India–The Current Trends and Future Prospects. *Indian Journal of Agricultural Economics, 76*(1), 92–108. DOI: 10.63040/25827510.2021.01.004

Bene, C., Cannon, T., Davies, M., Newsham, A., & Tanner, T. (2013). *Social protection and climate change*. OECD Development Co-Operation Workinp Paper., DOI: 10.1787/5jz2qc8wc1s5-

Berthe, A., & Elie, L. (2015). Mechanisms explaining the impact of economic inequality on environmental deterioration. *Ecological Economics, 116*, 191–200. DOI: 10.1016/j.ecolecon.2015.04.026

Besnili, M. O. (2023). İklim Değişikliği ve Sosyal Adalet: Sosyal Politika ve Dayanıklılık Çerçevesinden Bir İnceleme. *Uşak Üniversitesi Uygulamalı Bilimler Fakültesi Dergisi, 3*(2), 20–37.

Bevan, D. (2012). *Aid, fiscal policy, climate change, and growth*. Research Papers in Economics.

Bhate, I. A study of Mahila e-haat|| portal for encouraging women entrepreneurs. *General Management*, 467.

Bhatia, M. (2012). Domestic Violence in India: Cases Under the Protection of Women from Domestic Violence Act, 2005. *South Asia Research, 32*(2), 103–122. DOI: 10.1177/0262728012453489

Bhoi, D. (2022). Economic Growth, Development, and Education of Scheduled Castes: Line Drawn from Neoliberal Era. *Contemporary Voice of Dalit*. https://journals.sagepub.com/doi/full/10.1177/2455328X211073207

Bhoi, S. Gender Based Discrimination and Gender Differences in India.

Biljanovska, N., Fu, M. C., & Igan, M. D. O. (2023). *Housing affordability: A new dataset*. International Monetary Fund.

Binuomote., O. E. (2023, May). Interconnectedness of Girl-Child Education and Poverty Alleviation: Exploring the Dynamics. In *Lead City University Postgraduate Multidisciplinary Conference Proceedings* (Vol. 1, No. 2, pp. 400-408).

Biswas, S. (2021). Effect of mobile financial services on financial behavior in developing economies-Evidence from India. arXiv preprint arXiv:2109.07077.

Biswas, S. (2021). She Innovates-Female owner and firm innovation in India. *arXiv preprint arXiv:2109.09515*.

Bittencourt, M. (2015). Determinants of government and external debt: Evidence from the young democracies of South America. *Emerging Markets Finance & Trade*, *51*(3), 463–472. DOI: 10.1080/1540496X.2015.1025667

Blanco-Mesa, F., Merigó, J. M., & Gil-Lafuente, A. M. (2017). Fuzzy decision making: A bibliometric-based review. *Journal of Intelligent & Fuzzy Systems*, *32*(3), 2033–2050. DOI: 10.3233/JIFS-161640

Blau, B. M. (2015). Income inequality and stock market volatility. SSRN *Electronic Journal*. DOI: 10.2139/ssrn.2708500

Blau, B. M., Griffith, T. G., & Whitby, R. J. (2021). Income inequality and the volatility of stock prices. *Applied Economics*, *53*(38), 4404–4416. DOI: 10.1080/00036846.2021.1904110

Blesch, K., Hauser, O. P., & Jachimowicz, J. M. (2022). Measuring inequality beyond the Gini coefficient may clarify conflicting findings. *Nature Human Behaviour*, *6*(11), 1525–1536. DOI: 10.1038/s41562-022-01430-7 PMID: 36038775

Blickle, K., & Brown, M. (2019). Borrowing constraints, home ownership and housing choice: Evidence from intra-family wealth transfers. *Journal of Money, Credit and Banking*, *51*(2-3), 539–580. DOI: 10.1111/jmcb.12566

Bourguignon, F. (1999). Crime as a social cost of poverty and inequality: A review focusing on developing countries. *Revista. Desarrollo y Sociedad*, (44), 61–99.

Bouzarovski, S. (2014). Energy poverty in the European Union: Landscapes of vulnerability. *Wiley Interdisciplinary Reviews. Energy and Environment*, *3*(3), 276–289. DOI: 10.1002/wene.89

Boyce, J. K. (2019). *The Case for Carbon Dividends*. Polity Press.

Brady, D. (2023). Poverty, Not the Poor. *Science Advances*, *9*(34), eadg1469. https://www.science.org/doi/pdf/10.1126/sciadv.adg1469. DOI: 10.1126/sciadv.adg1469 PMID: 37611106

Breusch, T. S., & Pagan, A. R. (1980). The Lagrange Multiplier test and its applications to model specification in econometrics. *The Review of Economic Studies*, *47*(1), 239–253. DOI: 10.2307/2297111

Browning, C. R., Dietz, R. D., & Feinberg, S. L. (2004). The paradox of social organization: Networks, collective efficacy, and violent crime in urban neighborhoods. *Social Forces*, *83*(2), 503–534. DOI: 10.1353/sof.2005.0006

Buchanan, J. M., & Wagner, R. E. (1977). *Democracy in deficit: The political legacy of Lord Keynes*. Academic Press.

Burke, T., Nygaard, C., & Ralston, L. (2020). Australian home ownership: past reflections, future directions. AHURI Final Report, (328).

Butler, E. (2022). *Introduction to Economic Inequality*. Institute of Economic Affairs.

Cai, Y., & Lontzek, T. S. (2019). The social cost of carbon with economic and climate risks. *Journal of Political Economy*, *127*(6), 2684–2734. DOI: 10.1086/701890

Callon, M., Courtial, J. P., Turner, W. A., & Bauin, S. (1983). From translations to problematic networks: An introduction to co-word analysis. *Social Sciences Information. Information Sur les Sciences Sociales*, *22*(2), 191–235. DOI: 10.1177/053901883022002003

Camilletti, E., Nesbitt-Ahmed, Z., & Subrahmanian, R. (2022). Promoting gender-transformative change through social protection.

Carrera, J., & de la Vega, P. (2021). The impact of income inequality on public debt. *Journal of Economic Asymmetries*, *24*, 1–16. DOI: 10.1016/j.jeca.2021.e00216

Carrera, J., de la Vega, P., & Toledo, F. (2024). Income inequality and fiscal policy over the political cycle. *Empirical Economics*, *66*(1), 301–325. DOI: 10.1007/s00181-023-02455-1

Carter, M. R., & Janzen, S. A. (2018). Social protection in the face of climate change: Targeting principles and financing mechanisms. *Environment and Development Economics, 23*(3), 369–389. DOI: 10.1017/S1355770X17000407

CESCR. (1999). General Comment 12: On the Right to Adequate Food. *E/C.12/1999/5*. https://digitallibrary.un.org/record/1491194?ln=en&v=pdf

Cetintas, H., Bicil, İ. M., & Türköz, K. (2016). Türkiye'de CO2 Salınımları Enerji Tüketimi ve Ekonomik Büyüme İlişkisi. *Finans Politik ve Ekonomik Yorumlar*, (619), 57–67.

Chadwick, A. (2021). Human Rights, Poverty, and Capitalism. In Egan, S., & Chadwick, A. (Eds.), *Poverty and Human Rights: Multidisciplinary Perspectives* (pp. 68–90). Edward Elgar.

Chakrabarty, K. 2. (2013). Financial Inclusion in India: Journey so far and way forward. *Key note address at Finance Inclusion Conclave Organised by CNBC TV, 18.*

Chakraborty, L. (2014). Gender-Responsive Budgeting as Fiscal Innovation: Evidence from India on'Processes'. *Levy Economics Institute, Working Paper*, (797).

Chamorro Narváez, R. A. (2017). Crecimiento económico y política fiscal: Una revisión crítica de la literatura. *Estudios de Economía Aplicada, 27*(51), 79–107. Advance online publication. DOI: 10.15446/ede.v27n51.69104

Chancel, L., & Piketty, T. (2019). Indian Income Inequality, 1922-2015: From British Raj to Billionaire Raj? *Review of Income and Wealth, 65*(S1), S33–S62. https://onlinelibrary.wiley.com/doi/full/10.1111/roiw.12439. DOI: 10.1111/roiw.12439

Chancel, L., Piketty, T., Saez, E., & Zucman, G. (2022). *World Inequality Report*. World Inequality Lab.

Charlot, O., Naiditch, C., & Vranceanu, R. (2022). Migrant smuggling to Europe: A matching model. ESSEC Business School Research Paper.

Chaturvedi, S. (2015). *Quality of Obstetric Care in India's Janani Suraksha Yojana Cash Transfer Program to Promote Facility Births: Studies from Madhya Pradesh Province*. Karolinska Institutet.

Chaudhary, M. N. Comprehensive Examination of the Educational Situation of Women in Uttar Pradesh, with a Special Emphasis on Women's Empowerment and Progress.

Chauhan, R., & Charanda, M. (2023). Women Empowerment and Urban Local Self-Governance in the light of 74th Amendment. *Bayan College International Journal of Multidisciplinary Research, 3*(2), 109–114.

Chen, C. (2017). Science mapping: A systematic review of the literature. *Journal of Data and Information Science, 2*(2), 1–40. DOI: 10.1515/jdis-2017-0006

Chen, D. H. (2004). *Population age structure and teh budget deficit. (World Bank Policy ResearchWorking Paper No. 3435).* The World Bank. DOI: 10.1596/1813-9450-3435

Chen, N.-F., Roll, R., & Ross, S. A. (1986). Economic Forces and the Stock Market. *The Journal of Business, 59*(3), 383–403. DOI: 10.1086/296344

Ching, S. L., Lau, L. S., & Choong, C. K. (2023). Income inequality, educational attainment and environmental degradation: Evidence from global panel. *Environmental Science and Pollution Research International, 30*(15), 43056–43067. DOI: 10.1007/s11356-022-19256-1 PMID: 35508851

Chisadza, C., Clance, M., Sheng, X., & Gupta, R. (2023). Climate Change and Inequality: Evidence from the United States. *Sustainability (Basel), 15*(6), 5322. DOI: 10.3390/su15065322

Chiu, W. H., & Madden, P. (1998). Burglary and income inequality. *Journal of Public Economics, 69*(1), 123–141. DOI: 10.1016/S0047-2727(97)00096-0

Cho, E. Y. N. (2018). Links between poverty and children's subjective wellbeing: Examining the mediating and moderating role of relationships. *Child Indicators Research, 11*(2), 585–607. DOI: 10.1007/s12187-017-9453-z

Christophers, B. (2024). *Our lives in their portfolios: Why asset managers own the world.* Verso Books.

Christou, C., Gupta, R., & Jawadi, F. (2017). Does inequality help in forecasting equity premium in a panel of G7 countries? *The North American Journal of Economics and Finance, 55*, 101456. Advance online publication. DOI: 10.1016/j.najef.2021.101456

Cigdem-Bayram, M., Whelan, S., & Wood, G. (2025). The Bank of Mum & Dad–intergenerational transfers and first-time homeownership in Australia. *Review of Economics of the Household, 23*(1), 1–29. DOI: 10.1007/s11150-024-09732-7

Cingano, F. (2014). Trends in Income Inequality and Its Impact on Economic Growth. *OECD Social, Employment, and Migration Working Papers*, no. 163. https://www.oecd.org/en/publications/trends-in-income-inequality-and-its-impact-on-economic-growth_5jxrjncwxv6j-en.html

Cloward, R. A., & Ohlin, L. E. (1960). Illegitimate means and delinquent subcultures. *Social Deviance: Readings in Theory & Research, 5*, 45–49.

Cobham, A., & Sumner, A. (2013). Putting the Gini back in the bottle? 'The Palma' as a policy-relevant measure of inequality. King's College London International Development Institute Working Paper. Retrieved from https://citeseerx.ist.psu.edu/document?repid=rep1&type=pdf&doi=7ceaa0d76e8c0f2fbb9a53aa7043108c857890b3 at 25.07.2025.

Cobo, M. J., López-Herrera, A. G., Herrera-Viedma, E., & Herrera, F. (2011). An Approach for Detecting, Quantifying, and Visualizing the Evolution of a Research Field: A Practical Application to the Fuzzy Sets Theory Field. *Journal of Informetrics*, *5*(1), 146–166. DOI: 10.1016/j.joi.2010.10.002

Coccia, M., Cohn, E. G., & Kakar, S. (2024). How immigration, level of unemployment, and income inequality affect crime in Europe. *Crime, Law, and Social Change*, *82*(2), 363–385. DOI: 10.1007/s10611-024-10144-y

Cohn, E. G., Coccia, M., & Kakar, S. (2021). The relationship between crime, immigration and socioeconomic factors. *Rassegna Italiana di Criminologia*, (3), 180–191.

Congregado, E., Esteve, V., & Prats, M. A. (2023). *Optimal public deficit and tax-smoothing in the Spanish Economy, 1850-2022 (EIQ Papper No. 184)*. London School of Economics and Political Science.

Cookson, T. P., Ebner, N., Amron, Y., & Kukreja, K. (2024). Social protection systems and gender: A review of the evidence. *Global Social Policy*, *24*(1), 25–45. DOI: 10.1177/14680181231180507

Cooray, A., Dzhumashev, R., & Schneider, F. (2017). How does corruption affect public debt? An empirical analysis. *World Development*, *90*, 115–127. DOI: 10.1016/j.worlddev.2016.08.020

Cooray, A., & Özmen, I. (2024). The role of institutions on public debt: A quantile regression approach. *International Review of Economics & Finance*, *93*, 912–928. DOI: 10.1016/j.iref.2024.03.065

Costella, C., McCord, A., Van Aalst, M., Holmes, R., Ammoun, J., & Barca, V. (2021). *Social protection and climate change: Scaling up ambition. Social Protection Approaches to COVID-19 Expert Advice Service (SPACE)*. DAI Global UK Ltd.

Cowell, F. A., & Flachaire, E. (2007). Income distribution and inequality measurement: The problem of extreme values. *Journal of Econometrics*, *141*(2), 1044–1072. DOI: 10.1016/j.jeconom.2007.01.001

Cuevas, P. F., Lucchetti, L., & Nebiler, M. (2020). What Are the Poverty and Inequality Impacts of Fiscal Policy in? (World Bank Policy Research Working Paper No. 9300). Washington, DC: World Bank.

Cukierman, A., & Meltzer, A. H. (1989). A political theory of government debt and deficits in a neo-ricardian framework. *The American Economic Review*, *79*(4), 713–732.

Dabla-Norris, E., Kochhar, K., Suphaphiphat, N., Ricka, F., & Tsounta, E. (2015). Causes and consequences of income inequality: A global perspective (IMF Staff Discussion Note SDN/15/13). International Monetary Fund. https://www.imf.org/external/pubs/ft/sdn/2015/sdn1513.pdf

Dabla-Norris, E., Daniel, J. F., & Nozaki, M. (2021). *Fiscal policies to address climate change in Asia and the Pacific*. International Monetary Fund., DOI: 10.5089/9781513511955.001.A001

Daim, T. U., Rueda, G., Martin, H., & Gerdsri, P. (2006). Forecasting emerging technologies: Use of bibliometrics and patent analysis. *Technological Forecasting and Social Change*, *73*(8), 981–1012. DOI: 10.1016/j.techfore.2006.04.004

Daly, M., & Wilson, M. (1988). Evolutionary social psychology and family homicide. *Science*, *242*(4878), 519–524. DOI: 10.1126/science.3175672

Dasgupta, A., & Sharma, A. (2021). *Can legal bans on sex detection technology reduce gender discrimination* (No. 58).

Dayal, D. (2023). Empowering Hindu Women: Unveiling the Legacy of Ancestral Property Rights. *Nyaayshastra L. Rev.*, *4*, 1.

De Beckker, K., De Witte, K., & Van Campenhout, G. (2019). Identifying financially illiterate groups: An international comparison. Sustainability & Economics eJournal. DOI: 10.2139/ssrn.3360483

de Schutter, O. (2021). A Human Rights-based Approach to Measuring Poverty. In Davis, M. F., & Kjaerum, M. (Eds.), *Research Handbook on Human Rights and Poverty* (pp. 2–20). Edward Elgar. DOI: 10.4337/9781788977517.00010

de Vita, A. (2007). Inequality and Poverty in Global Perspective. In Pogge, T. (Ed.), *Freedom from Poverty as a Human Right: Who Owes What to the Very Poor?* (pp. 103–132). Oxford University Press. DOI: 10.1093/oso/9780199226313.003.0005

Debnath, K., & Chatterjee, S. Marginalised Groups in India.

Deidda, M. (2015). Economic hardship, housing cost burden and tenure status: Evidence from EU-SILC. *Journal of Family and Economic Issues*, *36*(4), 531–556. DOI: 10.1007/s10834-014-9431-2

Demir, G., Chatterjee, P., & Pamucar, D. (2024). Sensitivity analysis in multi-criteria decision making: A state-of-the-art research perspective using bibliometric analysis. *Expert Systems with Applications*, *237*, 1–18. DOI: 10.1016/j.eswa.2023.121660

Demirgüç-Kunt, A., Klapper, L., Singer, D., Ansar, S., & Hess, J. (2018). *The Global Findex Database 2017: Measuring financial inclusion and the fintech revolution.* World Bank., DOI: 10.1596/978-1-4648-1259-0

Dennis, B. N. (2022). *Climate change and financial policy: A literature review.* Finance and Economics Discussion Series. DOI: 10.17016/feds.2022.048

Desbonnet, A., & Weitzenblum, T. (2012). Why do governments end up with debt? Short-run effects matter. *Economic Inquiry*, *50*(4), 905–919. DOI: 10.1111/j.1465-7295.2011.00410.x

Desmond, M. (2018). Heavy is the house: Rent burden among the American urban poor. *International Journal of Urban and Regional Research*, *42*(1), 160–170. DOI: 10.1111/1468-2427.12529

Destek, M. A. (2019). Türkiye'de gelir dağılımının çevre kirliliği üzerindeki etkileri üzerine bir inceleme. *Journal of Social Sciences*, *6*(2), 117–134. DOI: 10.21547/jss.556006

Dogan, B., Tekgüç, H., & Yeldan, A. E. (2023). Toward a green income support policy: investigating social and fiscal alternatives for New Perspectives on, 68, 7–29.

Donadelli, M., Jüppner, M., Riedel, M., & Schlag, C. (2017). Temperature shocks and welfare costs. *Journal of Economic Dynamics & Control*, *82*, 331–355. DOI: 10.1016/j.jedc.2017.07.003

Dorfman, A. (1984). The criminal mind. *Science Digest*, *92*(10), 44–47, 98.

Doss, C. (2014). Collecting sex disaggregated data to improve development policies. *Journal of African Economies*, *23*(suppl_1), i62–i86. DOI: 10.1093/jae/ejt023

Drabek, Z. (2024). Is the WTO Terminally Ill? Threats to the International Trading System. *Asia and the Global Economy* 4(1), 100078. https://www.sciencedirect.com/science/article/pii/S2667111524000021

Drazen, A., & Grilli, V. (1993). The benefit of crises for economic reforms. *The American Economic Review*, *83*(3), 598–607.

Dumitrescu, E.-I., & Hurlin, C. (2012). Testing for granger non-causality in heterogeneous panels. *Economic Modelling*, *29*(4), 1450–1460. DOI: 10.1016/j.econmod.2012.02.014

Dzikowski, P. (2018). A bibliometric analysis of born global firms. *Journal of Business Research, 85*, 281–294. DOI: 10.1016/j.jbusres.2017.12.054

Eitle, D. J. (2002). Exploring a source of deviance-producing strain for females: Perceived discrimination and general strain theory. *Journal of Criminal Justice, 30*(5), 429–442. DOI: 10.1016/S0047-2352(02)00146-0

Ellis, L. (1982). Genetics and criminal behavior evidence through the end of the 1970s. *Criminology, 20*(1), 43–66. DOI: 10.1111/j.1745-9125.1982.tb00447.x

Elsinga, M., & Hoekstra, J. (2015). The Janus face of homeownership-based welfare. *Critical Housing Analysis, 2*(1), 32–41. DOI: 10.13060/23362839.2015.2.1.174

Enamorado, T., López-Calva, L. F., Rodríguez-Castelán, C., & Winkler, H. (2016). Income inequality and violent crime: Evidence from Mexico's drug war. *Journal of Development Economics, 120*, 128–143. DOI: 10.1016/j.jdeveco.2015.12.004

Errami, E., Ochir, G., & Peppoloni, S. (2021). Achieve gender equality and empower all women and girls. *Geosciences and the sustainable development goals*, 105-126.

Errol, Z., Madsen, J. B., & Moslehi, S. (2021). Social disorganization theory and crime in the advanced countries: Two centuries of evidence. *Journal of Economic Behavior & Organization, 191*, 519–537. DOI: 10.1016/j.jebo.2021.09.017

Ersoy, I., & DOĞAN, F. İ. (2016). Impact Of EU Governance Reforms And ECB Policy Reactions On European Government Bond Markets. *International Journal of Economic Perspectives, 10*(1), 116–130.

Escudero, V., & Mourelo, E. L. (2015). *The Youth Guarantee programme in Europe: Features, implementation and challenges*. ILO.

Fadun, S. O. (2014). Financial inclusion, tool for poverty alleviation and income redistribution in developing countries: Evidences from Nigeria. *Academic Research International, 5*(3), 137.

Fagan, J., & Freeman, R. B. (1999). Crime and work. *Crime and Justice, 25*, 225–290. DOI: 10.1086/449290

Fan, S., & Cho, E. E. (2021). Paths Out of Poverty: International Experience. *Journal of Integrative Agriculture, 20*(4), 857–867. https://www.sciencedirect.com/science/article/pii/S2095311920632956. DOI: 10.1016/S2095-3119(20)63295-6

Farha, C., McCoy, J., & Rodziewicz, D. (2025). First-Time Homeownership Became Less Affordable Across Most of the United States in Recent Years. *Economic Bulletin*, •••, 1–4.

Felson, M., & Clarke, R. V. (1998). *Opportunity Makes the Thief, Practical Theory for Crime Prevention*. Police Research Series.

Ferreira, I. A., Gisselquist, R. M., & Tarp, F. (2022). On the Impact of Inequality on Growth, Human Development, and Governance. *International Studies Review, 24*(1), viab058. https://academic.oup.com/isr/article/24/1/viab058/6460467. DOI: 10.1093/isr/viab058

Fields, D. (2015). Contesting the financialization of urban space: Community organizations and the struggle to preserve affordable rental housing in New York City. *Journal of Urban Affairs, 37*(2), 144–165. DOI: 10.1111/juaf.12098

Fields, D., & Uffer, S. (2016). The financialisation of rental housing: A comparative analysis of New York City and Berlin. *Urban Studies (Edinburgh, Scotland), 53*(7), 1486–1502. DOI: 10.1177/0042098014543704

Fisher, C. S. (1975). The effect of urban life on traditional values. *Social Forces, 53*(3), 420–432. DOI: 10.2307/2576584

Flango, V. E., & Sherbenou, E. L. (1976). Poverty, urbanization, and crime. *Criminology, 14*(3), 331–346. DOI: 10.1111/j.1745-9125.1976.tb00027.x

Floden, M. (2001). The effectiveness of government debt and transfers as insurance. *Journal of Monetary Economics, 48*(1), 81–108. DOI: 10.1016/S0304-3932(01)00064-2

Forrest, R., & Hirayama, Y. (2015). The financialisation of the social project: Embedded liberalism, neoliberalism and home ownership. *Urban Studies (Edinburgh, Scotland), 52*(2), 233–244. DOI: 10.1177/0042098014528394

Freeman, R. (1995). The labor market. *Crime*, 171-92.

Freeman, R. B. (1999). The economics of crime. *Handbook of labor economics, 3*, 3529-3571.

Freeman, M. A., Rudolf, B., & Chinkin, C. (Eds.). (2012). *The UN convention on the elimination of all forms of discrimination against women: A commentary*. Oxford University Press. DOI: 10.5422/fso/9780199565061.001.0001

Gans, H. (1962). *The Urban Villagers*. Free Press.

Gartaula, H. N., Atreya, K., & Puskur, R. (2025). *Women's empowerment through technology-enabled rural financial services: A systematic review*. npj Sustainable Agriculture, 3(1), 22.

Gartaula, H. N., Atreya, K., Sapkota, A., Mukhopadhyay, P., Chadha, D., & Puskur, R. (2025). A systematic review of agricultural projects' contributions to women's empowerment. *npj Sustainable Agriculture, 3*(1), 22.

Gaviria-Marin, M., Merigó, J. M., & Baier-Fuentes, H. (2019). Knowledge management: A global examination based on bibliometric analysis. *Technological Forecasting and Social Change, 140*, 194–220. DOI: 10.1016/j.techfore.2018.07.006

George, B., & Thomachan, K. T. (2018). Financial inclusion and women empowerment: A gender perspective. *International Journal of Research-Granthaalayah, 6*(5), 229–237. DOI: 10.29121/granthaalayah.v6.i5.2018.1443

Giang, D. H. (2024). Poverty as a Concern for Human Security: Vietnam's Policies on Multidimensional Poverty. *VNU Journal of Foreign Studies* 40(4), 58-73. https://jfs.ulis.vnu.edu.vn/index.php/fs/article/view/5346/4533

Goh, L. T., & Law, S. H. (2023). The crime rate of five Latin American countries: Does income inequality matter? *International Review of Economics & Finance, 86*, 745–763. DOI: 10.1016/j.iref.2023.03.036

Golley, J., & Meng, X. (2012). Income inequality and carbon dioxide emissions: The case of Chinese urban households. *Energy Economics, 34*(6), 1864–1872. DOI: 10.1016/j.eneco.2012.07.025

Gottfredson, M. R., & Hirschi, T. (1990). A general theory of crime. In *A general theory of crime*. Stanford University Press. DOI: 10.1515/9781503621794

Gough, J. A., & Eisenschitz, A. (2021). Poverty in the High-Income Countries: A Marxist Alternative to Mainstream Ideologies. *Class, Race, and Corporate Power* 9(2), art. 2. https://digitalcommons.fiu.edu/classracecorporatepower/vol9/iss2/2/

Grabia, T. (2019). Why do richer EU countries have a higher public debt ratio than their poorer counterparts. *Research Papers of Wroclaw University of Economics and Business, 63*(12), 35–48. DOI: 10.15611/pn.2019.12.03

Gráda, C. Ó. (2007). Making Famine History. *Journal of Economic Literature, 45*(1), 5–38. https://www.aeaweb.org/articles?id=10.1257/jel.45.1.5. DOI: 10.1257/jel.45.1.5

Groot, W., & van den Brink, H. M. (2010). The effects of education on crime. *Applied Economics, 42*(3), 279–289. DOI: 10.1080/00036840701604412

Grossman, G. M., & Krueger, A. B. (1991). Environmental Impacts of the North American Free Trade Agreement. *John M. Ohlin Program Discussion Paper*, No. 158, Princeton. https://www.nber.org/papers/w3914.pdf

Grunewald, N., Klasen, S., Martínez-Zarzoso, I., & Muris, C. (2017). The trade-off between income inequality and carbon dioxide emissions. *Ecological Economics, 142*, 249–256. DOI: 10.1016/j.ecolecon.2017.06.034

Gruszczynska, B., & Gruszczynski, M. (2005). Crime in enlarged Europe: Comparison of crime rates and victimization risks. *Transition Studies Review, 12*(2), 337–345. DOI: 10.1007/s11300-005-0065-9

Gruszczyńska, B., & Heiskanen, M. (2018). Trends in police-recorded offenses at the beginning of the twenty-first century in Europe. *European Journal on Criminal Policy and Research, 24*(1), 37–53. DOI: 10.1007/s10610-018-9370-9

Guiso, L., Sapienza, P., & Zingales, L. (2008). Trusting the stock market. *The Journal of Finance, 63*(6), 2557–2600. DOI: 10.1111/j.1540-6261.2008.01408.x

Gürer, E., Satıoğlu, B., Voyvoda, E., & Yeldan, A. E. (2025). Beyond the quest for a technological holy grail: Patterns of income inequality and the household carbon footprint in Turkey. *New Perspectives on Turkey*, 1–28. Advance online publication. DOI: 10.1017/npt.2025.14

Hailemariam, A., Dzhumashev, R., & Shahbaz, M. (2019). Carbon emissions, income inequality and economic development. *Empirical Economics, 59*(3), 1139–1159. DOI: 10.1007/s00181-019-01664-x

Hai, X. (2016). Dynamic research on China's Gini coefficient. *International Conference on Humanities and Social Science (HSS 2016).* DOI: 10.2991/hss-26.2016.98

Hallegatte, S., Rentschler, J., & Rozenberg, J. (2020). Adaptation Principles: A Guide for Designing Strategies for Climate Change Adaptation and Resilience. World Bank. https://doi.org/DOI: 10.1596/978-1-4648-1674-7

Hao, Y., Chen, H., & Zhang, Q. (2016). Will income inequality affect environmental quality? Analysis based on China's provincial panel data. *Ecological Indicators, 67*(8), 533–542. DOI: 10.1016/j.ecolind.2016.03.025

Hasell, J., Roser, M., Ortiz-Ospina, E., & Arriagada, P. (2022). Poverty. *One World in Data*. https://ourworldindata.org/poverty

Hausman, J. A. (1978). Specification tests in econometrics. *Econometrica, 46*(6), 1251–1271. DOI: 10.2307/1913827

Headey, B., Goodin, R. E., Muffels, R., & Dirven, H. J. (2000). Is There a Trade-Off Between Economic Efficiency and a Generous Welfare State? A Comparison of Best Cases ofThe Three Worlds of Welfare Capitalism'. *Social Indicators Research, 50*(2), 115–157. DOI: 10.1023/A:1007005619530

Hepburn, C., O'Callaghan, B., Stern, N., Stiglitz, J., & Zenghelis, D. (2020). Will COVID-19 fiscal recovery packages accelerate or retard progress on climate change? *Oxford Review of Economic Policy*, *36*(Supplement_1), S359–S381. DOI: 10.1093/oxrep/graa015 PMID: 40504141

Hickey, A. (1991). *Serial murderers and their victims*. Wadsworth.

Hick, R., Pomati, M., & Stephens, M. (2022). Severe housing deprivation in the European Union: A joint analysis of measurement and theory. *Social Indicators Research*, *164*(3), 1271–1295. DOI: 10.1007/s11205-022-02987-6 PMID: 36039339

Hick, R., Pomati, M., & Stephens, M. (2024). Housing affordability and poverty in Europe: On the deteriorating position of market renters. *Journal of Social Policy*, •••, 1–24.

Hochstenbach, C., & Aalbers, M. B. (2024). The uncoupling of house prices and mortgage debt: Towards wealth-driven housing market dynamics. *International Journal of Housing Policy*, *24*(4), 642–670. DOI: 10.1080/19491247.2023.2170542

Huang, Z., & Duan, H. (2020). Estimating the threshold interactions between income inequality and carbon emissions. *Journal of Environmental Management*, *263*, 110393. DOI: 10.1016/j.jenvman.2020.110393 PMID: 32174532

Hubacek, K., Baiocchi, G., Feng, K., & Patwardhan, A. (2017). Poverty eradication in a carbon constrained world. *Nature Communications*, *8*(1), 912. DOI: 10.1038/s41467-017-00919-4 PMID: 29066777

Hunter, R. (1904). *Poverty*. Macmillan.

Igan, D., Kohlscheen, E., & Rungcharoenkitkul, P. (2022). Housing market risks in the wake of the pandemic. BIS Bulletin, (50).

Igan, D. (2024, December). The Housing Affordability Crunch. *Finance & Development*, 21.

Immervoll, H., & Richardson, L. (2011). Redistribution policy and inequality reduction in OECD countries: What has changed in two decades? OECD Social, Employment and Migration Working Papers, No. 122. DOI: 10.1787/1815199X

INED. (2023). Increasingly unequal levels of home ownership between poor and wealthy young households in France. Retrieved May 17, 2025

International Monetary Fund. (2014). Fiscal policy and income inequality. IMF Policy Paper. Retrieved from https://www.imf.org/external/np/pp/eng/2014/012314.pdf at 25.07.2025.

IPCC. (2013). Summary for policymakers. In Stocker, T. F., Qin, D., Plattner, G. K., Tignor, M., Allen, S. K., Boschung, J., Nauels, A., Xia, Y., Bex, V., & Midgley, P. M. (Eds.), *Climate Change 2013: The Physical Science Basis. Contribution of Working Group I to the Fifth Assessment Report of the Intergovernmental Panel on Climate Change*. Cambridge University Press.

IPCC. (2021). Climate Change 2021: The Physical Science Basis. Contribution of Working Group I to the Sixth Assessment Report of the Intergovernmental Panel on Climate Change [Masson-Delmotte, V., P. Zhai, A. Pirani, S.L. Connors, C. Péan, S. Berger, N. Caud, Y. Chen, L. Goldfarb, M.I. Gomis, M. Huang, K. Leitzell, E. Lonnoy, J. B. R. Matthews, T. K. Maycock, T. Waterfield, O. Yelekçi, R. Yu, and B. Zhou (eds.)]. *Cambridge University Press*, Cambridge, United Kingdom and New York, NY, USA, 2391, https://doi:DOI: 10.1017/9781009157896

IPCC. (2022). *Climate Change 2022: Impacts, Adaptation and Vulnerability. Contribution of working group II to the Sixth Assessment Report of the Intergovernmental Panel on Climate Change. H.-O. Pörtner* (Roberts, D. C., Tignor, M., Poloczanska, E. S., Mintenbeck, K., Alegría, A., Craig, M., Langsdorf, S., Löschke, S., Möller, V., Okem, A., & Rama, B., Eds.). Cambridge University Press.

Isidore, R., & Arun, C. (2022). Does the annual income earned influence the decision-making in the Indian secondary equity market? *Journal of Business and Economic Studies*, *6*(1), 24–40. DOI: 10.53462/AZNZ9904

Iskandar, I., Anas, A., Bahri, S., Menne, F., & Baharuddin, T. (2024). Social vulnerability and climate change: A bibliometric analysis. *Cogent Social Sciences*, *10*(1), 1–15. DOI: 10.1080/23311886.2024.2402849

Iskenderian, M. E. (2022). *There's Nothing Micro about a Billion Women: Making Finance Work for Women*. MIT Press. DOI: 10.7551/mitpress/12278.001.0001

Jabłoński, Ł. (2013). Nierówności dochodowe a zadłużenie publiczne krajów OECD. *Management and Business Administration*, *21*(2), 64–81.

Jaimes, R. (2023). Optimal climate and fiscal policy in an OLG economy. *Journal of Public Economic Theory*, *25*(4), 727–752. Advance online publication. DOI: 10.1111/jpet.12637

Jakob, M., Steckel, J. C., & Edenhofer, O. (2022). Equity and distributional effects of carbon pricing: Review of evidence and policy design options. *Environmental Research Letters*, *17*(4), 043002. DOI: 10.1088/1748-9326/ac5c36

Jolliffe, D., & Prydz, E. B. (2021). Societal Poverty: A Relative and Relevant Measure. *The World Bank Economic Review*, *35*(1), 180–206. https://openknowledge.worldbank.org/server/api/core/bitstreams/604d5856-5214-4b7c-a64e-1925b161ba4d/content. DOI: 10.1093/wber/lhz018

Jorgenson, A. K., Schor, J. B., & Giedraitis, V. (2017). Income inequality and carbon emissions in post-soviet nations, 1992-2009. *Ekonomika (Nis)*, *96*(3), 33–43. DOI: 10.15388/Ekon.2017.3.11557

Kaas, L., Kocharkov, G., & Preugschat, E. (2019). Wealth inequality and homeownership in Europe. *Annals of Economics and Statistics*, (136), 27–54. DOI: 10.15609/annaeconstat2009.136.0027

Kaeding, M., Pollak, J., & Schmidt, P. (Eds.). (2020). *Euroscepticism and the Future of Europe: Views from the Capitals*. Springer Nature.

Kährik, A., & Pastak, I. (2023). Access to homeownership in decline—Rising housing inequalities for young people in the neoliberal housing market of Tallinn. *Frontiers in Sustainable Cities*, *5*, 1149087. DOI: 10.3389/frsc.2023.1149087

Kandpal, P. C. (2024)... *Discover Global Society*.

Kant, I. (1795). *Perpetual Peace: A Philosophical Essay*. B.F. Trueblood (Tran.). American Peace Society.

Karakuş, Ö., & Başıbüyük, O. (2010). Social disorganization theory and human trafficking: A systemic control approach to the phenomenon. *Polis Bilimleri Dergisi, 12*(2).

Karapınar, B., Dudu, H., Geyik, Ö., & Yakut, A. M. (2019). How to reach an elusive INDC target: Macro-economic implications of carbon taxation and emissions trading in Türkiye. *Climate Policy*, *19*(9), 1157–1176. DOI: 10.1080/14693062.2019.1635875

Katz, M. B. (2013). *The Undeserving Poor: America's Enduring Confrontation with Poverty* (2nd ed.). Oxford University Press.

Kaur, L., & Anthony, S. B. (2021). Offences Against Women Viz-A-Viz the Criminal Law (Amendment) Act, 2018.

Kaymak, H., & Dökmen, G. (2021). The effect of change in population age structure on budget deficities. *Research of Financial Economic and Social Studies*, 459-476.

Kelly, M. (2000). Inequality and crime. *The Review of Economics and Statistics*, *82*(4), 530–539. DOI: 10.1162/003465300559028

Kelly, P., & Lobao, L. (2021). Whose need matters?: The local welfare state, poverty, and variation in US counties' social service provisioning. *Social Currents*, *8*(6), 566–590. DOI: 10.1177/23294965211047886

Kemeny, J. (2001). Comparative housing and welfare: Theorising the relationship. *Journal of Housing and the Built Environment*, *16*(1), 53–70. DOI: 10.1023/A:1011526416064

Keynes, J. M. (1936). *The General Theory of Employment, Interest, and Money*. Macmillan.

Khan, I., & Sahu, M. (2025). Enhancing financial inclusion in India: The impact of socioeconomic and macroeconomic factors. *Journal of financial economic policy*, *17*(2), 270-294.

Khan, S., Yahong, W., & Zeeshan, A. (2022). Impact of poverty and income inequality on the ecological footprint in Asian developing economies: Assessment of Sustainable Development Goals. *Energy Reports*, *8*, 670–679. DOI: 10.1016/j.egyr.2021.12.001

Kim, B., Seo, C., & Hong, Y. O. (2020). A systematic review and meta-analysis of income inequality and crime in Europe: Do places matter? *European Journal on Criminal Policy and Research*, •••, 1–24.

Kim, S. J. (2021). Environmental shocks, civil conflict and aid effectiveness. *Conflict Management and Peace Science*, *38*(6), 674–695. DOI: 10.1177/07388942211015240

Kissoon, P. (2010). From persecution to destitution: A snapshot of asylum seekers' housing and settlement experiences in Canada and the United Kingdom. *Journal of Immigrant & Refugee Studies*, *8*(1), 4–31. DOI: 10.1080/15562940903575020

Kistner, N. (2007). The Sources and Consequences of Public Perceptions of Corruption. Continuity and Change in Social Life: Structural and Psychological Adjustment in Poland. Warsaw: IFiS Publishers.

Klein, N. (2014). *This changes everything: Capitalism vs. the climate*. Simon and Schuster.

Knight, K. W., Schor, J. B., & Jorgenson, A. K. (2017). Wealth inequality and carbon emissions in high-income countries. *Social Currents*, *4*(5), 403–412. DOI: 10.1177/2329496517704872

Kobakiwal, S. (2018). Inward FDI stock and income distribution: An analysis from an income group perspective [Master's thesis, Lund University].

Koç, N., Koç, Ö. E., Virlanuta, F., Bıtrak, O. O., Çiçek, U., Kovacs, R.-O., Vasile, V.-A., & Vrabie, T. (2025). Agricultural value added, renewable energy, and the Environmental Kuznets Curve: Evidence from Turkey. *Energies*, *18*(13), 3291. DOI: 10.3390/en18133291

Kopp, T., & Nabernegg, M. (2022). Inequality and Environmental Impact-Can the Two Be Reduced Jointly? *Ecological Economics*, *201*, 1–12. DOI: 10.1016/j.ecolecon.2022.107589

Kouadio, H. K., & Gakpa, L.-L. (2022). Do Economic Growth and Institutional Quality Reduce Poverty and Inequality in West Africa? *Journal of Policy Modeling*, *44*(1), 41–63. https://www.sciencedirect.com/science/article/abs/pii/S0161893821001095. DOI: 10.1016/j.jpolmod.2021.09.010

Kousar, S., Bhutta, A. I., Ullah, M. R., & Shabbir, A. (2023). Impact of economic and green growth on poverty, income inequalities, and environmental degradation: A case of South Asian economies. *Environmental Science and Pollution Research International*, *30*(12), 35200–35213. DOI: 10.1007/s11356-022-24191-2 PMID: 36527550

Krueger, P., Sautner, Z., & Starks, L. T. (2020). The importance of climate risks for institutional investors. *Review of Financial Studies*, *33*(3), 1067–1111. DOI: 10.1093/rfs/hhz137

Kumar, S. (2022). Financial inclusion of women: Current evidence from India.

Kumari, S. (2022). Financial inclusion: An initiative towards women empowerment against social norms. Economics, Business. *Accounting & Society Review*, *1*(2), 88–95.

Kutlu, G., & Örün, E. (2023). The effect of carbon dioxide emission, GDP per capita and urban population on health expenditure in OECD countries: A panel ARDL approach. *International Journal of Environmental Health Research*, *33*(12), 1233–1242. DOI: 10.1080/09603123.2022.2083088 PMID: 35635518

Kutty, N. K. (2005). A new measure of housing affordability: Estimates and analytical results. *Housing Policy Debate*, *16*(1), 113–142. DOI: 10.1080/10511482.2005.9521536

Kuusela, H. (2020). The hyperopia of wealth: The cultural legitimation of economic inequalities by top earners. *Socio-economic Review*. Advance online publication. DOI: 10.1093/ser/mwaa047

Kwa, E., Howes, S., & Lin, S. (2011). *Climate change and fiscal policy*. World Bank (APEC Finance Ministers' Policy Initiatives).

Laengle, S., Merigó, J. M., Miranda, J., Słowiński, R., Bomze, I., Borgonovo, E., Dyson, R. G., Oliveira, J. F., & Teunter, R. (2017). Forty years of the European Journal of Operational Research: A bibliometric overview, *European Journal of Operational Research,* 262(3), 803-816, ISSN 0377-2217, DOI: 10.1016/j.ejor.2017.04.027

Lambert, P., & Decoster, A. (2005). The Gini coefficient reveals more. SSRN *Electronic Journal*. DOI: 10.2139/ssrn.809004

Larch, M. (2012). Fiscal performance and income inequality: Are unequal societies more deficit-prone? *Kyklos*, *65*(1), 53–80. DOI: 10.1111/j.1467-6435.2011.00527.x

Lawrence, P. (2021). The Global and National Inequality Faultlines: The Economic Dimensions of (In)security. *Journal of Global Faultlines*, *8*(1), 23–33. https://www.scienceopen.com/hosted-document?doi=10.13169/jglobfaul.8.1.0023. DOI: 10.13169/jglobfaul.8.1.0023

Lee, I. (2022). Does political polarization lead to rise in government debt? *Review of Public Economics*, 3-25. DOI: 10.7866/HPE-RPE.22.2.1

Lee, Y., Kemp, P., & Reina, V. (2022). Drivers of housing (un)affordability in the advanced economies: A review and new evidence. *Housing Studies*, *37*(10), 1739–1752. DOI: 10.1080/02673037.2022.2123623

Levin, A., Lin, C.-F., & Chu, C.-S. J. (2002). Unit root tests in panel data: Asymptotic and finite-sample properties. *Journal of Econometrics*, *108*(1), 1–24. DOI: 10.1016/S0304-4076(01)00098-7

Li, J., & Chen, C. M. (2016). CiteSpace: Text Mining and Visualization in Scientific Literature. *Capital University of Economics and Business Press.* 193-206.

Licchetta, M., Martins, V. D., & Vašíček, B. (2025). Selected Macroeconomic and Social Aspects of Housing Affordability. *Inter Economics*, *60*(2), 101–106. DOI: 10.2478/ie-2025-0020

Liebenberg, S., & Slade, B. (2023). Applying a Human Rights Lens to Poverty and Economic Inequality: The Experiences of South African Human Rights Commission. *Federal Law Review* 51(3), 296-314. https://journals.sagepub.com/doi/full/10.1177/0067205X231188637

Lim, W. M., & Kumar, S. (2023). Guidelines for interpreting the results of bibliometric analysis: A sensemaking approach. *Global Business and Organizational Excellence*, *43*(2), 17–26. DOI: 10.1002/joe.22229

Liu, M. (2017). Inclusive Growth and Poverty Eradication Policies in China. UNDESA. https://www.un.org/development/desa/dspd/wp-content/uploads/sites/22/2017/04/MLiu-DESA1-30Apr2017.pdf, Malthus, T. (1798). An Essay on the Principle of Population.

Liu, X., Zhang, L., & Hong, S. (2011). Global biodiversity research during 1900-2009: A bibliometric analysis. *Biodiversity and Conservation*, *20*(4), 807–826. DOI: 10.1007/s10531-010-9981-z

Li, X., Wu, K., & Liang, Y. (2023). A Review of Agricultural Land Functions: Analysis and Visualization Based on Bibliometrics. *Land (Basel)*, *12*(3), 561. DOI: 10.3390/land12030561

Long, J., & Zhuang, L. (2025). Housing finance and inequality: Mortgage debt in urban China. *Habitat International*, *161*, 103411. DOI: 10.1016/j.habitatint.2025.103411

Lucas, R. E.Jr, & Stokey, N. L. (1983). Optimal fiscal and monetary policy in an economy without capital. *Journal of Monetary Economics*, *12*(1), 55–93. DOI: 10.1016/0304-3932(83)90049-1

Lusardi, A., & Mitchell, O. S. (2014). The economic importance of financial literacy: Theory and evidence. *Journal of Economic Literature*, *52*(1), 5–44. DOI: 10.1257/jel.52.1.5 PMID: 28579637

Lux, M., Sunega, P., & Kážmér, L. (2021). Intergenerational financial transfers and indirect reciprocity: Determinants of the reproduction of homeownership in the post-socialist Czech Republic. *Housing Studies*, *36*(8), 1294–1317. DOI: 10.1080/02673037.2018.1541441

Manduca, R. (2018). Income inequality and the persistence of racial economic disparities. *Sociological Science*, *5*, 182–205. DOI: 10.15195/v5.a8

Marcuse, P., & Madden, D. (2024). *In defense of housing: The politics of crisis*. Verso Books.

Martínez-López, F. J., Merigó, J. M., Valenzuela-Fernández, L., & Nicolás, C. (2018). Fifty years of the European Journal of Marketing: A bibliometric analysis. *European Journal of Marketing*, *52*(1/2), 439–468. DOI: 10.1108/EJM-11-2017-0853

Massey, D. S., & Denton, N. A. (1988). The dimensions of residential segregation. *Social Forces*, *67*(2), 281–315. DOI: 10.2307/2579183

Masud, M. M., Kari, F. B., Banna, H., & Saifullah, M. K. (2018). Does income inequality affect environmental sustainability? Evidence from the ASEAN-5. *Journal of the Asia Pacific Economy*, *23*(2), 213–228. DOI: 10.1080/13547860.2018.1442146

Mednick, S. A., Gabrielli, W. F., & Hutchings, B. (1987). Genetic factors in the etiology of criminal behavior. *The causes of crime: New biological approaches*, 74-91.

Medrano-Sánchez, E. J., Jerez Rivero, W., & Medrano-Sánchez, G. M. (2024). A literature review of public policies on climate change and the environment during the 2019–2023 period. *Migration Letters : An International Journal of Migration Studies*, *21*(1), 73–85. Advance online publication. DOI: 10.59670/ml.v21iS11.8651

Méjean, A., Sowah, P. C., Guivarch, C., Piontek, F., Soergel, B., & Taconet, N. (2024). Climate change impacts increase economic inequality: Evidence from a systematic literature review. *Environmental Research Letters*, *19*(4), 1–22. DOI: 10.1088/1748-9326/ad376e

Merigó, J. M., Pedrycz, W., Weber, R., & de la Sotta, C. (2018). Fifty years of Information Sciences: A bibliometric overview, *Information Sciences*, 432, 245-268, ISSN 0020-0255, DOI: 10.1016/j.ins.2017.11.054

Merigó, J. M., Blanco-Mesa, F., Gil-Lafuente, A. M., & Yager, R. R. (2017). Thirty Years of the International Journal of Intelligent Systems: A Bibliometric Review. *International Journal of Intelligent Systems*, *32*(5), 526–554. DOI: 10.1002/int.21859

Merigó, J. M., Gil-Lafuente, A. M., & Yager, R. R. (2015). An overview of fuzzy research with bibliometric indicators. *Applied Soft Computing*, *27*, 420–433. DOI: 10.1016/j.asoc.2014.10.035

Merton, R. K. (1938). Social Structure and Anomie. *American Sociological Review*, *3*(5), 672–682. DOI: 10.2307/2084686

Messner, S. F. (1989). Economic discrimination and societal homicide rates: Further evidence on the cost of inequality. *American Sociological Review*, *54*(4), 597–611. DOI: 10.2307/2095881

Messner, S. F., & Rosenfeld, R. (1997). Political restraint of the market and levels of criminal homicide: A cross-national application of institutional-anomie theory. *Social Forces*, *75*(4), 1393–1416.

Mészáros, Á., Dósa, N., & Péterfi, A. (2023). *Prospects of food taxes for planetary health: A systematic review of modeling studies. Research Square*. DOI: 10.21203/rs.3.rs-2787374/v1

Metelski, D., & Sobieraj, J. (2024). Trading volume concentration across S&P 500 index constituents: A Gini-based analysis. *Journal of Risk and Financial Management*, *17*(8), 325. DOI: 10.3390/jrfm17080325

Meyer, P. B., Piacentini, J., Frazis, H., Schultz, M., & Sveikauskas, L. (2025). The Effect of the COVID 19 Pandemic on Inequality. *Review of Income and Wealth, 71*(1), e12707. Advance online publication. DOI: 10.1111/roiw.12707

Mikeladze, N., & Bedianashvili, G. (2024). Assessing the effectiveness of fiscal policy tools in facilitating inclusive economic growth. *Economics, Ecology. Socium, 8*(4), 30–44. DOI: 10.61954/2617-7107-2024-8-4-1

Millennium Ecosystem Assessment. (2005). *Ecosystems and Human Well-being: General Synthesis*. Island Press.

Miyandazi, V. (2023). Human Rights and Equality Commissions in Kenya and Their Role in Tackling Poverty and Economic Inequality. *Federal Law Review* 51(4), 422-441. https://journals.sagepub.com/doi/full/10.1177/0067205X231212026

Moatsos, M. (2021). Global Extreme Poverty: Past and Present since 1820. In OECD, *How was Life? Volume II: New Perspectives on Well-being and Global Inequality since 1820* (pp. 186-215). OECD Publishing.

Moatsos, M. (2025). Global Poverty: A Review of Measurement, Levels, and Trends in a Historical Perspective. *Journal of Economic Surveys, 39*(2), 706–766. https://onlinelibrary.wiley.com/doi/pdfdirect/10.1111/joes.12644. DOI: 10.1111/joes.12644

Mohajer, N., & Culty, M. (2024). Impact of human-relevant doses of endocrine disrupting chemical and drug mixtures on testis development and function. [aop]. *Reproduction*, 1. PMID: 39454032

MOHANAN, P., & MOHANAN, R. (2025). Technological Advancements and Women Entrepreneurs: A Historical Odyssey. *Entrepreneurship and Sustainable Business Development*, 127.

Muinelo-Gallo, L., & Roca-Sagalés, O. (2011). Economic growth and inequality: The role of fiscal policies. *Australian Economic Papers, 50*(2–3), 74–97. DOI: 10.1111/j.1467-8454.2011.00412.x

Mukhopadhyay, U. (2023). Disparities in Female Labour Force Participation in South Asia and Latin America: A Review. *Review of Economics, 74*(3), 265–288. DOI: 10.1515/roe-2022-0061

Murray, C., & Herrnstein, R. J. (1994). Race, genes, and IQ–An apologia. *New Republic (New York, N.Y.), 211*(18), 27–37.

Musterd, S., Marcińczak, S., Van Ham, M., & Tammaru, T. (2017). Socioeconomic segregation in European capital cities. Increasing separation between poor and rich. *Urban Geography, 38*(7), 1062–1083. DOI: 10.1080/02723638.2016.1228371

Nandi, A., Haberland, N., & Ngo, T. D. (2023). The impact of primary schooling expansion on adult educational attainment, literacy, and health: Evidence from India's Sarva Shiksha Abhiyan. *International Journal of Educational Development, 102*, 102871. DOI: 10.1016/j.ijedudev.2023.102871

Narayan, D., Chambers, R., Shah, M. K., & Petesch, P. (2000). *Voices of the Poor: Crying out for Change*. Oxford University Press. DOI: 10.1596/0-1952-1602-4

Network, T. E., & Tanzania, M. W. E. (2024). Gender responsive budget analysis of the education sector.

Newman, E. (2021). COVID-19: A Human Security Analysis. *Global Society, 36*(4), 431–454. https://www.tandfonline.com/doi/pdf/10.1080/13600826.2021.2010034. DOI: 10.1080/13600826.2021.2010034

Newman, M. E. J. (2001). Scientific collaboration networks. I. Network construction and fundamental results. *Physical Review. E, 64*(1), 016131. DOI: 10.1103/PhysRevE.64.016131 PMID: 11461355

Nigam, A. D. S. (2023). *Dowry Is a Serious Violence: Rethinking Dowry Law in India*. Shalu Nigam.

Nordhaus, W. D. (2018). Projections and uncertainties about climate change in an era of minimal climate policies. *American Economic Journal. Economic Policy, 10*(3), 333–360. DOI: 10.1257/pol.20170046

Norris, M., & Oppenheim, C. (2007). Comparing alternatives to the Web of Science for coverage of the social sciences' literature. *Journal of Informetrics, 1*(2), 161–169. DOI: 10.1016/j.joi.2006.12.001

Nunen, K. V., Li, J., Reniers, G., & Ponnet, K. (2018). Bibliometric analysis of safety culture research. *Safety Science, 108*, 248–258. DOI: 10.1016/j.ssci.2017.08.011

OECD. (2021). *Brick by Brick: Building Better Housing Policies*. OECD Publishing., DOI: 10.1787/b453b043-

OECD. (2025), OECD Affordable Housing Database - indicator HM1.3 Housing tenures, https://oe.cd/ahd

OPHI & UNDP. (2024). *Global Multidimensional Poverty Index 2024: Poverty Amid Conflict*. Oxford University Press.

OPHI. (n.d.). What is the Global MPI? https://ophi.org.uk/what-global-mpi

Ostendorf, W., Musterd, S., & De Vos, S. (2001). Social mix and the neighbourhood effect. Policy ambitions and empirical evidence. *Housing Studies*, *16*(3), 371–380. DOI: 10.1080/02673030120049724

Ozili, P. K. (2025). Can monetary and fiscal policy reduce CO_2 emissions? Analysis of regional country groups. *China Finance Review International*. Advance online publication. DOI: 10.1108/CFRI-09-2024-0564

Pal, M., Gupta, H., & Joshi, Y. C. (2022). Social and economic empowerment of women through financial inclusion: Empirical evidence from India. *Equality, Diversity and Inclusion*, *41*(2), 294–305. DOI: 10.1108/EDI-04-2021-0113

Pandey, B. (2025). Impact of Federalism on Women's Empowerment in Nepal: Case of Chandragiri Municipality. *Academia (Caracas)*, *5*(1), 15–28.

Pandey, V., & Shekhar, S. (2024). Gender Neutrality of Indian Laws-A Myth or Reality? *Educational Administration: Theory and Practice*, *30*(5), 3204–3213.

Parolin, Z., Pintro-Schmitt, R., Esping-Andersen, G., & Fallesen, P. (2025). Intergenerational Persistence of Poverty in Five High-Income Countries. *Nature Human Behaviour*, *9*(2), 254–267. https://www.nature.com/articles/s41562-024-02029-w. DOI: 10.1038/s41562-024-02029-w PMID: 39468279

Parry, I., Minnett, D., & Zhunussova, K. (2023). *Climate Mitigation Policy in Türkiye* (IMF Working Paper No. 2023/108). Washington, DC: International Monetary Fund.

Parsons, B., & Rabhi, A. (2024). Shifting sands: How exchange rate volatility shapes income distribution in high-income countries. *Structural Change and Economic Dynamics*, *67*, 203–219. DOI: 10.1016/j.strueco.2024.12.021

Pata, U. K., Yilanci, V., Hussain, B., & Ali Naqvi, S. A. (2022). Analyzing the role of income inequality and political stability in environmental degradation: Evidence from South Asia. *Gondwana Research*, *107*, 13–29. DOI: 10.1016/j.gr.2022.02.009

Patel, R., & Patel, N. (2020). Impact of microfinance on women empowerment: A study from the decision—making perspective. *Indian Journal of Finance*, *14*(8-9), 52–68. DOI: 10.17010/ijf/2020/v14i8-9/154948

Pazarlıoğlu, M. V., & Gürler, Ö. K. (2007). Telecommunication investments and economic growth: A panel data approach. *Finance Politics & Economic Comments*, *44*(508), 35–43.

Persson, T., & Svensson, L. E. (1989). Why a stubborn conservative would run a deficit: Policy with time- inconsistent preferences. *The Quarterly Journal of Economics*, *104*(2), 325–345. DOI: 10.2307/2937850

Pesaran, M. H., Shin, Y., & Smith, R. P. (1999). Pooled mean group estimation of dynamic heterogeneous panels. *Journal of the American Statistical Association, 94*(446), 621–634. DOI: 10.1080/01621459.1999.10474156

Pesaran, M. H., & Smith, R. (1995). Estimating long-run relationships from dynamic heterogeneous panels. *Journal of Econometrics, 68*(1), 79–113. DOI: 10.1016/0304-4076(94)01644-F

Phillimore, J., & Goodson, L. (2006). Problem or opportunity? Asylum seekers, refugees, employment and social exclusion in deprived urban areas. *Urban Studies (Edinburgh, Scotland), 43*(10), 1715–1736. DOI: 10.1080/00420980600838606

Pigato, M. A. (2019). *Fiscal policies for development and climate action*. World Bank Group., DOI: 10.1596/978-1-4648-1358-0

Piketty, T. (2014). *Capital in the 21st Century*. Harvard University Press. DOI: 10.4159/9780674369542

Piketty, T., & Zucman, G. (2015). Wealth and Inheritance in the Long-Run. In Atkinson, A., & Bourguignon, F. (Eds.), *Handbook of Income Distribution* (Vol. 2, pp. 1303–1368). Elsevier.

Pimkina, S., & de La Flor, L. (2020). *Promoting female labor force participation*. World Bank. DOI: 10.1596/34953

Pogge, T. (2011). Are We Violating the Human Rights of World's Poor? *Yale Human Rights & Development L.J* 14(2), 1-33. https://openyls.law.yale.edu/handle/20.500.13051/5760

Pogge, T. (2005). World Poverty and Human Rights. *Ethics & International Affairs, 19*(1), 1–7. https://onlinelibrary.wiley.com/doi/abs/10.1111/j.1747-7093.2005.tb00484.x. DOI: 10.1111/j.1747-7093.2005.tb00484.x

Poylov, N. A. (2023). *Fiscal policy and economic growth in the short and long run: A literature review*.

President's Commission on Law Enforcement and Administration of Justice. (1967). The Challenge of Crime in a Free Society. Washington: U.S. Government Printing Office.

Quigley, J. M., & Raphael, S. (2004). Is housing unaffordable? Why isn't it more affordable? *The Journal of Economic Perspectives, 18*(1), 191–214. DOI: 10.1257/089533004773563494

Raihan, A., Bala, S., Akther, A., Ridwan, M., Eleais, M., & Chakma, P. (2024). Advancing environmental sustainability in the G-7: The impact of the digital economy, technological innovation, and financial accessibility using panel ARDL approach. *Journal of Economy and Technology*, 1-26. DOI: 10.1016/j.ject.2024.06.001

Ramos-Herrera, M. D. (2024). *Economic growth and deviations from the equilibrium exchange rate: A panel ARDL and panel NARDL approach.* Applied Economic Analysis., DOI: 10.1108/AEA-02-2024-0065

Ramos-Herrera, M., & Sosvilla-Rivero, S. (2020). Fiscal sustainability in aging socities: Evidence from Euro Area Countries. *Sustainability (Basel)*, *12*(24), 1–20. DOI: 10.3390/su122410276

Rangarajan, C. (2008). Report of the committee on financial inclusion. *Ministry of Finance, Government of India*, 155-167.

Rathi, P., Rathi, A., Sidana, S., Tailor, R. K., & Hariharasudan, A. (2025). *Shaping Atmanirbhar Bharat (Self-Reliant India) through Atmanirbhar Nari (Self-Reliant Women): A Roadmap for Empowering Women-Led MSMEs through ICT.* Financial Access, and Skill Development.

Rausch, S. (2013). Fiscal consolidation and climate policy: An overlapping generations perspective. *Energy Economics*, *40*(S1), S134–S148. DOI: 10.1016/j.eneco.2013.09.009

Ravallion, M., Datt, G., & van de Walle, D. (1991). Quantifying Absolute Poverty in the Developing World. *Review of Income and Wealth*, *37*(4), 345–361. https://onlinelibrary.wiley.com/doi/abs/10.1111/j.1475-4991.1991.tb00378.x. DOI: 10.1111/j.1475-4991.1991.tb00378.x

Ravallion, M., Heil, M., & Jalan, J. (2000). Carbon emissions and income inequality. *Oxford Economic Papers*, *52*(4), 651–669. DOI: 10.1093/oep/52.4.651

Rawat, V. S., & Kumar, M. (2022). Women empowerment through pradhan mantri ujjwala yojana (PmUY)–a study of LPg refills. *Review Journal Philosophy & Social Science*, *47*(2), 407–415. DOI: 10.31995/rjpss.2022.v47i02.046

Ray, A., & Chowdhury, S. R. (2022). Impact of Financial Inclusion on Women's Economic Empowerment: Evidence from Self Help Group-Bank Linkage Programs in West Bengal. *International Research Journal of Economics and Management Studies IRJEMS*, *3*(11).

Reddy, S. G., & Pogge, T. (2010). How Not to Count the Poor. In Anand, S., Segal, P., & Stiglitz, J. E. (Eds.), *Debates on the Measurement of Global Poverty* (pp. 42–51). Oxford University Press. DOI: 10.1093/acprof:oso/9780199558032.003.0003

Reinhart, C. M., & Sbrancia, M. B. (2015). The liquidation of government debt (IMF Working Paper No. 15/7). *International Monetary Fund.*

REN21. (2023). *Renewables 2023 Global Status Report Collection.* Renewables in Energy Supply.

Rennó Santos, M., Testa, A., & Weiss, D. B. (2021). Inflation and cross-national homicide: Assessing nonlinear and moderation effects across 65 countries, 1965–2015. *International Criminal Justice Review, 31*(2), 122–139. DOI: 10.1177/1057567720981624

Reserve Bank of India. (2004). *Report on trend and progress of banking in India* (Vol. 2004). Reserve Bank of India.

Riitsalu, L., & Murakas, R. (2019). Subjective financial knowledge, prudent behaviour and income. *International Journal of Bank Marketing, 37*(6), 1431–1448. DOI: 10.1108/IJBM-03-2018-0071

Rodríguez-Pose, A., & Storper, M. (2020). Housing, urban growth and inequalities: The limits to deregulation and upzoning in reducing economic and spatial inequality. *Urban Studies (Edinburgh, Scotland), 57*(2), 223–248. DOI: 10.1177/0042098019859458

Rogerson, P. A. (2013). The Gini coefficient of inequality: A new interpretation. *Letters in Spatial and Resource Sciences, 6*(2), 109–120. DOI: 10.1007/s12076-013-0091-x

Röhrs, S., & Winter, C. (2017). Reducing government debt in the presence of inequality. *Journal of Economic Dynamics & Control, 82*, 1–20. DOI: 10.1016/j.jedc.2017.05.007

Rolnik, R. (2013). Late neoliberalism: The financialization of homeownership and housing rights. *International Journal of Urban and Regional Research, 37*(3), 1058–1066. DOI: 10.1111/1468-2427.12062

Roser, M. (2022). The History of the End of Poverty has just Begun. *Our World in Data.* https://ourworldindata.org/history-of-poverty-has-just-begun

Roser, M. (2023). Extreme Poverty: How far have we come, and how far do we still have to go? *Our World in Data.* https://ourworldindata.org/extreme-poverty-in-brief

Sacco, V. F., & Kennedy, L. W. (1998). *The Criminal Event.* International Thomson Publishing.

Sachs, J. D. (2005). *The End of Poverty: Economic Possibilities for our Time.* The Penguin Press.

Sachweh, P. (2012). The moral economy of inequality: Popular views on income differentiation, poverty and wealth. *Socio-economic Review, 10*(3), 419–445. DOI: 10.1093/ser/mwr023

Sadler, A., Ranger, N., Fankhauser, S., Marotta, F., & O'Callaghan, B. (2024). The impact of COVID-19 fiscal spending on climate change adaptation and resilience. *Nature Sustainability, 7*(3), 270–281. Advance online publication. DOI: 10.1038/s41893-024-01269-y

Salt, J. (2000). Trafficking and human smuggling: A European perspective. *International Migration (Geneva, Switzerland), 38*(3), 31–56. DOI: 10.1111/1468-2435.00114

Sarma, M., & Pais, J. (2011). Financial inclusion and development. *Journal of International Development, 23*(5), 613–628. DOI: 10.1002/jid.1698

Scanlon, K., Whitehead, C., & Arrigoitia, M. F. (Eds.). (2014). *Social housing in Europe*. John Wiley & Sons. DOI: 10.1002/9781118412367

Scarpa, S. (2015). The spatial manifestation of inequality: Residential segregation in Sweden and its causes (Doctoral dissertation, Linnaeus University Press).

Schaffrin, A. (2014). The new social risks and opportunities of climate change. In *International Handbook on Social Policy and the Environment*. Edward Elgar Publishing. DOI: 10.4337/9780857936134.00007

Schasfoort, J. (2020). Stock market volatility and wealth inequality. SSRN *Electronic Journal*. DOI: 10.2139/ssrn.3452599

Schlosberg, D. (2007). *Defining Environmental Justice: Theories, Movements, and Nature*. Oxford University Press., DOI: 10.1093/acprof:oso/9780199286294.001.0001

Schneider, M. (2021). The discovery of the Gini coefficient. *History of Political Economy, 53*(1, S1), 179–206. DOI: 10.1215/00182702-8816637

Schoder, C., & Tercioglu, R. B. (2024). A climate-fiscal policy mix to achieve Türkiye's net-zero ambition under feasibility constraints. *European Journal of Economics and Economic Policies: Intervention, 21*(2), 331–359. DOI: 10.4337/ejeep.2024.02.07

Sengül, B., & Murat, G. (2024). Küresel İklim Krizinin Sosyal Boyutu ve Sosyal Politika Önlemleri. *Süleyman Demirel Üniversitesi Vizyoner Dergisi, 15*(41), 342–358. DOI: 10.21076/vizyoner.1310015

Seven, Ü., & Yetkiner, H. (2016). Financial intermediation and economic growth: Does income matter? *Economic Systems, 40*(1), 39–58. DOI: 10.1016/j.ecosys.2015.09.004

Sharma, D. (2024). Unveiling Saving and Credit Dynamics: Insights from Financial Diaries and Surveys among Low-Income Households in Unauthorized Colonies in Delhi. *arXiv preprint arXiv:2412.03033*. DOI: 10.2139/ssrn.5020724

Sharma, H. (2024). *Digital Financial Services: Unveiling the Collective Potential in Rural Landscape of India* (Doctoral dissertation, Doctoral dissertation, Auckland University of Technology).

Shaw, C., & McKay, H. (1942). *Juvenile Delinquency and Urban Areas*. Univ. Press.

Siallagan, W. A. (2021). The role of fiscal policy in the crisis: A literature review. *CosmoGov*, *6*(2), 186. Advance online publication. DOI: 10.24198/cosmogov.v6i2.29509

Singh, S. Women in Panchayati Raj Institutions: A study of two villages in Rajasthan.

Singh, C., & Sanyal, A. (2023). An Analysis of Financial Inclusion of India. *Productivity*, *64*(3), 309–320.

Singh, P. (2021). Aadhaar and data privacy: Biometric identification and anxieties of recognition in India. *Information Communication and Society*, *24*(7), 978–993. DOI: 10.1080/1369118X.2019.1668459

Sivakumar, I., & Manimekalai, K. (2021). Masculinity and challenges for women in Indian culture. *Journal of International Women's Studies*, *22*(5), 427–436.

Smith, H. J., Pettigrew, T. F., Pippin, G. M., & Bialosiewicz, S. (2012). Relative deprivation: A theoretical and meta-analytic review. *Personality and Social Psychology Review*, *16*(3), 203–232. DOI: 10.1177/1088868311430825

Soh, W. N., Muhamad, H., & San, O. T. (2021). The impact of government efficiency, corruption, and inflation on public debt: Empirical evidence from advanced and emerging economies. *Pertanika Journal of Social Science & Humanities*, *29*(3), 1551–1570. DOI: 10.47836/pjssh.29.3.05

Speth, J. G. (1998). Poverty: A Denial of Human Rights. *Journal of International Affairs*, *52*(1), 277–292. https://law-journals-books.vlex.com/vid/poverty-denial-of-human-rights-52647503

Statista. (2025). Ranking of the Gini index by Country 2024. https://www.statista.com/forecasts/1171540/gini-index-by-country

Steffen, W., Grinevald, J., Crutzen, P., & McNeill, J. (2011). The Anthropocene: Conceptual and historical perspectives. *Philosophical Transactions. Series A, Mathematical, Physical, and Engineering Sciences*, *369*(1938), 842–867. DOI: 10.1098/rsta.2010.0327 PMID: 21282150

Stiglitz, J. E. (2012). *The price of inequality: How today's divided society endangers our future.* W.W. Norton & Company.

Stiglitz, J. E. (2016). Inequality and Economic Growth. *The Political Quarterly, 86*(S1), 134–155. https://onlinelibrary.wiley.com/doi/10.1111/1467-923X.12237. DOI: 10.1111/1467-923X.12237

Stone, M. (2010). *Shelter poverty: New ideas on housing affordability.* Temple University Press.

Stone, M. E. (2006). A housing affordability standard for the UK. *Housing Studies, 21*(4), 453–476. DOI: 10.1080/02673030600708886

Stone, M. E. (2006). What is housing affordability? The case for the residual income approach. *Housing Policy Debate, 17*(1), 151–184. DOI: 10.1080/10511482.2006.9521564

Storper, M. (2005). Society, Community, and Economic Development. *Studies in Comparative International Development, 39*(4), 30–57. https://link.springer.com/content/pdf/10.1007/BF02686164.pdf. DOI: 10.1007/BF02686164

Tabellini, G. (1991). The politics of intergenerational redistribution. *Journal of Political Economy, 99*(2), 335–357. DOI: 10.1086/261753

Tabellini, G., & Alesina, A. (1990). Voting on the budget deficit. *The American Economic Review, 80*(1), 37–49.

Tatoğlu, F. Y. (2012). *Panel data econometrics: With Stata applications.* Beta Publishing.

Tekgüç, H., & Eryar, D. S. (2024). Redistribution trends in: Regressive taxes, structural change, and demographics (CEQ Working Paper No. 134). New Orleans, LA: Commitment to Equity Institute.

Tetlow, G. (2018) Rising burden of housing costs shown by 60-year UK spending survey. FT.Com. Available at https://www.ft.com/content/32d71316-fc5f-11e7-9b32-d7d59aace167

Thornton, A., Bhorat, H., Lilenstein, A., Monnakgotla, J., & van der Zee, K. (2023). Crime, Income, and Inequality: Nonlinearities under Extreme Inequality in South Africa. *Economic Development and Cultural Change, 72*(1), 207–240. DOI: 10.1086/719646

Tong-Yu, Z. (2010). Empirical analysis on the relationship between income changes of high-income group and stock market index in U.S. *The Theory and Practice of Finance and Economics, 32*(6), 34–37.

Tonry, M. (2014). Why crime rates are falling throughout the Western world. *Crime and Justice*, *43*(1), 1–63. DOI: 10.1086/678181

Torrente, D., Gallo, P., & Oltra, C. (2017). Comparing crime reporting factors in EU countries. *European Journal on Criminal Policy and Research*, *23*(2), 153–174. DOI: 10.1007/s10610-016-9310-5

Townsend, P. (1979). *Poverty in the United Kingdom: A Survey of Household Resources and Standards of Living*. Penguin Books. DOI: 10.1525/9780520325760

Tsushima, M. (1996). Economic structure and crime: The case of Japan. *Journal of Socio-Economics*, *25*(4), 497–515. DOI: 10.1016/S1053-5357(96)90041-4

Tur-Porcar, A., Mas-Tur, A., Merigó, J. M., Roig-Tierno, N., & Watt, J. (2018). A Bibliometric History of the Journal of Psychology Between 1936 and 2015. *The Journal of Psychology*, *152*(4), 199–225. DOI: 10.1080/00223980.2018.1440516 PMID: 29611782

Tuttle, J. (2022). Inequality, concentrated disadvantage, and homicide: Towards a multi-level theory of economic inequality and crime. *International Journal of Comparative and Applied Criminal Justice*, *46*(3), 215–232. DOI: 10.1080/01924036.2021.1942103

UN General Assembly. (2005). World Summit Outcome. Resolution Adopted by the General Assembly, 24 October (A/RES/60/1). https://www.un.org/en/development/desa/population/migration/generalassembly/docs/globalcompact/A_RES_60_1.pdf

UNDP. (2022). *New Threats to Human Security in the Anthropocene: Demanding Greater Solidarity*. https://hdr.undp.org/content/2022-special-report-human-security

UNDP. (n.d.). Human Development Index (HDI). https://hdr.undp.org/data-center/human-development-index#/indicies/HDI

United Nations. (2020a). UNDESA World Social Report 2020a. Retrieved from https://www.un.org/development/desa/dspd/world-social-report/2020a-2.html

United Nations. (2025). The 17 goals. Retrieved from https://sdgs.un.org/goals

UNTFHS (United Nations Trust Fund for Human Security). (2021). About the Trust Fund. https://www.un.org/humansecurity/

Vold, G. B., & Bernard, T. J. (1986). *Theoretical Criminology* (3rd ed.). Oxford University Press.

Wacquant, L. (2008). *Urban outcasts: A comparative sociology of advanced marginality*. Polity Press.

Wang, J. (2024). Renewable energy, inequality and environmental degradation. *Journal of Environmental Management*, *356*, 1–14. DOI: 10.1016/j.jenvman.2024.120563 PMID: 38479288

Wetzstein, S. (2017). The global urban housing affordability crisis. *Urban Studies (Edinburgh, Scotland)*, *54*(14), 3159–3177. DOI: 10.1177/0042098017711649

Wilkinson, R., & Pickett, K. (2010). *The Spirit Level: Why Equality is Better for Everyone*. Penguin Books.

Wilson, J. Q. (1983). Crime and American culture. *The Public Interest*, *70*, 22.

Wilson, J. Q., & Herrnstein, R. J. (1985). Crime &. *Human Nature (Hawthorne, N.Y.)*.

Wirth, L. (1938). Urbanism as a way of life. *American Journal of Sociology*, *44*(1), 3–24. DOI: 10.1086/217913

Wolde-Rufael, Y., & Idowu, S. (2017). Income distribution and CO2 emission: A comparative analysis for China and India. *Renewable & Sustainable Energy Reviews*, *74*, 1336–1345. DOI: 10.1016/j.rser.2016.11.149

Woo, J., Bova, E., Kinda, T., & Zhang, Y. S. (2013). Distributional consequences of fiscal consolidation and the role of fiscal policy: What do the data say? IMF Working Paper WP/13/195. Retrieved from https://www.imf.org/external/pubs/ft/wp/2013/wp13195.pdf at 25.07.2025.

Woo, J. (2003). Economic, political, and institutional determinants of public deficits. *Journal of Public Economics*, *87*(3-4), 387–426. DOI: 10.1016/S0047-2727(01)00143-8

Wooldridge, J. M. (2010). *Econometric Analysis of Cross–Section and Panel Data* (2nd ed.). MIT Press.

World Bank. (2023). CO_2 emissions (metric tons per capita) – World Development Indicators. https://databank.worldbank.org/source/world-development-indicators

World Inequality Database. (2019). Data. Retrieved from https://wid.world/data/. Accessed: 12 Apr 2025.

Wu, R., & Xie, Z. (2020). Identifying the impacts of income inequality on CO2 emissions: Empirical evidences from OECD countries and non-OECD countries. *Journal of Cleaner Production*, *277*, 123858. DOI: 10.1016/j.jclepro.2020.123858

Xepapadeas, A. (2021). Climate change and the financial system: A note. *Economia e Politica Industriale*, *78*(4), 867–872. DOI: 10.1007/s40812-020-00158-7

Yan, L., & Zhiping, W. (2023). Mapping the Literature on Academic Publishing: A Bibliometric Analysis on WOS. *SAGE Open*, *13*(1), 21582440231158562. Advance online publication. DOI: 10.1177/21582440231158562

Yao, S. (1999). On the decomposition of Gini coefficients by population class and income source: A spreadsheet approach and application. *Applied Economics*, *31*(10), 1249–1264. DOI: 10.1080/000368499323463

Yared, P. (2019). Rising government debt: Causes and solutions for decades-old trend. *The Journal of Economic Perspectives*, *33*(2), 115–140. DOI: 10.1257/jep.33.2.115

Yoganandham, G. (2022). Global Economic Inequalities and Environmental Problems in relation to the Job Market, The Economy, and the Ecosystem as a whole-Atheoretical Assessment. *Mukt Shabd Journal*, *11*(8), 640–658.

Yu, J., Hassan, M. K., & Sanchez, B. (2012). A re-examination of financial development, stock markets development and economic growth. *Applied Economics*, *44*(27), 3479–3489. DOI: 10.1080/00036846.2011.577019

About the Contributors

Oytun Meçik is a Professor at Eskişehir Osmangazi University, Department of Economics. Meçik completed his undergraduate education at Eskişehir Osmangazi University in 2008, his master's degree at Uşak University in 2010, and his doctorate in Economics at Anadolu University in 2014. He received the title of Associate Professor in Macroeconomics in 2017 and became a Professor in 2023. Meçik, who has many studies in the fields of labor market and social and economic networks, currently works on social capital, education-job mismatch in the labor market, the effects of digital transformation, and innovation economics. Meçik serves as editor and editorial board member in national and international journals and publishing houses. Meçik is a member of the Turkish Economic Association and the Regional Science Turkish National Committee. In 2024, he received the title of Sworn Social Mediator.

***

Arun Agrawal is an accomplished academic in the field of Computer Science & Engineering, Currently serving as an Assistant Professor at the Institute of Technology & Management, Gwalior. With a strong educational background including a B.Sc. in Electronics, M.Sc. in Computer Science, and M.Tech. in Information Technology, Agrawal is currently pursuing his Ph.D. His career spans over two decades, beginning with five years in the industry as an Embedded Engineer before transitioning to academia in 2007. Over the past 17 years, he has progressed from a Lecturer to his current role as Assistant Professor, demonstrating expertise in areas such as vehicular networks, image processing, and cloud computing security. Agrawal's academic contributions include numerous patents, book chapters, publications in international journals and conferences, as well as presentations at IEEE international conferences. His ongoing research and teaching efforts continue to shape the field of computer science and nurture the next generation of technology professionals.

Fethiye Burcu is an Assistant Professor of International Development at Ahi Evran University, Türkiye, and serves as the Faculty R&D Coordinator. She holds a PhD from the University of East Anglia, School of Global Development, where she remains an affiliated researcher. Her interdisciplinary work bridges public health, climate change, and development economics, with a focus on fiscal policies and social inequality. Fethiye has published in leading Q1–Q2 journals and contributed to policy-relevant research with UN agencies, including FAO. Her recent work explores the socio-economic impacts of crises such as the COVID-19 pandemic, and she regularly collaborates in international research consortia.

Pinar Deniz joined the Department of Economics at Marmara University in 2016. She received her Ph.D. in Economics from Marmara University in 2014. Her area of expertise is applied macroeconomics. She is the editor of Journal of Research in Economics. Some of her articles have been published in journals such as Economics Letters, Regional Studies, Empirical Economics, European Journal of Political Economy.

Prabha Dixit holds an M.Sc., M.Phil., and Ph.D. in Chemistry from Jiwaji University, Gwalior. With over 18 years of teaching experience, she currently serves as Assistant Professor in the Department of Chemistry at ITM Gwalior. Her research focuses on electrochemical studies and antimicrobial agents, supported by a major MPCOST-funded project. Dr. Dixit has authored several academic books and contributed to national and international conferences. She has also served in key academic roles including NAAC and Exam Coordinator. A recipient of the Dr. Shankar Dayal Sharma Shrijan Award, she is an active contributor to curriculum development and science outreach through workshops and FDPs. Her dedication to teaching and research continues to shape aspiring scientists.

Fadime İrem Doğan is an Assistant Professor and Department Chair in the Department of Economics and Finance at Bahçeşehir University. She holds a PhD in EU Economics from Marmara University and has additional graduate training in Forensic Sciences and Management of European Affairs. Her research spans the economics of crime, labor and health economics, and applied and regional economics, with a strong emphasis on empirical and spatial analysis. She has published in Sociology Compass, The Indian Journal of Labour Economics, and Employee Responsibilities and Rights Journal, among others. Dr. Doğan has been a Senior Research Fellow for an EU- funded labor migration project with the Oxford Centre for Technology and Development and actively contributes to European

COST Action networks. Her ongoing research explores topics such as crime and inequality, labor market outcomes for marginalized groups, and the socioeconomic determinants of mental health.

Kavita Indapurkar is a Professor and Head of Amity School of Economics at Amity University Noida Campus.

Jipson Joseph has a PhD in Ethics from DVK Bangalore. Currently, he is a Research Scholar at School of Law, Christ (Deemed to be University), Bangalore, India. His research interests are in the fields of ethics, gender studies, constitutional law, human rights, human security, environmental justice, SDGs, developmental policies, and global poverty.

Achyutananda Mishra is a Professor at the School of Law, CHRIST University, Bangalore. His areas of research interest are Constitutional Law, Human Rights, Legal Theory, Globalization, Human Security, and Democracy.

Emre Örün, PhD, is an Assistant Professor at Yozgat Bozok University, Department of Economics. He completed his Master's degree from Süleyman Demirel University, Department of Economics, and his PhD from Yildiz Technical University, Department of Economics. Örün started his academic career at Yozgat Bozok University, Department of Economics, where he has seven years of experience. His main research areas are economic policy, economic inequality, and health economics.

Orhan Özaydın is currently serving as an Associate Professor at Istanbul Medipol University in the Department of Economics and Finance. His academic focus lies in the field of Financial Economics, where he combines rigorous theoretical insight with extensive industry experience. Before transitioning into academia, Dr. Özaydın held senior roles in financial management across several international corporations, amassing over 15 years of professional experience in corporate finance. This practical background enriches his academic work, enabling a strong connection between real-world applications and scholarly research. He earned his B.Sc. in Mathematics from Middle East Technical University, followed by an M.Sc. in Business Administration from Istanbul Bilgi University. He completed his Ph.D. in Financial Economics at Istanbul Commerce University. Dr. Özaydın's teaching and research interests include financial markets, corporate finance, financial risk management, and econometrics, with a particular emphasis on applied methods using R.

Şeyma Sertçelik completed their bachelor's and master's degrees at Istanbul University, in the Department of Econometrics. Currently, they work as a Research Assistant at Istanbul Esenyurt University, Faculty of Business and Management Sciences, Department of Business Administration. Their academic interests include machine learning and econometric modeling. They are also a PhD student in Quantitative Methods. They aim to combine data-driven approaches with social science perspectives in their research. Additionally, apply interpretable machine learning methods to real-world problems.

Neha Sharma is a mathematics postgraduate from South Asian University, New Delhi, where she completed her M.Sc. in Applied Mathematics with a SAARC scholarship. She holds a B.Sc. (Hons.) in Mathematics from the University of Delhi. Her academic interests include optimization methods, particularly Spider Monkey Optimization, Gravitational Search Algorithm and Biogeography-Based Optimization (BBO), and expertise in abstract and linear algebra. Neha is proficient in C, C++, Mathematica, and MATLAB, and experienced in both Windows and Linux environments. She has participated in international conferences and workshops on applied mathematics and computational techniques. Beyond academics, she has performed on Doordarshan, volunteered with SPIC MACAY, and achieved the Rajya Puraskar in scouting. Passionate about research, she completed her dissertation on BBO, exploring its real-world applications.

Özge Filiz Yıldırım is an Assistant Professor of Economics at İzmir Katip Çelebi University and a current visiting researcher at King's College London. She holds a PhD in Economics from Ege University, where her doctoral research focused on DSGE modeling of macroeconomic shocks and capital controls. Her research interests include open economy macroeconomics, monetary policy, housing markets, and the macroeconomic effects of climate change.

Mustafa Ozan Yıldırım is an associate professor at the Department of Economics, Pamukkale University, Turkey. They hold a Ph.D. degree in economics from Pamukkale University-Turkey. They graduated from Dokuz Eylül University, Department of Economics in 2008. They hold a master's degree in economics from Dokuz Eylül University in Turkey. They spent eight months as a visiting Ph.D. student at the Center for Research in Econometric Analysis of Time Series (CREATES) at Aarhus University, Denmark in 2016. Their research focus on housing economics, monetary policy, time series econometrics and dynamic stochastic general equilibrium (DSGE) modeling.

Index

B

C

D

E

F

G

H

I

P

R

S

T

U

V

W

www.ingramcontent.com/pod-product-compliance
Lightning Source LLC
LaVergne TN
LVHW060003031026
849161LV00025B/1339